WORLD CRISIS

WORLD CRISIS
and
BUDDHIST HUMANISM

End Games:
Collapse or Renewal of Civilisation

JOHN H. CROOK

Foreword by
ROSHI JOHN DAIDO LOORI

New Age Books

ISBN: 978-81-7822-325-4

First Indian Edition: 2009

© John H. Crook

The Buddha image on the cover drawn by Ros Cuthbert

Published by
NEW AGE BOOKS
A-44, Naraina Phase I
New Delhi – 110 028 (INDIA)
Email: nab@vsnl.in
Website: www.newagebooksindia.com

Printed in India
at Shri Jainendra Press
A-45, Naraina Phase I, New Delhi – 110 028

This book is dedicated to
The Venerable Chan Master Sheng Yen
with affection and gratitude

CONTENTS

PART IV: THE SEARCH FOR A FUTURE

Foreword

We are in a unique period of human history. For the first time, the major threats to our existence are not the natural disasters that were the biggest fears of our predecessors a thousand years ago, but human-created dangers. This places us at a critical time in evolution, a time that could decide the fate of both the human race and the planet we all share. The paradox that we're facing is that, on the one hand, we possess a degree of knowledge and technological capability hardly dreamed of only decades ago. We understand complex data about the furthest reaches of space and the subtlest workings of subatomic particles. On the other hand, millions of us starve. Our environment is polluted. The earth's natural resources are being plundered at an alarming rate, and the specter of global ecological catastrophe looms over us, threatening to extinguish our species and indeed all of life.

No matter how much we think we know of the universe and its functioning, it is obvious that we have barely begun to scratch the surface of our human existence and the nature of our relationship with the ten thousand things that make up the phenomenal world. For millennia, our perception has remained largely dualistic and virtually static. We see ourselves as our bag of skin, and everything and everyone outside of it as "other". As a result of that separation, our philosophy, art, science, medicine, ecology, theology, psychology, politics, sociology, ethics, and morality also operate within a dualistic framework. The consequence of this dualism is the kind of world we now live in.

The issues of war, pollution, global warming, addiction, poverty, starvation and immorality all share the basic premise of a distinct and separate self. The way we understand the self is the way we understand the universe, and the way we understand the universe will determine how we relate to it and how we combust our lives within it.

Very recently in the West, we've become aware of the existence of a way of understanding reality that goes beyond our deeply entrenched dualistic view. Its origins go back to seventh-century Chinese text called *The Flower Garland Sutra*. In it, a universe is described in which everything interpenetrates with everything else – there's not a single speck of dust separate from the whole. In the sutra's most powerful metaphor, the Diamond Net of Indra, all existence is seen as a vast net of diamonds that extends throughout the universe, not only in the three dimensions of space, but also in the fourth dimension of time. Each point of this huge net contains a multi-faceted diamond that reflects every other diamond, and as such, contains every other diamond in the net. The diamonds represent the entire universe of past, present, and future. When one thing arises in this net, all things arise simultaneously. Everything has a mutual causality – what happens to one thing, happens to the entire universe. It's a self-creating, self-maintaining, self-defining organism – a universe in which all of its parts and the totality are a single entity.*

Predictably, not too many people have taken this teaching seriously. Yet, the Diamond Net is not some kind of holistic hypothesis or idealistic dream. It's not a philosophical postulation. It is a description of reality that has been directly experienced by thousands of Buddhist men and women for more that two thousand years. And more recently, it has also been corroborated by science through the discovery of the hologram.

Twentieth century scientists found that when laser light was transmitted through a photographic plate, a three-dimensional image would be projected into space – an image that you could literally walk into. This in itself seemed pretty remarkable, but what was even more remarkable was the fact that when they cut that photographic plate in half and projected laser light through half of it, the whole image was projected. They then cut the half in half, the quarter in half, the eighth in half and so on, down to the smallest piece of that photographic plate, and still, when laser light was projected through it, the whole image was projected. Not a single element was missing. This could mean only one thing: each section of the plate contained all the information of the whole, just like each diamond in the Diamond Net contains every other diamond.

As a result of this discovery, scientists have also begun to exmine biology, physics, neurology and chemistry in terms of the holographic modal, providing additional verification of the validity of the ancient teaching of the Diamond Net. I call this realization of the holographic universe "twenty-first century mind"–the realization that we are responsible for the whole universe. We have created the whole catastrophe–every blessed bit of it. And until we take responsibility for what we've created, we will not be able to do anything about it.

Each of us has the ability to see this mind. When we realize the interdependent nature of the universe, there is no way to avoid responsibility for it. It becomes crystal clear that what we do and what happens to us are exactly the same thing. And when we deeply realize this truth, it's no longer possible to postpone, blame, or victimize. It's no longer possible to look outside for the answers to our questions.

It is easy to feel overwhelmed by the problems we now face. But a true sense of empowerment and understanding can arise from taking on our

---

* For further discussion of Hua Yen thought see chapter 8.

feelings of despair and hopelessness. This is our challenge–to go beyond the bag of skin, beyond the words and ideas that merely describe reality and realize the truth of our human existence.

As a practitioner and teacher of Buddhism, accomplished scientist and professorial researcher in behavioral biology and evolutionary psychology, Dr John Hurrell Crook has boldly taken up this challenge in his book *World Crisis and Buddhist Humanism*. John Crook is eminently qualified to synthesize a compelling argument for a Buddhist humanism that eloquently integrates modern science and the practise and philosophy of Buddhism, resulting in a fresh way of understanding our responsibility as global citizens. As he points out in his Preface, "Today all of us stand on high terraces as witnessess of our civilization facing its greatest threat... [a] threat created by human beings." We are the source of this threat. What will we do about it?

It is no small thing to be born human. With this human consciousness comes a tremendous responsibility. Each of us has the power to not only change our lives and bring them into harmony with the ten thousands things, but also to nourish others and to heal this planet. We have created destruction; we can create life. All it takes is the will to do it. We can realize ourselves; all it takes is the determination to do it. In both cases, we're fully equipped. We have everything needed to realize ourselves and transform this planet. We should not take this responsibility lightly.

I swear the earth shall be complete to him or her who shall be complete,

The earth remains jagged and broken only to him or her who remains jagged and broken,

I swear there is no greatness or power that does not emulate those of the earth,

There can be no theory of any account unless it corroborates the theory of the earth

No politics, song, religion, behavior, or what not, is of account, unless it compares with the amplitude of the earth.

– Walt Whitman
Roshi John Daido Loori

Mount Tremper, New York
June 2007

PREFACE

In Jean Giraudoux' play, 'The Tiger at the Gates'*, two statesmen meet near Troy in an attempt to avert the Trojan War. Hector for Troy hosts the occasion, Ulysses represents the Greeks. The situation is at crisis point yet the two of them create a plan that could have saved the situation had the forces of history, the passions of enflamed peoples, not determined otherwise. They know the chances of success are very slim and that destiny bears down upon them. Ulysses reflects, "One of the privileges of the great is to witness catastrophes from a terrace."

Today it is not only politicians who stand on terraces commanding views of human tragedy; scholars too are witnesses and indeed anyone with enough concern can join them. Modern communication, television and the web, make everything clear for those who wish to stand there. Today all of us stand on high terraces as witnesses of our civilisation facing its greatest threat.

As with war, this threat is created by human beings. There is here no fate other than the consequence of human stupidity. In spite of repeated denial, it is clear that we are ruining the planetary ecology upon which our style of life if not the very lives of our grandchildren depend. Preoccupied with personal, institutional and national gain, attempting to deal with worldwide discontent and terrorism, politicians and their short-term administrations fail to grasp the severity of the situation. The ships are drifting on the rocks while the captains ignore the far off coast or play chess in their cabins. Without meeting the planetary challenge, no safe harbour can be reached and any imposition of a rule of law will be valueless.

It is not the case that we lack the scientific knowledge to avert this crisis. Many means for correction are actually at our disposal. The difficulty is that there is insufficient collective will to engage the problem with the seriousness it demands. One or two politicians are perhaps waking up but most are comatose. The very world view of the West appears to be the cause of massive illusion. The faraway frontier has long been reached and the resources of the planet will not for long support the civilisation our grandchildren will inherit. There is much grief to come. Indeed the suffering has already begun.

This book is an advocacy. We need to look beyond the parochial wisdom of the West. Western insight, in spite of its great material success and

---

* La Guerre de Troie n'aura pas lieu. 1936. Translated by Christopher Fry. 1955. Methuen. London.

indeed partly because of it, seems unable to conceive the means to a necessary restraint that would permit us to discover other ways of utilising universal energy and other modes of planetary governance.

Asian wisdom sees the human world through different eyes and has created perspectives that challenge Western assumptions in ways that can be extremely useful. Among these ways, Buddhism stands out as pre-eminent. Buddhist ideas have followed an independent path of globalisation almost as impressive as that of the West and are now penetrating Western consciousness. In this book we will argue the case for taking them totally seriously in the construction of a world view that may help us adapt once more to the demands of the planetary environment in which our species has evolved.

Niko Tinbergen, Nobel Laureate in Behavioural Biology, was one of the first to express doubt as to whether humanity can survive this crisis without major changes in attitude and world view. Today, many would agree with his vision, which at the time was dismissed perhaps as mere depression. Tinbergen, however, was not familiar with a system of Eastern thought that can now provide a basis from which to build and this book presents a case for its robust consideration.

After exploring the nature of the problem, we examine the tenets of Buddhist thought carefully. In particular, we note it's subjective empiricism that places it with science as a major form of human enquiry. In Part 2, we survey the global range of Buddhist ideas taking care to look closely at their basis and adaptability within differing cultures. In Part 3, we imagine the Buddha with us today as he discovers many aspects of scientific knowledge that would fill gaps in his original proposals. We evaluate viewpoints and their supporting evidence that could only have been metaphysical speculation in his time. We look at contemporary ideas regarding human social and ethical evolution, psychology, economics, philosophical nihilism and the nature of contemporary suffering.

The Buddha would be interested in those ideas that relate most closely to his original insights. We undertake therefore a tour through key themes in contemporary scientific and humanist perspectives and link them to themes in Buddhist thought. Starting with biological evolution, we examine the origin and expression of the human person and go on to investigate the nature of the self in which they are anchored. Consciousness and culture are profoundly underpinned by economics and the ethics by which we govern our lives and these in turn are expressed through the philosophical enquiries that have come down to us through recent centuries. We find the Western world view to be astonishingly split by a pattern of dualisms that divides economics from ecology, self from body, facts from values, and humanity from a sense of the divine' in the universe. To emerge from this schizoid mentality we need to create a world view that may meet the challenges we face with a broadly based holism that re-integrates what our Western culture has set asunder. We end by proposing that this will require a system of world wide education based in a Buddhist humanism fundamental to scientific enquiry. Is such a humanist revisioning possible and can it help reduce the planet-wide destructiveness of human beings in time?

The book as a whole attempts to show how Buddhist ideas can be related to modern knowledge to create a world view that offers hope, a perspective that relieves modern alienation and an opportunity to re-enchant our world.

Finally, a personal point: on his death bed during the oil crisis of the nineteen seventies my father remarked lucidly that he no longer wished to return in the future to see how we were getting on. Things just looked too bleak. I have resisted my father's vision over the years but have recently become inclined to agree with him. I am aware however of the immense privileges I have experienced in my life as an academic enabled to study, research and to think with others in world class universities in Europe, India and in the United States. At 75 years, I wish to pay back something of that debt in a summary of what I believe I have learnt – full of errors as that undoubtedly may be.

John Hurrell Crook

ACKNOWLEDGEMENTS

Years of concerned contemplation about the state of the world have led me to this book. Needless to say, many people have inspired it, helping me to reach the perspective I present here. I am especially grateful to Louise Barrett whose enthusiastic response to an earlier draft, read while on a field study of baboons in Africa, rekindled my endeavour in a time of doubt. My old friend Yiu Yannang engaged me in a vigorous re-examination of key chapters making many valuable criticisms resulting in shifts of emphasis in the text. Peter Reason enlivened me many times through creative discussion alerting me to unexplored themes. Mike Masheder laboured helpfully and critically through many chapters helping me polish my prose and commenting on errors. Bill Grimstone kindly commented on Chapter 11. Colin and Carol Evans reviewed certain chapters and introduced me to the plays of Jean Giradoux, leading me both to begin and end the text with quotes from his highly relevant works. I am also deeply grateful to Crispin Goswell for assistance in preparing the camera ready copy for the publisher.

The friendship of the 'Western Academy', our mutual support group, has in many wonderful meetings over the years provided intellectual stimulation assuring me that what I was about was at least worthwhile: the Peters Reason; Tatham; and Hawkins; and Malcolm Parlett.

Within my own field of evolutionary biology, David Lack, Niko Tinbergen, Reg Moreau and Arthur Cain particularly influenced me, while my original teachers at Cambridge, Robert Hinde and Bill Thorpe, also showed me how scientists can contribute very effectively to discussions of world problems and other issues well outside the immediate field of their specialisation.[*] Joseph Needham, Lawrence Picken and Carmen Blacker showed me how especially important is discipline in academic thought when embarking on cross-cultural studies.

My concern with therapeutic psychology was stimulated in workshops organised by the Esalen Institute at Stanford University during my year there as a Fellow at the Center for Advanced Study in Behavioral Sciences. Both there, and subsequently through the creation of the Bristol

---

[*] Thorpe, W.H. 1978. *Purpose in a World of Chance.* Oxford University Press.

Hinde. R.A. 1999 *Why Gods, Persist: a scientific approach to religion.* Routledge.

Needham, J.1954 *et seq. Science and Civilisation in China.*, Cambridge University Press.

Encounter Centre, I benefited from the teachings, advice and friendship of numerous American and British group leaders: James Fadiman; Jay Stattman; Jeff Love; Michael Wilson; Hazel Russell and many others.

Meetings with Krishnamurti in intimate workshops in India were eventually to lead me in the direction my life has taken. Over the years I have been extraordinarily fortunate in receiving teachings from outstanding Zen teachers and Tibetan lamas: Yen Shiliang; Roshi Jiyu Kennett; Irmgard Schloegl; Chan Master Sheng yen; Lama Thubten Yeshe; HH Dudjom Rimpoche; Geshe Damchos Yontan; Staglung Rimpoche; Khamtag Rimpoche; Reb Anderson; Stephen and Martine Batchelor; James Low; the yogins Nochung Tse and Gonpo of Stagrimo Gonpa, Zanskar; and Shri Tashi Rabgyas of Leh, Ladakh. In recent years, my root teacher has been Chan Master Sheng yen of Dharma Drum Mountain, Taiwan and New York, to whom this book is dedicated, and it is to him that I owe such understanding as I may have of Chinese Zen (Chan). My colleagues in the Western Chan Fellowship, Simon Child, Ken Jones, Hilary Richards, Jake Lyne, Eddy Street, Fiona Nuttall, Charles Vincent and others, inspire me through our joint programme of retreats and teachings.

Finally, I owe an immense debt to my parents for their care, kindness and tolerance especially when as a young man in the Far East I became interested in forms of spirituality that differed markedly from their own. Their trusting involvement in what I was about was always a great spur to an exploration of world views lying way outside my culture of birth.

I am well aware that my choice of themes to discuss with the Buddha during his imaginary reappearance in London (Part 3) reflects personal interests and that others may well have focussed on very different ideas. I believe however that I have covered at least some of the ground that would concern him were he actually to return among us. Needless to say, I am frequently no expert in the fields that attracted me and I beg forgiveness for any serious errors of interpretation and doubtless also for an often inadequate coverage of complex issues. I trust that the broad approach to the whole may carry conviction.

Finally, this work is an offering to my grandchildren who will face the rigours of the upcoming world and all its problems. I wish them and all future generations well and trust they may come to forgive the failures in world management that currently disfigure my time.

I thank the following publishers for permitting the use of quotations as epigraphs to Parts 1-3: Penguin for a text from Marcus Aurelius "Meditations' translated by Maxwell Staniforth; Oxford University Press for a text from Lucretius's 'On the nature of things' translated by Sir Ronald Melville; Taigen Daniel Leighton for his translation from Hongzhi's 'practice instructions'. Leighton, T.G with Yi Wu. 1991. Cultivating the Empty Field. The Silent illumination of Zen Master Hongzhi. North Point Press. San Francisco.

John Hurrell Crook
Wednesday, May 28, 2008

PART I

TINBERGEN'S DOUBT

"Think of your many years of procrastination; how the Gods have repeatedly granted you further periods of grace, of which you have taken no advantage. It is time now to realise the nature of the universe to which you belong, and of that controlling power whose offspring you are; and to understand that your time has a limit set to it. Use it then... or it will be gone, and never in your power again."

MARCUS AURELIUS
Meditations Book 2[1]

1

UNCERTAINTY AND DESPAIR

In 1973 the Dutch biologist Niko Tinbergen and Konrad Lorenz of Germany were jointly awarded a Nobel Prize for founding the scientific study of animal behaviour. Niko had specialised in conducting elegant field experiments demonstrating how even the most subtle aspects of wasp or bird behaviour could be interpreted as adaptations to the habitat of the species, while Konrad preferred studying captive animals at his research station in Germany and pioneering important theories concerning the motivation responsible for instinctive activity. In the years after World War II the two of them took the study of evolution into a new arena, the biology of behaviour.

Towards the end of his remarkably creative career,[2] Tinbergen became interested in our own species, contributing new ideas about the causation of autism and asking serious questions about the sufferings of our time. From readings in anthropology, it was clear to him that the basic, behavioural adaptations of the human species must have evolved over immense lengths of time, primarily in the savannahs of Africa. Many features of human behaviour are social adaptations to the communities in which early humans lived. In Africa, the context of these adaptations appeared to have been societies characterised by low densities, small groups of family parties and organisation strongly supportive of collaborative endeavour. Puzzled by the psychological stresses of our times: neurosis, anxiety, social violence, the breakdown of marriage and the difficulties of relations between genders, Tinbergen wondered whether the contemporary development of cultures permitting high densities, complex institutionalised groups and extremely fast communication in all aspects of life had not generated a social environment to which our behavioural biology was simply no longer adequately adapted. Was there perhaps some fault in the evolutionary design of humans that prevented us from meeting such challenges?

"We all have grown up in times of rapidly increasing efficiency, of growing mastery over our environment, and so of increasing security. But now we begin to see that this security cannot be taken for granted, that we have been lulled into an attitude of complacency, and even of arrogance – and we are feeling an uneasy sense of doubt. This feeling of unease is the more disconcerting because, unlike the tight rope walker, we do not know the nature of the threats."[3]

He knew of course that the prime feature of human behavioural biology was the outstanding capacity of our species for social flexibility based on exploratory learning. Indeed it had been this capacity that allowed our species to spread through all inhabitable regions of the globe in spite of the enormous physical and climatic contrasts between them. Behavioural evolution through exploration and learning occurs in other mammals too, but it is the additive effect, generation after generation, through culture, that marks out the human species. What is peculiar to our species is that each generation adds accumulatively to this supplementary programming.

It seemed to Tinbergen that the genetic endowments upon which this adaptability depended remained essentially those of the ancient savannahs. So long as gradual environmental adaptation was required, the innate capacity for flexibility could cope, he thought, but, as cultures increased in complexity in modern times at a speed much greater than genetic change could follow, so adaptability to the pressures of modern civilisation seemed to be failing. Changes in culture have been so great that adaptations for healthy survival and reproduction seem increasingly unable to cope. Could we be maladapted to the civilisation we had created for ourselves? "We are creating a habitat that diverges more and more and with increasing speed from that to which genetic evolution has adapted us. ... can the cultural evolution continue unbridled, or will our survival, or at least our well being, be threatened?" Indeed, could this maladaptation lead, like the debilitating huge antlers of the ancient Irish Elk, to our eventual extinction?

Ending his 1972 review Tinbergen wrote," ... the behaviour student considers it very well possible, indeed likely, that we are reaching a point where the 'viability gap' – the gap between what our new habitat requires us to do and what we are actually doing – is becoming so wide that our behavioural adjustability is already being taxed to the limit. ... Knowing what we do about political decision-making, I believe it will be useless to call upon people's altruism or use other arguments of a moral nature. Rather, the scientist will have to point out that the prevention of a breakdown, and the building of a new society is a matter of enlightened self-interest, of ensuring survival, health and happiness of the children and grandchildren of all of us – of people we know and love."[4]

In 1976, Tinbergen returned to his theme.[5] His paper, amounts to a chilling vision of human future. He exhorted his fellows to investigate the roots of these problems in human evolution and psychology. Scientists are perhaps more deeply embedded in their parochial concerns than Tinbergen may have realised and few have responded in relation to the scale of the task he set them. Indeed, so vast is this canvas that it requires a thinking-together by evolutionary ethologists, psychologists, sociologists and philosophers across boundaries few have been tempted to cross.

In this second paper, Tinbergen stresses the anonymity of life in large megalopolises compared to the intimacy of earlier cultures, the increasing complexity of human relationships and roles in relation to institutionalised work, the lack of inspiration in repetitive tasks in offices and on factory floors. He discusses the increased competitiveness, high speed of change, and the endless creation of dissatisfaction through social envy stimulated by rising incomes, commercial needs, advertising and psychological manipulations by capitalist business. He points out that these dissatisfactions are associated with increasing levels of violence. Tinbergen argues, "I am convinced that our species, in spite of all its cultural achievements, has now reached a stage at which a variety of dangerous pressures threaten to overwhelm all the advantages that our cultural evolution has for so long carried with it. We are entering one of the great, if not the greatest, discontinuities of our entire history."

In turning to the possibility of remedial measures, Tinbergen points out that what will be needed is a "new type of citizen." Only a thoroughly renewed outlook on life and its problems can make a difference. There are many issues here that go beyond Tinbergen's account and some of which we will try to address in this book. How far do the material and social circumstances affect our motivation to change or merely depress us? In what way is human identity affected by despair and regret? What is the relation between politics and philosophy? Are there deeper issues here to do with the evolution of humanity, the conduct of the human self, both personally and institutionally? How do ideologies control us? At root, what is suffering? As an ethologist, Tinbergen thought in terms of behavioural changes but these are often based in profound movements within the human psyche not easily visible on the surface. May be it is within the underlying mechanisms of a 'depth' psychology that we need to look.

Since Tinbergen first expressed his impassioned doubts, the human situation has deteriorated further. Today our major concerns focus upon actual or potential disaster mostly due to human interference with the natural environment of our planet. Together with climate change, over population, the pace of technological and social change, political conflicts and the nuclear threat, we face a terrorism based in religion operative at ever-new levels of impact and inhumanity. There is an extraordinary inability and lack of will on the part of politicians and governments to initiate adequate remedial measures. Instead, there is the making of major errors of political judgement. This is not because we lack scientific understanding of the world processes now in train.

Joanna Macy neatly encapsulates our dilemma and the grief it may impose: "It has always been assumed as an integral part of human experience, that the work of our hands and heads and hearts would live on through those who came after us, walking the same earth under the same sky. – Now we have lost the certainty that we have a future. I believe that this loss, felt at some level of consciousness by everyone – is the pivotal psychological reality of our time."[6]

The American Zen Master John Daido Loori writes: "We are in an unique period of human history. For the first time, the major threats to our existence are not the natural disasters that were our biggest fears for our predecessors a thousand years ago, but human created dangers. This places us at a critical time in evolution, a time that could decide the fate of the human race and the planet we all share. The most compelling paradox we are encountering is that, on the one hand, we possess a degree of knowledge and technical capability hardly dreamed of only decades ago. We understand complex data about the farthest reaches of space and the subtlest workings of the minute fragments of atoms. On the other hand, millions of us starve. Our environment is polluted. The earth's natural resources are being plundered at an alarming rate and the spectre of global ecological catastrophe raises the possibility of the extinction of our species and all life. In spite of our understanding so much about the universe and its functioning, we've barely begun to scratch the surface of understanding who we are, what our life is, and what our relationship is with the 'ten thousand things' that comprise phenomenal existence"[7] The need to reverse our gaze to examine what lies within becomes obvious.

Reflecting on the life and insight of Gregory Bateson Stephen Nachmanovitch[8] has written: "It is a crisis of mind. It's a case of wake up or die. We have the whole night mare history of political revolutions against bloody regimes, replacing them by still more bloody ones, to teach us that *that* is not the way out. The only way out is a spiritual, intellectual, and emotional revolution in which we learn to experience as biological facts, first-hand, the interlooping connections between person and person, organism and environment, action and consequence – when we are able to talk a language that includes the context in each thought. Our present language *excludes* context."

To consider an example: the current American administration has been most reluctant to participate in international endeavours that could start to reduce global warming and retains policies of commercial maximisation known to pollute the environment in potentially disastrous ways. How can it be that the most intelligent and creative of sentient beings are so stupid when it comes to their own ultimate welfare? It is not difficult to perceive that much of this non-enabling reluctance is embedded in the institutional structure of the western world through which consumer capitalism operates. This economic system, based in a competitive ethos necessitated by companies required to maximise dividends to shareholders, has a major difficulty in restructuring itself to meet the needs of collective sustainability in a world of ultimately limiting resources. The gross self-interest of vast military-industrial corporations dominates capitalist politics so as to encourage short-sighted policies of environmental exploitation, world dominance over unsustainable resources and militaristic bullying. The neglect and failure to meet these challenges poses the paradoxical dilemma of our times because, after some two hundred years of unremitting technological advance bringing immense benefits to humanity, it appears that the entire paradigm of thought underpinning Western civilisation needs a radical overhaul if not total replacement.

There are those who argue that market forces will eventually ensure change but it is far from clear that this alone can shift the paradigm in the way required. From a fragmentary, competitive, short sighted, exploitative system encouraging uneven distribution of wealth without adequate concern for the future, we have to develop policies that are global, multicultural, rooted in collaborative endeavours and aimed at an optimisation of use of world resources, physical and social, rather than at maximisation for the profit of the few. Furthermore, it needs long-sight into the future.

Yet, it is precisely in the future that we sense our deepest fears. Long gone is the widespread public optimism and belief in 'progress' of the Victorian era. Susan Greenfield, currently Director of the Royal Institution, in her book *Tomorrows People* fears that in the economically advanced parts of the planet an increasing public reliance on electronic gadgetry and immersion in virtual worlds could sap the human character by a process of dumbing-down wherein active intelligence is replaced by a self-indulgent but meaningless life machined for comfort. Such self-indulgence, she argues, would negate any effort for renewal in poorer parts of the world thereby fuelling more resentment and violence.[9] Sir Martin Rees, cosmologist and Astronomer Royal, has gone further suggesting that the twenty first century could be our last and this because of our totally uncontrolled scientific genius in producing fantastic new discoveries that, aside from their often-debatable benefits, have the potential of causing worldwide disasters.[10] The issues here are not so much economic or political but rather lie within Science itself – human genius may lead to the self destruction of humanity – or at least of civilisation as we know it today. Two fields in particular, the biology of genetic modification and disease transmission and nanotechnology are so potentially threatening that Rees believes some lines of research need careful control or even complete abandonment. The danger arises not so much among scientists themselves, he argues, as from the fact that the relatively accessible skills of such technologies could easily spread to and be applied by compassionless destroyers with the mindset of contemporary Islamic terrorists.

"Choices on how science is applied – to medicine, the environment and so forth – should be debated far beyond the scientific community," writes Rees. "This is one reason why it is important that a wide public should have a basic feel for science, knowing at least the difference between a proton and a protein. Otherwise such debate won't go beyond slogans – The views of scientists should not have special weight in deciding questions that involve ethics or risks: indeed, such judgements are best left to broader and more dispassionate groups." Yet, we have to ask whether, if we are indeed maladapted to our fast moving world, such groups are up to such a task.

Is this so? Is there really a design fault in human evolution that needs to be faced and overcome? Or is it that to adapt to contemporary circumstances we need to develop a comprehensive and radically daring new world view pitched against the conservative tendencies of self-concern? And upon what basis could a fresh world view be constructed?

These broad issues crop up in many contemporary circumstances. In his bold, inaugural lecture in the University of Bath (January 2002) Professor Peter Reason of the Department of Management quoted from a student essay:

> As I approach the end of my studies, I can't help feeling that freedom is a fallacy, and that somehow I have been walking a predetermined path to mortgage repayments and commuting nightmares. Further, I'm not alone. Despite a whole array of 'graduate opportunities' there is a growing mood of claustrophobia and sense of powerlessness; for all the relative luxuries of the western world, we are still unsatisfied; there is an unmistakable sense of longing, a deep craving for some kind of release or escape. (Sarah Atkins, 2001)

Commenting on this Reason asks: "What is it that this bright young woman, and at least some of her contemporaries, want to escape from? I want to suggest to you that it is from the all-encompassing frame of the modern world view, which stops us listening to the world. It is a way of doing and being in the world which has made extraordinary contributions to human affairs in the flourishing of culture, scientific endeavour and material well-being, but has brought in its wake human alienation, ecological devastation, and spiritual impoverishment. In particular it has brought the twin global crises of justice and sustainability. I want to suggest to you that these two crises represent an enormous challenge, and one that cannot be fully addressed within the modern worldview because it is that world view that has substantially brought about these crises."[11]

As we can see from Peter Reason's student's essay, these issues are not merely to do with instrumental failures, errors in correcting environmental damage or educational inadequacies for which the application of practical knowledge may make a difference; rather there is something profoundly personal at stake, the very worthwhileness of the self, of life itself and the mode of being that contemporary Western ways appear to prescribe for us.

Archbishop Rowan Williams in his perceptive work *'Lost Icons'*[12] points out that in modern culture many traditional patterns of western thought, conventions governing almost all aspects of life from the language of kinship, child care, gender relations, the disposal of corpses, and the various *'rites de passage* involved in maturing and ageing, have been undergoing fundamental restatement so that contemporary texts, even when using the words of these old iconic patterns, are based in a very different ideological condition than was the case for previous generations. In particular, he mourns the loss of a language of the 'soul' by which he means a reflective inner life very different from the reactive emotionality in relation to passing desires generated by the overpowering influence of capitalist consumerism that presses in upon us from all sides and especially through the identity creating power of the media. The absence of self-questioning, the avoidance of "spiritual discipline in favour of an increasing superficiality of religious thought" are all in play here. The Archbishop is not alone in his misgivings. Senior educationalists also mourn the loss of high culture and it's replacement by cheap populism usually simplistic and reductionist in character, however cleverly presented. They ponder the deep mistakes in education policy that have encouraged such decline.[13]

In my book of 1980, *'The Evolution of Human Consciousness'*, I too reflected on these issues.[14] "It is in the particular quality of contemporary alienation that the deepest roots of the malaise lie. The speed of change in the meanings individuals attribute to life itself has resulted in an almost total absence of those old legitimations of life and praxis that were the constants of traditional societies. Science has replaced religion with the scholastic metaphysics of an empiricism, which – leads to no certainty. The great unknown, like an abyss, yawns before the enquirer. Theology, too, retreating into parallel abstractions or existentialist visions of despair – no longer provides the simple heart with the meaning of what lies before it."

All this of course is the continuing expression of what the great sociologist Max Weber called the 'disenchantment' of the world, the loss of wonder. Morris Berman (1981) describes well what that old enchantment was like, "Rocks, trees, rivers and clouds were all seen as wondrous, alive, and human beings felt at home in this environment. The cosmos in short was a place of belonging. A member of this cosmos was not an alienated observer of it but a direct participant in its drama. This type of consciousness – involves merger or identification with ones surroundings and bespeaks a psychic wholeness that has long passed from the scene."[15] And moving beyond this evocation of animism and shamanic responsiveness, even the more controlling figure of God, which in high Christianity provided a sense of safety and involvement with the divine, has become largely irrelevant.

Yet it seems as if we are already moving beyond the 'post-modernism' that followed the breakdown of the materialist assumption of progress inherent in the Cartesian assumption of mind's separation from nature, whereby everything was to be made use of, exploited in some way. In post-modernism, everything became of equal value or no value, meaning was relative, and the task was to build an 'authentic'self, independent of others' values, an individual as created by himself or herself alone. Some at least of today's students, by contrast, seem seriously concerned with the tragedy of the world situation and actively seeking a way beyond the hedonism, the conceited authenticities of the 80s-90s and the gross capitalism of U.S.A. Even if it is primarily only the student generation that is looking ahead, there does seem to be a new seriousness, perhaps powered by the ever-growing global climate crisis, for which the philosopher Charles Taylor would be grateful.

In *The Ethics of Authenticity* (1991)[16] Taylor argues that a way beyond the expressions of merely hedonistic individualism is essential if Western civilisation is not to decay further with a loss of everything gained from the European Enlightenment. Contemporary perspectives need to be replaced, he argues, by a more discerning viewpoint that would value the advances in self-expression, openness and personal freedom, the permissiveness achieved in the 20th century. It would have to counter the more recent, facile assumptions of an illusory, personal autonomy. Behind the contemporary facade of cheap individualism, argues Taylor, lie serious moral motives that tend to be forgotten or submerged. Many modes of contemporary self-fulfilment function without regard to ties with others or consist merely in fantasised aspirations that are deeply self-defeating. One might think here of much 'new ageism'. Taylor proposes that we look behind these facades to the original sources of our search for authenticity in the freedoms from tyranny, obscuration, emotional sterility and bigotry that the Enlightenment 'turn' in Western thought provided. He seeks something like a middle way that is a re-engagement with these earlier values and their source. He points out that the search for such renewed meaning will be a struggle through which the positive advantages of scientific instrumentalism and an awareness of life as being personal can be related in a commitment to social good. He sees that, without such commitment, the effectiveness of the democratic process will decrease leaving room for a tyranny of institutions that vie for governance to take control. Meanwhile the planetary crisis grows and grows.

The essence of the matter lies in establishing what an involvement with the good of the planet actually comprises. This indeed is the key question that will concern us throughout this book and it is not a matter for merely intellectual speculation. Action is needed NOW. We all face a situation in which our grand-children will inherit a world profoundly damaged by our current activities. Not only will the rising sea levels have destroyed immense areas of land including several world-class cities but also the climate of whole continents could be radically altered. Indeed, we do not yet know the extent of the potential disasters because we have yet to understand the thresholds within change that may act as tipping points for cataclysmic shifts in the nature of the physical environment. Gaia is reacting to several centuries of abuse. Further more the essential supplies of energy upon which civilisation depends need to be based in new, non-polluting technologies for which adequate investment has yet to be secured. To this is added the political and religious unrest and terrorism resulting from intolerant, unthinking fundamentalisms that have the potential for ending civilised life with both bangs and whimpers.

End Notes

1. Marcus Aureleus (Trans: M. Staniforth). 1964. Meditations. Penguin.
2. For an excellent biography of Niko Tinbergen see: Kruuk, H. 2003. *Niko's Nature.* Oxford University Press.
3. Tinbergen, N. 1972. Functional ethology and the human sciences. The Croonian Lecture. *Proc. R. Soc. B.* 182:385-410.

4.   Tinbergen, N. *Ibid.* 407.
5.   Tinbergen, N. 1976. Ethology in a changing World. In: P.P.G. Bateson and R.A. Hinde (Eds). *Growing points in Ethology.* Cambridge. p. 507-528
6.   Macy, Joanna. 1991. *World as Lover, World as Self.* Parallax. Berkeley. p. 5.
7.   Loori, J.D. 1999. *Teachings of the Insentient. Zen and the Environment.* Dharma Communications Press. Mt. Tremper. New York: p. 31.
8.   Nachmanovitch, S. 2001. *Gregory Bateson: old men ought to be explorers.* Free Play Productions. Ivy. VA.
9.   Greenfield, S. 2003. *Tomorrow's people.* Allen Lane. Penguin. London.
10. Rees, M. 2003. *Our Final Century.* Heinemann. London.
11. Reason, P. 2003. Inaugural lecture. Bath University.
12. Williams, R. 2000. *Lost Ikons: reflections on cultural bereavement.* T and T Clark. London.
13. Haldane, J. (Ed.). 2004. *Values, Education and the Human World.* St Andrew's Studies in Philosophy and Public Affairs. Imprint Academic. Exeter.
14. Crook, J.H. 1980.*The Evolution of Human Consciousness.* Clarendon. Oxford.
15. Berman, M. 1981. *The Reenchantment of the World.* Cornell University Press. Ithaca and London.
16. Taylor, C. 1991. *The Ethics of Authenticity.* Harvard University Press. Cambridge Mass and London.

2

THE NATURE OF WORLD VIEWS

The question for this book is what world view could replace or modify the prevailing Western one with any likelihood of making a difference. The dominating world view is a product of Western cultural history, thought and economics. In a sense, it is local. We need to consider how far its totalising application on a global scale is adequate or even relevant to the profound issues raised in the last chapter. 'Globalisation' is the current buzzword in economics and it implies the spread of the Western world view over all cultures, replacing ancient ways of doing things, negating contemporary local alternatives, causing the extinction of traditional ways of life and languages. The resistance to it is increasingly vocal, violent and often with well stated reasons. But what to do?

We need, first of all, to ask what a world view actually is. Two Prussian brothers, the Barons Alexander and Wilhelm von Humboldt (1769-1859, 1767-1835), set this discussion going with their concept of *weltanschauung*. Both men made major contributions to enlightenment thought in the nineteenth century. Alexander travelled widely, especially in South America and Russia, carrying out pioneering anthropological studies focussing on the comparisons of cultures. In his old age, he attempted a vast encyclopaedic work summarising the totality of knowledge about the universe, the planet and society. He named it 'Kosmos'.[1] He sought to present a complete *weltanschauung*, a world view of contemporary scientific knowledge that would be a basis for future study and world development. He was perhaps the last 'renaissance man' to attempt a total summary of world knowledge. His elder brother, Wilhelm, more philosopher than anthropologist, suggested that the contrasting world views of differing cultures that Alexander had described were based in language differences. The languages in which experiences were presented were the shapers of cultural ideas – a view foreshadowing the Whorfian hypothesis in linguistics and influencing the language theory of Chomski. Today we use the term *weltanschauung* or 'world view' in a variety of ways. We have *weltanschauungen* of individual persons, of institutions, of religions, of cultures, of philosophical systems such as communism or capitalism. The term gathers up in an inclusive summary the ideas and attitudes of the entity in question to suggest a cultural form governing expression and policy.

It seems that more is involved in the creation of a world view than simply the language in which it may be couched, important as that may be. The nature of family life, the structure of society, the modes of livelihood and the environment of exploitation all seem to be creators of experience to which language then gives expression. The world view of a tribe will be related to the manner in which it exploits the resources of the environment. Farmers have a world view very different from nomads; jungle dwellers differ from inhabitants of savannah. In their interpretation of the forces operating in their world, tribal peoples create differing shamanic systems in which projections of god-like figures will demand of them sacrificial, petitionary or placatory rituals. Such rituals express their interpretation of being in their world, their ontologies, and give rise to manners, fetishisms and the shaping of ethical codes. In complex civilisations with extensive marketing arrangements, long distance travel, frontier relations with other systems, elaborated religious thought and state policies linking state and religion, the overall world view is correspondingly complex. Furthermore, world views differ in their flexibility. Some, such as that of the Roman Catholic Church, are remarkable rigid, barely noticing or even resisting the advances of scientific understanding. Others are quite fluid changing with new discoveries as Kuhn has shown in his analysis of changes in scientific paradigms.[2] World views also drift as cultures change under economic or demographic pressures and here we face the issue of the adequacy of our Western perspectives at the present time.

WORLD VIEW, ECOLOGY AND POPULATION DENSITY

A world view is shaped in the environment within which people exploit their habitat. Habitat includes the demography of a people, the density of settlements and the availability of sustaining resources. This relationship is a dynamic one as ecological studies of both animals and humans show. For example, as a rat population increases in numbers and the availability of resources such as holes and food decreases so the behaviour of the animals changes. Simple ranking of males according to dominance changes to include territorial occupation and the defence of holes accompanied by the aggressive retention of females for mating. If rats could speak, they would doubtless change their philosophies too!

Among the nilo-hamitic peoples of East Africa social life and organisation depends on their density. As numbers increase, pastoralists seek to extend their ranging. Greater dispersal means that families live in small, separated units. When they meet neighbouring peoples who oppose range expansion, their population density necessarily increases within the restricted area to which they are then confined. Competition within their restricted range then forces changes in patterns of social organisation and settlement.[3] Comparable social changes have been recorded in other vernacular societies such as the Shoshone Amerindians and the complex societies of Papua.[4-5]

In small island populations of the Pacific, newly arrived peoples gradually increased in number to produce intense competition leading to the creation of hierarchies and complex political organisation accompanied by interpretive systems that supported the religious authority of the hierarchs. In some cases, such societies stabilised but in others, they broke down, as on Easter Island, and the population reverted in strife to forms that are more primitive. In all such cases, the world views of the people change to suit their unavoidable circumstances.[6]

These examples are all illustrations of the complex relations between environment, habitat exploitation, population density, social organisation and the sustaining beliefs that comprise vernacular world views. In populations that are numerically well below the carrying capacity of their habitats, competition is slight and reproduction fast causing high rates of population increase. By contrast, where populations are close to the maximum supportable by the carrying capacity of the habitat, competition is keen, mortality increases with density, reproduction slows and social organisation becomes complex. Efficiency in competition rather than productivity becomes a prime characteristic. Among humans, world views of relatively simple societies are strongly determined by density in relation to resources.

When we look at the modern world, we can see that humanity has largely filled the usable planetary habitat and that non-renewable resources are diminishing. The history of humanity has been one of extensive global expansion for millennia. In recent centuries, the prime movers have been European peoples forcing their expansion into regions sparsely occupied by others. The mercantilist thrust driving these movements was expressed in a world view accepting no limiting frontier either physically or philosophically – witness the immense optimism of the European enlightenment together with its extraordinary success in exploring all realms of knowledge.[7] In the youthful USA, all this was expressed as the 'frontier spirit'. Unfortunately the 'frontier' has been reached – not only on the Pacific coast but also in terms of global population density. The European expansion has been halted by the failure of imperialism in lands already occupied by effectively resistant cultures. Today the Chinese are expanding into the lightly populated regions of Central Asia. Yet, the legacy of Western expansionism remains an economic theory and a psychology only appropriate to earlier conditions when resources seemed unlimited and the frontier still far away. It needs replacing today.

The consequent failure of economic theory to relate to the laws of socio-ecology lies at the root of the social tensions that press everywhere. Until we develop a world view that responds to the dependence of the human population on patterns of density and their social concomitance, such tension with all its ramifications at the personal level will continue.

EXPLORING THE SOLUTION

One approach is to take globalisation truly seriously by looking more widely at what world culture as a whole can offer. Reason and insight are by no means Western attributes alone. Can other cultures offer clues to a better way? Just as food products from all over the world are easily available in our emporia so Asian philosophies and viewpoints are today easily discovered in our bookshops. Western academic work tends to be amazingly slow to catch on to such perspectives. Even major works in philosophy and ethics commonly reflect solely on Western history and culture as if no one else ever had a creative thought: and this in spite of our understanding that the structure of personal identity is highly culturally dependent.[8] Reading such works, one might suppose that any culture worth considering arose solely from that of the ancient Greeks. The contributions of India and China are usually sidelined and not considered seriously. Eastern thought is something towards which a Western academic may genuflect but not take too seriously lest one be considered beyond the pale. Yet, even a slight acquaintance with Asian thought reveals paradigms so strikingly at variance with Western perspectives, and often interestingly subversive of them, that to ignore their potential global contribution is tantamount to arrogance. In challenging this stance, this book takes a risk. Yet, let us see what the outcome may be.

In 'The Evolution of Human Consciousness' (1980) I attempted to reflect on the cross fertilisation that could emerge by taking seriously a three way relationship between biology, especially evolutionary biology, social psychology-anthropology and an eastern vision of the self, in particular Buddhism.[9] It seemed to me that what the East could offer was a functional phenomenology, a subjective empiricism that had never developed in Western thought, one that might be more responsive to the stresses of our times. Although the book was warmly welcomed in some circles and used for a while in University courses, perhaps the time was not yet ripe for such a synthesis. It did not make the impact that essentially the same argument was to make a decade later. I wrote against a background of prevailing instrumentalism in science and relativism in philosophy. Only a few doors were opening.

By 1991, ignorant of this prior work and in a more relaxed climate of scientific understanding, Francisco Varela, Evan Thompson and Eleanor Rosh were claiming successfully that: "It is our contention that the rediscovery of Asian philosophy, particularly of the Buddhist tradition, is a second renaissance in the cultural history of the West, with the potential to be equally as important as the rediscovery of Greek thought in the European renaissance. Our Western histories of philosophy, which ignore Indian thought, are artificial since India and Greece share with us an Indo-European linguistic heritage as well as many cultural and philosophical preoccupations."[10] They justified their position in much the same way as I had done by showing that the prime feature of Buddhist thought is based in direct experience and not merely speculation or philosophising about experience. Both works argue for a subjective empiricism that balances the objective empiricism of the European tradition, a practical phenomenology in fact. While the West contributes to the science of matter, the East has deeper, traditional insight into the science of mind. Together they can initiate a new enquiry into the creation of human values.

Does this proposal really make a difference? Buddhist phenomenology is particularly concerned with the nature of the self and we may well contend that it is the self in either personal or institutionalised forms that produces the problems we are enduring, particularly since a solution requires a self restraint entirely absent in prevailing Western economics. If Tinbergen was right in arguing that a "new type of citizen" is required to put the world to rights, then clearly it is through an examination of what the 'self' comprises that we must proceed. Let us look then at what Asian thought may be able to offer. The one Asian perspective that transcends regional cultural constraints and has proved itself to be of universal relevance is the message of the Buddha.

End Notes

1. Humboldt, A. von 1850-1859. *Cosmos: A sketch of a Physical Description of the Universe.* 5 vols. Harper. New York. Original in German.

2. Kuhn, T.S.1970 *The Structure of Scientific Revolutions.* Chicago University Press. Chicago.

3. Dyson-Hudson, R. 1989. Ecological influences on systems of food production

and social organisation of South Turkhana pastoralists. In: Standen, V. & R.A. Foley. (Eds.) *Comparative Socioecology: the behavioural ecology of humans and other mammals.* Blackwell. Oxford.

4. Maitland-Bradfield, R. 1973. *A Natural History of Associations: a study in the meaning of community.* Duckworth. London.

5. Feil, D.K. 1987. *The Evolution of Highland Papua New Guinea Societies.* Cambridge University Press. Cambridge.

6. Forde, C.D.1934. *Habitat, Economy and Society. A geographical introduction to Ethnology.* Methuen. London.

   Reader, J. 1988. *Man on Earth.* Collins. London.

7. Sloan, K. 2003. *Enlightenment: discovering the world of the eighteenth century.* British Museum. London.

8. Neisser, U. and D.A. Jopling (eds.). 1997. *The Conceptual self in Context: Culture, experience, self understanding.* Cambridge University Press.

9. Crook, J.H. 1980. *The Evolution of Human Consciousness.* Clarendon. Oxford.

10. Varela, F. Thompson, E. & E. Rosch. 1991. *The Embodied Mind: Cognitive science and Human experience.* MIT Press. Cambridge. Mass.

3

ASIAN PERSPECTIVES:
THE CASE FOR BUDDHISM

Surprising as it may seem, the first person to seriously question the sources of human suffering in ignorant stupidity was not some long sighted, contemporary scientist with global concerns but a minor Indian prince who lived some 2500 years ago. Siddhartha Gautama, known later in life as the Buddha, asked fundamental questions about the nature of the ignorance that underlay suffering. The insights he achieved have lain at the root of some of the most peaceful and creative cultures the world has known and in which matters of psychological depth were explored over a time period numbering more than two thousand years.

At around the same time as Heraclitus in Greece was pondering the nature of the Universe and coming to some remarkably similar conclusions, the Buddha's "Law of Co-dependent Arising" emerged as perhaps the very first scientific law based on personal empiricism. He argued that the universe expressed the patterning of change through time, one event determining another in a matrix of causation 'co-dependently'. The past has gone, the future unborn, only the present exists impermanently as the flux of change. He was arguing against the 'eternalist' thinkers of his time who focussed on an external cause (a form of god or gods) and who therefore argued dualistically and against the nihilists who denied causation. Human life comprised a participatory element in a flux of time perceived as a holistic system of 'interdependent origination'.[1]

Unlike Greek thinkers, whose intellectual orientation was mostly outward to the world and which led heroically to the objective empiricism of Western science, the Buddha derived his 'Law' from an inward investigation of the mind, a 'subjective empiricism'.[2] This was however no mere introspection, a review of thoughts, feelings and ideas, but a profound exploration of the nature of experience itself utilizing the yogic methods already current in Indian religious practice and which had come down from shamanic origins. This subtle, yogic methodology, to which the Buddha added his own insightful practice, gave him access to phenomena of consciousness and mental functioning that an objective rationalism could never have reached. Basically, he came to realize that our world was very far from what it seemed to us to be and that this profound illusion was a product of our seemingly helpless persistence in an erroneous way of seeing. Even today, after some fifty years of rapidly increasing sophistication in the appreciation of Buddhism in the West, many critical thinkers still think of Buddhism as a 'religion' or as a metaphysical philosophy of an outdated culture unlikely to be of significance in a world dominated by Western thought and practice. Of course, just as science is embedded and merged with non scientific aspects of Western culture, so these Eastern systems are often socially embedded in traditional cultures of village life that interpret the world in relatively primitive ways. Yet, when one looks at the outstanding philosophical work of great oriental thinkers, one comes across interpretations of humanity that are radical in the extreme and profoundly insightful, especially in the domains of psychology and social life. In science, it is expected that writers will refer carefully to the relevant work of others and to acknowledge the work of precursors. Tinbergen was not familiar with Eastern thought or the nature of its concerns. Contemporary thinkers do not have that excuse. Translations of major texts are no longer difficult to obtain and critical scholarship has developed based upon them. Buddhist thought, the Buddha Dharma, has much to say about human suffering and if we are to develop a global perspective, as indeed we must, these views need careful examination in relation to Western viewpoints. When one viewpoint is reflected in the mirror of another, unusual insights begin to make an appearance generating creative and novel ideas.

I argue that of the several important Asian thought systems, Buddhism is today the most valuable due to its cross-cultural reach, the clarity of its logical presentation and the yogic nature of its practices, its empiricism and its social and political implications. Hinduism is too firmly embedded in the Indian social system including that of caste to be exportable on a wide scale, although it has important similarities to Buddhism and shares with Buddhism a common origin in the cultural resistance to Vedic thought in ancient times. Philosophical Taoism today lacks effective institutions and is largely modified through relating to Chinese Buddhism. Islam suffers from similar problems to those of Christianity when called to account by science and has yet to experience a humanist renaissance. The Buddhist analysis of suffering as a consequence of illusion throws up a perspective on Tinbergen's doubt of the greatest interest. It may be that the design fault at the root of contemporary problems lies in the nature of self-knowledge, the very seedbed of human thought and motivation. This was certainly the Buddha's viewpoint and we need to examine it closely.

THE BUDDHIST DIASPORA

In 2500 years, the Buddha Dharma (teaching) has spread cross culturally around the world. From India it penetrated China mingling with indigenous Chinese thought, Taoism and Confucianism, and went on to Japan. There it became deeply rooted, generating artistic skills and martial arts shaped by the Japanese character. It went north into Tibet, again to produce a specific methodology of mental yoga based on the character of Tibetan civilization. A westward extension was blocked by the European dark ages, the spread of Islam, the vigour of Christianity and the emergence of Cartesian dualism but the recent arrival of Buddhism in the West has in a few years yielded temples, meditation centres and practice groups in virtually all major cities and, particularly in U.S.A, advanced interpretive scholarship. So far Buddhist thought in the West remains close to its origins: little amalgamation or assimilation with Western paradigms has yet emerged, although there are signs that this is beginning in the philosophical work of Joanna Macy, Stephen Batchelor and David Loy. In the main this is due simply to the difficulty Westerners have had in taking on the Dharma (teaching) in its subtle profundity and specific focus so often counter intuitive to Western ideas. In these distressing times, in which traditional Western religion has so sadly and severely failed, people are looking for comfort, spiritual succour and insights into their hurt and often believe that Buddhism holds at least some answers. Western Buddhists are mostly naive, floating along with great expectations and idealizations and usually fail to realize that Buddhism requires hard work, a struggle with internal, personal contradictions.

This book makes the case that once vital linkages are established between Buddhist thought and Western sciences, especially biology, psychology and sociology, we will have in the making core proposals for a revolution in social attitudes of great relevance for the remedial treatment needed if we are to avoid the planet wide disaster to civilization Tinbergen so clearly foretold. As he said, this may involve nothing less than the creation through education of a "new type of citizen". The emphasis must focus then on new systems of education, multicultural, international, economically and sociologically critical, participative and innovative, which will enthuse the young for an essential work of transformation inevitably political in nature. In such a process, a fresh world view will be in the making. I am not here making a case for Buddhism as such, nor for some sort of Buddhist take over, but rather I will attempt to show how key Buddhist ideas can and must play a major role in creating an influential 'buddhistic' perspective on the problems we have been considering.

Already key figures in Western thought have acknowledged the significance of Buddhist paradigms. In the eighteenth century, philosophers Schopenhauer and Nietzsche considered some key ideas of Buddhism as highly relevant in response to the growing nihilism of the time. In the last century, Carl Jung on his deathbed was reading D.T Suzuki with enthusiasm. Martin Heidegger too has been reported as saying that had he read Zen earlier he would not have needed to write his philosophy! Christmas Humphreys' book 'Buddhism' in the Pelican series from Penguin (1951) introduced the subject to a wide readership.[3] Gifted writers such as Alan Watts,[4] Joanna Macy,[5] Jack Kerouac[6] and poets Alan Ginsburg and Gary Snyder have touched many hearts[7]. Recent thinkers, such as the Oxford philosophers David Parfitt and Iris Murdoch, have paid respects to the Buddha and the environmentalist Maurice Ash has created a Buddhist college on his estate.[8] Gregory Bateson, one of the greatest of contemporary holistic thinkers, spent his dying days in the San Francisco Zen Centre and his ashes were scattered on the shore at Big Sur by Zen Master Reb Anderson. Through their scholarship, academics such as Herbert Guenther, Peter Gregory, Bernard Faure, Steven Heine, Steven Collins, Richard Gombrich, Jeffery Hopkins, Dale.S.Wright, Michael Carrithers and others have given precision and analytical depth to our understanding. Joanna Macy, Stephen Batchelor and David Loy and a surprising number of American thinkers[9] have begun the task of relating Western thought to Buddhist ideas. There is also an increasingly popular genre of writing that draws on Buddhist perspectives or practices but with a more limited presentation of their meaning. The ideas appear as genuflections to sources known to be important but only partially digested. Some of the best examples of these writings include Alan Watt's popular work, Kerouac's beat Zen and Persig's impressive *Zen in the art of Motorcycle maintenance* and *Lila*. Such texts draw fragmentary Buddhist ideas within the frame of the Western consensus often in the way that yoga has become popular in beauty parlours or meditation used as a calming practice 'mainstreamed' in hospitals, asylums or prisons, yet their significance is not trivial but rather expressive of a general trend. Additionally the new approach to cognitive science in the work of Varela (Chapter 2) and Austin[10] suggests that Science too is opening its doors.

To push a concern with Buddhist insights further it is essential to relate Buddhist practice to contemporary thought in a more embracing way, to suggest precisely how the premises and hypotheses of this ancient system may integrate with Western paradigms. It must be argued straight away that Buddhist thought is not a religion in the sense that the 'religions of the book', Judaism, Christianity and Islam are so called: rather it is an enquiry into human nature and experience. It presents no dogmatic theism in which divinity is imagined as an external cosmic source for inspiration but focuses on human existence from a phenomenological perspective. There is here no string puller, confessor, father or tyrant, no heaven and no hell. Instead, there is the mind in all its wondrous complexity, subtlety and potential, a mind furthermore capable of uncovering its own 'salvation'.

BUDDHISM AND THE WEST

Why should it have taken Buddhism so long to have an impact on Western thought? To answer this question we need a brief outline of the curious story of Buddhist history (See further Chapter 11). The Buddha's Dharma was never a folk religion like Hinduism, Bon or Shinto. It began almost as a protest movement against the dominance of the Brahmins in Indian life and thus the caste system. Even so, it was essentially a top-down movement founded by a highborn revolutionary and, although open to all, it attracted many from the higher reaches of Indian society indeed from among Brahmins themselves. Buddhism has an elitist tendency and its major successes have been associated with support from rulers, some of them great emperors.

Monasteries are always at risk in periods of major social or political strife when folk religions tend to re-assert themselves or the belief systems of a conqueror eliminate that of an earlier educated elite. In India the great Buddhist universities did not survive the advance of Islam and much of what we now have of Mahayana Buddhism owes its survival to its refuge in Tibet and its entry to China. Monks and lay followers need teachings if the superstitions of folk belief are not to submerge them. In India under Islam, the Hindu folk beliefs gradually re-absorbed the remains of Buddhist culture eventually to fertilize an intellectual revival in the teachings of the great Hindu thinker Shankara. Buddhism itself did not re-appear in strength in India until Dr Ambedkar, leader of the 'untouchables' in the last century, adopted it as a religion that would bypass the social discrimination of the Hindu caste system.

Before its demise in India, Buddhism had spread along the silk routes and by sea to China. Its spread and influence there fluctuated according to the extent of the support provided by emperors and mandarins. Contending with the indigenous beliefs of Taoism and Confucianism, Buddhist monasteries were always liable to assault on the grounds of being of foreign origin or because of the effect of large monastic estates on the economy.[11] Its monastic rather than folk basis posed a risk to its continuance whenever politics took a negative turn. Even so, in China, long after its demise in India, Buddhist creativity again flourished producing new philosophical perspectives and practices of an often highly pragmatic nature.

The southern schools of the Theravada containing the earliest teachings flowered in Burma, Thailand and Sri Lanka beyond the influence of Islam but in Indonesia it was absorbed into Hinduism following the spread, once again, of Islam. It was this Theravada Buddhism that first impressed Europeans. The imperial West derived its earliest understanding of Buddhism from these countries. Between the seventeenth and nineteenth centuries, Europe extended its influence in Asia at first along trade routes and later in the development of British and Dutch empires. The effectiveness of Western technologies, military control and the vigour of missionary Christianity with its intolerance of other faiths, comprised a power that could not then be matched by anything the East could offer. Yet, already by the end of the nineteenth century doubt was spreading, confidence starting to fade and belief in an innate superiority fading. In Europe the emergence of rationalist philosophy, the Western 'enlightenment', generated a new liberalism and a tolerance that was eventually to express itself in the emergence in India of the Indian National Congress of which some of the founder members were British. In Europe, the philosophical movement through Hume to Kant unseated an arrogant Christianity leaving the questioning doubt of Nietzsche and Kierkegaard in its place. The rapid expansion of experimental science provided extraordinary advances in material knowledge leaving the world of the spirit to languish.

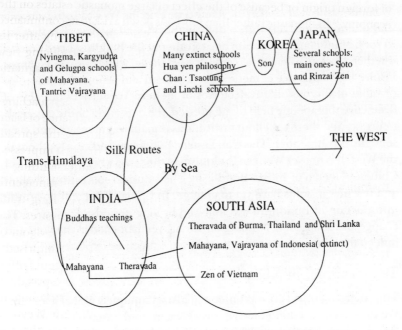

The Global Spread of Buddhist Thought

Although humanist liberalism and an increasingly democratic polity was linked to a social conscience that abolished the slave trade, the thrust of the British industrial revolution increased the power of empire, the exploitation of resources and the implicit subjection of non-European peoples. Only gradually did the ethics of European imperialism and the consequences of fascism and communism became clear so that the failure of the Christian West became evident, and a search for an alternative viewpoint began. Ready to hand were the thoughtful philosophies of the orient.

Yet Buddhist thought had been stagnant for centuries: the last creative phase in the long history of Buddhist philosophy had occurred in China with the Hua yan philosophers developing the ideas of the old Indian Avatamsaka Sutra in new and fascinating ways (7th Century CE). [12] Buddhism as discovered by the West was simply circling slowly within its own heritage. Even so, embedded in that heritage were insightful jewels that, once glimpsed, stimulated Westerners to the creative investigation running at full spate today.

Buddhism as practised in the many centres in the West today is primarily a lay phenomenon, very different from the oriental monasticism that was its root. Many centres recreate one or other of the Buddhist orientations, whether Tibetan, Theravada, Zen or a new fangled version usually Japanese inspired. The practice of meditation is general and proven not only to be of value in the busy life trajectories of modern Westerners but also of distinctive therapeutic help to the stressed, the depressed or the anxiously neurotic. Yet, these excellent institutions remain fragmentary, and even sometimes competitive. This is an Eastern Buddhism finding a foothold in the West. It is not yet Western Buddhism in the sense whereby we speak of Chinese, Tibetan or Indian Buddhism. The cultural roots remain shallow and few new insights have yet to emerge. In China, Tibet and Japan the introduction of Buddhism was followed by long periods of assimilation, change and adaptation. Nothing similar has yet happened in the West and indeed the time is so short that such could scarcely be expected.

THE NEED FOR A BUDDHISTIC ENQUIRY

The emerging world crisis is unique in history, uniquely global in extent. We need to understand in what ways Western and Eastern wisdoms can fertilise one another, perhaps to yield new orientations that can revolutionise current paradigms in ways that may protect global civilisation from the developing ecological, economic and political scenario that few doubt comprises threats never experienced before. It seems likely that emerging world wisdom will confront the culture of consumer capitalism head on, for therein lie some major psychological and sociological roots of the problem. Maybe too an investigation of this nature can rekindle that intellectual enthusiasm for life and thought that the bright young woman quoted in Peter Reason's lecture felt to have deserted her (Chapter 1). If the young cannot feel committed to a way of hope, then the likelihood of a future for them becomes remote.

Such an exploration needs to be undertaken now. The pace of socio-political and ecological change; the 'future shock' of these changes; the terrorist response of those whose fundamentalist theologies are threatened; the extraordinary vistas opened up by genetic engineering, electronic communication, robotics and brain physiology, are so far reaching and puzzling and generally so poorly understood, particularly perhaps by so called world 'leaders' with their often limited intellectual vision, that there is a real urgency about an enquiry that centres on human motivation, values, ethics and the nature of wisdom. Indeed, it seems there may be nothing more important than such an enquiry today.

In examining the way in which Buddhism can contribute to contemporary world culture we need to find out which questions the Buddha Dharma (teaching) tackles especially well and those which, researched in the West, are neglected in its teachings. As we have pointed out the world is becoming culturally, politically, economically ever more interdependent. We need a global vision for globalisation. Both Buddhism and Western thought contain much wisdom. We need to see if these distinctive wisdoms of East and West can speak to one another and thus to the difficulties of our times. Yet, first of all we need to understand that the philosophical project of Buddhism is of a very different nature from traditional Western thought.

Western thought today is deeply schizoid. On one side, Christianity and Christian values remain deeply rooted. In standard Christianity, the meaning of the world and human life is provided by the word of God in the Bible as related in the extraordinary story of the life and death of Christ. In this vision, the human soul stands as the focus of creation on a planet still implicitly the pivot of universal history and the especial concern of God. The symbolism of the Christian story runs very deep, full of archetypes that resonate with the daily experience of worldly life. Yet, the formal expression of the interpretive theology does not seem to relate in any clear way with our scientific comprehension of the Universe as revealed in modern times.

The mythology of the Churches and their authoritarian hold on the Western mind was originally broken through the emergence of a questing intelligence seeking to understand how things actually were.[13] Man became no longer the central figure, indeed in many ways his being appeared increasingly as an accident, a rarity, and a form of life that may perhaps be unique and transient. Loneliness before the vastness and ever changing nature of the cosmos and the separateness of the human spirit from the physical world is inevitably accompanied by a sense of loss. The ancient innocence has gone, we are 'disenchanted'. We seem adrift in ultimate unknowing, in total insecurity. Thinking Westerners attuned to science are for the most part living a form of stoicism, courageously facing the unknown and creating personal values from the practice of life itself, creating the 'authenticity' of humanism.

Buddhism by contrast is a soteriological phenomenology: an experientially based investigation into human life rooted in the belief that at the end of a knowledgeable, practice oriented path a personal solution to the problem of alienation and suffering can be found. The

Western paradigm prevailingly looks outward at the apparent things of this world; the Buddhist looks at their representation in experience and asks what that is and what it means.

One can see a convergence in these perspectives; while the external world is only known through the internal, the internal is clearly an aspect of that which is explored by the outward vision. As we shall see, Buddhism does not reduce outer experience to a mind alone in solecism but rather explores in what way outer and inner converge as one understanding. While Western thought is primarily dualistic, Buddhist thought tends to an ultimate monism of an acceptable unknowing. What however may be the outcome of convergence?

The power of the Western paradigm lies in the extraordinary way in which logic driven by mathematical description can comprehend physical mechanisms and, through experiment, demonstrate the accuracy of theory that can then be applied in creative technologies. We are enabled to split the atom, fly to the moon, clone living creatures. All this however has emerged only within the last century of our existence and such power does nothing to relieve the existential loneliness of individuals in the face of universal chance, nor does it provide roots for clear ethics with which to meet the problems of exploitation, violence and the many forms of strife. In a strange way all our scientific achievements are devoid of personal 'meaning' because all we have are utilitarian values.

The power of Buddhist thought lies in its close relationship to practice; its examination of the nature of experience, the depths of consciousness, the nature of self identity, and from these to construct values and a way of life that breaks free from dualisms that appear at first sight unavoidable. It returns us to a belonging in the natural world perceiving humanity as an integral part of nature. It operates, as did the Buddha, by questioning the very basis of knowledge and inference as experienced by the mind. It remains open to repeated experiential test, generation after generation, and may be expressed in varying ways in different cultures and different times without losing its root in the meditative quest.

During his teaching career, the Buddha was often expected to answer questions that his followers and interlocutors threw at him. He was quite surprisingly ruthless in his disciplined replies. Certain types of questions he would simply not answer. These were questions such as 'Does the world have a beginning and an end or does it go on for ever?' He rightly saw that such questions could receive no answer. They are purely metaphysical and he felt it useless to discuss them because they could only lead to a multiplicity of irresolvable contradictions. In addition, the form of such questions usually implied a dualism, which he had already rejected. He would however respond at length, in depth and with novel insight to questions about human life and experience. Buddhism therefore contains no theory about the nature of the universe or time. Rather it provides an experientially tested path for the relief of suffering through 'enlightenment', a path with social consequences, and it does, moreover, imply a theory of knowledge.

If the Buddha were to return today, he would find that many topics that could only be metaphysical speculations in his time have now received empirical investigation through the development of scientific methodologies. The responses we now have about these issues fill out the context within which the Buddhist paradigm works. For example, we have a much wider understanding of the universe and time, broader understanding of human psychology, deeper psychiatric knowledge. All of these would certainly fall within the Buddha's discourse today. Indeed, we can see the truth of this in the width and depth of the Dalai Lama's teachings that encompass most contemporary problems about which anything constructive can be said.

Table 1

FIELDS OF ENQUIRY IN WESTERN THOUGHT RELEVANT TO THE BUDDHIST PARADIGM

(1)   Evolutionary theory in relation to mind
(2)   Psychology of self and identity
(3)   Consciousness
(4)   Economics and ethics
(5)   Post-modernity and the global crisis
(6)   Transformation and cultural change

There are several main areas to examine. Since Buddhism is so focussed on mental phenomena, an important theme is the modern understanding of the origins and evolution of the mind. Evolutionary theory is synthetic based upon genetics, palaeo-ecology, and the study of adaptations, selection theory, and behavioural ecology. Its prime heuristic, its provocative idea of natural selection, defines the process whereby the progressive evolution of any replicating structure can occur. In an evolutionary perspective, we can provide a reasoned context for the origins of mind discussed in Buddhist theory. There has also been discussion about the origin of ethical systems based in field studies of behavioural control in animals. Ethical behaviour seems to be based in human universals that underlie contrasts between cultures. The similarity between the ethical systems of major religions suggests a common root not dissimilar from the basic precepts of Buddhism.

Buddhism is particularly concerned with the nature and shortcomings of the self and what happens to psychological identification in meditative states. The 'object-relations theory' of psychotherapy also describes the functions and nature of self in ways that parallel and even support a Buddhist interpretation of 'karma'. In many respects, the study of self and identity lies at the heart of both Buddhism and modern social psychology. Many issues arise here. How do Buddhist ethics relate to modern economics? Can the commitments of Buddhist practitioners influence the ethos of institutions within which they work? What sort of education is essential to bring about change in the world? How do Buddhist values relate to those of Christianity and humanist stoicism?

In examining these questions, we first need an account of the Buddha Dharma itself and the way in which it is presented by Western thinkers. The second part of this book therefore surveys the long journey of Buddhism from India to the West. We turn then first of all to asking who the Buddha was and what he actually said.

End Notes

1. Macy J. 1991. *Mutual causality in Buddhism and General Systems Theory.* SUNY. New York.

2. Crook, J.H. 1980. *The Evolution of Human Consciousness.* Clarendon. Oxford.

3. Humphreys, C. 1951. *Buddhism.* Pelican. Penguin. London.

4. Watts, A. 1972. *In my own way: an autobiography.* Pantheon. New York.

5. Macy, Joanna. 1991. *World as Lover, World as self.* Pantheon. New York.

6. Haynes, S. 2005. An exploration of Jack Kerouac's Buddhism: text and life. *Contemporary Buddhism,* 6.2.153-172.

7. Fields, R. 1986. *How the Swans came to the Lake. A narrative history of Buddhism in America.* Shambala. Boston & London.

8. Ash, M. 1992. *The Fabric of the World. Towards a Philosophy of Environment.* Green Books. Bideford. *Environment.*

9. Inada, K.K. and N.P. Jacobson (Eds.). 1984. *Buddhism and American Thinkers.* Sri Satguru Publications. Delhi . Originally published by SUNY.

10. Austin, J.H. 1999. *Zen and the Brain: Toward an understanding of Meditation and Consciousness.* MIT Press. Cambridge Mass.

11.   Gernet, J. 1995 *Buddhism in Chinese Society: an economic history from the fifth to the tenth centuries.* Columbia. University Press. New York.

12.   Cleary, T. 1983. *Entry into the Inconceivable. An introduction to Hua-yen Buddhism.* University of Hawai'i Press. Honolulu.

13.   Tarnas, R. 1991. *The Passion of the Western Mind.* Ballantine. New York.

PART II

GLOBAL BUDDHISM

In clarity the wonder exists, with spiritual energy shining on its own. It cannot be grasped so cannot be called being. It cannot be rubbed away and so cannot be called non-being. Beyond the mind of deliberation and discussion, depart from the remains of the shadowy images. Emptying one's sense of self existence is wondrous. This wonder is embodied with a spirit that can be re-enacted. This is how one must genuinely investigate the essence.

Chan Master Hongzhi.
Practice Instructions.[1]

4

THE CONTEXT OF THE BUDDHA'S TEACHING

The Buddha was born into an Indian civilisation that was already complex, sophisticated and undergoing a slow fermentation of social, political and cultural change. To understand the relevance of his teachings to his time we need to have a clear picture of the cultural background to which they relate, to which they contributed and from which they stand out so uniquely.

There is also another important reason for a clear comprehension of the context of the Buddha's life and thought. The social and economic changes occurring in his time were having consequences for the social psychology of self that resemble in some respects the changes going on today, some twenty-five centuries later. The manner in which personal identity was understood was changing in ways that remind us of our present situation. Of course we must not make too much of this point because the levels of global activity today are of an entirely different order from those of his time and the cultural basis different. Even so, such parallels suggest reasons why Buddhism is growing in influence in today's world and why a 'buddhistic' perspective is of importance to us.

Sources of Indian Civilisation

The civilisation of India goes back an astonishingly long time, indeed in common with the ancient civilisations of the Euphrates and China, it began in the third millennium BC on the banks of a great river that supplied ample soil, regular moisture and other conditions suited to agricultural development. The first great cities of India grew up on the banks of the Indus near present day villages known now as Mohenjodaro and Harappa. In time, this civilisation spread as far south as Gujarat and into the upper Ganges valley showing remarkable uniformity throughout. The peoples who created these cultures are believed to have been of ancient Indian stock, Dravidian peoples whose genes still course in Indian blood and especially in some of the tribal societies of the Deccan and among low caste people. These sophisticated cities, trading centres for an agricultural economy, were the seedbed for important features of Indian religious life that in mutant form have continued unto the present day.

We know from figurines and relief carvings on seals that yoga postures and presumably related practices were already present and that gods and goddesses similar in form to Shiva and others were already worshipped, although doubtless not in the way that developed in later Hinduism. The culture was probably 'shamanistic', with shamanic priests making contact with nature gods of the environment. Yoga may well have begun in association with the induction of altered states of consciousness by shamans during rituals of intercession perhaps involving 'journeys' to the lands of the gods. While no details of these early practices survive, they may have resembled the religious preoccupations of some tribal groups still extant in the sub continent. Transformations of mental activity, a feature so important in Indian religion and in various ways common to most forms of shamanism, thus seem to have been present at the very roots of Indian civilisation.[2]

The invasions of northern India by Aryan peoples seem to have begun around 2000 BC and continued for a long time. The old Dravidian civilisations faded away and the victorious Aryans imposed their own culture upon the land. A prime feature of this process was the creation of non-intermarrying castes, at first doubtlessly based on ethnic grounds, whereby the Dravidians were driven into servile roles in a world dominated by three superior and purely Aryan castes, landowners, traders and business people, warriors and priests. Caste was essentially a product of Aryan colonisation of a subject people. It was in fact a successful form of 'apartheid'.

The creation of caste was related to a world view containing two essential ideas forming what was essentially a rationalised justification for the social structure. The first of these ideas was that of cyclical rebirth, later known to the Buddhists as 'samsara'. The second was the idea that the natural order of life could only be maintained by the practice of sacrifice. At first sacrifice was undoubtedly made to the gods who were appeased or cajoled into sustaining the universe as a consequence of effective performance. Later, however, the gods' role diminished in importance: the performance of accurate sacrificial ritual itself became the means of 'sustaining the revolutions of the Universe'[3]

This was no easy feat! To achieve it, the complex ritual had to be performed with a precision in which the correct pronunciation of key words or phrases in chants was critical. Only the Brahmin priests knew the secrets of making correct sacrifice and received the training required. In theory, therefore, the sustainability of life itself depended on their activities and their purity.

The castes were required to maintain a certain moral integrity. One had to behave correctly in accordance with the rules of caste in order to have the possibility of a rebirth in a higher order. Good behaviour in a servile caste had its own reward in rebirth whereas any revolutionary act of resistance would ensure various forms of damnation. This was a system of moral coercion ensuring the extraordinary stability of social structure in Hindu India that survives in little altered forms even today. Generally, the caste into which one was born was believed to be a consequence of one's karma - that is of one's behaviour in both this and previous lives; yet ritual sacrifice, for those who could afford it, could sustain a person's status. The strength of this extraordinary, ethical system reflects the ability of the Brahmin priestly caste to sustain its relative integrity and its position on the moral high ground of this civilisation.[4]

Needless to say, there was one caste that tended to find the Brahmin superiority particularly irksome; the kshatriyas or warrior caste included kings, military captains and local rulers whose leadership behaviour was none the less held within bounds by the need for Brahmin support. Without the sacrifices conducted by Brahmins, no prince could be sure of success in any enterprise. It is therefore not surprising that resistance to the Brahmins pre-eminence came in due course largely from this quarter, although there were also those among the Brahmins who sought a way out of this tightly bound society in a quest to break the shackles of karma and thus to escape samsara.

THE INTERNALISATION OF RITUAL SACRIFICE

The way out of the Brahminical trap lay in the gradual emergence of points of view that radically shifted the interpretation of the role of sacrifice in human life. Stephen Collins has described this sequence of ideas through careful and exhaustive examination of the relevant ancient literature, the Vedas, Upanishads and Brahminical writings.[5]

He points, first of all, to an underlying, cyclical motif rooted in the movements of the sun and moon and their significance in agricultural cycles, the alternation of day and night, summer and winter. In the early literature, cosmic and personal cycles reflected one another. Efficacious practice of sacrifice ensured a passage to other worlds, either of the ancestors or of the gods. It was not, however, deemed possible to stay in such worlds without losing humanity through madness; a return to the human condition necessarily followed. Cyclic reincarnation was the norm.

There were essentially three births/deaths in a man's life; the first being the initiating sacrifice on entering his caste brotherhood, the second during further sacrifices that maintain such life and the third being physical death followed by the funeral pyre. A person was not thought to move into future existence in one piece, rather fragments of personality were believed to disperse separately. "At death a man's breath returns to the wind, his eye (sight) to the sun, his bones to the plants,–thus a (sacrificial) hymn to preserve a man's life calls back his breath from the wind and his sight from the sun."[6] In the natural cycles of life, these fragments are re-assembled on the return to earthly life. Certain sacrifices may enable a priest to re-assemble the person by calling back such functions from the worlds to which they have gone, essentially watery, airy and fiery. In the performance of sacrifice, the priest literally makes up a person during such a re-assemblage, presumably beneficially.

As time went on, the belief arose that high moral behaviour in this life would influence rebirth since moral behaviour was seen to have aspects of personal sacrifice in its performance. It followed that 'karma' shaped by moral choice became an important determinant of the quality of the return and a dominant eschatological idea.[7] Good behaviour became the basis for a more beneficial return. Furthermore, if the result of sacrifice depended on the correct knowledge of the magical acts of chant and sound, then knowledge of such skills was potentially equivalent to their performance. Maybe a sacrifice need not be performed at all if the inner knowledge and skills were already present? Such a thought seems to have been the basis for a major shift in emphasis among certain Brahmins - not so much a rejection of sacrificial ideas as a development from them. Action becomes internalised as an inner practice.

Collins tells us: "It should not be thought that this necessarily implies an outright opposition to the caste system of Brahminical society; rather it implies the beginnings of the alternative- and ultimately complementary type of religious practice; that is of those who 'went to the forest' dispensing with external rituals and caste-related behaviour, leaving the social world of the village in order to make their entire life into a sacred ritual act."[8]

When a person's entire life becomes a sacrificial act, then everything one does has its effect on the nature of the next life. Yet, this life sacrifice did indeed entail hardship. The renouncer opted out of caste society entirely. By becoming a 'home-leaver' he was no longer any sort of householder. He was socially 'dead' through the ritual act of renunciation and there was no way back. He lost all trace of name and past history as a person in the samsaric world, and indeed this is still true for those sadhus of India who truly renounce worldly life. They are the socially dead. And yet herein lies a deep paradox. In renouncing the social world of their birth, which essentially enslaved them, they become for the first time truly individuals - an individual with no name, creating himself in the inner fire of his own sacrifice. Renouncers were revered and supported by those they had left behind because of the admired purity of their endeavour.

Yet, there is more. Once knowledge is power, there is a question as to the limits of such power. In the earliest texts, the term 'Brahman' (later to mean the power of the universe or 'god') was used to indicate the potency of the Vedic hymns as embodiments of sacrificial power. When such practice became interiorised so did Brahman. The individual atman, 'soul', 'breath' or personal essence, thus became no different from the potency of Brahman itself. "Thou art that" as one scripture, proclaimed. Brahman became identified with universal creativity and the 'atman' seen as the individualised representation of that power. Immanence is omnipresent here but this immanence, although in a sense 'divine', is not derived from the gods but from the power of internalised sacrifice. The gods have been sidelined into merely commentarial roles.

The release from the samsara of caste through renunciation has therefore a 'higher' parallel, namely a release from individual being into universal participation. In the Kausitaki Upanishad, souls are depicted as going to the moon after death. On arrival, one is asked a question. If it is correctly answered, one goes on further but a failure results in a return to earth as rain to be reborn. The question is "Who are you?" and the correct answer is "I am you!" Success means release from the effects of good or bad actions, one is not reborn in samsara but becomes one with the all - Brahman.[9] As Collins rather dryly concludes, "Such an absorption in the 'all', and such an escape from time into timelessness, as part of the conscious inner feeling of individuals, is doubtless the sort of aesthetic feeling which has been described - in western terms- as 'pantheistic mysticism'. In a wider sociological perspective, it is clear that this sort of feeling is available only to a few individuals whose aspirations and skills tend in that direction. What turned this statistically unusual type of feeling into the commonly accepted religious goal in India was the particular social position and prestige of the world renouncer and his quest." We shall see that this was the arena into which the Buddha introduced his own specific and novel insights.

THE SOCIAL AND ECONOMIC SETTING OF THE BUDDHA'S WORLD

At the time of the Buddha's birth the high point of Indian civilisation lay in the middle reaches of the Ganges valley; a plain as rich as that of the Indus, watered by the monsoon and the perpetual rivers descending from the Himalayan glaciers and Tibet; an alluvial plain suitable for rice growing with ample lands to support an enlarging population. In those days it must have been a beautiful land, green for much of the year, covered by rich forests full of wildlife and flowering trees within which were spreading the villages and bright green fields of rice and through which cut the roads between major cities, trading centres situated at river crossings, road junctions and other places conducive for the exchange of goods and for trade. The area was divided between small states that were progressively reduced in number as neighbours swallowed each other up in competitive warfare.

Many of the cities were or had recently been capitals. They were surrounded by handsome defensive walls often of great height and along the streets and alleys were the shops and businesses of numerous trade guilds, workshops of numerous artisans, money lenders, some of the stature of bankers. The pivot of society would have been either a king's palace or a central assembly hall for quasi-republican governance. Many families were rich and supported extensive artistic creativity. Transportation between cities was mostly by foot but large wagons could shift heavier objects. This was the Iron Age and the metal was to be found in the southern hills. It was distributed throughout the area with appropriate customs charges en route. On the river, large boats sailed or rowed between ports. This growing cradle of civilisation did not extend much beyond the Ganges valley, hardly to the East as far as the sea or beyond Delhi to the West. The Deccan seems to have been barely incorporated into Indian civilisation at this time. Compared with later times, the horizons of the Buddha's world were quite small, although of course this would not have appeared so to the inhabitants of the period.[10]

This actively industrious, expanding world had developed from a more or less pastoral beginning with early agricultural settlement to an integrated if competitive economic system based on rice agriculture, ample surpluses, opportunities for trade exchange and extensive urban development. Two systems of governance operated in the contrasting polities of the time. The earlier system was more or less a tribal 'republicanism' with representatives of the entire tribal community meeting to make collective decisions. It seems such assemblies could elect a leader and the Buddha's father was evidently one such. Monarchs with large personal powers ruled other states with limited consultation. Unlike the 'republics', their rule did not include representation from the people. Yet, their governance could not be arbitrary since the rules set by the Brahmins imposed clearly determined duties in relation to sacrifice and the people's welfare. Concentration of power in the hands of an able monarch was evidently politically effective and led to the rapid conquest of neighbouring, less well-organised states. Monarchy was thus replacing republican government in the area during the Buddha's life. It was to continue to do so after Buddha's death until the vast Mauryan Empire was created and the Emperor Ashoka ruled the greater part of the entire sub-continent.

The Ganges valley was experiencing quite rapid and extensive social and cultural change. The old Vedic cults of sacrifice and the strict delimitation of castes had belonged to an essentially pastoral society gradually adapting to more settled agricultural life. With successful cultivation of rice in the riverine lands, the production of surplus allowed for social developments based in the growth of towns appearing where transportation links became naturally established. As the towns became centres for government so wealth accumulated; exchange of goods and money increased; wealth produced increased domestic sophistication; a flourishing of the arts; busy lives occupied in economic and political affairs and also no doubt in both romance and intrigue. Guilds for the manufactures of all sorts of goods from wood, leather, and iron or from precious metals and stones, tended naturally to have urban bases and their products moved upon the roads between the cities. Weapon manufacture and military bases were also doubtless established near the regional capitals. Bankers and moneylenders could create vast fortunes that could be used in the support of enterprises or of particular kings or rulers. All such activity produced a socio-economic style of life to which the old Vedic ways became less relevant and which threatened the old social divisions. Sophisticated sons of bankers with lots of money, fine clothes and material possessions now had the time to contemplate personal existence in a new context. What was the point of money? What was the value of life? Who held the secrets of the spirit–the Vedic Brahmins with their sacrificial cults and costly performances or the renouncers drifting about in the forests and occasionally appearing in the cities with provocatively tranquil demeanour? Such questions had not been asked before because the social conditions for them had not existed. Urban life was their father and time to think their mother. Their existence is reflected in the new doubts and queries appearing in the Upanishads so different from the confident authority of the Vedic hymns. Yet, doubt and enquiry had in fact been present throughout the Aryan search for meaning, the early Vedic Hymn of Creation, for example, provides thoughts on the creation of the world but then continues:

"But, after all, who knows and who can say
Whence it all came and how creation happened?
The gods themselves are later than creation,
So, who knows truly whence it has arisen?

Whence all creation had its origin
He, whether he fashioned it, or whether he did not
He, who surveys it all from highest heaven,
He knows – or maybe he knows not.[11]

In the writing of the Upanishads, such wonderings became pronounced.
We can see too that the renouncers' style of life was not the only form of
individualism developing in this culture. The effective practice of various
forms of business and banking, roles in governance, the direction of public
or princely politics all required an intellectual grasp of practical affairs in
which the development of strongly individualised points of view, capacity
for independent argument and the complex handling of subtle affairs all
required distinctive personalities. The rigidities of the Brahminical
conception of society with its strict and limiting codes of conduct were
inappropriate in this world requiring flexibility and unhampered insights.
Yet, it was still within a deeply conservative world that these people
functioned. Small wonder that there were signs of what today we would
call alienation, a sense of personal emptiness and an increasing need for
personal quest outside the strictures of society. The forest wanderers, the
original outsiders, beckoned.

THE FOREST WANDERERS

The Aryan invasions and their consequent spread within India lasted a
long time. During most of this period, their culture had something of a
frontier spirit about it, expansive confidence and a dominating presence.
Yet, in the Vedic writings there are hints of a contrasting development for
not everyone under the new dispensation accepted it. There are reports
of attempts to harass the sacrificers and the protection of the gods
sometimes may have had to be invoked. The Dravidians did not disappear
and their relation to the new culture was often highly ambivalent, as might
well be expected. In addition, not all Aryans were purely Vedic sacrificers.
There were several elements in this mix. Some Aryans adopted Dravidian
ways but without completely abandoning their own tradition and there
was the possibility that different waves of Aryan invaders had differences
in belief and practice occasioning dispute or divergence. There may even
have been some originally non-Vedic Aryans around to stir the pot. The
Dravidians too were far from uniform, without doubt there were cultivated
descendants from the old Indus civilisation but there were also primitive
tribes of little sophistication. Some supported sacrifice while retaining

original beliefs. All these people may be described as 'marginal' in that they occupied a periphery of the society. Many of them practised austerities, extreme asceticism or sexual practices involving either a prominent promiscuity or extreme celibacy. Some of them may have used yogic means to their conception of salvation or have worshipped one or other of the gods of the Indus people. There is an account of one of these people, a type known as a 'muni'. He is reported as having long hair, clad in dirty, tawny coloured garments, walking in the air delirious from drinking poison in the company of a god, and ecstatic following the paths of sylvan beasts: a figure indeed reminiscent of a contemporary 'New Age' Hare Krishna adept![12]

The Vedic religion was fundamentally practical and concerned with the life of the householder. The sacrificial rituals were designed to ensure the welfare of such people. The Brahmans held to this ideal even when frequenting the forest and practising internalised sacrifice. The true wanderers tended however to deny the Vedic assumptions, rejecting caste, the value of sacrifice and pursuing a personal pursuit of salvation. With such a complex mix outside orthodoxy, some attempt at synthesis was needed and the questioning that underlies the Upanishads has some of its origins within such a synthesis. In particular, the acceptance of the role of karma in the outcomes of a life in samsara was influential. The acceptance of these doctrines caused "a veritable spiritual revolution. The early Vedic religion was life affirming; the post-Vedic attitude is more of life negation – If the moral quality of an action is the sole and irrevocable determinant of the future, man becomes the arbiter of his destiny and priests and sacrifices cease to be indispensable." Several schools of philosophical thought, mostly tied to either yogic practices or mortifying austerities, gradually developed and their teachers became famous figures with considerable followings. It was into this world that the Buddha was born.[13]

End Notes

1. Leighten, T.D. and Yi Wu. 1991. *Cultivating the Empty Field: The Silent Illumination of Zen Master Hongzhi*. North Point Press. San Francisco. p. 29.
2. Crook, J.H. 2007. Shamans, yogins and indigenous psychologies. In: L. Barrett and R. Dunbar (eds.). *The Oxford Handbook of Evolutionary Psycholog*. Oxford University Press.

3.   The idea is deeply persistent. This functional interpretation in exactly this
     phrase was given me by a Buddhist monk in the Gelugpa monastery of Rangdom
     in Zangskar, Ladakh, in 1980 as an interpretation of a ritual they were performing
     at the time.

4.   Singh, M.M. 1967. *Life in North-East India in Pre-Mauryan Times.* Motilal
     Banarsidass. Delhi.

5.   Collins, S. 1982. *Selfless Persons. Imagery and thought in Theravada Buddhism.*
     Cambridge University Press.

6.   Collins, S. *loc cit.* p. 49

7.   Eschatology = Christian theological theory of the four last things, *i.e.* death,
     judgement, heaven, hell: hence, more generally, doctrines determining destiny
     or afterlife.

8.   'See Collins, *loc cit.* p. 57. Indeed a yogin in Lamayuru Gompa was to tell me in
     1981. "We are consecrated persons."

9.   Collins, S. *loc cit.* p. 62.

10. Chakravarti, U. 1987. *The Social Dimensions of Early Buddhism.* Oxford University
     Press. Delhi.

11. Basham, A.L. 1956. *The Wonder that was India. A survey of the culture of the Indian
     sub-continent before the coming of the Muslims.* Sidgwick & Jackson. London. p. 248

12. Goyal, S.R. 1987. *A History of Indian Buddhism.* Kusumanjali Prakashan. Meerut.

13. Goyal, S.R. 1987. *loc cit.* p. 48.

5

THE BUDDHA'S LIFE AND AWAKENING

The early Buddhist literature, composed many years after the events of the Buddha's life, contains little in the way of biography. The main thrust was always upon the statement and clarification of the Buddha's teachings – the Dharma. Even so, diligent research within the few accounts of his life that do exist, together with the examination of comments in other texts regarding situations and relationships in which he appeared, have provided us now with a moderately comprehensive understanding of the life and times of a remarkable man. In this chapter, I attempt to summarise the main events in the life bringing out features of particular interest today.

The Gautama family were kshatriyas, members of the so called 'warrior' caste to which kings, princes and other rulers traditionally belonged. It seems that most of the Shakya people considered themselves well borne and this was doubtless related to their republican style of governance. They were a hill people living in the foothills of the Nepalese Himalayas and, ethnically, they may not have been completely Aryan. Their state affairs were settled in assembly, originally a tribal assembly in which open discussion took place. Siddhartha's father, Suddhodhana, was, it seems, *primum inter pares* among the noble Shakyas and plausibly the little state was moving towards becoming a monarchy like so many others around it. Be that as it may, Siddhartha was born into a wealthy, ruling family with at least three palatial buildings to live in, courtiers and numerous attendants.

CHILDHOOD

At Siddhartha's birth, some seer prophesied that the child would become either a great king or a religious teacher. Suddodhana, not surprisingly, appreciated the first idea but was worried by the second. It appears that he made every attempt to ensure that the young prince grew up to be a sound, earthly ruler. Siddhartha appears to have been a handsome lad, athletic, skilled at arms, popular and intelligent. Yet, something in his early life was to tilt his inclinations away from palatial joys. Perhaps this began with the death of his mother during his infancy and the fact that a relative living in his father's harem reared him. Stemming from this loss suffering may have started early, as indeed has often been the case in the childhood of religious leaders.

It seems likely that his father imposed upon him so many delights, concubines, dancing, games, sports with the intent of attaching him to the life style of a prince, that he began to be bored by such an existence, seeing nothing in it. Suddodhana neglected to educate the boy in the ways of life among his people. It thus came about that when he went out from the palace Siddhartha came unsuspectingly upon all too visible instances of sickness and death, perhaps strikingly displayed at the roadside. His teachers answered his questions in a matter of fact manner. Did you not know people got sick – and eventually died? These basic facts had been unknown to the sensitive lad and he must have been severely shocked by such discoveries. He became oppressed by the realization of the extent of suffering in this world. He suffered himself, secluded by his father's command in the palace. On one of his outings, he is said to have observed a holy man, one of the forest wanderers, perhaps one of the wilder 'munis'. He was told that this strange person believed he had solved the mystery of life. Siddhartha was left wondering whether this could be so. In Zen terms, these events created for him his life koan "How may one pass beyond suffering?"

THE SCEPTICAL RENOUNCER

Dutifully, Siddhartha married and in due course, his wife bore him a son thus securing a male heir. Yet, even the love he had for them could not restrain his need to solve the burning question of his life. So, he left and sought out a leading teacher among the wanderers. He is later said to have told his monks:

"Before my awakening, monks, I was simply a living being seeking to understand the meaning of birth. I was myself ageing so I sought for the meaning of age. I sometimes got ill and knew that I would die so I sought the meaning of that too. I said to myself, suppose I, being thus, seek out the not born, the beyond sorrow and pleasure and the undefiled extinction of all these principles. After some time when I was little more than a boy, black haired, a healthy youth in my adolescence, I went forth from home into homelessness, my parents weeping at my departure. I shaved off my beard and hair and donned these brown clothes."[1]

As Michael Carrithers remarks: "The unexamined and uncontrolled life of the home leads only to sorrow and despair, endlessly repeated. Only the renouncer's life offers hope, the hope of looking down upon a mass of desire and suffering from an eminence of knowledge and dispassion."[2]

Arada Kalama was a teacher living beyond society in the forests. He had a sound reputation and the young home-leaver asked him to teach him his doctrine and his way of life. Siddhartha took up the challenge vigorously, applying himself with critical attention to both his teacher's ideas and to his practices of profound yogic meditation. Surprisingly, we are given little information concerning whatever views on the human condition Arada may have had. Probably he was basically a Brahmana teaching essentially Upanishadic doctrines, perhaps even the Samkhya philosophy. The aim of yoga practice is the purification of the self, the element of being that transmigrates, so that it merges with a greater self, the absolute or Brahman. In the Samkhya system beyond the atman lies the wider self. The means of unification is yogic.

We know that Siddhartha studied and practised yogic meditation under Arada's guidance. He asked Arada how far he himself had attained his ends through directly experiencing them in meditative investigation. Arada replied that he had reached the 'meditative plane of nothing-ness'. Siddhartha practised hard, achieved this plane and so pleased his teacher that Arada wanted him to become his fellow teacher. Siddhartha, perhaps due to having experiences of illusory happiness at home, was of a very sceptical turn of mind. He reflected that Arada's teaching did not lead to dispassion or the ending of desire, to direct experience of final accomplishment, to an awakening. It led only to this meditative plane of nothing-ness. And he left. Joining another teacher who had reached the 'meditative plane of neither perception nor non-perception', Siddhartha achieved this also and came to a similar conclusion. He left once again. This forest life, meditating in the jungles, was far from easy. In one text, the Buddha remembers "It is hard to respond adequately to these remote abodes, the woods and hills of the forest. Solitude is hard. It is hard to enjoy being alone. It is as if the woods steal the mind of the monk who does not concentrate."[3]

These yogic meditations were well established before the time of the Buddha. As we have already remarked, yoga itself probably goes back to Dravidian times. In the Upanishads, and later in Buddhism, the meditations formed a series that remains similar to the one commonly practiced today. Adopting the traditional lotus posture, the meditator concentrates on some object, at first physical, then later a mental one, maybe a mantra, the breath, some inner sound or that which lies in the heart as small as a golden mustard seed, the self. All other thoughts or feelings are to be rigorously excluded. Modern research confirms that such practices bring about profound changes in conscious experience. Classically they are described as rising through four levels to reach two meditative 'planes'. Originally, these planes may have been conceived as special realms, spheres, spaces for astral travel or the realms of gods or, later on, of bodhisattvas, but in the Buddhist accounts they are mostly quite laconically described. These deep states of Samadhi are those in which Indian yogis perform a number of feats, slowing the heart rate, stopping the breath, generating internal heat. Advanced states as some of them may be, Siddhartha found that they led to no clear conclusion. They were merely temporary abidings in the present moment. The practitioner returns to his normal mental condition little altered. This was not that for which the young wanderer was looking. Such states had little effect on the moral or intellectual character in daily life either, he realised.

Yet, Siddartha was far from rejecting meditation as useless. Although the methods were inadequate to reach a final resolution, they did provide a deep understanding of the varieties of conscious experience and the extraordinary capacity of mind. The forest wanderers of Brahminical orientation followed the essential thought of the Upanishads. In meditation, they reached states that seemed tranquil, oceanic ultimates in which the lesser attachments of everyday self became submerged and disappeared. The subject of practice then witnesses only a state without diversity. The maps of inner states provided by the books suggested that such was the ultimate merging with Brahman. But, asked Siddhartha – Why was there no subsequent liberation?

In much later conversations, the ascetic Potthapada[4] asks him whether the frame of mind in deep meditation comes first and the knowledge of where one is on the map second or vice versa. The pragmatic Buddha opts for the former reply. Yet, here comes the problem. The meditator knows the path he took to reach that state, and he knows about the return to normality. This is what happens in actuality. Why call the state an ultimate one since it is dependent on skilled practices and is not enduring? If meditative states can be intended and created by practices of yogic skill, they cannot be the ultimate – for that should be independent of the causes and consequences of living in this world. One can see the precision of Siddhartha's mind in following through his thought on this subject.

THE ENLIGHTENMENT

It was probably only gradually that Siddhartha developed a fresh meditative skill that was to overcome these difficulties in novel and surprising ways

and which in the end led to his 'enlightenment', the liberation that he
sought. If meditative states were dependent on conditions created by the
mind what was it that the mind actually did, and what was driving it?
Siddhartha relaxed into a gentle, meditative equipoise he had originally
experienced quite casually as a child. He simply sat and watched in clarity
the machinations of his own mind, their comings and their goings. In this
way, rather than forcing his mind into deliberately induced states, he
became familiar with the whole phenomenology of the mind's life. This
practice developed in two aspects, the first, samatha, is essentially a period
of calming the mind. Maybe it enters one or more of the absorptions but
these are not to be pushed in the direction of the trance-like samadhi of
the 'planes'. Rather, once calm is established, the flow of phenomena is
simply witnessed. This 'vipassanna' then allows the practitioner to see
what is actually happening; provides insight into his own nature freed
from the preoccupations of thought.

At this time, Siddhartha was wondering whether the yogic methods
were perhaps adequate to reveal the ultimate of which the teachings
spoke. Other wanderers had undertaken the path of extreme asceticism,
physical mortification, and this Siddhartha now attempted. He persisted
till he was little more than a walking skeleton, every technique exhausted.
He realised that he was quite simply on a path of suicide. His wandering
brought him to a beautiful grove near a river with a comfortable farmstead
nearby. A young woman took pity on his condition, gave him some rice
gruel and arranged grass beneath a large tree where he could sit.
Abandoning asceticism and after bathing, Siddhartha sat down to review
his endeavours and once more to focus the mind in meditation. It is said
that he practiced there for some forty-nine days.

What then happened in the early hours of the last morning has been
described in many ways. Some writers give an intellectual, academic
account rooted in texts, some list the teachings that sprung forth, others
have written in high-flown poetry about the wonders of that night. Perhaps
the best way is through a straight-forward story, the paradoxical simplicity
of which may then need further explication, for the story indeed becomes
a koan.

At first, it seems his mind was wildly troubled with speculation,
daydreaming and erotic fantasy all described as the temptations of Mara
and well known to any meditator who attempts a really long 'sit'. At last,
Mara asked him to provide evidence of his goodness. Siddhartha touched
the earth as witness and the earth confirmed him. The gesture suggests
that the Buddha already felt at one with the Earth and the Earth itself
could never be described as bad. Mara fled and the renouncer's mind fell

into a calm and spacious state. Plausibly Mara's flight symbolises a dropping of all anxiety arising from a differentiated self and its qualities. Just before first light, he opened his eyes and there before him in the early morning sky shone the morning star in all its brilliance. Suddenly he broke free from all his labouring and in sharp clarity, he is said to have cried: " Ah! The Morning Star! When the morning star first shone there was I." A little later, as the experience he was undergoing became clear to him, he is said to have exclaimed: "Oh house builder you have now been seen! You shall build the house no longer. All your rafters have been broken, your ridgepole shattered. My mind has attained unconditional freedom and the end of craving is achieved."[5]

The two exclamations, whether he actually ever said them or not, tell us something about his momentous experience. Intellect, mindfulness and yogic absorption had combined to break up both the attachments that hampered his mind and his ego-based efforts to resolve them. In an ineffable freedom, his experience was no longer that of a circumscribed self or ego; the very categories of time withdrew so that the moment of sitting and the moment of creation seemed one and the same to him. Like a house from which the rafters have fallen, the structures of his mind had fallen away, opening up as it were to the vast sky, a freedom from self-concern. There were no more walls, no more restrictive self, no more concern, to hold him. There were no conditions to shape experience because indeed there was no longer a problem, no need for thought. In the collapse of the categorisations of thought, he went beyond the conceptual. There was a vastness beyond telling. In Zen terms, he had indeed 'seen the nature'.

The three events in this sequence recall stages in meditative practice. Touching the earth and receiving confirmation of his natural goodness suggests a total acceptance of himself and what he was about, a cessation of doubt. Both the Earth touching and the seeing of the morning star were moments in which outer and inner became 'one mind' as the categories by which experience is measured in space and time came to a halt in a moment of limitless clarity. The falling rafters point to the moment when the experience of his selfhood dropped away, removing all concern for any previous attachments. In effect, what the Buddha had discovered was neither conditioned by the external nor was it an inner absorption in trance or thought, rather it was a completely radical condition in which all concerned attachment to his own life story and its resolution simply melted away. With no basis in ego and no concern for his personal past or future, all activities of mind and body formerly occupied with such objects ceased. In that cessation lay complete and utter freedom.

Sometimes a reader may wonder what joy could be found in such emptiness. The answer lies in this experience of freedom from all mental elaboration regarding the comfort, security or achievements of either mind or body. Such release is naturally an end to mental suffering. The Buddha also found that while such a state of mind was not permanent in that the concerns of the self returned and thought about them would start up again, the moment of freedom was indeed his solution because it could always be recalled. Its influence permeated his waking life, his social relationships and his teaching with a changed understanding. There was indeed an ending of ignorance.

We need to trace this back to its beginnings to understand the meaning. Siddhartha had realised that the mind was nothing other than a continuous flow of experience of all kinds, thoughts, images, worries, memories; a flow like a river that never stops. Nowhere was it possible to catch the river as something separate from the water's flow. Sensations, perception, preoccupation with intentions, consciousness itself were names for aspects of this cognitive flow; the 'self' was just a name for all of it just as 'river' was a name for water in movement. And what is a name? Where is a name? Looking at the flowing water – where is the river?[6]

A label is just a convenience, a 'cognitive construct'. Omit the label, the process continues. Apart from process, there was no separate 'self'. The 'reification' of process as a thing and consequent attachment to that name was simply an error. In this realisation, there was a sudden bursting out into a freedom from reification. Liberation lay in the dropping of the innate preoccupation with self-reference. Self-concern itself was driven by desire for security and attainments rooted in attachments to whatever was conceived as desirable. Nothing now remained to be found; the river just kept on flowing in freedom from conceptualisation.

We can understand something of this moment from accounts of great insights by philosophers and scientists. Profound and prolonged concentration on a problem or a paradox may go so deep that it is sustained unconsciously. There, worked upon in sleep and under the surface of life, the mind may suddenly hit upon a radical reframing, a reconstruction of the problem. Suddenly the answer is obvious. And the joy of discovery at so deep a level can transform a life.

Siddhartha realised the momentous implications of his insight both for himself and for others. Freedom lay in a total release from self-concerned conception rooted in attachment. Such emptiness was not anything particular; it was simply the freedom inherent in letting go of the reifying tendency of the mind, the lamp blown out, 'nirvana'. Whatever the wordless was, it just went on without any secondary description in thought. In the absence of words creating duality, Siddhartha was indeed just 'thus'. Herein lay release, enlightenment, 'bodhi'. Thereafter he knew himself as the Buddha. The Zen teachers are right: oddly, the deep quest ends in a great laugh. There was no problem!

THE BASIC FORMULAE

The Buddha, as we must now call Siddhartha, is believed to have spent some weeks in the caves among the hills of Bodhgaya[7] thinking through the implications of his insight. We must remember that during his lifetime there was as yet no writing, no note taking therefore. Learning was entirely verbal. Analysis, memory, hypothesis, synthesis were all done in thought alone or in discussion, debate or Socratic teaching. Not till centuries later were the memorised stories of his sermons and talks actually written down so that textual examination and study could begin. The Buddha realised that his conclusions were subtle, would not be easily received by others. He had doubts about speaking of them, let alone teaching.

In myth, the Buddha's hesitancy so disturbed the gods that Brahma himself came down to persuade the Buddha that, out of compassion, he must teach his insight to others. So he set off to Sarnath near Varanasi (Benares) where his five former companions in asceticism were staying. As he approached, they resolved to ignore him believing him to have abandoned the search. Yet, as he came near, they saw his extraordinary radiance and knew something had occurred to him. He sat among them and gave them his first teachings. First of all, he stressed that neither the path of sensuous indulgence nor the path of mortification could lead to release. His discovery was that of a third way, the middle way.

The early talks of the Buddha are sometimes called the basic 'formulae', that is the first formulations of his thought based on his direct experience of insight. Each formula can be considered separately but they are all in fact extensions of one basic insight and interdependent with one another. Starting from any one of them, one is led also to the others. Let us put them in the order in which they may well have occurred to him.

(i)   The Law of Co-dependent Arising. *Pratityasamutpada*
(ii)   Impermanence and no-self. *Annica* and *Annata*
(iii) The Chain of Causation. The nature of "rebirth." *Karma.*
(iv)   The Four Noble Truths: Suffering, the Cause of Suffering, the
       Ending of Suffering and the Eightfold Path.

1. *Co-dependent arising*

The Buddha probably reasoned as follows. In meditation, it is clear from direct observation that all phenomena have a cause and that all causes have effects. Yet, it is also true that the relation between cause and effects is influenced by conditions. An acorn will not grow into an oak tree unless the soil is right, rain yields adequate moisture and the sun shines sufficiently on young leaves. When these conditions are present the oak tree can grow and the acorn as cause will produce tree as effect. Every thing arises dependently upon its causes and conditions. Furthermore, given that events in one chain of causation interact with those in another, so one event can produce many consequences in progressive elaboration. Related events of many kinds are co-dependently arising. This is a basic law of interdependent origination. Nothing arises from its own side by itself but only within the manifestation of this law. There is therefore no need to look for some hidden essence, Brahman or God, responsible for the occurrence of events or things; the process of causation is sufficient.

2. *Impermanence*

There is then a further implication. Since everything is in movement, no one thing can possibly be permanent. The interdependent process sustains endless change. Everything we know is impermanent. Of course some things endure more than others, rocks last longer than flowers, people live longer than dogs and cats, but viewed in the round everything is impermanent – even this great world itself. And looking back in time one can see that the present is already implicit in the past just as it is in the future. Thus when the "morning star first shone there too was I". Such a sense of the vastness of change can be felt in the heart in meditation. When clarity arises in timeless experience this is more than just a bright idea.

Looking at the self in meditation one can see that it too is made up of contributory processes. These too are impermanent, fluctuating, subject to birth and death. Indeed in meditation that which is observed consists in nothing more than the several ways of experiencing: sensation, as when you pinch me in the bum; perception, as when I realise what has happened; cognition as when I understand it is a joke and not an attack; pre-conception when I understand the whole matter in the light of friendship and our personal histories of joking together; and consciousness, the awareness of it all. These are the basic components of experience (*skandha*). So where is the self? Well, there is no self as a separate entity. The self is just a name for the interactive complex of being. Process but no agent. The agent is an imputation. In disidentifying from this imputation, there is freedom from the implications of agency.

The illusion of self has been compared to a wave moving across the ocean. There appears to be something called a wave moving along. In fact, the water remains where it is, it is simply the energy of the wind that drives the apparently moving wave. So it is that the skandhas drive the self, but there is no such 'thing' as a self that moves. Water simply arises and falls as the pulse of energy flows through.

3. *The chain of causation: samsara and rebirth*

In the Theravadan analysis the transience of human life is described in terms of a twelve linked chain of causality that cycles through repeated rebirths. Ideas that produce karma are conditioned by the fact of ignorance. The quality of consciousness is determined by karma and mental and physical phenomena are realised in experience. Mental experience depends on sensation determining perception. Perception leads to differential feelings, which result in craving and clinging. Craving and clinging constitute becoming – that is the continuing round of karmic formations that end in old age and death and which are reconstituted in 'rebirth'.

Since there is no self but only process, there is no person as an entity that can be re-incarnated. It is rather that the unfinished business of one cycle of life remains active after death and rekindles in another life as sparks do when flown from a fire. It is not the old fire as such that is reborn but a new one – yet the sparks of unexpended energy coming down through time condition the new. This is the inner meaning of rebirth. It is not a re-incarnation of pre-existing persons.

Sentient beings, believing in their possession of a self, long for some meaning for it and the certainty of its continuity in some form of salvation. Impermanence creates suffering because of the desire for security. Few understand that if there were permanence there could be no change, hence no experience either. Craving (*tanha*) is the cause of suffering (*dukha*) in this world misperceived through ignorance (*avidya*) of its actual process. The endless re-birth of error presents an awe-inspiring picture of a process of endless suffering. Only when attachments to the objects of craving cease and self-concern dies away is release obtained.[8]

The concept of rebirth does however seem to contradict the Buddha's insight into no-self, until one realises that the Buddha includes endless rebirth within his perspective. Plausibly the Buddha felt that his teachings were already challenging enough without taxing his hearers' patience further by rejecting reincarnation of self out-right.[9] His perceptive ideas needed to be transmitted through the common understandings of his time.

Rebirth remains a problem for many Westerners who otherwise accept

the Buddha's teachings fully, yet it is not difficult to perceive in the traditional account a metaphor for psychological processes well known to modern life, in particular the prime concepts of developmental psychology
defining an intergenerational transmission of psychological attitudes.
Ever since Freud, psychologists have focussed on the manner in which
childhood experiences lie at the root of adult behaviour, preoccupations
and neurosis. The factors involved are both genetic and acquired through
social interaction. Genetic endowment is an important determinant of
mental disposition inherited directly but, equally if not more critically,
are the ways in which a child is treated by its prime care givers – parents,
teachers, friends, whose attitudes, capacity for empathy and kindness, or
disinterest and even cruelty, mould the character of a young adult as he or
she processes the world (see Chapters 14 and 18).

The modern account resembles the karmic theory closely.
Predispositions acquired through social conditioning are directly
comparable with the volitional factors (*samskara*) in the Buddhist model.
The difference is that in the Western account the influencing factors
from the past are not regenerated as it were internally but are responses
to social conditioning through interaction in development. Most of the
programs involved are not seen as arising through descent into the zygote
at conception or at birth but rather acquired throughout the course of
the child's experience. Yet, genetic dispositions may determine how
experiences have effects.

The causes, conditions and consequences in play as one generation
succeeds another comprise genetic templates, behavioural information,
themes and ideas that evoke responses of acceptance or rejection during
the child's dependency on caregivers. Responsibility for personal
behaviour is usually seen in the West as attributable to an individual only
when he or she is sufficiently adult to understand the effects of his or her
behaviour on others. Responsibility is here not back dated into previous
existences The information that determines distress may be derived from
personal interactions, from situations of birth in a particular economic
class, ethnicity or within the character shaping patterning of a national
culture or all of these contexts. The suffering of one generation produces
further suffering in the next in multiple ways. The notion of rebirth may
be said to be a metaphor for this continuous process of the influence
one–generation bears upon the next.

4. *Interpreting the Noble Truths*

The first noble truth is the assertion that impermanence is the prime
characteristic of life. Since we all experience the conventional illusion of

a substantial self, the fact of impermanence is naturally distressing. The second noble truth asserts that it is the craving for security in the face of inevitable impermanence; quests for immortality; the pleasing or desirable; or, alternatively, the craving not to experience whatever is unpleasant, which is the cause of suffering. The third truth asserts that there is a way out of this trap that leads to clarity, detachment, and peace of mind. The direct way out is through the insight by which illusive ignorance in hankering after permanence is broken and the direct awareness that attachment to things is indeed based in reifying illusions. This insight is however more than intellectual. It arises from the yogic practice that provokes or allows the collapse of the structures of ego attachment. The Buddha's metaphor of the collapsing roof is apt. What remains is not a nihilistic void but rather a vast open sky empty of the noise of self. It cannot be described because no thoughts operate here. Such insight when fully realised confers an ineffable, inner freedom but for most practitioners a more gradual path is the way to a realisation. The fourth truth therefore outlines eight thoughtful ways designed for those deep in the mire whereby escape may be achieved. It is through the steps of right behaviour, speech and thought that one prepares oneself to proceed towards a freedom that emerges as right livelihood, wherein training in meditative concentration eventually yields realisation.

The basic training in Buddhist ideas amounts to a gradual appreciation through intellectual and experiential training of the truth of the basic propositions. Within this context, the practice of meditation allows the arising of experiences that are a consequence of the mental yogas involved and which function in confirmation of the path. In summary the key ideas are as follows:

IMPERMANENCE

All phenomena in continual flux.
Causes and conditions: all events in co-dependent arising.
INSIGHT shows:
Mind is continuous movement in sensation, perception, cognition, karmic pre-occupation and consciousness.
The inferred self is the name for these processes unitarily experienced as attachment to "me'.
Freedom is liberation from concepts of self as a thing-like entity. Dropping attachments to self is realisation: holding on is ignorance
IGNORANCE is maintained through craving or clinging to continuity, status, prestige, immortality resulting from karmic conditioning .
REALISATION is perception of self and things as labels within a universal

virtuality:, hence form is emptiness while emptiness as the 'suchness' of things expresses itself in form.

Abandonment of clinging brings tranquillity and allows the growth of wisdom.

MINDFUL MEDITATION

The Buddha left his followers a profound meditation practice that he himself had used in solving the problem of suffering. The surviving Pali text is the 'Greater Discourse on the Foundations of Mindfulness', the *Mahasatipatthana Sutta*.[10] This practice is the forerunner of other meditation systems in Buddhism and differs in several important points from the earlier methods of the Brahmins. It does not focus on the attainment of profound states but rather encourages direct awareness of what is happening in the present moment. This is 'mindfulness'.

The Buddha introduces his monks to the 'Four Foundations of Mindfulness' as follows: "What are the four? Here, monks, a monk abides contemplating body as body, ardent, clearly aware and mindful having put aside hankering and fretting for the world; he abides contemplating feelings as feelings; he abides contemplating mind as mind; he abides contemplating mind objects as mind objects, ardent, clearly aware and mindful, having put aside hankering and fretting for the world."

The practice begins by mindfulness of the body through observing the flow of the breath while sitting in a comfortable meditation posture. A monk trains himself, thinking: "I will breathe in, calming the whole body process." He trains himself thinking. "I will breathe out, calming the whole body process." Just as a skilled carver senses the movement of his knife along the wood so a monk breathing in a short breath observes the breathing in of a short breath – or a long breath, in or out. The practice continues in the same way taking various themes as a focus for mindfulness in the present moment. A monk observes in a dispassionate manner all the parts of the body, its composition, and its decay observed in the charnel grounds.

So, he abides contemplating body as body internally, contemplating body as body externally, and contemplating arising phenomena in the body. Or else he practices simple mindfulness that "there is a body" present to him, "just to the extent necessary for knowledge and awareness". No extrapolation or descriptive thinking is required- awareness alone is the focus.

In the same manner, the monk contemplates feelings, the qualities of his mind state, the objects arising in mind, their origin in the consciousness of the sense organs. The monk observes the rising and fading away of all these things. He practices without any grasping as he observes the arising of peaceful states. He then proceeds to contemplate the existential facticity of the Four Noble Truths in himself – the arising of suffering, its root in the attachment to self, the dropping of self-concern and the cessation of hurt. In further extension of this practice, the lay-person is advised to contemplate mindfulness of his daily work, his livelihood, thereby undoing his attachment to the everyday in the same manner. Mindfulness training forms the basis for insight in Vipassana meditation. There is clearly a deep ethical significance in this meditation.

Indian meditation calms the body into Samadhi and deep one pointed states of trance. Attachment to such states can be undone through perceiving them as transitory appearances just like all other phenomena. In this Sutta we find the fundamental basis for mind training in Buddhism all the way from that of the beginner right through to that of an adept. The roots of training go right back to the Buddha's words.

The Buddha tells us that the fundamental root of human suffering lies in attachment to the illusion of a permanent self and the painful struggle

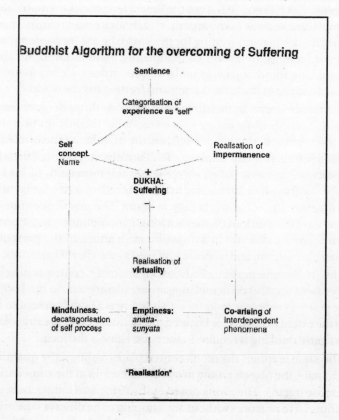

Buddhist Algorithm for the overcoming of Suffering

Sentience

Categorisation of experience as "self"

Self concept. Name

Realisation of impermanence

+
DUKHA:
Suffering

Realisation of virtuality

Mindfulness: decatagorisation of self process

Emptiness: anatta-sunyata

Co-arising of interdependent phenomena

"Realisation"

to preserve some sense of identity in the face of endless flux. Today, we have indeed inherited this illusion and its consequences from our ancient past. Is the Buddha's solution relevant and if so how to use it?

End Notes

1. Warder, A.K. 1970. *Indian Buddhism*. Motilal Banarsidass. Delhi. See p. 46.

2. Carrithers, M. 1983. *The Buddha*. Oxford.

3. Quoted by Warder. *loc cit*. p. 47.

4. Walshe, M. 1995. *The Long Discourses of the Buddha. A translation of the Digha Nikaya*. Wisdom. Boston. See the Potthapada Sutta. p. 159-170.

5. Byrom, T. 1976 *The Dhammapada*. Wildwood House. London. p. 56.

6. *As philosopher Gilbert Ryle was to comment centuries later. After viewing the colleges of Oxford, the laboratories, libraries, games fields, boat sheds and boats racing on the river one might well ask, "So well and good – but now, where is the university?"*

7. *A visit to Bodhgaya really does bring the story to light. It has all the environmental features still visibly there to support imagination. And in the hills, you can still find the caves – if you are prepared to risk meeting a dacoit or two.*

8. *In this account, we are focussing on the prime features of the Buddha's discovery. Specialists might have two objections: firstly we are not emphasising the more mythical elements in the story, the appearances of gods and miracles, and, secondly, we are not detailing in full the rich complexity of the psychological model as presented in the commentaries on the Suttas. We need to recall that the Buddha was a man of his time and made full use of the standard interpretations of life current in his society. The Buddha himself tells conventional stories of his past lives as a Buddha. As we have seen the concepts of samsara and reincarnation were commonly held in his time but, as we have noted, even before the Buddha considered the issue, it was not traditionally a person that reappears but rather those aspects that are reassembled through sacrifice. The idea of an individual reincarnation was already in doubt.*

9. Kolm, S.C. 1979. *La philosophie bouddhiste et les 'homes economiques'*. Social Science Information 18. 4/5: 489-588.

10. Walshe, M. 1995. *The Long Discourses of the Buddha. loc cit*. p. 335-350.

6

DHARMA DEVELOPMENTS
WITHIN INDIA

The Buddha sometimes addressed his monks in assembly with the talks that form the substance of many of the suttas (discourses). I suspect however that his chosen method of teaching was through dialogue. Many suttas depict him in conversation with individuals whom he comes across in his travels or who, having heard that he is in the neighbourhood, seek him out. The variety of people is great, kings, princes, bankers, brahmins, forest renouncers, teachers of other orientations and ordinary folk are all there in a fascinating cross section of the people of his time – lively, intelligent, respectful, keen to resolve the meaning of existence. Should we so wish, we can go and see their depiction carved centuries later on the magnificent panels of the gateways to the great stupa at Sanchi.

His five friends at Sarnath were not all immediately convinced by the Buddha's first teachings yet, after some days with the Buddha, all of them realised in their own being the insight that he had achieved. They became the first arhats, enlightened ones. Soon after, others came to him, invited him to visit their houses where he met their friends, and, gradually, when some sixty had joined him and understood his message, he was able to create the Sangha or body of monks. The word 'Sangha' originated from the quasi-republican form of government that the Shakya and other peoples still practised. It meant assembly and implies participatory discussion. The Buddha told the monks to go forth as wanderers and to teach their insights to others.

The development of the Sangha went through several stages. At first these wanderers behaved very much like other renouncers, but, gradually, they established bases in which to stay during the rains of the monsoon season when travelling was very difficult. These proto-monasteries were often on land given them by rich landowners. We will not provide a detailed account of their history here. It is more important for our purpose to describe the nature of the teachings as they developed. Suffice it to say, as the Sangha grew in strength in the centuries following the Buddha's death, there were several grand assemblies to determine the orthodox form of the teachings, which then remained for hundreds of years as memorised 'texts' and not as written documents. We are fortunate that the Buddha's cousin, Ananda, evidently had a photographic memory of great help to the first assembly in deciding what it was the Buddha had said. The Suttas remembered by Ananda begin with the words, "Thus have I heard –" The great Emperor Ashoka used the teachings of the Buddha as the ethical cement for his Indian empire and during his time the teachings spread far and wide within the sub-continent and reached Sri Lanka.

Given the slow speed of communication, the Sanghas of different areas tended to diverge in the emphasis they put on aspects of the teachings and gradually schools or 'sects' arose differing primarily in their modes of practice. Only to a limited degree did the conclaves settle these differences. In any case, the Buddha had given directions that, rather than submerging disputes by majority decisions, Sanghas might split if there was no other way to settle differences. Eventually two main strands arose which became known as the great vehicle, Mahayana, and the lesser vehicle, Hinayana. The latter consisted of the more conservative teachings based strictly in the original suttas and is more respectfully known as the Theravada, "Doctrine of the Elders". Geographically, it has its focus today in Sri Lanka, from where it later spread to Burma and Thailand. The Mahayana with its innovative teachings spread from India along the trade routes; the overland Silk Road to Central Asia and China, and the sea route to Java and again to China, eventually also to Japan. Mahayana thought and practice thus mingled with every other sort of belief that travelled along the key routes of the time. It became truly global within Asia and the monks were immensely successful in transmitting the teachings, founding new monasteries and making careful translations into Central Asian languages, Tibetan and Chinese, and thence Japanese. It also reached the boundaries of Christendom along the routes leading West through the Greek lands of the Middle East, as several Byzantine tales such as that of Barlaam and Jehosavat show.

In this and the following chapter we will follow the development of the Buddha's teachings as they were gently spread by itinerant monks in India and beyond during the centuries after his death. Such a task is immense and the best we can do is to aim at presenting certain essentials especially relevant to the theme of this book.

THE ABHIDHARMA

The Buddha's discourses often had a decidedly philosophical tone, and indeed Indians of his time clearly loved metaphysical debate. The teachings were collected into three main groups: the actual discourses, Sutta Pitaka or 'basket' of suttas; the Vinaya Pitaka, that is the rules of conduct for monks and nuns; and detailed examinations of the inner meaning of the teachings known as the Abhidharma (Abhidharma Pitaka), a word meaning discourse about the teachings. This was additional teaching elaborating on the nature and relationship of the 'dharmas', the elementary events of experience. It is said that Sariputra, considered to be the most philosophically minded of the Buddha's disciples, initiated these elaborations of the discourses. Certainly whoever started this train of thought was a thinker of no mean calibre.

These supplementary teachings are very important for our purpose since they established the mode and set the tone for much further philosophical development in the centuries to come. Furthermore, they still provide a valuable basis for meditation today. The Abhidharma originated before the splitting of the Sangha into its later components within India so that most schools had some version of these texts. In this presentation, we will consider only the main thrust of the arguments because in the end they all point in the same direction, a rather formal account of the process of liberation.

The Abhidharma is not at all easy for a Westerner to enter and indeed, at first sight, it is a very off-putting form of literature consisting largely of enumerated lists of mental factors and their complex interactions. The casual reader may come to the conclusion that all this seemingly static enumeration of mental attributes cannot be related to contemporary psychology. While this would certainly be a serious mistake, we do need to ask what kind of a literature this is and what it's function is intended to be.

The modern reader will be used to studies purporting to describe some process in a personally disinterested, 'objective' manner without considering the position of the observer or participant. If one hopes to find in the Abhidharma an objective account of human psychology in this manner, there will be disappointment. No reductionism to brain mechanisms or physiology is to be found here, although there is no objection to such an analysis by others. These texts are simply not of such a kind. Rather, as with Buddhism in general, the Abhidharma is a phenomenological enquiry with a soteriological intention. That is to say it is entirely concerned with an examination of human experience with the intention of finding a way to move that experience out of suffering into liberation. The texts have the function of showing the way to a release from suffering; from the mental confusion of 'samsara' to the insightful freedom of 'nirvana'. They contain a dynamic model of the processes of mind intent upon enlightenment expressed in terms of precise experiences and their relations on the path. The difficulties for the reader lie in the method used, listing fine distinctions in what at first seems to be an unending and pedantic analysis.

For the Western reader without meditative experience there is a further problem. The technical terms of the discourse refer to events and processes in consciousness that arise in yogic practices of mental examination. Such terminology refers to matters that are entirely subjective and intrinsically puzzling to the inexperienced. The system is based in a subjective empiricism and can be verified by following the same practice as one's instructor – much as an objective èxperiment is open to checking by repetition in several laboratories. The reader needs to realise that this is not a metaphysical argument but rather a description of an advanced method of mental analysis, a yogic phenomenology, and in this sense it is thoroughly scientific. It is important therefore to recognise the logical consistency of these analyses and to see how the argument coheres.

Indian theorists other than the Buddha tended towards two extremes known respectively as 'eternalism', arguing for the persistence and reality of perceived things, or as 'nihilism', arguing for their non existence and non reality. When it came to examining human experience the Buddha saw that neither of these ways of thinking was valid. Taking one or the other of these positions, or both, or neither, cannot describe an experience accurately or fully. If I look at an egg boiling in a pan and examine the experience I am undergoing, I can neither assert that the egg exists in itself as a reality outside myself nor as non-reality only created by my mind. Events in consciousness cannot be accurately described in either of these ways because they are appearances.

The Buddha himself emphasised a distinction between the way in which we all talk conventionally in terms of 'you' and 'me', self and other, as if such words referred to things existing in themselves, and, by contrast, an analytical perspective referring to the processes that such words denote. For example, to discuss personal consciousness in terms of sensation, perception, cognition and so on, is to take an analytical view of the object identified in common sense as 'me'. He sometimes spoke in what we might call 'common sense' terms, and sometimes he spoke in terms of processes underlying the conventional view; this choice depending on who his hearers were and what they could understand. In Western psychology a similar distinction is made between theories of 'agency' that speak of agents in interaction and 'motion theories' that speak in terms of the process that underlies the appearance of agents.

The Abhidharma constructs a middle way between the extremes of Eternalism and Nihilism and works out the implications of such a position.

It does this in many ways and the argument we pursue here is only one theme with which we are presented. It does however introduce us to some fundamental concerns of this literature. If we begin by asking what an experience is, we can get a grip on the issues involved.

An experience only exists 'now'. Past events are dead; they are only represented in memory 'now' while the future is only existent as hope or fear. Neither past nor future can be directly experienced. There is only one experiential moment in time and it is constantly passing. The Buddha described it as like the point of contact between a large cartwheel and the road. Only at the point of contact does experience actually manifest. Furthermore, within that moment, the discrete, minimal events in consciousness (known as the dharmas) are said to flash on and off momentarily, sometimes maintaining their appearances, sometimes giving way to fresh ones. One might liken this idea to the ever-moving activity within an atom. Like flowing water or the moving wind there is nothing here that can be grasped. The objects of hopes and memories are cognitive constructions that do not actually exist in present experience other than as appearances. The Abhidharma is a discourse on the nature of experience as a virtual flow and describes the way from ignorance to liberation through insight (*prajna*) into its ultimate ungraspability.

Two methods of practice are described by the Abhidharma discourse on meditation.

(1) The first is analytical observation of experience in terms of types of mental event and how these condition and shape one another. Some mental events are derived from the senses and refer to what we might call the 'outer' world. Others are internally generated as in dream, fantasy and imagination. Both modes influence one another. A rope in dim light might be experienced as a snake. A visualisation of Buddha may convert an encounter into one of kindness rather than aggression.

In applying this first method, the qualities of the object of awareness are seen to be determining appearances in consciousness. Objects are commonly qualified by mental categorisation, as when mental events arising in relation to an outer state are modified by an inner one such as a judgement or prejudice. They may thus provide a basis for preferences and attachments that can then be analysed.

(2) The second method perceives experience as a single process, understanding it to be empty of any solid, separately differentiated particularities. The flow of the mind is observed as one continuity. Such understanding is known as insight or *prajna*. Whatever arises in perception is doing so in correlation with everything else, as the Law of Co-dependent Arising states. The insight known as *prajna* is the ability to see all mental

phenomena as mutually relating in co-arising. If everything is co-arising in interdependence then every thing is 'empty' of a particulate, separable identity. The practice involves becoming aware of the unity inherent in all transient experiences as a continuity of endless change. An important consequence is that such awareness naturally undermines tendencies to form attachments. This second method is not usually applied before expertise in the first has been acquired.

In relation to the first method, the Abhidharma, classifies mental objects under five categories.

(a) The first class of object derives from the stimulation of sense organs and sense awareness during the apprehension of forms.

(b) The second identifies the desires that arise during the differential discrimination of sense objects.

(c) The third comprises the complex forms so produced.

Classes (a,b) and c) are thus focussed on form.

(d) In this fourth class there is meditative absorption during which the focus on forms is progressively abandoned while the mind state as a whole is observed in one-pointed concentration.

(e) The fifth category is that of nirvana where experience goes beyond all forms entirely. No forms appear within the experience of vivid awareness.

Between the fourth and fifth class several further formless spheres are also mentioned in each of which fewer subjective characteristics arise into consciousness. The movement between (d and e) is essentially a progressive loss of the categorisations whereby form appears in consciousness.

These categories of experience are qualified by the subjective conditions that accompany objective appearances. There are three modes of experience here: appearances considered unwholesome because of selfish attachment; those called wholesome because of detachment and those lacking either negative or positive qualities.

The five main classes of experience (a)to (e) comprise a developing series with respect to the practice of meditative absorption. The senses provide the basis for desire, which entails attachments to forms or their rejection. Through meditative absorption in single pointed concentration, forms become formless and insight may then lead to a relative liberation from all attachments to form. Whether this happens or not depends upon the quality of the subjective involvement. On the one hand, experiencing a boiling egg may be simply a case of observation and no more than functional in a neutral context. On the other hand, it may be correlated with greed, in which case it would be considered unwholesome, or it may arise in compassionately cooking for an old person, in which case wholesome. The unwholesome or wholesome involvements are labelled such because they have karmic consequences, basically either increasing involvement with attachments or a letting go of self-concern.

When a Dharma practitioner undertakes meditation following the first method, it will normally be conducted in a wholesome state of mind. Under such conditions, meditation can move through a series of developing changes.[1] The mind may move from a fragmented state with many ideas and images whizzing about chaotically linked to some distress, anxiety or maybe happy memories, towards a more focussed, controlled and unified condition. There are four stages in this progression known as (a) Initial Application, (b) Sustained Application, (c) Stable state of interest, rapture or bliss and (d) One-pointedness. (These stages are common to most Buddhist meditation systems and we will come across them again when we examine these in detail. Chapter 23)

Initial Application means a mindful observation of what precisely is going on by means of a steady focus on the senses. With Sustained Application, the quality of the meditative experience changes as involvement with sensory data, wants and desires and fantasies diminishes and the mind stabilises, becoming effortlessly one pointed on the object of meditation (a material object, a mantra or an internally created state that is no longer being judged, or an enquiry.) At this point, the meditator shifts his or her attention off the object and onto the experience of limitless space that has arisen as its context. This occurs when a fully stable one-pointedness is attained and the first formless sphere appears, a condition known in India as Samadhi.

Shifting attention onto looking into the 'limitless consciousness that observes this limitless space as its correlate' moves the meditator into the second formless sphere. The third is an experience of the emptiness of limitless consciousness and the fourth entails neither perception nor non-perception, presumably a paradoxical experience of nothing at all. The practice as a whole is known as samatha or mind calming.

Samatha is therefore a gradual rarification and unification of consciousness ending in one ineffable state attained through abandoning all roots of preference, judgement and attachment. The progressive states are produced by a deliberate practice that, depending on its efficacy, may yield increasingly beneficial results in terms of knowing the capacities of mind and how to attain release from perplexity. Yet it was states similar to these that the Buddha had found wanting in his training. They merely provide experience of the complexity of mental events in consciousness training. Hence they are mostly 'mundane' or worldly and are not in themselves liberating.

The application of *prajna* (*i.e.* the second method) to the advanced spheres of the first approach enables the practitioner to abandon blind beliefs in the inherent existence of objects without any residual doubt. The continuity of all apparent entities in their unending dynamism is then clearly known.

Liberation from attachment ('nirvana') is now within sight. Rituals and rules of behaviour are no longer required. At this point, it is said that the stage of Stream Winner is reached. As practitioners continue to weaken their sensual desire, they reach the state of Once Returners. Going on to eliminate these negative states completely leads to becoming a Non-Returner and dropping all attachment to both form and formlessness leads to the condition of an Arhat who requires no more training, lives out a life and is said to return no more.

When *prajna* insight is applied to any of the listed stages (A-E) of the first method, glimpses of nirvana (liberation) may occur, the awareness becoming clearer as the practitioner eliminates attachments. The two methods are now working together. What then is nirvana? It is the condition in which all attachments to either form or formlessness are blown away through the awareness that all elements in mind, whether form or formless, are co-dependently arising. They cannot be thought of as separable entities unrelated to one another. The practice progressively synthesises and integrates experience through the abandonment of conceptual distinctions. That which then arises is said to become signless through acceptance of impermanence, wishless through seeing through suffering without wanting any particular result and empty through abandoning the reifications of self. Such liberation is ineffable and beyond description; naturally enough for words fail! The mind has gone beyond language.

The Abhidharma model makes clear that liberation requires the initial mind trainings of samatha to be examined by *prajna*; the insight into the interdependent co-arising of all 'dharmas', impermanence and no separate self. As this insight becomes clearer, so glimpses of liberation arise. It seems that for the Arhats this is the end of the matter. It is said that their earlier karma continues to be present, although inactive, within their transformed personalities until everything disappears at death. For them there is no more rebirth; liberation from the samsaric cycle of ignorance is complete.

Yet, as we shall see, penetrating thinkers were to realise an odd paradox here. The meditator has 'seen the nature' of the conventional as emptiness. The insight itself is a sudden cognitive apprehension rather than a state reached by following a gradual path.

SUMMARY OF KEY ASPECTS OF ABHIDHARMA

Progressive stages of Dhyana practice.

MEDITATIONAL MODE	APPLICATION

ANALYTICAL APPROACH:

Samatha	*Mundane spheres*
1. Application.	A.Sense spheres
2.Sustained application	B.Desire spheres.
3.Stable state	C.Form spheres
4. One pointedness	

+

SYNTHETIC APPROACH

Prajna	D.*Formless spheres:* supramundane
= *Vipassana*	
	1.Limitless space
ie. Mundane spheres seen in	2.Limitless consciousness
the light of co-dependent arising.	3. Neither perception nor non-perception.
	E. Nirvana

The application of Prajna to either Mundane or Supramundane spheres may occur at four levels of depth each realisable either as intentional, as on a path with a goal, or as the resultant fruit- the goal attained.

i. Streamwinner   ii. Once returner.   iii. Non-returner.   iv.Arhat .

Application in these four ways to five(A-E) spheres yields 20 types of experience.Result attained through fours ways in approaching five spheres yields 20 types also .
Total 40 possibilities of insightful realisation.

Explanation: The application of insight (prajna) to each of the spheres, whether mundane or supramundane, yields the understanding that each is co-dependently arising and lacking in inherent selfhood. Emptiness of inherent being in all perceived entities necessarily eliminates attachment to them and the freedom called nirvana arises.

Nirvana was already implicit in Samsara. At the end of this training then, the practitioner discovers that Samsara is Nirvana and indeed has always been so. The end of the path lay right at the beginning; ignorance alone obscured it. So why do we need a path?

It was the implications of these insights that stimulated the constructive intellects of those philosophers of later generations who, in their own time, were making their way to the end and back again.

THE EMERGENCE OF THE MAHAYANA

The Abhidharma was a prime teaching for the 'religious virtuosi' who specialised in meditation. Many monks were however of a more practical disposition and acted furthermore as guides and teachers to the lay supporters upon whom the Sanghas depended. As the years passed there were subtle changes in Indian society and it is a beautiful example of the Buddha's Law of Co-dependent Arising to work out how these social changes and the nature of the Sangha altered in an interactive tandem. During the Buddha's lifetime the prime centre of Vedic religion and Brahmin power lay to the northwest, further up the Ganges River, but already the influence of the Brahmins was central to the local culture of his period. Surprisingly perhaps, the Buddha does not attack Brahmin beliefs directly in the Suttas but rather demonstrates through dialogue the inadequacy of their system and the greater moral relativity to his time of his own.

In the Vedic system, karma meant behaving appropriately within the ritual life proper to one's caste. The benefits achieved by well-performed sacrifice were in a sense automatic. The Buddha however persuaded his interlocutors that the true Brahmin would be one who lived an ethical life, one whose karma varied according to his morality. Furthermore, the merit from good living leads in the end not so much to beneficial rebirth as to clarity and nirvana. This is inevitably so because the practice of insight is impossible so long as moral turbulence remains. As Richard Gombrich has put it,[1] the Buddha 'ethicised' karma and thus invalidated in one move any magical salvation through ritual or sacrifice. Furthermore, by denying any particularity to the atman, the Buddha also denied the equivalence of a human essence with that of the cosmos. The relativity of samsara and nirvana refutes the hidden essences so loved by the Vedantists. To the Buddha the main force in karma was intention and once intention becomes paramount so does choice. Individuals make choices. Brahmin and Sudra may both choose the good and share in the common karmic effects of good intention. Ethics in Buddhism are thus no longer caste bound for, as the Buddha told his hearers, without good intention a Brahmin becomes unworthy of the name.

Richard Gombrich has put it this way; "It is this purifying action - which brings the good Buddhist rewards in this and future lives. But since acting is really mental, doing a good act is actually purifying one's state of mind.

In meditation, such purification is undertaken directly, without any accompanying action. Thus there is a logical continuum between the moral actions of a man in the world and the meditations of a recluse." Ethical behaviour is the cornerstone for spiritual advance.

Such an emphasis is all of a piece with the social changes happening around the Buddha as he grew up. The development of trade guilds, government bureaucracy, banking and the growth of urban commerce and trade between centres of production was accompanied by the emergence of a new kind of individual to whom the caste allocations of rural India barely applied. As Gombrich opines, the earliest forms of the caste ideology had no place for trade, an increasingly important stratum of urban society not catered for or even recognised by Brahminism. The practical individualism implicit in trading called out for the parallel spiritual individualism of the Buddha's teachings. Indeed, scholars have compared the spread of his message to the growth of Protestantism in the increasingly mercantile centuries later in Europe. The autonomous individual reveals through his intentions not only his honourable status as a righteous man but also his subscription to Buddhist values. In the Buddha's perspective on karma any misfortune may be attributed to an ethical lapse and therefore a result of karma and hence of personal choice. There is no such thing as chance. Honesty in business furthermore turns out to be the best policy yielding trust in transaction, loyalty and stability in enterprise. It is not so surprising that the Buddha was commonly to be found in the houses of 'business' men and residing in the suburbs of cities.

The Buddha had much to say about the conduct of life by the laity. In the Sigalaka Sutta [2] he advised a young man that proper 'sacrifice' consists in appropriate behaviour in relation to parents, teachers, wives and children, renouncers and Brahmins. A husband must care for his wife and she must look after his earnings. Servants should not be given work beyond their ability, they should be provided with food and wages, and given care when ill. They in turn should rise before the master and retire after him, take only what is due and support him in his affairs. Householders should befriend renouncers and supply their material needs without bothering about whatever creed they pronounced. Economic life should be carefully controlled with enough saved for the future, debt should be avoided and the good life led. There is, as Gombrich suggests, a sort of spiritual monetisation here, the good man sustains his positive karma much as he might his bank account.

Main contrasts between Theravada and Mahayana

Theravada	Mahayana
Buddha as human	Buddha as supramundane.
One 'body' of Buddahood	Three bodies
One life	Recurrent avatars
Asceticism	Social emphasis
Emptiness	Compassion
Goal-Nirvana	Bodhicitta

One may wonder why early Buddhism emphasised the ascetic life so strongly when the path was of the Middle Way rather than the extremes followed by other renouncers. While, as Gombrich suggests, misery may well have increased through ill health in the growing cities, this seems hardly sufficient to account for the ascetic trend in Indian life. In the years after the Buddha's death, the Sangha seemed to forget that the Buddha's first acquaintances became arhats within a few days. The brahmin hold on society was very strong and the homeless life seemed to demand almost superhuman effort if one was to attain liberation in a lifetime. One must remember that the renouncers were essentially rebelling against the dominant brahminical system with its caste exclusiveness and ritual. The renouncer undertook responsibility for his own liberation but such rebellion was hard for the only way out of a suffocating apartheid was through escape. The Middle Way avoided extremes but essentially the Sangha provided such an escape for bankers and even kings. Describing the way as a 'refuge' had real social meaning. It certainly favoured the Buddha's own caste, the original warrior landowners.

In the Mahayana, the ideal and the purpose of the life of a practitioner shifted away from earlier Buddhism. Instead of a focus on nirvana attained through practices leading to arhatship through the recognition of impermanence, emptiness and no-self, the prime goal became the cultivation of Bodhicitta – the mind set of Buddha. This required a practice of imitating Buddha in his compassion for others through kindness, charity and teaching. The aim was to become a Bodhisattva who works out his repeated lives in the service of others; shepherding them towards ultimate liberation and only accepting liberation once all others have attained it. Although arhats were undoubtedly compassionate, the Mahayana emphasis was on an unlimited altruism – which led naturally to an abandonment of self-concern including a concern for one's own enlightenment. The path to Bohisattvahood involved the practice of the Six Perfections, generosity, morality, patience, energetic application, meditation and especially *prajna*, the perfection of wisdom that gave insight into the emptiness of all things and the application of which made each of the other perfections transcendental.

The Buddha certainly knew that the practice of the good was valuable advertisement in inducing faith in his teachings. And it was the teachings rather than the teacher that he always emphasised, especially at the end of his life. He did not appoint a successor or establish a lineage of persons. The monks were to work out their salvation with diligence through following the Dharma. Further more, according to Theravada Buddhism, the Buddha had completely disappeared on his death in a final departure from the round of samsara. Seemingly, only the Dharma and the Sangha remained as 'refuges'.

In the early centuries, no effigy was to be found on the empty thrones that depicted the Buddha-dharma in stone. Yet, it was the charismatic person of the Buddha in death as well as in life that moved hearts to faith in the teachings. The human need for godlike icons was perhaps more resistant to change than he knew. Probably it was the stories of the Buddha in his past lives, as he himself recounts in the Jataka tales and some suttas, that were one source of the growth of the idea that many Buddhas had existed in time, avatars who descended when their time was ripe. This idea was to become a central pivot of the Mahayana. And of course future Buddhas, current bodhisattvas, became figures of great interest. The notion gradually developed that the Buddhas were recurrent representatives of 'Buddha nature', the underlying essence of Buddhahood. Such beings could determine their rebirth, appearing in many forms as bodhisattvas representing compassion, wisdom, awareness or the capacity to heal. These figures emerged as the great icons of the Mahayana and appear in the development of wonderful arts that depict them throughout Asia. Although these great icons were essentially archetypes of ideal persons they none the less represented a style of holy life liveable by anyone who trained mindfully in the path.

In Mahayana thought, archetypical Buddhas were believed to live in their respective spiritual lands or realms to which one might go after living a meritorious life. Amitabha, the Buddha of the Western paradise, was said by some to live in a 'pure land' to which one could go simply through faith and by repeating his mantra. Here we observe a move away from an inner path to an outer path of faith and devotion functioning as a simple religion for many. For the virtuosi however the whole story was seen as a functional myth metaphorically representing processes of mind and not to be dislocated from the true Dharma of the inner path.

The five Buddha icons primarily used for meditative contemplation, the so called Dhyani Buddhas, are of especial interest because they derive from the five attributes of mind, the skandhas of sensation, perception, cognition, volition and consciousness/form. In perfected form these attributes are said to become the Buddhas Akshobya, Ratnasambhava, Amitabha, Amogasiddhi and Vairochana, who can be arranged in a circle with one of them as a central core, becoming a mandala for purposes of meditation. Such mandalas were to become highly significant in the practice of Tantra (see Chapter 10). In their visualisation, each of them has particular attributes and realms representing states of mind. Meditating on these Buddha icons transcends the mundane activity of the skandhas.

While the Mahayana was developing, the Indian world was again changing. Although the castes remained, the country had gone through periods of great empires, destructive wars and major invasions from the North West. Some of these dynasties had supported Buddhism, some not. The revival of ancient Indian gods, often of Dravidian origin, and the emergence of a Hinduism of devotion (*bhakti*) provided the people with many images, icons of spiritual power and consoling faith in hard times. The new Buddhist icons matched those of resurgent Hinduism and for many doubtless served the same function.

THE LOTUS SUTRA

The idea of 'skilful means' (*upaya*) now became highly significant. In the chaos of a world so full of illusion, the skilful means of the Bodhisattvas were the multiple arts by which they taught a great variety of persons with methods appropriate to their needs and understanding. This is clearly demonstrated in the colourful text of the Lotus Sutra (*Sadharmapundarika Sutra*) where all these Mahayanic trends emerged in full force. What remains surprising is that in all this turmoil and religiosity the heart of the Buddha's message remained intact, great scholars reconciled past themes with shifting needs. The basic formulae of the Buddha's earliest teachings remained the core of the Dharma, the seat of philosophical and ethical development.

Several features of the Mahayana involve *bhakti*, devotion. Doubtless derived from a common inheritance of devotion to the gods within Hinduism, the Buddhist emphasis was to couple devotion with selfless service for others. Such a trend is visible also in the Bhagavad-Gita and especially in the Vaishnavite tradition centring on Krishna, the avatar of Vishnu. Like Krishna, the Buddha in the Lotus Sutra is depicted shedding brilliant light throughout the universe, surrounded by gods and angelic beings showering him with flowers.

This 'superabundance' was reconciled with his mundane presence through the doctrine of the three bodies of a Buddha. The Dharma body

(*Dharmakaya*) was the immaterial essence of Buddhahood, the Resplendent body (*Sambhogakaya*) was his idealised, archetypical form as the shining one etc while the *Nirmanakaya* was his material, incarnated presence as a normal human being. The new tantric rituals of visualisation could move from a focus on one level of devotion, the abstract, through the archetypical to the personal and back again, giving the practice of meditation a fresh, emotional depth. The practitioner endeavoured to cultivate the intentional mind of Buddha (*bodhicitta*) through visualising the mundane self as a Bodhisattva practicing on earth in compassion, love and wisdom. A true Bodhisattva does not seek enlightenment until all have attained enlightenment before him/her.

The Buddha had shown that this self does not exist as an entity; the five characteristics of cognition revolve continuously giving rise to an erroneous imputation of self-hood. No-self is the root of the Theravada enlightenment of the Arhat. Manhayana thinkers showed that not only the self but also all manifold things and ideas were interrelated and hence equally empty of inherent selfhood. Nothing and no one could stand-alone in the world. This impermanent 'inter-being', as Thich Nhat Hahn puts it, is the suchness (*tathata*) of all things in which all appearances are empty (*sunya*) of any isolated existence. The practice of a Bodhisattva's compassion goes on within this realisation as his form of relatedness with it. From this resounding insight, one major philosophical line developed focussing on emptiness, while a more psychological perspective emphasised this very emptiness as the 'Buddha essence' basic to mind. In this latter perspective mind was therefore already Buddha, only the obscurities of ignorance prevented one from achieving the insight that constitutes selfless enlightenment.

The Lotus Sutra focuses on the multifarious skilful means of the Buddhas. In this narrative drama, the scenes are always changing and numerous Bodhisattvas meet together in multiple circumstances with both human beings and Buddhas. The Buddha is eternal and his descent to earth a mere expedient in a vast cosmic, soteriological play. All Dharma vehicles are one vehicle and all are empty. The Buddha activity of compassion combined with skilful means is repeatedly demonstrated. In one story, the people are dancing and partying in a great house when it catches fire. They are so absorbed in the partying that no one notices. The Buddha creates an even finer building outside with an even more exciting party going on. Everyone comes out and runs towards it. When at last all are safe, the illusion disappears leaving them to contemplate smoking ruins. The parable is repeated in several such entertaining stories.

This brief introduction to Mahayana perhaps reveals why this form of Buddhism was so successful in Central Asia and in China. Buddhist institutions comprised monasteries and temples with strict rules and ethics. They were increasingly filled with magnificent art, mural paintings, tankas, carving and led by men of undoubted sincerity and often deep spiritual attainment. The habit of travelling and spreading the Dharma ensured that the ideas spread widely along the trade routes of the time. Traders and men of religion travelled together, strong and determined individualists sharing the hardships of Silk Road travel. The openness of Buddhism to lay and Sangha membership without discrimination between ethnic origins or class pretensions meant it was available to virtually anyone moving around on these immense journeys.

The simple ideal of an ethical life with benefits in terms of karmic outcomes and the possibility of beneficial rebirth opening the way to ultimate Buddhahood would have appealed to men whose capacity for self development was apparent already in their manner of livelihood. For those with a more inward disposition there were the heart-warming rituals in temple and monasteries and the availability of personal practices that tested and confirmed the premises of the Dharma. Those skilled in the arts of calligraphy, painting and carving could readily find a home among the monks and did so – as, for example, the extraordinary painted grottos of Dunhuang on the edge of the Gobi desert and the giant statues of Bamyan in Afghanistan, recently destroyed by the Taliban, testify.

In Central Asia, such an ideology stood opposed by local shamanism with its closeness to nature. Where these interact positively Buddhism is associated with the notion of personal development as well as adaptation to the rhythms of nature. In the cities that stood along the Silk Road, new schools, temples and monasteries could be established and supported by local rulers and householders of influence. Sangha creation spread steadily as leading citizens became attracted to the Dharma. There was also a complex interaction with other religions, Manicheeism, Zoroastrianism and Nestorian Christianity reflected in carvings and residual documents.

Men and women with spiritual inclinations had the possibility of joining the Sangha as a monk or nun. It was then of course that the depth of the soteriological philosophy with all its subtlety and depth of meditative yoga became apparent to the practitioner. The emotionally appealing, less ascetic, approach of the Mahayana stimulated a renewal of philosophising. In monasteries, great scholars studied the texts and wrote commentaries and treatises upon them. By the time, Buddhism reached China new philosophical texts had originated in India and Central Asia; whole Mahayana sutras that carried these deep thoughts ever further east. These texts were, on the one hand subtly analytical, sometimes with an amazingly penetrating insight into the nature of language and thought and, on the other hand, psychological, based in yogic insights. There were also devotional texts, which, while well suited to men of little academic attainment, could also be interpreted in the light of psychological philosophy.

We have already seen that the Buddha sometimes talked quite conventionally and sometimes with an emphasis on ultimate causation. This distinction is important in the Mahayana where some of the practices seem quite worldly, attaining pure lands, obtaining meritorious rebirths. Such activities were all skilful means by which the institutions of Buddhism related the Sangha to the laity upon whom the monks depended. Yet anyone with the wit to penetrate beyond appearances soon came face to face with the transcending wisdom whereby the impermanence and emptiness of all things was perceived as the liberation of the Buddha mind, the discovery of the basis. This uneasy and paradoxical relationship between the conventional and the transcendental forms a key theme in Mahayana and it preoccupied numerous philosophers. The great Tibetan scholar Tsonkhapa, the founder of the reformed Gelugpa Order, indeed claimed that the most difficult thing in Buddhism was to see clearly how the appearances of the self were at the same time the manifestation of the emptiness of not-self. As we shall see this insight was often lacking, as when Bodhidharma abruptly informed a Chinese emperor that all his practical support of monasteries and the Sangha had no relation to his possible enlightenment. The poor Emperor was completely at a loss.

In China, there already existed the major philosophical perspectives of Taoism and Confucianism so it is not surprising that, as Buddhism began to take hold there, so began a profound discussion between these viewpoints, sometimes leading to syncretism and sometimes to conflict. It took many years of careful translation before the meanings of the sutras were properly understood, and, even then, the influence of Taoism in particular often remained. Buddhism began to incorporate the Taoist love of nature within a Dharma perspective, a viewpoint that gradually emerged as Chan/Zen with its sensitivity to the natural world and the wilderness.

End Notes

1. *This progression has much in common with the descriptive accounts of mental yoga practiced quite generally in India but especially associated with Yoga and Samkhya philosophy.*
2. Gombrich, R. 1988. *Theravada Buddhism. A social history from Ancient Benares to modern Columbo.* Routledge and Kegan Paul. London.

7

THE GREAT PHILOSOPHERS

The Buddha had shown that the self exists only conventionally: on meditative examination nothing more than the prime characteristics of mental activity, sensation, perception, cognition and the complexes of will can be found. They are continuously and interactively moving in a process of appearance in consciousness. The self is an imputation inferred within the awareness of this process; it is no more than a conceptual reification. A capacity to realise a state without attachment to self (No-self -*anatta*) is then perceived as the root insight of enlightenment experienced by an Arhat within the Theravada.

Mahayana thinkers, as we will now see, were to go further showing that not only the self but all manifold things and ideas were interrelated, relative, subject to impermanence and hence equally 'empty' of any inherent selfhood. Nothing and no one could stand alone as an independent object in the world. This flux came to be known as the suchness (*tathata*) of all things in which all appearances are empty (*sunya*) of any isolated, independent existence for all experience is relative. The unattached practice of a Bodhisattva's compassion goes on within this realisation of emptiness (*sunyata*) as the co-arising of the myriad phenomena in relativity. When viewed conventionally with attachment to an 'I', this whole matter constitutes 'samsara', the realm of suffering. When seen with the eye of insight (*prajna*) as to its true nature it constitutes enlightenment – 'nirvana'. The process of awakening is thus initially seen as a move from samsara into nirvana as if in a temporal progression.

As we have mentioned, one major philosophical line focussing on emptiness developed directly from these resounding insights while another emphasised this very emptiness as the universal 'Buddha nature' basic to mind. Mind in this latter perspective is therefore already 'Buddha'; only the obscurities of ignorance prevent one from achieving the insight that constitutes seltless enlightenment. Nirvana is already present within samsara and the requirement is simply to awaken to this fact. Here, no temporal progression is needed.

We need to examine these two contrasting perspectives for they provide the basic theoretical understanding of Mahayana practice and of a later development in Chinese philosophy, which has significance for our view of the self, and the environment in Western Buddhism today.

NAGARJUNA: REDUCING PHILOSOPHY TO ABSURDITY

The Mahasanghikas, early Buddhists of eastern India, were the first to develop the philosophy of total emptiness (*sunyata*) by emphasising ancient teachings on the Perfection of Wisdom (*Prajnaparamita*) that some argue had been secret or hidden since the Buddha's time, possibly because they had been taught only to adepts. The actual history of these texts remains uncertain and modern scholarship remains unclear as to what extent they may have been taught by the Buddha or developed from his tenets in a later age. Certainly, they have a clear foundation in the Buddha's idea of the emptiness of self. According to a recent understanding, elements in Greek thought ultimately stemming from Parmenides (475 bc) very plausibly influenced Buddhist philosophy during the years of Greek predominance in Gandhara in the Indus valley, Bactria and the region of contemporary Afghanistan, at around the same time as the Greek style of dress and imagery created the conventional representation of the Buddha in statuary (100-200ce). The emerging philosophy of the Mahayana may thus have resulted from an amalgam of Indian and Greek ideas.[1]

These *Prajnaparamita* Sutras appeared over some thousand years from around 100 bce till the 5th century ce.[2] They began with elaborations of a central idea in which the names of the discussants in the texts are those of individuals known to the Buddha. Later they became unbelievably unwieldy as repetitions were inserted for the purpose of chanting. As time went on, the names of the protagonists in dialogue became those of idealised Bodhisattva figures such as Avalokiteshvara, the icon or archetype of Compassion. Near the end of the period, manageable condensations of the essential tenets were written to provide the classic sutras of the genre – the Heart Sutra (*Hrdaya Sutra*) and the Diamond Sutra (*Vajracchedika Sutra*). The key idea is that the basic elements of existence (dharmas) figured in the primordial events of experience and which had been viewed as really existent in the Theravada, are, like the self, inherently transient, insubstantial, empty of any sort of particularity or permanence. They come and go, emerge and change in endless process. There is nothing that can be grasped as an object independent from context. As the Law of Co-dependent Arising argues, phenomena are dependent on conditions, causes lead to consequences under the influence of context. The nature of reality itself is thus 'emptiness' and nothing can be grasped.

As the Heart Sutra puts it: "Form is emptiness and emptiness is form. Form is precisely emptiness and emptiness precisely form."

This root idea is then applied to everything that in the Theravada retained a quality of inherent 'thingness':

"So also are sensation, perception, volition and consciousness. This emptiness of all dharmas is not born, not destroyed, does not increase nor decrease. In emptiness...there is no sight, sound, touch, thought...no realm of cognition, no ignorance and no ending of ignorance, no suffering and no ending of suffering, no ageing and death and no ending of ageing and death. No wisdom or any attainment. No path..."

And thus with nothing to attain, Bodhisattvas relying on such insight, "have no obstructions in their minds and departing far from confusion and imagining they reach ultimate nirvana." Yet, one must never forget the returning line "emptiness is form": the empty process manifests in the forms that appearances take in the mirror of consciousness.

The understanding of this view is no mere intellectual exercise, it depends on deep meditation until the experiential awareness of its meaning arises as personal insight. At this point even the idea of emptiness is abandoned as a mere raft that had carried one across to the other shore. This indeed is a radical position, as Shariputra the Theravadin Arhat must have found when, in the Heart Sutra, Avalokiteshvara first put it to him.

The great philosopher Nagarjuna (Second century CE) pondered deeply upon such ideas and wrote two great works exploring their logical implications. He saw that any assertion, whether positive or negative, would simply dissolve in the light of the transcending wisdom of emptiness. His method was therefore to reduce any proposition to 'absurdity' – the method of *prasanga* as it was called. He would take any thesis presented by either a non-Buddhist or a Buddhist thinker and, by the use of subtle syllogism, show that it was simply untenable because inherently inconsistent. Being utterly consistent himself, he applied the same method to his own thought and thus had no position to propose whatsoever. Accused of mere nihilism by some of his critics, Nagarjuna was actually making the powerful and logically incontrovertible point that whatever 'reality' may be it remains ultimately beyond thought construction since no metaphysically conceived entity can possibly exist. The applications of Nagarjuna's method continue to be a fundamental Mahayana philosophical position, with minor commentarial diversions, till the present day.

Nagarjuna's insights had begun from contemplating the questions that the Buddha himself had refused to discuss. These were:

(1) Whether the world is eternal or not (or both or neither);

(2) Whether the world is finite or infinite (or both or neither),

(3) Whether the Buddha exists after death or not (or both or neither) and

(4) Whether the self is identical with the body or different.

Altogether these comprise fourteen questions derived from four basically opposed alternatives.

The Buddha, in refusing to answer, stated that he could neither affirm or deny any such position and that his viewpoint was the middle way – from which we get the name Madhyamaka for Nagarjuna's thought system. Reflection on any one of these positions shows that no one of them can be reasonably and conclusively held as true. They are simply speculative, veering from an eternalist to a nihilist position. Any belief based upon any one of them is thus necessarily untenable. Since most religious tenets are based in such beliefs it follows that nearly all religions remain non-demonstrable. They are merely one-sided 'faiths'. Any assertion becomes meaningless in the awareness of its contextual dependence, its 'empti-ness'. Whatever might be called the 'Absolute' in Western translations is thus, to Nagarjuna, completely void of meaning.

Nagarjuna was followed by a number of eminent thinkers. Buddhapalita continued to develop the *prasanga* viewpoint but Bhavavivika believed that the reduction to absurdity of any viewpoint was not enough to establish absolute truth. He tried to compose independent, logical arguments additional to Nagarjuna's dialectic to silence an opponent. Candrakirti was having none of this, demonstrating that such a position could not be held against further application of Nagarjuna's method. Philosophy in these centuries was very much alive and a prime concern in the great university of Nalanda and elsewhere.

The positive point in Nagarjuna's Madhyamika philosophy is that in adopting a third position, that of total non assertion, the practitioner transcends dualities and gains freedom from their implications. This practice of finding a third place transcending the dualities of opposites is a vital move in Mahayana thinking and also in meditative practice. Freedom from any one-sided conceptuality emerges as the key to Nirvana and yet living in a world of appearances we have to deal with the conventional. Here then we return to the problems of finding a path in the paradoxical awareness that no such 'Path' can ultimately be found!

THE 'EMBRYO' OF BUDDHAHOOD – TATHAGATAGARBHA

There were thinkers who felt that this *via negativa*, this negative way of expressing ultimate truth, was unsatisfactory because it failed to express the joy of positive discovery, of realisation and relief, inexpressible logically but none the less there, which attended the insight giving rise to freedom.

How could what has been discovered be expressed? The issue here is more psychological than philosophical. In Tibet this unease became focussed in a debate between a) 'self emptiness' (rang tong), that is the emptiness of self in all things as found in the Heart Sutra and discussed by Nagarjuna, and b) a comprehensive basis which could be said to be there even though all its expressions were 'self empty'. This basis was called 'other emptiness' (sheng tong). 'Other emptiness' means something that is empty of every characteristic other than its own existence. The argument asserts a 'reality' even though all its expressions are self-empty, thereby creating an interestingly positive position much less precisely intermediate between nihilist and eternalist viewpoints. Unfortunately Buddhists are as prone to prejudice as anyone else and this divergence of view occasioned much disputation between monasteries in Tibet, some of it violent, a divergence still apparent in the thought of lamas today.

The Buddha himself had from time to time strongly argued that although the self was empty this did not mean that it was void-that is to say nothing at all. In a famous quotation from the Udana (VIII.3) in the Khuddaka Nikaya he said: "There is an unborn, unbecome, unmade, uncompounded; for if there were not this unborn, unbecome, unmade, uncompounded, there would be no escape from this that is born, become, made and compounded".

We have here the basis for a positive assertion of an ontology affirming that ultimate being exists even though it must remain ineffable because any assertion made about it is captured by Nagarjuna's reduction to nonsense. It was the relation between this assertion and the negations of Nagarjuna that troubled these thinkers. The theme crops up in numerous writings in the early Mahayana and scholars have yet to thoroughly understand the intricacies and roots of these various arguments. We can only trace the main theme here.

The arguments circle around a puzzling question: if all things are relative to one another is this relativity also relative? We have seen that all phenomena (and all concepts) are viewed as relative to one another, hence, contextually co- determined and 'empty' of an independent self-nature. Nothing stands alone. Yet, if everything was relative, the concept of relativity necessarily depends on the notion of non-relativity. Candrakirti, a great follower of Nagarjuna, indeed says that so long as we argue that relativity is the common characteristic of all existents, we must also argue that there is no existent which could be non-relative. Yet, because relativity has no object with which it could be contrasted it becomes as unsubstantiated as a flower in the sky. He goes on to ask whether this means that relativity should therefore be rejected. No, he argues, because the assertion of relativity is the only way to get rid of arbitrarily existent conceptions. Yet, clinging to relativity is to fall back once more into ignorance. It would be as if a shopkeeper said, "I have nothing to sell." and the shopper replied, "OK, then sell me this nothing itself."

The Gelugpa of Tibet say that to argue for a positive basis for the relativity of things is merely a device in argument to aid those lost in the puzzles of emptiness. Yet, others argue, as we have already seen, for a more assertive stand as being genuinely useful to understanding. In effect what troubles these thinkers is the ungroundedness of thought based in the relativity of 'emptiness' and their sense that some positive ontology is needed if only to provide psychological security for believers in the Dharma.

The Buddhist assertion of groundedness appears to have developed through a progressive series of ideas that emerged gradually over centuries. We have seen that a prime move in the development of the Mahayana was the notion that the historical Buddha was a representation, along with many previous Buddhas, of a universal Buddha-mind or nature that was transcendent. Since this Buddha-mind was held to be universal, it could be said to be potentially present in all sentient beings. This potential became known as the 'embryo' of Buddhahood that in each and every person remains unseen because of ignorance.

This embryo or womb of Buddha at the heart of every person can be interpreted from a 'sheng tong' position as being the ultimate ground of being, while emptiness refers simply to the impermanence of moral and spiritual hindrances. Defilements can be read as empty and merely adventitious to the root conceived as pure, blissful and permanent. There is a sharp divergence here from the *Perfection of Wisdom and Nagarjuna*.

Examining the etymology of terms is useful here. The Sanskrit word for this basic Buddha nature in everyone is *Tathagatagarbha*. Breaking this word down to its components, we have: *garbha* meaning embryo or womb and *tathagata* meaning the 'thus (*tathata*) going (*gata*) one', a title of the Buddha which he had attributed to himself. The whole word means the 'embryo or womb of the one who comes and goes' or more simply 'the basis in coming and going', i.e. impermanence. Therefore, although this word points to the Buddha-mind in everyone, this mind is in no sense a self as entity but rather the principle of impermanence lying at the heart of being. It seems we have here a sort of short hand whereby the assertion of the Buddha-mind in everyone codes for the presence of impermanence as a potential to be realised in enlightenment. Yet, the concept fills the role of an assertive ontology for those requiring one.

This dispute or contrast in perspectives re-appears also in Chinese Buddhism. Master Yinshun of the last century argues that in Buddhism there is a distinction to be made between definitive and non-definitive truth. The former expresses an ultimate or conclusive understanding while the latter is useful for helping a practitioner overcome obstacles. Yinshun opines that *tathagatagarbha* is a non-definitive teaching designed to overcome peoples fears about emptiness. The teaching is expedient to circumstances and has a soteriological function. It is not that the idea of *tathagatagarbha* is false or misleading but rather that it is incomplete. The 'rang tong' position here retains its ultimate hold. Yinshun would point us back to the Diamond Sutra as definitive while Nagarjuna might well point to the relativity of 'rang tong' and 'sheng tong' and press the case that neither can be true exclusively of the other. Their mutual dependence points beyond both of them. [3]

There appear to have been sociological reasons for this gradual shift towards a dualism in the understanding of the Buddha's message. During periods of imperial stability in north India (the Kushan and Gupta empires), there had been a resurgence of confidence in life and livelihoods and the re-emergence of a folk pantheon of gods to form the roots of what in modern times became known to the West as Hinduism. In addition, newly asserted philosophical views within Brahminism emphasised a view of the 'ultimate' as Brahman, an all-pervasive godhead. It seems the times required a more positive ontology as a basis for Buddhist values than that supplied by the Theravada. The shifts in philosophical argument seem therefore to be the result of a social selection of ideas under the influence of changes in society. Unfortunately, we have no clear picture of the nature of these changes so that much of this argument remains surmise, but the presence of large Buddhist universities teaching a wide curriculum additional to Buddhist thought must have encouraged reflection and innovation among the professors of a cultured elite and a tendency to divergence in doctrine. Anyone today who attempts to enter the surviving literature of these centuries will be impressed by its sophistication, subtlety and philosophical drive.[4]

Among these developments was a tendency that current Westerners may find difficult; namely the idea that the universe can be interpreted as mind rather than as matter. The hefty assault on dualism had lead to a monistic picture of reality as the relativity of co-dependent arising. But what was 'doing' this co-dependent arising? The yogic basis of Buddhist thought inclined thinkers towards seeing experience itself, rather than the experienced, as basic to understanding. Which came first, observer or observed? If the observer was not separate from the observed then these two shared the same nature. Since the approach was through the yogic activities of mind, it became logical to view the seen as an aspect of the seer. Inversely, the seen included the seer. Hence reality could be considered to be the same as mind, indeed was Mind (capitalised!) of which individual minds were, one might say, mere reflexes, like waves on the surface of the ocean.

As we have already remarked, a Buddha could be described in three ways: as the actual physical and historical person, as the iconic or archetypical emanation of the principle of Buddhahood, or as the basic universal Buddha mind, the pervasive and essential nature of all.Within this perspective, the *tathagatagarbha* became a term for an embryonic aspect within the as yet deluded individual mind that had the potential of blossoming into full comprehension of its apparent self as Dharmakaya. We can see in this metaphysical vision a shadow of Brahmanism but must then immediately recall that the perspective of Nagarjuna has not been lost. The *tathagata* remains 'empty', even though conventionally reality is positively here as such (*tathata*).

Several sutras reveal the progression of ideas that led to this *tathagatagarbha* perspective but the question as to how the individual person might come to comprehend it experientially was not at first answered in them. A further perspective however emerged that did provide an epistemological argument, indeed a model of mind, to show how the experience of personal 'enlightenment' as the recognition of the Buddha within could arise. Several names outline this viewpoint: Yogacara, emphasising the use of mental yoga, Mind Only (Cittamatra) school, or the Consciousness school (Vijnanavada).

THE YOGIC APPROACH TO 'MIND ONLY'

The gradual shifts in Mahayana philosophy towards an apparently more idealist position did not stand in contradiction to the teachings of the *Prajnaparamita* sutras and Nagarjuna. Earlier teachings were always preserved but new terminologies and emphases developed within them providing what amounts to a superstructure. In the Yogacara endeavour to meet the needs of Gupta period Buddhists, the ideas of emptiness were relegated more to the back burner. More positive assertions enabling effective meditation praxis came to the fore.

The large body of Yogacara literature developed from the major teachings of two brothers Vasubandhu and Asanga who are known as the main founders and synthesisers of this school. The earlier writings had asserted the 'embryo' as the self-evolving root of the mind. Later the identity of this root with the pervasive Buddha mind of the universe became emphasised and, finally, the psychological process whereby this could be perceived was provided. Ontology thus came to be reinforced by an effective epistemology of the process of awakening.

A major advance in this direction is found in the famous Lankavatara Sutra, which, as we will see later, became a foundation text for Zen and the emergence of vital trends in Chinese Buddhism (Chapter 8). The sutra includes a well-elaborated model of mind discussing the psychological dynamics of enlightenment itself.[5]

The Buddha had listed the mental faculties as sensation, perception, cognition, preconceived attitudes (the samskaras) and consciousness all based on the faculties of seeing, hearing, smelling, touching and mental awareness each of which was described as a sense organ linked to the consciousness appropriate to that sense organ. To this basic picture the Yogacara added two further faculties, a basic storehouse of impressions of all kinds (the *alayavijnana* or *alaya* for short) and the cognitive construction (*manovijnana*) of the relations between the contents of this storehouse created by an attentive consciousness (*manas*). Put simply, the idea is that we all live within a world of perceptions, cognitions and ideas constructed by mind out of an incredibly vast store of dynamic and interactive memories. As attention is directed to some aspect of this store so the links between it and a wide reaching scenario including ongoing perceptions of an 'outer' world are created. Basically, we are living in a virtual world created by the biased patterns of attentiveness of our own minds.

Yet, what is the fundamental process of this mind? The imagery in the sutra suggests that incoming information from the sense organs is like a perfume that scents the storehouse. This perfuming activity creates 'seeds' (*bija*), which may grow into complex associative structures. This approach emphasises the intangible nature of memory and hints at the arbitrary character of the world we create from it. There is a sense here that we are 'imprisoned' by the patterns of associations we make in constructing a personal view of the (apparent) world. Some 'seeds' are thought to be innate or universal and to provide a basis for the construction of a picture of 'reality'. Others arise in the course of interaction to create the conditioned world within which we live. This early recognition of an innate and an acquired origin of the contents of mind foreshadow similar discussions today (Chapter 15) and again demonstrate that in the world of ideas there is very often rather little new under the sun.

Yet we must persist, what is the nature of this perfuming process? The Yogacara view argues that the process is none other than the pervasive universal mind (Buddha nature, *Dharmakaya*) in perpetual motion. Direct apprehension of this flux is normally obscured by the masking construction of the world of ideas concerning the everyday world of 'things', a view none the less beset by an uneasy apprehension of their insubstantial nature. Such unease is perhaps the motivating root activating the 'embryo' of enlightenment to an expansive investigation.

Within this perspective, meditative training leads ultimately to a 'turning around' (*paravritti*) of the mental apparatus so that consciousness (*manas*) suddenly becomes aware of the storehouse no longer as a matrix of complex relations but simply as an unlimited network empty of any particulate, inherent reality. This moment is an enlightened awakening to the total relativity of all self-concern and the pointlessness of any attachments within it. Grasping at the ungraspable becomes foolish, like trying to catch the wind or cook sand. And in the release of freedom from mental constructions, unconditioned bliss appears as the basis for the career of a Bodhisattva.

MENTAL CONSTRUCTION

Careful study of these sutras reveals that the basis of mind is viewed from the twin perspectives of its basic nature and its capacity for knowing (epistemology). These are the two aspects of sentience. Sentience emerges from insentience; both are expressions of ineffable Buddha mind or nature.[5] Such a viewpoint presents the mind as constructing its understanding of reality in three ways:

(1) Perceptions based in sensation create objects of cognition leading to both the idea of the graspable and a self as grasper, thereby creating a dualistic picture of phenomenal reality. A constructive imagination (*parikalpa*) builds up the conventional world of samsara from the reifications inherent in thought and language. Seemingly really existing objects appear to face seemingly really existing subjects in a world of subject-object duality.

(2) Meditative practices enable the mind to observe the flow of mere perceptions (*vijnapti*) prior to their conceptualisation as objects. Under disciplined yogic control, thought is observed in its actual dependency upon this perceptual flow.

(3) The Yogacarins say that this perceptual process must itself be dependent on an underlying stratum or basis, a really existent ground of phenomena. They reject the Madhyamika analysis of Nagarjuna as too strong a negation. The essential basis is suchness (*tathata*) itself, the *Dharmakaya* or universal Buddha nature, which however is not something that can be characterised as a thing.

The Yogacarins argue, reasonably, that without such a basis the misconstructions of thought could not exist and, correspondingly, neither could the awakening that arises when its illusions are abandoned. There would be absolutely nothing at all. Since there is something existent as an inexpressible suchness, it seems wise to say so.

The major implication of these Mahayana philosophies is that there is no need to progress in time from samsara (illusion) to nirvana (insight) because samsara and nirvana are already co-present as inherent potentials of mind. They are in effect the same process observed from contrasting perspectives, with or without the grasping motivation. There is no need to 'go' anywhere. The vital move is to look directly at what is present without activating the dualistic mode of thought, effectively to remain at the point of contact between cartwheel and road. Such a revolutionary view has had wide implications in the further history of Buddhist thought and practice, particularly in China, Korea and Japan.

End Notes

1.   McEvilley, T. 2002. *The Shape of Ancient Thought. Comparative studies in Greek and Indian Philosophies.* Allworth. New York.

2.   Conze, E. 1959. *Buddhist Scriptures.* Penguin. London.
     Also: 1968. *Selected sayings from the Perfection of Wisdom.* Buddhist Society. London. and 1973. *Buddhist Thought in India.* University of Michigan. Ann Arbor.

3.   For further discussion see: Hookham, S.K. 1991. *The Buddha Within.* State University of New York Press. New York. Also: Brown, B.E. 1991. *The Buddha Nature: A study of the Tathagatagarbha and Alayavijnana.* Motilal Banarsidas. Delhi. Also: Yin shun, Master 1998. *The Way to Buddhahood: instructions from a Modern Chinese Master.* Wisdom. Boston. Also: Hurley, S. 2004. The doctrinal transformation of Twentieth century Chinese Buddhism: Master Yinshun's interpretation of the tathagatagarbha doctrine. *Contemporary Buddhism* 5, 1: 47-64.

4.   See further: Warder, A.K. 1997. *Indian Buddhism.* Motilal Banarsidass. Delhi. Also Goyal, S.R. 1987. *A History of Indian Buddhism.* Kusumanjali Prakashan. Meerut.

5.   Suzuki, D.T. 1930. *Studies in the Lankavatara Sutra.* Routledge. London. Also: Suzuki, D.T. 1932/1973. *The Lankavatara Sutra. A Mahayana text.* Routledge and Kegan Paul. London.

8

ENTRY INTO CHINA

SILK ROAD ADVENTURES

The gradual spread of Buddhism and its great philosophies in Asia began with the missionary endeavours of the great Mauryan Emperor Asoka (274-236 BC). Under his influence monasteries became established and the Dharma flourished in Kashmir and Gandhara, now in Pakistan. To the west of Gandhara was the kingdom of the Bactrian Greeks, descendants of Hellenes who had conquered these lands during the great Asian adventure of Alexander the Great but who had subsequently become isolated from Europe through the intervention of the Parthians. A political and military weakness in India in the second century bc had enabled these Greeks to extend their rule into the Indus valley and some areas further east. Their great king, Menander, became famous, not so much because he was an effective ruler, but because of the extensive interest, he took in Buddhism. He debated Buddhist tenets with the monk Nagasena, their discussions becoming an important text revealing the extent to which Greek and Buddhist thought intermingled in Bactria before the birth of Christ. The melding of Greek thought and Buddhist ideas led both to the development of philosophy and to the development of Mahayana art in both India and China , particularly the well known Buddha image in Greek clothing, perhaps modelled on Apollo.

The Scythians, who had originated in North West China and been driven southwards by the Turkish Xiong-nu, eventually conquered the Greeks. By 130 BC they had established an empire covering not only large parts of Central Asia but also an even greater area of India than had the Greeks. Their emperor, Kanishka of the Kushan dynasty, became a great supporter of Buddhism and the Dharma gradually spread into Central Asia along the Silk roads running west, eventually to Rome, and eastwards through Kashgar and Khotan to Turfan and ultimately to the borders of China at Dunhuang. These large oases in the vast Central Asian deserts were well watered in those days, supported agriculture and fruit and were often well governed as independent fiefdoms each isolated from the next by savage wilderness. They already had an ancient history having been colonised at first by Indo-European peoples. Here caravans would pause, monks could settle and spread their ideas, monasteries were established and great schools of translation of Buddhist scriptures into Central Asian languages developed. From Kashgar to Dunhuang was a long haul but it was probably there that Buddhism first encountered China[1].

Dunhuang lies at the far Western end of the Great Wall of China at the junction of the northern and southern branches of the Silk Road around the Taklamakan desert. Here, in the Mogao grottoes, Chinese culture and that of countries to the West met and fertilised one another, eventually attracting great scholars and translators as well as the artists who have given us wonderful murals that still adorn the walls of the 'caves of the thousand Buddhas'. The famous explorer Sir Aurel Stein was able to obtain ancient scriptures here, long hidden in a walled up cave. Their study has opened the door to our understanding of Central Asian Buddhism,the interactions between the various Buddhist cultures and the advent of Buddhism in China.[2]

An Indian or a Central Asian Buddhist scholar arriving in China was to encounter a civilisation totally different from that with which he would be familiar. In particular, China already had advanced systems of thought with which Buddhism was to interact down to the present day. By the time of the Han dynasty (206 BCE – 6 CE), China had already established an advanced system of bureaucratic control that was perhaps the key to its greatness in Asia. The Emperor was envisaged as the Son of Heaven appointed to ensure the welfare of mankind. To lose the Mandate of Heaven was the cause of the state falling into chaos. To assist him, the state appointed scholars upon whom the conduct of state depended. Confucius supplied the way of thought that underlay the loyalty and discipline of these often finely disciplined administrators. The relationship between heaven and humanity was believed to be such that human dislocations caused natural disturbances. Human morality was thus crucial to the maintenance of natural equilibrium. Flood, earthquakes, famines and so on comprised warnings to the ruler and people that their poor behaviour threatened the mandate under which the state was licensed. Heaven had sharp eyes. Confucianism emphasised filial piety and loyalty to the imperial power to such an extent that individualism was firmly suppressed in favour of a mutual understanding. Such an attitude is still a marked tendency of Chinese identity favouring collective solutions and negotiation towards mutual agreement rather than individualistic effort, personal excellence and competition.

The other key element in Chinese thought was Daoism (Taoism). The Dao is the natural way of nature with which it is the aim of a mystical practitioner to unite in a confluence conceived to be eternal. Philosophical Daoism has some resemblance to Buddhism in that it discusses the ontology of human experience rather than a right way of social action. Indeed, as Buddhism first lapped upon the shores of China, Daoist terminology was widely used in translations of texts. In Chan (Chinese Zen) particularly, Daoist themes, especially the love of nature, remain important. The middle classes and literati supported the arts, poetry, essay writing and painting expressing many Daoist themes. Chinese yoga, part of Daoism and in many ways as powerful as Indian yoga, could quickly penetrate the meditation practices and ideas of Buddhists. Among the less sophisticated, Daoism focussed on the preservation of corporeal life so as to achieve physical immortality. In addition, ancestor worship generated cults whereby the well being of the dead could be assured.

The history of Buddhism in China is very much one of comparative evaluation and competition between these three streams of thought and indeed others that took up further contrasting positions. The rich culture of China was far from monolithic and the potential for a creative interaction between ideas always present. Unfortunately, more often than not, one tradition or another would gain the favour of the imperial court, sometimes leading to the suppression of other points of view. As a foreign system of tenets, Buddhism was often stigmatised and made to suffer indignity, repression, loss of property and social position. Yet, at other times, it spread widely enjoying imperial favour. A main element in Buddhism's survival has been its support among the laity and the relative independence of monks from public support through their own labour.[3]

THE FLOWER ORNAMENT SCRIPTURE

Naturally enough the two main themes that dominated the emerging Buddhism in China were the Madhyamaka and Yogacara perspectives (Chapters 6-7). Yet, a key to how Buddhist philosophy developed such originality in China was the arrival of the extraordinary Mahayana scripture known as the Avatamsaka Sutra, the 'Flower Ornament Scripture'. This extraordinary work, vast in dimension, is really a whole library of sutras of varying kinds amalgamated into an immense text written with all the flowery exuberance of Sanskrit literature in the dream like creativity of the Indian imagination. Thomas Cleary[4] has recently translated this corpus into English to provide a volume that runs to one thousand five hundred pages of closely printed text. As yet, few Western studies of this work have been made in spite of its great significance.

Parts of the great compilation were probably composed in the Kushan period and partial translation into Chinese began in the second century CE. From then until the eighth century several further partial translations and one of the whole scripture were made. So profound were the spiritual intimations in the Avatamsaka that each of the several Buddhist perspectives that were entering China was influenced by it. Chinese Zen, Chan, was not only deeply affected by its ideas but conversely the meditation practices of Chan were found to be of value by those studying the scripture. A considerable convergence between the Avatamsaka perspectives and those of Chan eventually emerged. In Chinese this work is known as Hua-yan, a name translating the title of the sutra, that became attached to a whole philosophical school based upon its themes.

When compared to the *Prajnaparamita* Sutras, the Lankavatara or even the Lotus Sutra, the Flower Ornament Scripture presents us with a radical change of climate. The great Daisetz Susuki writes, "We are no more in this world...we are miraculously lifted up among the heavenly galaxies. The ethereal world is luminosity itself...When the Buddha enters a certain kind of Samadhi, the pavilion where he is situated all of a sudden expands to the fullest limits of the Universe...while the Universe itself is dissolved into the being of the Buddha. And this is no mere expanse of emptiness...for the audience before the Buddha is not a mortal one but a huge gathering of spiritual beings," archetypical bodhisattvas assembling from countless universes. The ground is "paved with diamonds, the pillars, beams, railings·etc are inlaid with all kinds of precious stones sparkling brilliantly and glittering with the reflection of one another." As the Buddha enters that Samadhi, all those present find themselves placed in galaxies of mutual reflection in which each one contains the Buddha and in every atom of which the whole realm of universes is replicated. Although impermanence rules, there is no time other than an eternity of the present and space is no longer a container of particularities but rather an infinite fusion of mutual penetrations and replications in which everything is luminous and transparent. Such a vision represents the *Dharmadhatu*, the realm of the infinite Dharma insight, as opposed to the *Lokadhatu* or realm of conventional appearances. Yet, not all can see this vision equally; it depends upon their spiritual attainments![5]

The books of the Avatamsaka explore this realm from many perspectives. The final work, by far the largest, describes the descent of Manjusri, Bodhisattva of Wisdom, from such an assembly to the human world where he finds a youth called Sudhana who has the potential of becoming a Bodhisattva. Manjusri gives him some instruction and then sends him off in search of enlightened beings each of which has a vision and a practice. These illumined ones come from every walk of life, beggars to kings, seeming fools to great monks, some human and some from far beyond the human world, some men and some women; each one passes Sudhana on to the next who is said to possess even deeper knowledge. This tale of an extraordinary journey reveals the wide reach of Mahayana thought and its rich inclusiveness, an understanding of an extraordinary range of human perception, sometimes deep sometimes relatively shallow. Sudhana eventually reaches the abodes of great beings; Maitreya; the Buddha of the Future, and Samantabhadra, the Bodhisattva of Great Vows, who represents spiritual action in the world. Sudhana is shown a miraculous tower inside of which are countless other towers each one a replica of all the others in unending mutual reflection. None of them obstructs any other one, yet all retain their individuality and each may fuse with all. Sudhana sees himself in all the towers and experiences an emancipation that goes beyond all limits. He finds himself experiencing great selfless compassion for all beings emanating from a wisdom world of unlimited insights powering unlimited potentials for the good.

A reading of such work is a reading of great religious poetry and although the style is foreign to a modern Western reader, it can have a compelling, almost hypnotic quality and the power to entrance through its profound conviction. To its original readers it became a source of faith and inspiration especially in its persuasive account of the lives, morality, achievements and insights of the Bodhisattvas busying themselves in saving the world. Yet, its immense bulk, seeming indigestible wealth of imagery and profuse metaphor was a challenge to the essentially practical Chinese mind.

The extraordinary wealth of contrasting and seemingly contradictory Buddhist ideas that were pouring into China prior to and during the Tang dynasty (7th–9th centuries) demanded some sort of classification, review and condensation. A string of eminent monks of philosophical inclination undertook to unravel the intricacies and to set out clearly the metaphysical principles that underlay these works. Interpreters of the Avatamsaka were of especial importance to the future of Buddhism in China. In particular five names stand out as the founders or 'patriarchs' of the Hua-yan perspective: Du-shun (557-640), Zhi-yan (600-668), Fa-zang (643-712), Cheng-guan (738-839 approx) and Zong-mi (780-841). A further author Li-Tongxuan (8th century) wrote further commentarial works that had a deep influence some centuries later.[6]

Thomas Cleary summarises the significance of these works as follows: "The hua-yen doctrine shows the entire cosmos as one single nexus of conditions in which everything simultaneously depends on and is depended on by, everything else. Seen in this light, then, everything affects and is affected by, more or less immediately or remotely, everything else; just as this is true of every system of relationships, so it is true of the totality of existence. In seeking to understand individuals and groups, therefore, Hua-yen thought considers the manifold as an integral part of the unit and the unit as an integral part of the manifold; one individual is considered in terms of relationships to other individuals as well as to the whole nexus, while the whole nexus is considered in terms of its relation to each individual as well as to all individuals."

Cleary goes on: "*The accord of this view with the experience of modern science is obvious, and it seems to be an appropriate basis upon which the question of the relation of science and bioethics – may be resolved.*"[7] Important words which we shall explore anon. But first, how is this vision constructed?

The essential basis is impermanence as the synonym of emptiness or suchness of all phenomena. As we have seen, impermanence means the momentary arising and simultaneous annihilation of phenomena (dharmas) in an unending yet timeless cosmic process in which all apparent entities are 'empty' of any inherent existence (Chapter 6 &7). The Hua -yan philosophers explore the implications of this idea further than did their forerunners in the Madhyamika or Yogacara traditions from which the sutra emerged. They do this in ways which, although at first seemingly very odd indeed, are in fact well based in logical argument from the initial premises.

Two root premises are Totality and Non Obstruction.[8] Since all phenomena are both instantaneously self-arising and self destructing, description in terms of temporal processes and dimensions become irrelevant in this vision. There is one cosmic whole and that whole is in its suchness 'empty'; furthermore, as phenomena arise and depart they do not obstruct one another but co-emerge without mutual interferences.

The Empress Wu, a great sponsor of Buddhism in the Tang dynasty and a woman of great intelligence, had had a copy of the Avatamsaka imported to the capital from distant Turkestan. The great sanscritist Siksananda undertook the immense task of translation. Wanting to understand the tenets, the Empress requested Master Fa-zang to explain them to her. In attempting to describe them Fa-zang found that the empress, perhaps unsurprisingly, remained puzzled even though she had grasped some essential ideas. She asked him whether he could arrange a demonstration of the key idea as a sort of metaphorical expression. After some thought, Fa-zang had the brilliant idea of using a hall of mirrors. He prepared a room with mirrors on all four walls, in the corners and on the ceilings. In the centre, he placed a Buddha image and a brightly burning torch. As she gazed at this inspiring panorama of receding mutual reflections, the empress exclaimed in wonder. Fa-zang told her that the room demonstrated very clearly that all realms of experience reflect one another and are thus contained in one another while also interpenetrating. Realms embrace realms to infinity and different realms arise simultaneously and all in a harmonious and quite natural pattern. He also demonstrated that the big could be contained in the small as well as the small within the big. Taking from his sleeve a large multifaceted crystal, he showed how all the manifold images in the big mirrors were also represented in the small crystal. On another occasion, he used the statue of a golden lion to demonstrate how the gold pervaded all parts while each part participated in the same gold.

Garma Chang has provided a valuable explanation of the Sanskrit word *dhatu* translated as 'realm' and used frequently in the scripture as in – "the realm of Buddhahood is the totality of non obstruction", or '*dharmadhatu*' – the realm of Dharma. A 'realm' is a term for an area, sphere or perspective within which certain beings, functions, activities, thoughts, or descriptions are manifest. A woodland is an area within which numerous trees and plants support insects, which support birds or small mammals that in turn support larger predators. Each of these comprises a 'realm' and each is dependent on the other and, in view of death, decay and the creation of humus, all are interdependent in one manifold process. Furthermore, the whole process may be expressed through other perspectives, realms of thought this time, providing a descriptive vision in terms of food chains, chemical equilibria, energy conservation, gain or loss or even in terms of a physical analysis. Again, the wood might be seen through the eyes of a poet or a painter. All these realms are contributory to a holistic vision and are both independent and mutually interdependent at the same time. Chang gives the example of a cup of water which may be seen as thirst quenching, contributing to a cooking process, made of H_2O, appearing as ice or snow or steam and so on. All of these 'realms' are independent yet all can manifest harmoniously without contradiction or 'obstruction'. In a 'totalistic' vision, therefore all perspectives or 'realms' concur without interference with one another yet all contribute to and relate within the whole.

Chang then asks what it is that comprises 'obstruction'. In Hua-yan speak, an obstruction is a boundary, wall, barrier or threshold beyond which a realm no longer applies. These barriers may be of many kinds and could perhaps be classified in terms of the distinctions they make. A poetic vision of daffodils is very different from a biological account of them.

> 'Year after year
> Daffodils
> On the road to Pant-y-dwr.'

Such a verse evokes a very different response from a statement regarding the climatic conditions that stimulate their appearance. What is in play here is what Wittgenstein called a difference between language 'games'. There is a barrier between two forms of verbal expression through their contrasting modes of insight and focus.

What distinguishes a barrier is the presence of distinctive 'being'. To 'be' normally means to 'be something' or to be in a certain manner. Distinctions acquire names and names soon enough evoke preferences or biases for one perspective or another. Such distinctions are constitutive of the way the human mind normally perceives or constructs its world. Our human mode of being is in itself a 'realm' among many others. The world of owls, or frogs, for example are very different from the world of humans as a study of their eyes and ears makes plain. Human minds, furthermore, are highly distinctive in themselves, each running according to a contrasting karma or conditioning. What one human sees another cannot imagine. In the wood, bird watchers see and hear birds, entomologists see a world of insects and the hunter of mushrooms keeps his eyes on the ground. They live in separate 'realms' yet all these realms arise together and penetrate mutually without obstruction. Indeed, they are also interchangeable. Clinging to one realm or another is a product of karmic roots generating distinctive evaluations and preventing the possibility of wider vision. A totalistic vision is only possible when such discriminations are entirely dropped. What is then seen is a whole without barriers yet it is no different from that seen categorised, as it were, through coloured glasses a moment before.

Garma Chang explores the inner dynamics of the totalistic or 'round' view as presented in Du-shun's perceptive essay *On the Meditation of Dharmadhatu*. The meditation first of all distinguishes between the realm of phenomena (*Shi*); that is events as normatively experienced, oak trees, admiral butterflies, cars on motorways, the song of the robin, hot fire and freezing ice, and the realm of the underlying principles (*Li*) that sustain phenomena; laws of gravity, inertia, temporal patterning, linguistic structure, brain processes that are invisible yet which are the determinants of events as perceived. This is then a distinction between the phenomena that appear and the noumena that they express. There are many realms within Li and the phenomena of Shi are the multiple experiences we have of the world, yet all can be subsumed under these two general terms. The realms of Shi and Li are however not themselves realms with barriers between them for they are inseparable, interdependent aspects of one whole. This is the metaphor of the Golden Lion explained; the gold is Li-the underlying pervasive noumenon, while the form of the lion is Shi, the differentiated, phenomenal artefact.

Du-shun describes the relations between Shi and Li. Li does not obstruct Shi (*Li Shi Wu Ai*). An event is always the expression of some underlying principle. Du-shun elaborates characteristically in ten ways. The principle (Li) embraces the event (Shi)) just as the event embraces the underlying principle; when the event (Shi), appears it relies on Li, the principle. Events illustrate the principle yet the appearance of the event may obscure the principle just as realising the principle may obscure the significance of the event. The principle is present in the event just as the events are none other than the principle. Even so, the principle is distinguishable from the event just as events are distinguishable from the principle.

Each of these positions depends on whether one takes up a standpoint from the perspective of the event or its underlying causation or understanding. Each of these relations is then quite logically comprehensible. Modern writers have described this distinction in terms of theories of 'agency', people or objects doing things in the world, or 'motion', the underlying forces that drive the processes of agency. While such theories refer to contrasting data and use differing terms, they are not in contradiction with one another. The beheading of Charles the First may be discussed in terms of personal beliefs or in terms of underlying cultural and historical trends.

Yet there is a further proposition; the non-obstruction of Shi against Shi ; that is of one event against another, an insight based upon the preceding analysis. Given the nature of impermanence, every individual event (Shi)) enters into and merges with all other events in perfect freedom irrespective of the principles underlying them. In the end the only *dharmadhatu* that exists is this mutual penetration in *Shi Shi Wu Ai* (Non obstruction of Shi against Shi).

In Cheng-guan's 'Mirror of the mysteries of the universe of Hua-yan', a contemplation on Du-shun's works, we have the following summary: "*...when all completely enter into one, that causes the one also to be within all that are within itself, simultaneously, without interference. Moreover, because including the other is identical to entering the other, when one thing is completely in all, it causes the all to be always in the one, simultaneously, without interference. Ponder this.*" Indeed!

Thomas Cleary reviews such ideas: "*The Flower Ornament Scripture is like a hologram, the whole concentrated in all the parts, this very structure reflecting a fundamental doctrine – that this is what the cosmos itself is like, everything inter-*

reflecting, the one and the many interpenetrating....Were its method unlocked, ancient research into the mental cosmos...might have something to offer to modern investigations into the holographic nature of the brain and its linear and simultaneous modes."[9]

These Hua yan ideas were taken up within other Buddhist trends entering China. The principles of *Li Shi Wu Ai* and *Shi Shi Wu Ai* became a differentiating focus between viewpoints expressed by the Tian tai and the Hua yan schools and both were subsequently influential in Chan.

THE INVOLVEMENT OF THE LAITY

During the Tang and Song dynasties there were periods when imperial courtiers and literati favouring either Confucianism or Daoism succeeded in persecuting Buddhism as a foreign faith. Monks and nuns were disrobed, monasteries sacked and teaching suspended. These cataclysmic events effectively destroyed much of the wealth and cultural contribution to Chinese Buddhist culture that had been built up in the Tang. In the following Song period the surviving Buddhist traditions tended to compete with one another for influence, not so much from the court as from rich patrons among the literati. The significance of lay practitioners thus became greatly enhanced.

The relations between Buddhism and both Daoism and Confucianism were argued anew. In particular, the great Chan and Hua-yan master Zong-mi[10] was able to show that neither Confucianism nor Daoism were of much use in determining the fate of humans either in this life or in the next. The folk doctrines of karma and rebirth of ancient Indian origin, polished to a reformulation in China, did however provide essential solutions. Through following the moral precepts, the lay-person could reduce the risks of negative karmic retribution in favour of a better rebirth. One might return as a human or even a god instead of as a hell being, a donkey or a perpetually duelling fighter. Such ideas provided a meaning and an incentive for living a good life.

One must recall that in the great cities of ancient China there were many sophisticated men of letters as well as innumerable relatively wealthy people forming a middle class in society; shopkeepers, artisans, traders, big merchants. Their concern with ultimate questions of life and death could find a more helpful answer in basic Buddhism than they could elsewhere. As the significance of the laity increased, so Buddhist teachers and masters shifted their attention towards the provision of teachings suited to their needs. Simple practices such as repeating Buddha's name originated with the Tian-tai and developed into the Pureland schools.

the naive were encouraged to believe that by simply repeating a Buddha's name they would be reborn in the land of the western paradise where Amitabha presided. The sophisticated would however understand that this was actually a metaphor for a mental process of self-cleansing.

Some monks, often living solitarily, acquired functions more shamanic than Buddhist. Once the charisma of such men became established, attention was drawn to their practice. One monk, who took the Hua-yan Sutra as his Dharma root, encouraged others in reciting it until a large society came to be formed with many local groups dedicated to periodic meetings and feasts at which the sutra was chanted. The more sophisticated lay scholars developed close relationships with Buddhist masters and some extensive correspondence between them has survived.[11] Furthermore, women began to play a role in both monastic and lay Buddhism receiving transmission as teachers and exercising influence.

During the Song Dynasty the surviving traditions sought to bolster their influence and popularity by rethinking their histories, questionably anchoring their teachings in the lives of great names of the past and even composing sutras in their name. The Song was thus a time rich in competitive Buddhist politics that, far from being negative in effect, generated a new creativity and force that enabled Buddhism to survive and sustain its institutions in China.

End Notes

1.   Wood, F. 2002. *The Silk Road*. Folio Society. London. Also: Whitfield, S. (Ed.). 2004. *The Silk Road. Trade, Travel, War and Faith*. British Library. Also Neville-Hadley, P. 1997. *China: the Silk Routes*. Cadogan. London.

2.   Stein, A. Sir. 1982. *On ancient Central-Asian tracks*. Southern Materials Center. Inc. Taipei. Originally published 1933. Macmillan London. Also: Le Coq, A von. 1985. *Buried Treasures of Chinese Turkistan*. Oxford University Press. Hong Kong. Originally published 1928.Allen and Unwin. London. Also: Whitfield, R. and A. Farrer. 1990. *Caves of the Thousand Buddhas. Chinese art from the Silk Route*. British Museum. London.

3.   Gernet, J. 2002. *A History of Chinese Civilisation*. Vols. 1& 2. Folio Society. London. Also Cambridge University Press. 1982, 1996.

4.   Cleary, T. 1993. *The Flower Ornament Scripture. A translation of the Avatamsaka Sutra*. Wisdom. Boston.

5.   Suzuki, D.T. 1953. *Essays in Zen Buddhism*. (Third Series) Rider and Co. London. p. 75.

6.   Note: Chinese names are given in the modern Pin yin system favoured in China. Many authors still use the older Wade-Giles system of rendering Chinese characters that may be more familiar to some readers.

7.   Cleary, T. 1983. *Entry into the Inconceivable. An introduction to Hua-yen Buddhism.* University of Hawai'i Press. p. 2.

8.   Chang, G.C.C. 1972. *The Buddhist Teaching of Totality: The Philosophy of Hwa Yen Buddhism.* Allen and Unwin. London. p. 23-24. See further Cleary, T. 1994. *Entry into the Inconceivable. An introduction to Hua-yen Buddhism.* University of Hawaii Press. Honolulu.

9.   Cleary, T. 1993. *loc cit. The Flower Ornament Scripture.* p. 43.

10.   Gregory, P.N. 1995. *Inquiry into the Origin of Humanity etc.* Kuroda Institute. University of Hawaii. Honolulu.

11.   Cleary, C. 1977. *Swampland Flowers, the letters and lectures of Zen master Ta Hui.* Grove Press. New York.

ZEN: THE DIRECT APPROACH

ORIGIN AND DEVELOPMENT

The great importance of Zen within the history of Chinese Buddhism, its significance in Japan and its cultural impact on coming to the West, merits Zen a chapter in itself. Indeed, for many Westerners Buddhism essentially means Zen and vice versa. The word 'Zen' is the Japanese pronunciation of the Chinese 'Chan' (primitively Chan-a), which in turn is the Chinese pronunciation of the Sanskrit 'dhyana' meaning meditation. In Korea and Vietnam the word mutates similarly to 'Son' and 'Thien' respectively. It is a school of Buddhism devoted to meditation practice, which it ranks in significance high above scholarly knowledge whether philosophical or psychological – a conventional generalisation which we must however consider below.

Unlike other schools, Zen (Chan) is taught primarily through stories that illustrate personal openings to enlightenment and encourage students to emulate the lives of great masters by penetrating the meaning of their sayings and actions – basically becoming enlightened through recreating the awakened mind of the master. When, during military service at the time of the Korean War, I met my first Chan teacher in Hong Kong in 1954, he taught his small group in this manner. A businessman who later became a leading monk in Hong Kong, Yen Shi-liang* had sat with the revered Master Xu-yun in pre-communist China and was therefore a first generation, realised descendant of this great reformer. It was in small convivial meetings held after hours in a Chinese doctor's surgery that I first heard the legendary tales of Bodhidharma and Hui-neng. Our task was to penetrate these tales to perceive the Buddha mind hidden within them. We neither 'sat' nor contemplated koans but the talk was brilliant, totally bemusing to a 21 year old, biologically trained reductionist, and, as I also began to appreciate the aesthetics of the (then) remote

---

* Mr. Yen was later to become head of several monastic foundations is Hong Kong under the religious name Yen Wai Si.

monasteries on Lantau Island, I found myself discovering a new perspective on my life. In those meetings, we assumed we were examining history, however legendary, and that the stories were essentially 'true'.[1] Today we have a very different account, the result of outstanding textual research mainly by American scholars.[2] Their work has revealed a much more nuanced understanding in which the romantic allure of Zen in the fifties is being replaced by a carefully considered understanding which, in the end, strengthens our comprehension of Chinese Buddhism, its Japanese derivative and its significance in post-modern culture.

There is virtually no information about Chan in any precise Indian form although it clearly originated from within Indian Buddhism. The founding legend concerns the monk Bodhidharma who, it is said, on his arrival in China had an interview with the Emperor and told him that all his practical support for monasteries and monks, in which the Emperor took much pride, had no merit whatsoever being merely trivial practice. When the Emperor, not unreasonably, asked whom it was that was speaking to him in this fashion, Bodhidharma, evidently unwilling to enter into any discussion and sticking to his abrupt zen pronouncements, exclaimed that he did not know. Perhaps understanding that he had offended the Emperor, he went off to a distant mountain and faced a wall in meditation for nine years. The Emperor is said to have regretted the rapid departure of so strange a monk but his ministers told him that such monks only appear once, they do not return. After some years in front of his wall, Bodhidharma was sought out by the monk Hui-ke but refused to help him. In desperation, Hui-ke is said to have cut off his arm and offered it, whereupon Bodhidharma turned to him and asked what he wanted. Hui-ke told him that his mind was troubled. Could Bodhidharma pacify it? "First show me your mind", said Bodhidharma. When Hui-ke said he could not find it. Bodhidharma said, " Well then – I have pacified it for you." On hearing this Hui-ke became enlightened and eventually succeeded Bodhidharma as patriarch.

This story is in fact a creation of much later times. We have virtually no knowledge of who the real Bodhidharma may have been but from among the manuscripts found at Dunhuang there have emerged important references and texts attributed to him. Among them is a verse that states the nature of Chan in a very clear manner revealing the basis for Bodhidharma's seemingly uncouth abruptness with the Emperor. These texts provide an account of a method of practice that turn out to be the basis for many subsequent developments. The famous verse defining Chan reads:

A special transmission outside the scriptures

No dependence on words and letters

Direct pointing to the human heart/mind
Seeing one's (Buddha) nature.

Two things are established by these texts; firstly the direct understanding of one's true or basic nature is not to be gained, so it is argued, by reading descriptive or explanatory literature, secondly, understanding arises in a direct encounter with a master who knows and is thus able to confirm a realisation. When one perceives what the master knows such perception comprises both enlightenment and a transmission of the Dharma. The prototype story here is one in which the Buddha is said to have refused to answer monks' metaphysical questions but rather to have picked a flower and held it up. The disciple Mahakasyapa smiled and the Buddha gave him the flower, thereby establishing the Chan style of teaching.[3]

The image we now have of Bodhidharma was built up over many years. John McRae (2003) has dated the first textual appearances of differing aspects of the stories concerning him from between 547 CE and the first millennium. Seventh century assertions suggest Bodhidharma came to China around 480 CE, was in the capital Luoyang between 516-526 and died around 530. He may have been a monk from south India of Brahmin caste who taught a small group of students and was the author of a text 'The Treatise on Two Entrances and Four Practices' prepared probably after his the death by a disciple. We must realise that not only may there have been more than one monk of this name in China but that the stories, like many others, were almost certainly created retrospectively to cement a growing tradition in a largely but perhaps not completely imaginary origin.

The 'Two Entrances and Four Practices' provide a picture of the early Chan orientation and method. The two entrances are by 'Principle', that is directly seeing one's Buddha nature through intuitive insight, and 'Practice' in the use of certain meditative techniques or attitudes in daily life. The four practices entail accepting misfortune as the maturing of one's own past transgressions, accepting all circumstances whether of good or bad fortune, living without craving while knowing craving to be the source of suffering, and living a life based in the six perfections naturally and not through some enforced technical system. At the root of both Entrances lies a faith in the Dharma, which is here essentially the *Tathagatagarbha* interpretation of Buddha mind: the root of mind is Buddha nature itself. In this vision all sentient beings, whether ordinary or enlightened, are said to possess a fundamental nature which in ordinary people is obscured by false sense impressions and attachments to fixed ideas based upon them (Chapter 7). When the false is discarded, the underlying nature is seen. When a practitioner comprehends this directly, either through a non-discriminative, serene and inactive meditation or through living an active life within the four practices, he or she perceives enlightenment. Here then we have a dual approach that recurs throughout the history of Chan - one through meditative absorption and the other through perfecting life in the world through the dropping of craving concerns.

The foundation myths of the Chan sects are based in genealogies of enlightened masters traced back generation by generation to the Buddha himself. Although the more recent lineages are more or less historical, the earlier ones are not only myths but also stories created in the Song dynasty (960-1126) to authenticate the teaching of a monastic line by an appeal to an ancestry in ancient masters who lived in the Tang times (618-907). Study of extant texts reveals the nature of the teachings and practices associated with these masters and their study can give an account of the manner in which Chan developed in China. In the accompanying Figure the basic historical phases of Chan development as reconstructed by John McRae are shown superimposed on the conventional lineage tree of major masters. We must bear in mind the often fictional reconstructions that surround the lives of these masters who none the less appear within the presentations of ways of teaching that vary in a progressive manner through time.[1]

Proto-Chan 500-600 CE: The early formulations of teaching and practice attributed to Bodhidharma seem to have been taught in small, scattered groups in northern China suggesting perhaps an entry by way of Central Asia and the Silk route. The teaching was focussed on experiencing Buddha nature but there were no lineage claims. Our understanding of this time is based in later traditional accounts and documents discovered in the Dunhuang caves.

Early Chan 600-900 CE: Small monastic communities had now developed following varying paths to understanding the mind through yogic meditation. At this stage, there is little differentiation between any specific Chan approach and those of other schools although divergence is emerging during the period. Lineage theories began to appear as contrasting sectarian positions emerged. In the seventh century a famous monk, Shen-xiu (606-706), gained influence and prestige in the capital. Shen-hui (684-758), a vigorous and confrontational evangelist, attacked the sitting meditation methods of the impressive Shen-xiu monastics and advocated a more direct approach to insight. He attributed this to an otherwise little known monk Hui-neng who lived around 700 with whom he had been acquainted and perhaps studied. This alternative viewpoint became known as the 'southern' school focussing on direct insight through enquiry rather than the sitting meditation of Shen-xiu's 'northern' school.

Middle Chan 750-10000: The classic 'Platform Sutra of the Sixth Patriarch' (Hui-neng) appeared perhaps around 780 purporting to give an account of the origin of Shen hui's new approach through an autobiographical account of the life of Hui-neng. Although it is a retrospective and perhaps largely fictional interpretation, the idea of a sudden approach to enlightenment through direct enquiry rather than through the gradualism of sitting meditation catches on and a major split between the original Northern school and the Southern school of Hui-neng appears. While the 'northern' monks based their approach largely in the Lankavatara Sutra, those of the Southern orientation favoured the Diamond Sutra. The respective positions were subsequently described as the Gradual versus Sudden ways to enlightenment although such differentiation is questionable (see below). In this period, accounts of the 'encounter dialogues' between masters or masters and monk students became the prime method of teaching. The masters of this period were certainly among the most forceful presenters of the koan approach such as we still know it today. The 'southern' tendency thus gained prominence in Chan and the 'northern' approach almost became extinct.

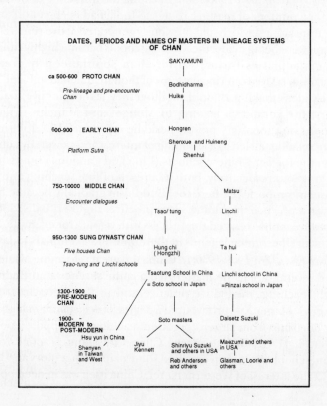

DATES, PERIODS AND NAMES OF MASTERS IN LINEAGE SYSTEMS OF CHAN

Song Dynasty Chan 950-1300: Major collections of encounter events were assembled becoming the basis for Koan stories used in contemplation. These stories largely concern the activities of the great Tang masters as retrospectively recreated and attached to genealogies by monks of the Song dynasty. Chan becomes the chief ideology of great monasteries favoured by government. Later, as government support waned, the differing sects competed for influence by wooing the great scholars and influential literati of the time. The competition between a reviving 'northern' and the established 'southern' Chan orientations contributed to the divergence of the two famous schools of Caodong (Tsao-tung) and Linji (Linchi) which in a later age became the Soto and Rinzai lineages of Japan. The Caodong school favoured Silent Illumination as its chief practice method while the Linji School favoured koans or rather the use of key phrases (huatou) from koan stories as themes for focussed meditation. The great advocates of these positions were Hong-zhi and Da-hui (Tahui) respectively.[5] There is considerable documentation from this period including letters between masters and learned disciples.

Pre-modern Chan/Zen 1300-1900: In China the influence of Buddhism waned for a number of reasons: routes to India had been cut off and no further translations, which had previously generated active research and discussion were being made; the existing schools became highly ritualised and their activities formal rather than spontaneously creative; Confucianism revived offering patterns of thought that had imbibed some Buddhist ideas making Buddhism altogether less distinctive; national disasters; the conquests leading to Mongol and Manchu dynasties; restrictions on monastery power; periodic rejection of Buddhism as a 'foreign' religion, all led to a lessening of interest and power. By contrast, in Japan the former Chinese schools (Linji and Caodong) flourished as Rinzai and Soto respectively, both as a result of fine teaching and from government support. Yet, here too, Buddhism gradually became highly formal and practice, including koan practice, highly ritualised. Some truly creative monks resisted this process with vigour (for example, Ikkyu and Ryokan), becoming legends in their time and exemplars today.

Modern Chan/Zen 1900-1950: In China the great reforming Master Xu-yun and several other fine masters led a cultural renewal in Buddhism through teaching, meditative practice and in the reconstruction of monasteries. Master Xu-yun favoured a degree of eclecticism in his revival, culling doctrines from largely forgotten teachings to support a popular perspective. He tended to merge Chan with some practices of the Pureland school. Buddhism regained some of its former glory and began to attract the interest of Westerners. Yet, China itself was in deep political and economic decline and subject to Western imperialist predation and the introduction of Christianity. The advent of Communism suppressed Buddhism completely but did not kill it. Like Daoism and Confucianism, it remained embedded in the hearts of the people and survived. In Hong Kong and Taiwan, Buddhism began to thrive as the post World War II economies grew. In Japan, before World War II, Zen became associated with the cult of the Emperor and developed growing links with Japanese militarism, a fact largely denied or ignored in the immediate post-war period of recovery and linkage with the West.[6] Since the war this emphasis has been abandoned. The Soto monks, unlike Rinzai, had been little influenced by such distortion.

In the West, the decline of Christianity allowed room for a growing and lively interest in Asian thought especially Zen and the formation of Buddhist societies. In London the well known judge, Christmas Humphries, and the writer Alan Watts, did much to encourage the popularity of Zen, which caught on within the hippie movement through the work of American writers Kerouac, Ginsberg and Snyder. The great Japanese teacher Daisetz Suzuki had become famous early in the century, promoting a view of Zen based almost entirely on the Rinzai viewpoint. His learned translations and his one-sided discussions of Zen remain influential today although subjected to considerable correction. After WWII, Phillip Kapleau, following some monastic training in Japan, compiled 'The Three Pillars of Zen', a highly influential contribution, and established a Rinzai style monastery in U.S.A. The head of the Soto church in Japan welcomed Peggy Kennet, an Englishwoman, to his monastery. She then trained, not without difficulty, in a male dominated institution eventually to become a local priest in Japan and to be the founder of a Soto derived monastic order in U.S.A. and in Britain.

Post-modern Chan/Zen (1950 – present): Zen centres now abound throughout the Western world and cater for the spiritual and often the psychological needs of numberless westerners. The movement is essentially secular and may be in danger of subversion by the prevailing spiritual materialism of the consumer culture – much as has happened to the humanistic sensitivity and growth group phenomena of the 1960s-70s. Many centres and lively masters abound but not without several reprehensible scandals arising from unwise transmissions to teach given to individuals who may have had 'enlightenment experiences' but who were clearly spiritually immature. Currently, a mature Chan is taught in New York by Chan Master Sheng-yen of Dharma Drum Mountain, Taiwan, with affiliated institutions world wide, while Japanese oriented Zen (for example, the San Francisco Zen Centre founded by the much loved

Shunryu Suzuki Roshi) flourishes in U.S.A. under the leadership of such teachers as Reb Anderson, John Daido Loori and Bernie Glassman. There are numerous Rinzai based groups, for example that led by the nun Myoko-ni in London (Irmgard Schloegl). There are signs of a major reappraisal of Zen/Chan history based on the work of textual scholarship reviewed in this chapter and of a rebirth of fresh Buddhist philosophy in the writings of Stephen Batchelor and David Loy. The social movement of 'engaged Buddhism' is largely Zen based, and attempts to ameliorate and criticise the materialism of our times.[7] In addition, both Korean and Vietnamese Zen flourish under good masters especially the renowned Thich Nhat Hahn of Plum Village in France.

There are reasons for thinking that Zen in homeland Japan, although still vigorous, may have declined somewhat due not only to the tide of consumerism enveloping that country but also because of the emergence of trendy post-modern sectarian novelties of dubious spiritual value. Indeed there may be a parallel here with the decline of Christianity and the emergence of New Age superstition in the West. In China, the restoration and renewal of practice in many monasteries bodes well for the future and receives considerable support from the laity. Conservative Chinese Buddhism together with traditional Daoism and Confucianism is no longer suppressed although closely supervised by the Chinese government.

KOANS, ORIGIN, USE AND MEANING

Daisetz Suzuki used to argue that solving koans led to an insight into a pure consciousness beyond any teaching yet fundamental to all religion. His philosophical approach ignored history since it focussed on an underlying nature of mind beyond thought and therefore beyond historical determination. Koans, he argued, essentially had no meaning because any successful response to a koan lay outside thought. The koan was an instrument for triggering insight into this hidden or obscured nature of mind. Such an interpretation did not encourage questions concerning the history of koans as a method nor an examination of the social history of the Chan School. It led some to a belief that Zen could be equally a basis for Christianity as for Buddhism. Such an attitude has allowed some Japanese masters to create Dharma heirs who were Christian rather than Buddhist and who mostly began at once to promote koans as instrumental in a Christian revelation. Such a use of koan decentres it from its position in Chinese and Japanese Buddhism and denies any connection between it and the ontology of mind found within Buddhist thought. Koans then become instruments for Christian theology potentially involving theist positions almost completely opposed to Buddhist understanding. Some theologians argue that while Zen is 'natural' religion, the Christian 'truths' are 'revealed' religion. Many have been confused by these sophistries, which remain unresolved.

Koans are best seen as instruments for a realisation allowing the student or monk to break out of his or her conventional assumptions into a freedom that is only possible to express through metaphors. Koans are themselves essentially metaphors. The Chinese 'gong-an', from which the Japanese word 'koan' originates, means a public case – such as a lawyer might present to a court. In the court of spiritual insight, the koan becomes the problem for the lawyer who sits as it were before the master as judge. Yet, here, the master already knows the resolution of the metaphorical paradox and the lawyer's job is therefore to align himself with the mind of the master who has trained in the same way in his own generation.

As one popular koan story has it, when the Master Joshu was asked 'Does a dog have Buddha nature?' He replied MU! This word MU meaning no or not (No, the dog does not HAVE Buddha nature) becomes the huatou or brief summarising phrase of the koan. The student's task is to penetrate the meaning of Mu. This does not entail searching for the reasons behind Joshu's answer if any, but rather a direct realisation of what is being negated. The dog has no essence, it is just the dog. What is NOT? There is no absolute dog abstracted from the living animal, the dog-process itself. One can create numerous interpretations of this koan all to no avail unless one discovers for oneself indeed what NOT is. It is not enough to seek recourse to philosophy arguing that MU represents the Buddha mind behind or beyond all thought, rather one has to realise MU directly and beyond words – the absence of an inherent being apart from process in anything. One is looking for a revelatory experience or insight of the mind before concepts arise within it – a pre-conceptual awareness.

Such stories do indeed have a history and were not used in early Chan. Bodhidharma had never heard of them and the story about the flower had not yet been invented. Where then did koans come from? Examination of extant texts reveals a gradual development beginning with the use of 'encounter dialogue' between a teacher and a monk in discussions of the meaning of Buddhist ideas. Some monks began recording such dialogues that became increasingly focussed on the gaining of a precise insight. In terms of Bodhidharma's 'Two Entries' this would be an entry through 'principle' that would not however invalidate entry through the methods of practice. The encounter stories eventually became a fictional and indeed a literary form, although a number of actual past events may underlie some of them.

There is a doctrinal background to this development. The Lankavatara Sutra was the favoured scripture of early Chan. One story relates how Bodhidharma on his deathbed told Hui-ke it was now time for him to read this sutra since his teacher would soon be gone. The Lanka is a very psychological text[8] (see Chapter 7) setting out a theory of mind and suggesting methods of meditation that hark back to the Indian methods of calming the mind (samatha) and gaining insight into it (vipyasanna). Students of the Lanka would have used such methods which included long periods of developing meditative equipoise through 'sitting'. The early East Mountain school, unlike other non-Zen Buddhist schools of the time, taught meditation and little else and seems to have become a base from which other monasteries with the same approach developed. The Lanka would have been a prime scripture for the Northern school of Shen-xiu. From the time of Hui-neng however emphasis shifted to the Diamond Sutra, a short text in the *Prajnaparamita* tradition. Here very little is said of the mind or its nature. The meditator is directed to see immediately why, for example, the Buddha never said anything at all! Consideration of such a matter did not require sitting but an immediate insight into the pre-conceptual basis of mind that can arise as all attachments are given up. In such an approach, we can see the essence of the koan dilemma that became the prime approach of the Southern school.

Even so, the divergence in monastic practices only developed gradually. Early on, every monastery had contained facilities for sutra study, recitation, ritual and manual labour in addition to meditation. This is true also today. On visiting the restored Yun-men monastery in 1997, my Chinese colleague and I found buildings allocated for these different purposes and monks could choose which activity was best suited to them. The options available suggested that Bodhidharma's 'Two Entries and four practices' are thus not merely theoretical but meaningfully expressed today in monastic life.[9]

The Platform Sutra of Hui-neng,[10] although now known to be a polemical document rather than either history or autobiography, remains a key text in understanding the emergence of these views. It appears that during the transition from early to middle period Chan, the use of sitting meditation as the key to enlightenment began to be popular and spread to a number of monasteries where individual teachers taught varying methods centred upon either calm sitting in the traditional Indian manner or more direct entries by principle. It seems that these contrasting patterns of practice may have coexisted in some monasteries connected to the practice of monks wandering between masters on pilgrimage. At the fifth patriarch Hung-ren's monastery, it seems plausible that an obscure and illiterate monk Hui-neng had a direct experience outside both scriptural study and long term sitting and that this was noticed by other monks. Unfortunately, so little is known of Hui-neng that we cannot be sure.

The story is none the less vivid. It depicts a monastery full of somewhat rivalrous monks without great initiative. When the master wished to transmit the patriarchate to a worthy fellow he asked the monks to compose short poems to demonstrate their insight. Shen-xiu, the head monk and instructor, is said to have written a verse in such trepidation that he wrote it secretly on a wall. It said:

> The body is the bodhi tree
> The mind a stand of mirror bright
> At all times must we polish it
> Let not the dust alight.

The master approved the verse but did not consider it profound enough to award the patriarchate. He exhorted Shen-xiu to greater efforts that were not forthcoming. Meanwhile Hui-neng, pounding rice as a labourer in the kitchen, heard of the verse and immediately saw its shortcomings. He was able to perceive its defects due to his prior spontaneous enlightenment experience, which had brought him to the monastery in the first place. Being illiterate he asked another to write his capping verse on the wall. It read:

> The body has no bodhi tree
> There's no stand of mirror bright
> Basically there is not a thing
> Where could the dust alight?[11]

Secretly the master approved the verse as revealing true insight but, due to fear that the jealousy of the monks might harm his chosen successor, he transmitted the patriarchate and its symbols (robe and bowl) to Hui-neng in the dead of night and rowed him away across the river. Hui-neng disappeared into obscurity for years and this may possibly be one reason for the lack of information about him. Shen-xiu (who may or may not have actually been at the monastery at the same time) meanwhile acquired great fame in the capital through his teaching of Chan based on the East Mountain meditative practice.

When Shen-hui eventually criticised this approach he did so in a very public and evangelistic manner seeking to establish an alternative direct approach to enlightenment based on the Diamond Sutra. His developing school used Shen-hui's apparent recollection of Hui neng's experience as a vehicle that became very popular. Eventually this Southern school largely displaced the Northern and developed encounter dialogue as a prime method leading gradually to the formal use of koan stories.

A famous case in the collection of koans called the Blue Cliff Record provides a fine demonstration. Master Nan-yue of the southern orientation observed his disciple, Ma-zu, sitting for many hours a day in silent meditation. He asked him why he was doing it. Ma-zu replied he was trying to become a Buddha. The master sat down and began rubbing a tile. "Why are you doing that?" asked Ma-zu. "I am making a mirror!" replied the master. This gave Ma-zu a shocked insight into his mistake and he became enlightened. Subsequently, as a great master in his turn, his method of teaching relied exclusively on koans. Neither he, nor the equally great master Lin-ji, relied on verbal answers, explanations or descriptions. Often a monk had to express his insight through means other than words and a whole repertoire of shouts, blows, castigations, developed with which to express insight or the rejection of a response. These non-verbal methods emerged as a kind of coded communication and their precise meaning in the stories is often lost to us now. Koans could be posed in disguised form during walks or manual work, the disciple being expected to penetrate them on the spot. Hours of sitting were not in the forefront of these endeavours.

The final development of the koan approach arose from the teaching methods of the great master Da-hui (1089-1163). He guessed that there was no need to labour with an entire koan story, some of which are quite lengthy. Rather one should focus on a capping phrase or a single sentence or word in the Koan story and investigate that. This use of such 'huatou' became the main Chan method following Da-Hui's teachings. Indeed it became a way of freeing koans from the literary forms into which they were developing. Simple huatou like "Who are you?" or "What is it?" became valid themes for investigation. When the monk Daikaku went from China to Japan to teach Chan to samurai he knew no Japanese and they did not know classical Chinese so he invented simple phrases based on their training, the so called warrior koans – which have become famous.[12]

We noted that the Northern or Caodong school had almost disappeared after the Tang dynasty. Indeed its last master failed to find a worthy Dharma heir and asked another monk to hold his transmission in trust as it were until one appeared. Eventually the monk did find a suitable candidate and handed the tradition down to him whereupon the school revived under several notable masters. Of these a contemporary of Da-hui was the famous Hong-zhi, who brought to perfection a method known as mo-zhao or Silent Illumination (or Shining Silence) clearly based in the orientation of the Northern school and a reinterpretation of the old Indian methods of calming (silence) and insight (illumination). They were brought together in a unified practice in which insight into the silenced mind constitutes an enlightenment experience much as did the solving of koans in the Lin-ji approach. In modern times, Master Sheng-yen of Dharma Drum Mountain, Taiwan and New York, has said that the method is a delicate one like seeking to catch a falling feather on an outstretched fan.[13] It is not easy to balance the silencing of the mind with insightful introspection, too much silence leads to drowsiness or trance while too much illumination sets going the orchestra of thought.

Da-hui (Ta hui) had rigorously attacked this practice arguing that it led to a nihilistic quietism without insight and indeed some teachers of the Song period may have been making such a mistake through denying the importance of effort in practice. Hong-zhi himself was quite clear that effort, or rather sustained focus, was essential if silence was to shine. It was essential to focus strongly on the silent practice to observe its fundamental nature. It seems Da-hui was not attacking Hong-zhi personally, and indeed it seems they greatly respected one another. He was objecting to a mistaken Silent Illumination practice consisting of tranquilisation alone. Even so there is little doubt that he felt his own method to be superior. There was a political motive in his assault. At the time, there was strong sectarian competition between the two schools for the favours of sponsors among the literati and Da-hui may have been alarmed by the renewed success of the Caodong school.

Shen-hui's attack on the northern orientation in Chan had introduced an atmosphere of rivalry to the Chan scene the shadow of which has continued to obscure the basic congruence of the two approaches even to this day. Particularly in Japan, the separation of the Soto and Rinzai sects has sometimes occasioned bitter disputes from which Daisetz Suzuki's silence on Soto derives. In China, the need to revive basic Buddhism led necessarily to a lessening of sectarian tensions: even so this deep and long enduring divide had yielded productive debate even as it was emerging.

The distinction between sudden ('subitist') methods and gradual ones has been a source of debate in modern as well as ancient times. To argue that Da-hui had favoured a sudden method and Hong-zhi a gradual one is misguided. The terms become meaningless when it is realised that a long time may have to be spent gradually with a koan before a 'sudden' breakthrough occurs. Likewise, when an insight is obtained in the illumination of silence it occurs suddenly. Furthermore, there are varying levels of insight in both cases. In either case, an insight may be of brief occurrence and lack complete loss of self-concern or it may consist in a full 'seeing of the nature' in which self- concern is totally absent. Either way, the learning that occurs is a substantial confirmation of the truth of the path. Today these terms, sudden versus gradual, need careful nuancing if they are to retain meaning.

The great master Zong-mi (780-841) upheld the Southern viewpoint but provided an understanding analysis of 'sudden' and 'gradual' that related it to the wider concerns of Chinese Buddhism in the Hua-yan and Tian-tai sects. He saw that fundamental to the division between Chan and other Buddhist approaches was an opposition between the ancient scholastic traditions of philosophy and the Chan emphasis on practice pure and simple. The devide lay between seeking understanding through devotion and intellect on the one hand and the evocation of a direct experience on the other.

Zong-mi was so distressed by the rivalry between the Caodong and Lin ji schools that he even argued that Buddhist teaching had become a barrier to enlightenment rather than as a means to assist people to understanding. He took the view, already present in the Pali Canon, that the Buddha had taught people of high perception in a way different from those for a duller mentality. The sudden methods were for the bright and the gradual for those less quick on the uptake. He also pointed out that the two terms imply one another and could be related in contrasting patterns of practice. After all, the experience of realisation is always sudden, while it seems that understanding it must be necessarily gradual. There could be varying paths in the manner in which experience and understanding were related.[14]

(1) *Gradual cultivation followed by sudden enlightenment* as when one travels gradually towards a city and suddenly sees it. Here then gradual refers to movement towards the goal while sudden is the moment of experiencing it.

(2) *Sudden cultivation followed by gradual enlightenment:* 'Sudden' here refers to directly seeing as when an archer aims his bow and sees the target clearly and 'gradual' to the practice needed before one can hit the bull's eye. Here a philosophical understanding precedes an experiential one.

(3) *Gradual cultivation and gradual enlightenment:* This is as if in climbing a tower one's gaze sweeps over an ever-increasing vista. Such an approach admits therefore of grades of enlightenment.

(4) *Sudden enlightenment followed by gradual cultivation:* Here 'enlightenment' means a glimpse of "seeing the nature" which needs to be followed by gradual study and practice to perceive its meaning.

(5) *Sudden enlightenment and sudden cultivation:* This occurs only in those of exceptional brilliance who both understand the "nature" conceptually and become fully realised experientially at the same time.

Zong-mi's analysis makes sense out of the counter claims of the contrasting advocates and clarifies the relations between the process of actualisation (Silent Illumination or Koans) and the experience of 'seeing the nature'.

It becomes clear that different teachers may prefer to emphasise one approach over another and indeed individual seekers may find one approach more suitable than others. Zong-mi's analysis is profound and merits close study today, yet his school did not outlast the Tang. Subsequent Chan teachers abandoned his syncretic approach and his sudden awakening/gradual practice approach – perhaps indeed because of the unusual breadth of his vision. He had been not only a Chan master but also a leading adherent of the Hua-yan school. Yet, in course of time, his viewpoint was resurrected by the great Korean master Chinul to encompass a broad approach to Chan practice related to Hua-yan theory in a truly ecumenical teaching, the basis of Korean Son still practiced today.[15]

KOAN AS LITERATURE AND ITS USE IN SERMONS

Modern scholars have noted that the structure of koans is essentially a brilliantly evocative literary device anchored in the Chinese love of word play. Moreover Koan stories and the huatou based on them were not always used solely in encounter dialogues or as themes for focussed contemplation. Nor for that matter was their use confined to the Linji and Rinzai descendants of the Southern school. Hong-zhi not only founded the practice of Silent Illumination but also built up a fine collection of koans now published in English as *The Book of Serenity* together with his own verse commentaries on them.[16] Its seems therefore that in talks and sermons he may well have referred to koan stories as themes for awakening the minds of his monks in addition to the practice of focussed silent sitting. Certainly, when the famous Japanese monk Dogen studied under Master Ru-jing, the Caodong master of Tiantong Monastery, and became enlightened in the Chan Hall, he returned to Japan not only with the method of Silent Illumination but also with a profound knowledge of Buddhist thought and especially koan stories, which he wove brilliantly into his numerous lectures from the platform. Dogen uses koans with great spiritual and philosophical insight but outside the confrontational technique so beloved by the Rinzai sect.

The Rinzai teachers in Japan developed a system of Koan use whereby a trainee monk had to pass a long series of koans in succession before receiving an acknowledgement of his insight.[17] Each response to a koan is moreover tested further by the use of a number of supplementary koans probing the depth of the monk's insight. The greatest exponent of this method was the great Hakuin from whom the koan system as used in the Rinzai tradition today is descended. Rinzai monks sit for long periods holding their koans in the meditation hall and are periodically summoned to confront the master. In a ritualistic rush, they queue up for a brief encounter. A skilled master is said to read the mind of a student even in the way he sounds the bell before his entry to the interview room. Most students are thrown out many times, sometimes with a shower of abuse, before any kind of verbal interaction actually develops. In Korean Son, a monk usually remains with a single koan for many years, even a lifetime, and there is no sense of rushing through a series.[18] None the less, many koans are available. The repetitive use of koans and their supplements shows this to be a gradual process based on an intentionality leading finally to a sudden realisation.

So, what is it that is seen whenever an experience of realisation occurs?

PATTERNS OF REALISATION

The newcomer to Zen arrives with a mind of conventional understanding believing in the identity of his self as the root and narrative of his life. This conception plays itself out in a network of social relations with other similarly composed identities. A Zen teacher will try to assist the beginner to a realisation that such a structure is underpinned by a pre-conceptual awareness that is the foundation of his being beyond identity. The beginner's understanding of mind is 'ignorant' in that he/she has no comprehension of the existence of such a basis to being in the world. She can relate to the social and natural world only through the structures that arise within her identification with her history and has no insight into a mode of awareness that does not structure the world in words, thoughts or symbols. The Korean Son master Chinul puts the intention of a master clearly.

"*When the Buddhas and the Patriarchs appeared, they had no teachings to offer. They only wanted sentient beings to see their original nature for themselves. The Avatamsaka Sutra says, 'You should know that all dharmas are the own-nature of the mind. The perfection of wisdom does not come from any other awakening.' Buddhas and Patriarchs did not let people get snared in words and letters; they only wanted them to put deluded thought to rest and to see the original mind.*"[19]

"Seeing the nature " (J: *kensho*) is to become purely aware of this pre-conceptual condition as the root of personal being – a no-mind. This is an awareness that perceives the everyday directly and without interpretation through conceptualisations in words or symbols. It is empty of all identifications because these become abandoned when the awareness arises. Approaching such a state through thinking about it can be scary since most people are unwilling to let go of their identity in so total a manner. Practitioners often stand back at the very moment when a realisation becomes possible. Pressing the delete button of the mind is not so easy yet the self does not die, it merely ceases to manifest for a while.

Such an opening is not easy to achieve because of the obsessive nature of self-regard. Indeed, it can never be an 'achievement' in the sense of obtaining something but rather arises as a consequence of letting go of everything. Practitioners have faith that such an event has great value. 'Entry to the inconceivable'[20] is accompanied by feelings of release as if one had escaped from a mental dungeon. This is why it is termed 'enlightenment' and it is often accompanied by feelings of amazement, wonder, perhaps bliss and love. It is a life turning moment as something has been uncovered that is quite fundamental and which may become the basis for a practice that turns to an active concern with others rather than oneself (*bodhicitta*).

The practices that lead to this insight are not so easy as this simple formulation would suggest. Indeed our account of the disputes that have arisen in Chan history makes that very clear. As the self clings fearfully to its identifications and its securities, there are numerous misapprehensions, deviations from a direct way and illusions to avoid. The self-obsessed mind is very busy in its defence and in promoting itself in whatever way possible. The anxieties, delusions, cravings and defences provide the would-be meditator with an exceedingly active mind within which an insight simply cannot arise. Calming this mind is essential. In the Silent Illumination practice the mind calms down and releases its rigid hold on self-protective manoeuvres. It may then experience a widening inner vastness of a spacious and timeless quality that reflects the abandoning of normal categorisations of space and time. It is not possible to achieve this by desire or thought and yogic concentration is essential. One objection to the koan method concerns its strongly intentional character and it's need for intense application before the mind simply gives in. The result is often dramatic and clearly 'sudden' while in Silent Illumination the mind seems to melt into awareness slowly although the final realisation is again sudden. An objection to Silent Illumination is that if the silence is too deep illumination may not be seen.

We have noted that some processes of training suggest that the outcome may arise at differing levels of completion. Sometimes there may be no more that a momentary glimpse of a total otherness not seen before. Another level is what Master Sheng-yen calls the 'One-mind' experience when a deep sensation of union with the world is felt very much as an expansion of self. In a complete experience of 'seeing the nature' there is a puzzling sensation of absence – the self has simply disappeared leaving the world shining in all its glory unprocessed by thought. In solving a negative koan such as Mu, the mind may simply and suddenly find that all thought, evaluation and endeavour has ceased in the great laugh of freedom. Such insights are however usually short lived as the conventional mind returns, perhaps leading to forlorn attempts to restore what one has glimpsed. Grabbing at such an experience is totally useless as it clearly results from the active presence of a desiring ego. Again as Master Sheng-yen puts it, all one can do is to practice, endure loss and then retrieve the practice again and again.

It is not a matter of the absence of thought alone. Sometimes there appears to be no active thought at all, yet there remains some feeling of constraint. Examination then reveals that some attachment to concept remains in place, albeit virtually unconsciously. Often this is an attachment to practice itself or to some idea of what 'emptiness' should be like. When this is given up then boundlessness arises. A smile arises with the discovery that there is absolutely nothing to do whatsoever.

The word 'enlightenment' has been used in at least three ways.[20] Firstly, it may refer to the underlying non-conceptual basis of mind, which in theory at least may be permanently available to a fully realised Buddha however active in the world. Secondly, it may refer to a brief experience either of 'seeing the nature' fully or perhaps merely in a brief glimpse of no-mind (*i.e.* no thought or attachment). Thirdly, it may refer to the training process whereby the ability to realise the meaning of training becomes apparent. Clearly, the contrasting meditation methods of the schools arising from the old Northern and Southern dispute are focussing on varying ways of expressing the process. There is however no real argument between them. Perhaps the contrasting methods are reflecting no more than differences in the temperaments of masters and the practitioners they attract.

The claims of the Chan and Zen schools to provide a way outside the scriptures is false in that they practice no more than what these scriptures claim to reveal. None the less, the methods are indeed probing beyond words and letters for such can never reveal more than descriptions of experiences or injunctions to follow particular ways. Zen is indeed a very direct and confrontational way with which to uncover the full reach of the mind and the meaning of transcendence.

End Notes

1. Crook, J.H. 1994. *Hilltops of the Hong Kong Moon.* Minerva. London.

2. The key sources for this chapter will be found in the following books or collections of articles:

    Welch, H. 1967. *The Practice of Chinese Buddhism. 1900-1950.* Harvard University Pess. Cambridge, Mass.

    Kennett, J. 1972. *Selling water by the River. A manual of Zen training.* Vintage. New York.

    Akishige, Y. 1977. (Ed.). *Psychological studies on Zen.* Zen Institute of Komazawa University. Tokyo.

    Buswell, R.E. 1983. *The Korean approach to Zen: the collected works of Chinul.* University of Hawai i Press. Honolulu.

    Gimello, R.M. & P.N. Gregory (Eds.). *Studies in Ch'an and Hua-yen.* Kuroda Institute Studies in East Asian Buddhism 1. University of Hawai i.Honolulu.

    Gregory, P.N. (Ed.). 1987. *Sudden and Gradual approaches to Enlightenment in Chinese thought.* Kuroda Institute. Studies in East Asian Buddhism 5. University of Hawai i Press. Honolulu.

    Faure, B. 1993. *The Rhetoric of Immediacy. A cultural critique of the Chan/Zen tradition.* Princeton University Press. Princeton.

    Faure, B. 1993. *Chan Insights and Oversights. An epistemological critique of the Chan tradition.* Princeton University Press. Princeton.

    Wright, D.S. 1998. *Philosophical meditations on Zen Buddhism.* Cambridge studies in religious traditions. Cambridge University Press. Reviewed: Crook, J. 1999. Language and freedom – meaning in Zen. *New Chan Forum* 19:29-37.

    Gregory, P.L. & D.A. Getz. (Eds.) 1999. *Buddhism in the Sung.* Kuroda Instutute Studies in East Asian Buddhism 13. University of Hawai i.Honolulu

    Heine, S. & D.S. Wright. 2000. *The Koan. Texts and contexts in Zen Buddhism.* Oxford University Press. Oxford.

    Sheng yen, Master, with Dan Stevenson. 2001. *Hoofprint of the Ox. Principles of the Chan Buddhist path as taught by a modern Chinese master.* Oxford University Press. New York.

3. The most comprehensive review of Chan teachings will be found in Sheng-yen, Master with Dan Stevenson. 2001. *Hoofprint of the Ox. Principles of the Chan Buddhist path.* Oxford University Press.

4. McRae, J.R. 2003. *Seeing through Zen. Encounter, transformation and genealogy in Chinese Chan Buddhism.* University of California Press. Berkeley.

5. Leighton T.D & Yi Wu 1991. *Cultivating the Empty Field. The Silent Illumination of Zen Master Hongzhi.* North Point. San Francisco.

    Cleary, C. 1977. *Swampland Flowers: the letters and lectures of Zen master Ta hui.* Grove. New York.

6. Victoria, B. 1997. *Zen at War.* Weatherhill. New York. Tokyo.

7. Jones, K. 2003. *The New Social face of Buddhism.* Wisdom. Boston.

8. Suzuki, D.T. 1930. *Studies in the Lankavatara Sutra.* Routledge. London.

    Suzuki, D.T. 1973. *The Lankavatara Sutra.* Routledge Kegan and Paul. London.

9. Crook. J.H. 1997. Ch'an revival in Mainland China. *New Chan Forum* 16:32-44. Also Crook, J.H. 2000. Revival of Buddhism in China. *New Chan Forum.* 23:11-35.

10. Wong, Mou-lam. 1953. *The Sutra of Wei Lang (Hui Neng)*. Lusac. London. Also Cleary, T. 1998. *The Sutra of Hui Neng Grand master of Zen*. Shambala. Boston & London.

11. McRae, J.R. 2003. *Seeing through Zen. Encounter, transformation and genealogy in Chinese Chan* Buddhism. University of California Press. Berkeley. p. 61-2 for precise textual translations.

12. Leggett, T. 1985. *The Warrior Koans: early Zen in Japan*. Arkana. London.

13. Crook, J.H. (Ed.). 1994. *Catching a feather on a fan*. Element. Shaftesbury. Also Crook, J.H. (Ed.). 2001. *Illuminating Silence. The practice of Chinese Zen*. Watkins. London.

14. Gregory, P.N. 1995. *Inquiry into the Origin of Humanity. An annotated translation of Tsung mi's* Yuan jen lun *with a modern commentary*. Kuroda Institute. University of Hawai i.Honolulu. Also Gregory, P.L. 1987. *loc cit.*

15. Buswell, R.E. 1983. *loc cit.*

16. Cleary, T. 1990. *Book of Serenity. One hundred Zen Koans*. Lindisfarne. New York.

17. Cleary, T. 2000. *Secrets of the Blue Cliff Record.*.Shambala. Boston and London.

18. For a detailed account of practice in a Son monastery see Buswell, R.E. 1992. *The Zen monastic experience. Buddhist practice in contemporary Korea*. Princeton University Press. Princeton.

19. Buswell, R. 1983. p.161 abridged.

20. This phrase is the title of a book by Thomas Cleary on the Avatamsaka Sutra. Note 7, Chapter 7.

10

TANTRA IN TIBET

BUDDHISM ENTERS TIBET

In the twelfth century, the advance of Islam across northern India destroyed the great Buddhist monasteries and universities, yet, in the few centuries prior to this cultural catastrophe Buddhism had slowly and hesitatingly crossed the snowfields of the Himalayas and entered the high plateaux of Tibet. It was this that enabled a very remarkable late development of Indian Buddhist practice, largely of East Indian and Bengali origin, to survive and flourish in a land markedly different from that of its origin. Everything about tantra seems tropical, yet this passionate engagement between asceticism and the sensuous, even sensual, life, developed most profoundly in the land of snows and constitutes one of its great gifts to world civilisation.

The wild men of Tibet had conquered much of central Asia, sweeping the Chinese aside and even, for a time, occupying the capital Chang-an (modern Xian). These fierce, largely nomadic 'barbarians' as the Chinese thought of them, lacked most of the niceties of their neighbouring civilisations. Fearful of the terrible gods of ice, snow, avalanches, flood and tempest, their shamans evoked ferocious nature spirits that needed placation and cajoling if anything was to go well. The period of the Yarlung kings (7th-9th centuries) was one of almost constant warlike activity and the war weary poetry of Po Chu-i, Li Po and Tu Fu expresses the Chinese fatigue at this time.

In the seventh century, the King Srong-brtsan-sgampo of Lhasa married two princesses, one from China and the other from Nepal. These valuable dynastic alliances brought Buddhism to the Tibetan court; both ladies were Buddhists. The king was impressed by the power of literacy and the depth of meaning in the Buddha's message and founded the still extant temple in Lhasa, the Jokhang, for his Chinese wife. Yet, it was not until the reign of King Khri-srong-lde-brtsan in the following century that Buddhism began to spread successfully and overcome local resistance. The king invited the scholar Santarakshita from India to educate the capital. Santarakshita was however quite unable to make any impression on the Tibetan farmers and nomads and his attempt to build a great stupa and translation centre at Samye was repeatedly frustrated by accidents and problems said to be due to the local demons. Santarakshita, according to tradition, then sent for a great tantric master, Padmasambhava, subsequently known to the Tibetans as Guru Rimpoche, who, using extraordinary skills and charisma, demonstrated such psychic power that he overcame the shamans and forced their gods to acknowledge the Buddha. Dangerous, demonic spirits were dismembered and their body parts scattered as odd shaped rocks all over the country, yet most of the local spirits remained in place only now under vow to support the Dharma. These stories are legendary perhaps refering to a historical process whereby Buddhism gradually spread over the countryside. Whoever he was, Padmasambhava achieved the merging of shamanism and Buddhism that characterises the religion of Tibet to this day.[1]

The entry of Buddhism to Tibet was thus considerably more dramatic and dependent on a 'depth' psychology than was the gradual percolation of Buddhism along the trade routes into China. From the first, there was in Tibet a unique blending of shamanic themes with a late form of Buddhism, itself 'shamanic' in many respects, yet one in which the scholarly tradition of the masters remained the bedrock. Purely 'karmatic' Buddhism, whereby meritorious behaviour ensures a better rebirth, was perhaps of less significance in Tibet than direct if not magical realisations of the holy through powerful yogic means often supported by tantric shamanism. The Indian concern with caste and the Chinese commercialised classes were absent from Tibet. Simple farmers and nomads needed to sustain their inner strength in the face of their fierce environment. They did this through direct placation, exaltation and enlightenment in relation to the powers of nature. The scholar Geoffrey Samuel has termed this spiritual amalgam 'shamanic Buddhism' and the Tibetans themselves 'civilised shamans'.[2]

THE ORIGINS AND SOCIAL EXPRESSION OF TANTRA IN TIBET

The earliest folk religions of the world took the form of animistic cults, beliefs and practices broadly known as shamanism. Unusually charismatic individuals conferred with the powers of nature often alone in the wilderness and some of them undertook long inner journeys often in trance to spiritual lands of ancestors or gods whose messages helped solve social and personal problems. In other forms, the gods descended on the shaman in trance who then healed the sick and pronounced oracles for rulers and villagers alike while manifesting feats beyond those of normal mortals.

In the centuries after Ashoka (Third century ce), the Indian religion of the common people became increasingly devotional and the gods resumed their pivotal place as bringers of salvation. Devotional '*bhakti*' became the root of so called 'Hinduism', although older elements persisted. The influence of *bhakti* also found its way into Mahayana Buddhism, indeed comprising one of the elements in its evolution. The Mahayanists focused on the innumerable Bodhisattvas whose idealised figures became a focus for devotion and evocation (Chapter 6). The main spiritual practice in both Hindu and Buddhist life became the *sadhana*, visualisation of holy beings, a method that is the defining hallmark of 'tantra'.

In visualisation, the image of the deity or Buddha is called to mind through invocations, often aided by the use of mantras and an offering ritual, and the imagined figure is invited to enter an effigy or indeed the priest-meditator him/herself. The deity is offered lights, incense, water, flowers and maybe food and wine, as would be an honoured guest. The deities are expressions of psychological power, which is thus transmitted to the worshipper. An enormous corpus of technical writings used in such evocations is known as the 'tantras'. Practical rather than theoretical in nature, they are usually associated with various forms of physical and mental yoga.

The way in which the tantric Buddhism of India penetrated and fused with Tibetan shamanism can be understood today through field study in remote locations in Himalayan Nepal where communities of shamans and Buddhists live side by side and influence one another. In addition, within the folk practice of Buddhism in Tibet and Ladakh many shamanic themes remain and their relationship to the Dharma is being investigated.

The anthropologist Stan Mumford was extremely fortunate in locating a village in the Gyasumdo region of the Nepal Himalaya where, on one side of the Marsyandi river lived a traditional shamanic community of Gurungs, who had themselves, centuries before, been immigrants from Tibet, while, on the other, lived a small population of recent Tibetan buddhist immigrants. In studying the interaction between these communities, Mumford traced parallels for what probably happened widely in Tibet in earlier centuries.[3]

Basic to both communities are very early shamanic themes common to the 'Siberian 'type widespread in central and northern Asia. Such themes and their Buddhist substitutions crop up in the ritual observances of both groups. The shamans' world view is focussed on sustaining a harmony with nature through animal and other sacrificial offerings to the nature spirits of the locality. The community practices exorcism and soul guidance to the land of the dead at the time of death while ritual journeys to the underworld are undertaken to recover lost or stolen souls. Mumford remarks that in the Gurung villages shamans still seek to live out the ancient way embedded within relationships between the community and the cosmos and signified in the local landmarks. The Gurung shamans offer no programme of extrication from such a world rather they mediate between forces, images and wills of various domains. By contrast, the Tibetan lamas across the river use rites and written scriptures of great sanctity to push into the foreground "a highly individuating religious identity". The rituals include means whereby this world can be transcended and the individual extricated from the matrix of village life and shamanic concern. The doctrine of karma allows individuals to accumulate merit through modified behaviour and practice a linear progression towards personal liberation. An implicit individualism thus replaces the communalism of the shamans. While the Buddhists see the shamans as remaining on the 'outer path' of samsara, they see themselves as self-liberating on the 'inner path' to nirvana. Never the less, the lamas in their teachings regularly interpose images and portrayals of affliction, sacrifice and augury that stem from the aboriginal shamanic base and which are persuasive among the people. In these villages, the ordinary Buddhist farmer is deeply embedded in a compromise between his nirvanic aspirations and his samsaric necessities. The shamanic visions thus remain attractive and the outcome is a complex dialogue between the two world and life interpretations.

Mumford interprets this process in the manner of Mikhail Bakhtin who, in his book The Dialogic Imagination (1981), envisaged the historical process as moving through three stages. The first primal experience of time and space took shape as an 'ancient matrix', the shamanic world view, in which personal identity is submerged in the communal interplay of persons and environmental characteristics. The need for harmony with nature is paramount. In the second phase, Bhaktin envisaged the development of a directional intention in individuals' lives towards some form of escape transcending this world, essentially a duel with death. The notion of an individual destiny arises and takes many shapes as in the salvation of Christianity, the nirvana of Buddhism, the wealthy life of the economic humanist or the 'individuation'sought in psychotherapy. In the third phase, the individual becomes aware of the relativity of changing circumstances, cultural belief and persons through time and takes this into account in a reflexive scepticism regarding any absolute values. It is the transition between the first two that Mumford finds particularly illustrated in his work.

Although the relative wealth of the Gurungs helped to sustain their shamanic approach, Mumford found that in Gyasumdo the personal meaning given to a trajectory through life as presented within Buddhism was gaining ground supported by the charisma of leading lamas, the power of written texts and in particular by the strong opposition to sacrifice that a leading lama had maintained. Yet, the influence ran in both directions and the cultural dialogue was beginning to produce an amalgam of belief neither purely one nor the other. It is this process that Mumford believes was paralleling the historical development of Tibetan tantric religion in its complex and highly creative merging of themes from Tibetan folk culture, Indian tantra and the Buddhism of the Sutras.

In Ladakh, the outcome of such a process of amalgamation can be readily observed in the religious life of villages. The monasteries high on precipices, cliffs or mountains overlook villages where exorcism, possession cured by shamans in trance and oracular pronouncements, are carried on as a regular practice. In particular, young women are commonly subject to dissociative states of possession that are attributed to witches. Research shows that for a young woman the transition from the paternal household to that of an husband on marriage can be unusually traumatic: women have little influence in their new homes yet they are expected to carry out important duties associated with household pride in hospitality while expressing exaggerated humility. They retain links with their natal homes but childbearing is entirely a matter for their new abode where a powerful mother-in-law may hold sway. In order not to cause household trouble, and a consequent loss of social esteem, the pressures to which young married women are subject are only shared with similar aged women among whom excessive dependencies develop providing the ground for mutual feelings of unexpressed jealousy, envy or paranoia. As these feelings become ever more inexpressible they may appear as hysterical symptoms of possession attributed to an unidentified witch, who, unknown to herself, may actually be a 'best friend'. There are many simple treatments in local use but, if the condition persists, a shaman known as a *lha.ba* ("one who lends his/her body to the gods") may be consulted. This individual has usually gone though a similar 'initiatory illness' followed by training from another shaman who in trance can call up local gods to assist in diagnosis and cure.[4]

The curing séance consists in a long, sometimes dramatic, interaction between the possessed 'patient' and the *lha.ba*, both of them mentally disassociated from 'reality' in trance. The process is a form of negotiation whereby the imagined 'witch' is placated or somehow relieved and the young woman, having received much healing attention all this time,

recovers a normal identity. Once a woman has had children and is well
established as the family mother such afflictions rarely occur.

Where a case is especially resistant and the 'patient' appears to have
become a vehicle for the appearances of higher beings such as local
demons or gods, then a Rimpoche (reincarnating lama) in a local
monastery may be consulted. He uses sacred texts, Buddhist sutras etc, to
come to an opinion. He may authorise the afflicted one to go into her
trance but only on occasions when the appearance of the *lha* (spirit) in
her trance can be helpful in curing another. Such a woman must then
undergo severe training similar to that of monks and work with an
established shaman. The Buddhist narrative thus imposes a limitation on
when the possession may occur (*i.e.* when it can be socially valuable).

We must remember that when Padmasambhava converted country
folk to Buddhism, he put the gods themselves under vow to support the
Dharma. A Buddhist metanarative has thereby come to supervise the
healing process. By placing the whole social situation in the realm of the
spirits, actual personal responsibilities are set aside while noumenal
forces act out the drama. In a society where the mutual relations of families
are important for their collective well-being such a ruse prevents direct
accusations against individuals being made. The assumed 'witch' is not
personally accused.

Men are less regularly afflicted by this form of possession but may also
become possessed in the context of family or personal misfortune, not
usually by 'witches' but by local spirits of which there are many kinds.
They thereby receive a lot of attention and on becoming *lha.ba* achieve
some social significance. Indeed one anthropologist, I M. Lewis, argues
that this is a main function of trance possession, a rise in social ranking
and a restoration of personal esteem.

The monastic system may also make use of trance possession to further
its influence and ensure the orthodox practice of the Dharma. At Mattro
monastery in Ladakh, two selected monks annually undertake a long
period of seclusion whereby, through repeated repetition of an invocatory
text, they gradually enter into trance as local spirits. At a major festival,
they then appear in trance majestically proclaiming the importance of
religious practice and morality, providing oracular judgements on harvests
and even politics and also performing strange feats and healing. The
Dalai Lama himself likewise consults a very powerful spirit that appears in
the trance of the Nechung oracle. Such oracles within the control of the
monastic system may indeed play a major role in political decisions. It is
fascinating that these monk-*lha ba* acquire their abilities through a training
procedure and not through an 'initiatory illness'. They usually appear in

festivals wherein the triumph of Guru Rimpoche over the original shamans of Tibet is celebrated through the performance of 'mystery plays'. The story of the intercourse between shamanism and the partial victory of Buddhism over the ancient ways is thus re-enacted every year.

TANTRA AND THE PASSIONS

The function of tantra is sometimes described by using a string of beads as a metaphor for the mind. The beads are of many forms and colours and obscure the string from view. The string is the clear basis of mind in enlightenment while the beads are the attachments we have for samsaric delights. The practice of tantra is said to render the beads translucent so that the inner string becomes visible.[5] The methods used are methods of transformation rather than of ascetic denial, avoidance, rejection or celibacy. Everything is accepted as real and wonderful, even disgusting things and those of moral questionability, but they are all transformed through mental yoga into the clear, empty, energies of the Buddha mind. Tantric Buddhism thereby contrasts strongly with the older, ascetic tendency of early Buddhism with its emphasis on moral form and chastity. Tibetans make a clear distinction between 'tantric 'and the 'sutric 'Buddhism of the earlier scriptures.

Tantra is however commonly said to be dangerous. One senior monk of Mattro Gompa in Ladakh, told me "Tantra is like the kiss of a beautiful woman with snake's fangs." The argument here is that indulgence in delights can become nothing more than that, a selfish, possibly addictive, practice harmful to self and others. Earlier Western commentators viewed tantric Buddhism as a repugnant, superstitious activity allowing sexual practices that were far from the pure thought of the Buddha or of serious monks. Recent research suggests however that these prudish opinions in no way accommodate the power and value of tantric meditative experience.

In order to understand Tantric Buddhism correctly, a prior training in the rigours of Sutric Buddhism is recommended because these provide the basis for the more complex practices. The meditative training consists primarily of the methods of samatha and vipassana that form the basis of Mahamudra, a system often taught within a tantric frame. Different schools present these methods in a number of slightly varying ways.[6]

In his valuable work on The Art of Tantra Philip Rawson presents a more positive picture.[7] He points out that lying at the root of much Indian culture is a theme that is not entirely absent from the West; namely that "human sexual libido is in some sense identical with the creative and beneficial energy essence of the universe"(p. 31). One prime Indian response to this idea is that sexual libido should be conserved, saved and not 'spent'. Hence, numerous practices developed in which orgasmic abstinence is linked to sensual delight, as in 'maithuna' – intercourse without emission. Here the semen is identified as the source of spiritual energy to be stored and not wasted in spiritual life. Some yogic practices in this mode may achieve the ejaculation of semen internally rather than externally in the belief that the power is thereby re-absorbed. Yet, alongside this retentive attitude may lie its exact opposite, the notion of sexual generosity, symbolised for example in the Holi festival when people sprinkle each other with red powders and water. In this perspective, ejaculation is considered as an act of sacrifice or as a way of anointing a spiritual object. Female companions to such activities are welcomed, in some cults especially during menstruation. To be complete a tantric experience is believed to require the presence of a consort or 'dakini' as an inspiratory, libidinous muse, mere visualisation of whom is thought of as inadequate. In the texts of such tantras, vivid sexual imagery of precise anatomical reference is to be found incorporated into the ritual. A recent Tibetan teacher, Lama Thubten Yeshe, was often entirely explicit in his references to Tibetan beliefs about human sexual anatomy in relation to yogic practice while emphasising that the purity of intention had to be present in both partners for the joint meditation to be valid. There is of course the ever – present danger of a moral lapse.

In India, a certain species of yogic heroism developed whereby yogins would test themselves in extremely demanding conditions to see whether the mind was capable of seeing through the bauble of experience to reach the clarity of the continuity within. In particular, charnel houses, cemeteries and cremation grounds where dead bodies, incompletely incinerated, were torn by feral dogs or other animals, were selected for rites in which wild dakinis associated with the yogins in self-denying ecstasies among the filth and the rotting corpses. While such practices are rare today, less gory forms of cemetery meditation persist as for example in the Chod ritual best performed in 108 cemeteries in succession. In the sadhanas of the great Tibetan tantric cycles, the imagery is still vividly present and sung in the deep chants of the initiatory ritual in shadowy, candle lit halls before a freezing dawn.

HIGHER AND LOWER TANTRA

The practice of *sadhana* extends to the visualisation of an internal anatomy, doubtless once believed to be actually physical but today understood to be an imaginary creation, within which dynamic experiences of energy flow occur. The body is experienced as laced through by numerous channels in which psychic energies flow. While these are connected to the outer air and sky, the energies are not to be completely identified with breath even when breathing exercises are employed. Two channels from the nostrils are imagined to run down within the body cavity close to the spine. At certain points, they cross over a central channel into which they ultimately flow by turning upwards to enter it in the lower belly. At the nodes formed by the crossover, minor channels fan out from a disc like plate on the central channel and radiate into surrounding organs and musculature. These 'cakras' (wheels) occur particularly just below the navel, at the level of the heart, the throat, behind the forehead and below the crown. The spiritual energy in these channels, *prana*, is brought up the central channel from the lower cakras to the upper ones, the manner in which this is done varying between the rites and whether they are Hindu or Buddhist inspired. Basically the rituals all incorporate, as it were, the visualised rising of spiritual semen from the generative organs to the higher cakras where it expands into bliss, blowing the mind into selfless delight. Indians say that the self is only truly transcended in birth, death and orgasm. The spiritual experience of self-loss in psychic orgasm is thus the basic object of this quest and from this basic model other considerations are derived. A unity of bodily expression in blissful passion is being emphasised here and used as powerful adjunct to traditional meditative absorption.

These tantric yogas can indeed have very powerful effects demonstrating the power of meditative visualisation over actual physiology. In the Six Yogas of Naropa, the first concerns the generation of blissful heat (gTumo). The method involves visualising the channels and cakras with a flame burning as if from a Bunsen burner at the point where the two lateral channels enter the central one. Special breathing exercises blow this 'flame' up the central channel to the head. As blissful delight arises, so the body flushes with heat. Tibetan yogins are known to practise in the snow dressed only in cotton cloth and to dry wet clothes in testing their abilities at generating this body heat. Western scientists have confirmed the efficacy of such practices. I myself tested one method that had been shown me and succeeded in generating a fierce heat flush. Without a teacher, I have not continued; a derangement of the sympathetic–parasympathetic nervous system is possible. The Tibetan yogis indeed warn that defects in method lead to illness.

Other practices of the Yogas of Naropa involve perceiving the body as a mirage of flowing energies, transferring consciousness into space and the induction of lucid dreaming. The results of these practices clearly show that they engage the physical nervous system in unusual ways to produce such feats. Although keeping warm in unheated rooms at 15000 feet in the Tibetan winter has practical implications, it is the state of spacious bliss that is the true object of this quest. The yogins say that these practices add power to methods of mindful calming and insight such as Mahamudra. "The bow of tantra makes the arrow of insight fly further," we were told. Even a slight acquaintance with using visualisation to enhance meditative practice can reveal the truth behind this suggestion. All such methods are only taught in secrecy and through initiation by a master – yogin. Errors are dangerous to practitioners in many ways and these methods should not be attempted without careful instruction.[8]

A fully developed Tibetan *sadhana* is a long, complex ritual that invokes the great Bodhisattvas to visit the worshippers where the practitioners internalise them. The monks are expected to visualise this process as they chant the texts and mantras, performing inner yoga while making expressive hand movements (mudras) signifying the pattern of internal changes. A novice westerner striving to follow a translated text through the freezing, early hours in a monastic hall may be spellbound by the deep, rhythmic chanting accompanied periodically by dramatic outpourings of wind instruments, drums, cymbals: a performance that ravages the inner world in ways impossible to describe, taking one down into vast silences, flying high in great spaces, or travelling in an utter blackness of a void so total that its seems endless, and surfacing into fields of light. One emerges cleansed, lightened, and extraordinarily open to the world. In such practices, it is clear that archetypes of ancient meaning embedded so deep as to be largely hidden are moved around by breathing techniques, bodily movement, inner visualisation and liturgical chant expressing a self-annihilating intellectual force that only the fully trained can understand.

These liturgies are classified in a series that begins with action: a real dakini is present, real foods are eaten, real offerings and elaborate rituals are enacted. Then the yogic element is introduced and much of the ritual is taken within as visualisation. Finally, the entire ritual is an internal visualisation leading one ultimately into deep, inner experiences of enlightenment. The evocations of unity with a visualised consort may be considered to be an internalised enactment of the deepest experiences of pure orgasmic love in which self is totally transcended. While not many Tibetan lamas reach these levels of knowledge, there are certainly some remarkable individuals who do so and radiate a selfless spirituality born of deep training. For them the world does not need re-enchantment – it is enchantment itself. To reach their levels from the triviality that characterises so much of modern life is a difficult path indeed.

TIBETAN RELIGIOUS ORDERS

Although tantra is the most striking aspect of Tibetan Buddhism, it is important to realise that the whole structure remains based in the classical scriptures of the Mahayana and the monastic rules of Vinaya variously interpreted. Indeed the validity of tantra has often been questioned and vigorous reform implemented when it seemed to be swinging out of the Dharma path. While Tibetan Buddhism owes its strength and creativity to tantra, its basis remains well anchored in the teachings of Buddha.

The early tantras had a tendency to slip into various forms of illusory self-indulgence that needed correction. The great teacher Atisa Dipankara came from the great Indian university of Nalanda to Western Tibet precisely for this purpose (1042 CE). He instituted a severe reform creating the indigenous order of the Khadampa in the process. The Khadampas were strictly celibate and ascetic even while practicing reformed tantra. One of their ideals was to be able to live in a cave and not worry whether villagers brought them food; to live in a cave and not worry about illness; to live in a cave and die there *i* and to live in a cave and not worry about dying there with no one ever knowing their names.

Other orders also reformed the relation between basic Mahayana teachings and the use of tantra. Lama Tsong khapa created the powerful Gelugpa order as a 'teaching' order strong in philosophical debate and ethical purity. The Sakyapa are similar. The Kargyupas and the Nyingmapas consider themselves 'practice' orders focussing on deep engagement in meditation and the use of tantra rather than philosophy. They transmit their teachings more by initiation and devotion to personal teachers than through lectures and debate. The Nyingmapa retain the use of some very ancient tantras but, together with the Kargyupas, they have also created an amalgam of scholarly teachings, the *rismed* approach, providing balanced instruction rivalling the well-organised corpus of the Gelugpas. While fierce philosophical debates have raged between these orders, occasionally leading to the sacking of rival monasteries, for the most part these varying trends in practice and teaching co-habit peacefully and have not fossilised into restrictive forms of closure. Indeed the frequent rediscovery of 'hidden texts' supposedly placed by Padmasambhava in rocks, cliffs or trees in ancient times, allows for cultural and spiritual renewal in successive generations particularly among the Nyingmapa.

While the sheer complexity and cultural embedding of Tibetan Buddhism may make it difficult to approach for some Westerners, the appeal of tantra, the emphasis on devotion and the depth of meditation practice, has led many to create new Tibetan centres world wide often led by highly eloquent teachers. In spite of the cultural holocaust following the Chinese occupation of Tibet and their continuing, strict political control of monasteries, there is no doubt that the vigour of Tibetan Buddhism, both outside and potentially within the Land of Snows, is undiminished.

End Notes

1. The following sources among others formed the basis for this chapter:

    Stein, R.A. 1972. *Tibetan Civilization*. Faber & Faber. London. Original in French 1962

    Tucci, G. 1980. *The Religions of Tibet*. Allied Publishers. New Delhi. Previously in German. 1970.

    Richardson, H.E. 1962, 1984. *Tibet and its History*. Shambala. Boston and London.

    Snellgrove, D. and H. Richardson. 1968. 1980. *A Cultural history of Tibet*. Prajna. Boulder.

    Snelgrove, D. *Indo-tibetan Buddhism. Indian Buddhists and their Tibetan successors*. Serindia.London

    Lopez, D.S. 1998. *Prisoners of Shangri-la. Tibetan Buddhism and the West*. University of Chicago Press.

2. Samuel, G. 1993. *Civilized Shamans: Buddhism in Tibetan Societies*. Smithsonian. Washington

3. Mumford, S.R. 1990. *Himalayan dialogue: Tibetan lamas and Gurung shamans in Nepal*. Tiwari. Kathmandu. Previously published by University of Wisconsin Press.

4. Lewis, I.M. *Ecstatic religion: an anthropological study of spirit possession and shamanism*. Penguin. London. Also:

    Kaplanian, P. 1981. *Les Ladakhi du Cashemire*. Hachette. Paris and Kaplanian, P. Undated. *Ladakh de la transe a l'extase*. Peuples du Monde. Hachette. Paris Also Day, S. 1989. *Oracles and possession ritual in Ladakh, North India*. PhD thesis. London School of Economics and Politics. Crook, J.H. 1997-1998. The Indigenous Psychiatry of Ladakh. *Anthropology and Medicine. 4.3:289-308 and 5.1:23-42.*

5. Crook, J.H. and J. Low. 1997. *The Yogins of Ladakh. A pilgrimage among the hermits of the Buddhist Himalayas*. Motilal Banarsidass. Delhi. p. 186.

6. Wallace, B.A. 1998. *The Bridge of Quiescence: Experiencing Tibetan buddhist Meditation*. Open Court. Chicago.

    Khyentse, D. 1992. *Enlightened Courage*. Padmakara. Peysac le Moustier.

7. Rawson, P. 1973. *The Art of Tantra*. Thames and Hudson. London.

8. Evans-Wentz, W.Y. 1969. *Tibetan Yoga and secret doctrines*. Oxford University Press.

    Govinda, Lama Anagarika. 1959. *Foundations of Tibetan Mysticism*. Rider. London.

    Govinda, Lama Anagarika. 1977. *Creative meditation and multi-dimensional consciousness*. Unwin. London.

    Cozort, D. 1986. *Highest Yoga Tantra. An introduction to the Esoteric Buddhism of Tibet*. Snow Lion. New York. (And other works).

11

ENTRY INTO EUROPE

The preceding chapters have told the story of the spread of Buddhism south and north from its origins in the Ganges valley through many lands and some five civilisations, India, China, Tibet, Japan and into the West. Clearly, this progress marks an extensive globalisation of the ideas and practices of Buddhism over many centuries. Among world religions, only Christianity, carried along on the tide of Western imperialism, has travelled so far; Islam, after its initial expansion, remaining focussed mostly in the Middle East and Indonesia but with numerous communities in the West resulting from immigration. Buddhist thought, moreover, was only rarely supported by a conquering tide, rather it seems that it was predominantly by reason of its essential ideas that it spread so far and achieved such success. There appears to be persuasiveness about the Dharma that once appreciated penetrates deeply, particularly among the educated of many contrasting worlds.

DELAYED ARRIVAL IN EUROPE

The advent of Buddhism in China was through an open door, even if one somewhat vigorously flung open by the Mongol invader, Kublai Khan. Not so its westward drift. The Dharma only reached Europe spasmodically, in a fragmentary fashion and against the tide of prevailing and intervening world views. Stephen Batchelor has provided an admirably detailed account of these various penetrations.[1] Although the post-Alexandrian Greeks in Bactria were the first Europeans to show great interest in Buddhism, their subsequent influence tended later to run along the Silk roads to Central Asia and not towards Europe. Certainly many of these Greeks were Buddhist and the dialogues between their King Menander and the erudite monk Nagasena reveal the subtleties of the speculations of the time. The Greek states faded away, re-absorbed into India, but there can be little doubt that some knowledge of Buddhism, albeit fragmentary, had managed to drift west. In particular, legends and stories coming in along the trade routes made some mark and the Gnostics seems to have been deeply influenced by ideas from the East. The Christian monk Basilides (2nd century CE), in particular, wrote a Christian Gnostic text with many seeming overtones of Buddhism plausibly derived from Indians living in community in Alexandria. His disciples, the Basilidians, were active in the Middle East and even in Gaul into the 4th century CE. Both the great theologians, Clement of Alexandria and Origen, made passing references to the Buddha.

The emergence of mutual intolerance between Christianity and Islam came eventually to form an effective cultural barrier against ideas coming from the East. Although various popes and kings sent missions to central Asia to locate the mythical land of Prester John or to solicit support against Islam from the court of the Mongol emperor Genghis Khan, indeed attempting to convert him, and thereby came across Tibetan Buddhism, such discoveries led to very little apart from a few travellers accounts buried in the libraries of the Vatican and the writings of Marco Polo. The Mongol rulers practised considerable tolerance towards the several faiths swirling around their courts so long as they did not impact upon their more worldly politics. Indeed the priestly travellers found the fundamental ideas of Buddhism so at odds with Christian assumptions that they were scarcely understood by them at all. As Batchelor remarks, the relationship between Christianity and Buddhism during the thousand-year period between the time of Buddha and Augustine was simply one of mutual ignorance tinged by the Christian assumption that all other peoples were barbarians.

It was not until 1720, when Peter the Great sent Ivan Licharov to search for gold near the source of the river Irtych in Siberia, that an intellectual interest in Buddhism was created. The explorer located a ruined temple and brought back a number of scattered pages of a manuscript written in Tibetan, which at that time no one could read. The Tsar was intrigued and began enquiries, which, in the course of time, came to the attention of oriental scholars elsewhere in Europe. Yet, the very concept of Buddhism did not yet exist.

As their empires spread in Asia, the Europeans began collecting materials from the newly colonised cultures. The British in India became interested in Tibet and the great Hungarian Csoma de Körös, following his lonely endeavours to read Tibetan in the wilds of Zangskar, was supported during his great work on Tibetan grammar at the Asiatic Society in Calcutta (1831). Meanwhile an interest was developing in the Theravada monks of Ceylon (Sri Lanka) and Brian Hodgson began studying and collecting ancient Sanskrit documents found lying about in Kathmandu. Although such manuscripts were now arriving in the research institutions of Europe, they were mostly stacked away and little studied. It was not until the great sanskritist Eugene Burnouf in Paris become engaged that Buddhism could be said to have been discovered and an understanding of it begun. His great book *L'introduction a l'histoire du Buddhisme Indien* (1844) was a major eye opener for many. Based on Hodgson's texts and his own first translation of the Lotus Sutra, Burnouf describes the new field of enquiry as "a completely new subject, with innumerable schools, an immense metaphysical apparatus, an endless mythology; everywhere disorder and a hopeless vagueness of place and time."[2] His work established Buddhism as a project within Western research using all the increasingly available skills of scholarship and science: and so it continues.

The impact of Burnouf's work was surprising. It was taken up very rapidly by thinkers, philosophers, historians, idealists and the composer Wagner to become a component of that spirit of investigation of all things in the known world rejoicing the name of the European "Enlightenment". Batchelor tells us that in 1853 the French writer Felix Nève was to proclaim that Buddhism was the only moral adversary that western civilisation would find in the Orient. Buddhism was being adopted by the Humanist enthusiasms of the time, yet the nobility of the Buddha's character was seemingly undermined by the apparently negative, life denying nature of his message – as it was first understood.

The irruption of Buddhism onto the European intellectual scene came at a time when the humanist assault on conventional religious belief was at its height and when industrialisation was creating social changes leading towards the revolutions of 1848. The philosophical concern with ethical nihilism arising from the 'death of God' was deeply disturbing at the time. Christian struggles with new ideas concerning the geological origins of fossils and biological evolution were opening up deeply schizoid tendencies. Ludwig Feuerbach had already argued that religious belief was merely superstition, a projection arising from wish fulfilment. Man invented God and not the other way about, his creation enshrining the anxious hopes and fears of mankind. The Buddhist ideas of 'emptiness', nirvana as extinction, and the purely nominal existence of self, reverberated with the philosophical doubts stemming from Hume and Kant to set up not only their approving adoption by as great a philosopher as Schopenhauer but also their vigorous rejection by Christian apologists.

Humanism itself was of course not new. As opposition to Christianity, it already had had a run of several centuries. Islamic scholars in the Dark Ages had preserved the ancient philosophies of the Greeks and these gradually became known in Christendom. A number of thinkers moved away from a Christological focus to resurrect the Greek concern with Man as the measure of all things, as Protogoras (490-421 BC) had proclaimed. Human beings were to determine their own values and moralities; these were not to be made dependent on metaphysical codes whether objective or subjective. Any attempt thenceforth to create an absolute authority through dogmatic assertions came up against similar refutation.

The church of Rome in medieval times had developed an authoritarian stance in relation to belief. Anyone not obeying the dictates of its dogma was a heretic and heretics could be treated with disdain, scorn, excommunicated or even executed. As resistance grew, the church became more prejudiced against any trend away from its doctrines and rooted its imposed morality in a focus on human sin, confession and forgiveness only through Christ – policed by the notorious Inquisition. Scholastic theories endeavoured to neutralise the humanism and individualism of the Greeks by incorporating Plato and Aristotle into theology as the great works of Augustine and Thomas Aquinas show. Yet, the openess of Greek thought was not easily suppressed and critical minds began to investigate the nature of the world independently from dogmatic assertion. William of Occam, Roger Bacon, Galileo and many Italian thinkers fathered an increasingly open minded 'renaissance' of classical thought rooted in studies of Roman and Greek texts.

The cruel response of the church was in the end to lead to its undoing. Philosophy itself in the work of Hume, Kant and others came to demonstrate that knowledge of the ultimate was finally unobtainable because all knowledge was dependent on the senses and reasoning of human beings. Internal church corruption led to resistance within the Church itself and the protestant reformation eventually precipitated the Thirty Years War that ravaged the heart of Europe. Afterwards Descartes, horrified by such chaos, created a philosophy in which matters of mind and consciousness were rigorously separated from objective material knowledge; thereby creating a dualism that was to leave the physical world open to morally unrestricted scientific investigation and economic exploitation.

The spread of science and utilitarian philosophy coincided with the assertive development of European mercantilism in global imperial projects. The excitement generated by creative European expansion into all manner of subjects, the outreach of research lining up with adventures into geography, geology and the awareness of far off civilisations, became known as the 'Enlightenment' (from the German 'Aufklarung'). Its values, now known as Humanism, focussed on the extraordinary capacities of human thought in exploration, in the freedom of the investigative and analytical mind and the development of rights for all.

Humanism may be described in many ways depending on a variety of emphases. We have secular humanism, religious humanism in which the function of religions in human life are acknowledged, humanistic psychology emphasising human capacity for spiritual growth and so on. There is even a humanist religious institution as a sort of church. Humanism is essentially a positive orientation that asserts the rights of human beings for individual expression and independence free from any priestly or lay hierarchs, or coercion by victimisation arising from dogmatic belief.

Sadly, humanism has not been a success, as the trials of our time testify. In spite of the genius of innumerable great humanists, Bertrand Russell, Albert Einstein, Carl Rogers, Abraham Maslow, Julian Huxley, John Boyd-Orr, Andrei Sakharov and contemporary scientists such as Stephen Jay Gould, Richard Leakey, Edward Wilson, Francis Crick and many others, the world is not a reformed place.

The reason lies in the split between the humanism of values on the one hand and the materialism engendered by human greed for endless ego enhancement, based perhaps ultimately on an unacknowledged fear of death without spiritual succour, on the other. Humanism does not provide an adequate understanding of human suffering, the stupidity of greed, and the institutionalisations of power that prevent political change. The dualism that Descartes established has created a schizoid Western mentality. Even if, as Charles Taylor (Chapter 1) wishes, we return to the positive values of the Enlightenment, unless these defects are corrected little progress can be achieved.

All this was becoming evident as early as the 1850s when Schopenhauer and Buddhism began to capture peoples' imagination replacing the interest in Hinduism that had preceded it. The mounting uncertainties that accompanied new scientific discoveries, Darwin's theory of evolution and social unrest consequent upon industrialisation, produced spiritual doubt, moral uncertainty and social anxieties. The Churches became increasingly defensive, spoiling for a fight, which Thomas Huxley eventually took to them in his effective defence of Darwin; while the Vatican produced a 'Syllabus of Errors' that consigned to the rubbish heap any idea that the Pope might reconcile himself with modernity. Buddhism was increasingly put forward as an antidote to the times and as a replacement of Christianity. Schopenhauer and Nietzsche became major background influences in this movement. Unfortunately, a focus on an Aryan rather than a Jewish origin for western spirituality was ultimately to have disastrous consequences in German nationalism. Buddhism was still poorly understood and the Theosophical Society based in the imaginative projections of Madame Blavatsky (1831-91) and Annie Besant (1847-1933) was offered more or less as an alternative. Eastern religions were drawn upon to suggest a religious orientation that might replace the old. The fantasies around this movement were blown apart by Krishnamurti's bold rejection of the role of a Messiah, which Annie Besant and her movement tried to impose upon him. His subsequent, inspired teachings had much in common with Zen. Yet Buddhism continued to fascinate many with serious concerns about their own spirituality and the future of the world, and various societies were formed. Even so, it was not until after World War Two, when Daisetz Suzuki's often puzzling works based in Rinzai Zen became extremely popular and the Chinese holocaust in Tibet projected learned lamas into a receptive world, that Buddhism started to fly. What is it then that the key ideas in contemporary Buddhism have to offer this confused and suffering world?

End Notes

1. Batchelor, S. 1994. *The Awakening of the West. The encounter of Buddhism and Western Culture.* Parallax Press. Berkeley.
2. Batchelor. *loc cit.* p. 240.

12

TRUTH CLAIMS OF
BUDDHIST THOUGHT

TRUTH, OPINION AND BELIEF

As we have argued, Buddhism is based essentially in the practice of a
subjective empiricism. It is a healing psychology focussing on the
transformation of human experience. The key ideas are open to test and
repeated test by people living in many differing cultures. The tests are
personal and convince by way of producing changes in mental attitude,
the quality of awareness and actions in the world. While individuals may
experience happiness as a result of 'taking refuge', the key intention is a
cultivation of equanimity within compassion. The American linguist and
anthropologist Melvyn Goldstein and his Tibetan colleague Paljor Tsarong
have argued with respect to Tibet that Buddhism – "represents one of
human history's most ambitious and radical social and psychological
experiments precisely because it attempts to achieve the creation and
perpetuation of a society in which basic ideals of non-attachment,
non desire, material renunciation and transcendental wisdom are
institutionalised. (It) therefore attempts to socialise recruits into an
alternative set of norms, values and standards for perceiving and evaluating
the world: a cultural template in which desire and wealth are renounced
as the source of misery and suffering." [1]

The same claim may be made for Buddhism in general and it is a
matter for historical research to establish how successful it has been. At
least one may say that the record of most Buddhist countries in terms of
limiting warfare and aggression and paying attention to the quality of life
has been relatively good. The question arises as to whether these aspects
of human life can develop further as this world view moves west and whether
it should therefore be actively promoted.

The subjective empiricism of Buddhism means that its value as a testable
set of propositions is not confined within the bounds of what Westerners

normally mean by the word 'religion'. The world religions, particularly the 'Abrahamic faiths', the so-called 'religions of the book', are very largely built up from dogmatic assertions that the 'faithful' must believe lest misfortune befall them and sustained by priestly hierarchies that may wield great social and political power. Such religions, competing for influence and recruits and based in contrasting dogmatic assertions, ensure that multiculturalism is often difficult to promote since the side by side existence of radically different interpretations of being becomes easily threatening. How can one's truth be absolute when one's neighbour, conditioned by education in some 'faith' school or another, is convinced of something else and when neither of us can produce conclusive proof except within ultimately dogmatic statements of belief? If a faith becomes little different from a fashion what then is its value?

Buddhist propositions are truth claims in the sense that anyone interested in them is able and encouraged to confirm them for themselves through personal assessment. Mere belief without a personal assessment rates poorly in Buddhist thinking. If the test is a failure, the individual is quite free to look elsewhere. Again, mutual assessment, rather than some authoritarian imposition, is the basis for the master – pupil relationship. The ideas of Buddhism can be checked out by anyone of whatever origin. Their relevance does not lie within a particular culture but is essentially domain-free. They are openly available to the whole of humanity.

The empirical basis for Buddhist propositions means that as a system of ideas they are closer to views of humanity put forward by great western psychologists than they are to the religious orthodoxies. Western psychologies are likewise rooted in testable propositions whatever dogmatic assertions have sometimes been based upon them. As we have argued, propositions derived from subjective empiricism cannot be evaluated in the same manner as objective empiricism in the hard sciences but they can be evaluated by comparisons of individual experience, much indeed as therapeutic systems may be assessed.

A truth – claim may be either an incontrovertible proposition that no one in their right mind would deny, or a proposition about the world or self that can be repeatedly tested. Kant would have considered an incontrovertible proposition to be a 'synthetic a priori statement' (Chapter 18) upon which an understanding of the world or of value can be based. Science also includes synthetic assumptions of this kind, although most scientific ideas are of the testable variety. In Buddhism, we find the system of thought rooted in a major incontrovertible assertion, the Law of Co-dependent Arising (Chapter 4), a generalisation that few would deny lies at the root of causality at least for macrophysical phenomena. In relation to this key idea, certain verifiable propositions arise from which the whole system of self-understanding and value is built.

These Buddhist ideas are however broadly situated within a set of social conventions that do take a form closely resembling the other major world religions – holy persons, temples and temple administration, the collection of alms, the ownership of land, simplistic renderings of the Dharma for the naive and those too busy to study carefully, communal rituals, comforting practices, counselling support and in some places a degree of wilful political influence. All these themes form part of Buddhist culture and they vary from one country to another as we have seen. As such, they do not claim universal interest; they are a matter of local convention, choice, taste or personal persuasion. It is in the key ideas of Buddhist thought and the means of testing them that we find something of universal appeal and relevance to all cultures. These are the themes that are of interest in this book, the institutional form of the 'religion' when compared to the practice of a testable way remains a matter of conventional aesthetics and need not concern us greatly here.

What then are the key propositions of the Buddha Dharma that may be considered to be universal statements about the human condition of significance to all of us? Considering them independently from the religious system of the monasteries and the temples allows us to come upon a practical philosophy for a way of life, we may call it a buddhistic way, which has relevance to the bewildering value-free world of the post-modern West. May be there is a perspective here that can help us to a 're-enchantment' of the world.

Although there is variation in the way buddhist ideas are presented almost all can be traced back to their origin in the Buddha's own teachings. The key ideas relate together comprehensively to create a perspective which we have called a soteriological phenomenology; that is a view of human experience which has the capacity to take us beyond suffering, particularly that form of suffering rooted in habitual self-concern. Essentially, the phenomenology comprises a practice the results of which are available for test. Each generation explores the assertions of those earlier masters who have walked the way previously. Buddhism resembles a therapeutic system evaluated in terms of the effectiveness of its cure. Indeed the Buddha is sometimes described as the 'Great Doctor'. The fundamental questions it asks concern the nature of mind and Buddhist methodology is the application of yogic mind exploration in the examination of contrasting states. Descriptive conclusions always arise from the practice rather than merely from metaphysical speculation. Let us list the main findings.

(1) Observation shows that in its normal state the mind undergoes continuous transformation. There is an unbroken flow of thought, imagery, planning, emotional feeling, going on all the time within states of varying alertness and clarity. If one looks for some permanent source or locus of control one cannot find such an entity apart from further sets of experiences. The self is a cognitive construction, an inference arising from the awareness of processes of sensation, perception and habit formation. The self appears as an observer that is itself unfindable, because it is imputed within experience itself

(2) Such an observation challenges assumptions that depend on the notion of a permanent entity or self, a controller or operator situated somewhere central to the system. Ideas and experiences follow from causes and exercise effects on subsequent experiences. There is no independent self. The mind responds through the senses to exterior circumstances and the observer infers that the observed process of change is going on in the world. Inner and outer are related. The universal process flows as such. There is no evidence for assuming some pivotal agent, being or god responsible for the endless co-dependent arising of phenomena in all their complexity. The view is monistic not dualistic, an implicit holism of a vast differentiating diversity.

(3) Yogic practices using methods honed by skilled yogins reveal depths of mental experience undetectable by the everyday mind. These practices form the basis of Buddhist understanding. Mind calming practices, often using physical posture and breathing techniques, lead to a gradual elimination of the normal manner by which the mind constructs its view of the world. Within the practice, time largely ceases and the normal awareness of space is replaced by a sense of vastness without horizons. The world given by the senses is no longer framed by such basic categorisations. The mind enters a deep experiential 'silence' in which conceptualisation is greatly reduced or may even stop. Yet, observation remains extremely acute and, lacking boundaries, experience appears to merge with or become essentially continuous with the world given by the senses. There is a feeling of a vast, timeless oneness. In some individuals a further happening may arise. The normal concern with an identified self as the pivot of experience may drop away. There is an odd awareness of absence in which all else continues as before in a oneness transcending everyday picturing, except that no one appears to be present within it. As we have seen, in Zen this moment is called 'seeing the nature', the basis of mind. All such experiences soon wane, coming to a natural end in a return to the everyday of self-identification in a world of objects and ideas.

(4) Such practice is commonly life transforming because the attachments to an egoic self conceived as a sort of 'thing' together with

the desire to satisfy its wants are now seen as essentially illusory. The mind normally functions through illusions, which none the less define our social and cultural worlds in an operational virtuality. We may assume that the mind has evolved to perform these functions in relation to environment but that in discovering how to withdraw from those functions a relative freedom from their control can be found. In Buddhist practice, people commonly find a new sense of freedom and consequent happiness and this undoubtedly is the greatest gift of the Buddha.

(5) Such practices suggest that self-concern need not be a habitual root of being in the manner that it usually is. The self attaches to likes and rejects dislikes, whether physically, socially or culturally, and these attachments easily lead to competition with others. In their infinite elaboration, attachments define a personal self-process that suffers because eventually it finds that nothing can be made permanent and its own existence as an entity is deeply questionable. The yogic investigation reveals this process to be merely a functional illusion floating in a timeless spaciousness, a 'vastness' in which an ultimate freedom from concern may be found. Persons fully trained in Buddhist practices find life to be play, serious play of course but play none the less.

(6) People who play are happy yet, in the awareness of others' inability to play, there is the experience of sadness and compassion. Furthermore, when, in ignorance of their implicit freedom, humans enter exploitative conflict, ego and nationalistic aggrandisement or the various dehumanisations of others, Buddhists face a choice – to act in relation to such violence and coercion or withdraw from all action. In the Theravada, there is an emphasis on non-harming through strategic withdrawal. In the Mahayana, there is an emphasis on compassionate action to enlighten the world.

(7) The split between everyday engagement in illusion and the yogic realisation of freedom reveals a profound paradox. The Buddha argued that in living a life it was essential to develop skilful means whereby the ignorance of living in illusion was comprehended within a wisdom that understands the emptiness of self-conception. Skilful means begin with self-understanding, and extend to understanding others. They work to create a world of non-harming activities, in effect a sustainable world for humans to live in. Such wisdom can of course be applied at whatever level in social organisation one has one's being, labour, caring, business or politics. There is an important ethical motivation at every level in such a life.

The truth-value of such claims cannot merely be asserted: we have to investigate them. They do however put forward a viewpoint that challenges

in a radical manner the inherent selfishness and greed that dominates
the religious bigotry, nationalism and capitalist enterprise that is ruining
our world today. We have here a subtle, healing perspective that needs
deep consideration. This is not some ancient belief system for the
historically curious but a living practice with the potential of intervening
in the mismanagement of our world.

Buddhist perspectives are not without their echoes in the modern
West. Christian monasticism has techniques and beliefs that support
spiritual development in many ways similar to the approach of Buddhist
practice. Both Christianity and Buddhism emphasise the practice of
compassion and a life of 'poverty'. Islam emphasises a brotherhood of
righteousness. Many Buddhist ideas find considerable support, both direct
and indirect, in contemporary science, in psychology and in some
philosophical perspectives. Perhaps the most important thing for a non-
Christian Westerner is that in Buddhist practices we have a spiritual path
not dependent on a conception of God. This means that for a humanist
who feels the need for an understanding of his or her inner world, a way
is open that leads to the investigation of little understood aspects of the
functioning of mind without requiring the abandonment of a basic
agnosticism.[2],[3]

To relate Buddhism to modernity we need to trace out some of the
Western themes that relate to Buddhism and then to assemble an
integrated perspective from which a more hopeful world view can be
suggested. The relationship between Buddhism and Western Humanism
is a key feature in such an enquiry.

End Notes

1. Goldstein, M.C. & P. Tsarong. 1985. Tibetan Buddhist monasticism; social,
   psychological and cultural implications. *The Tibetan Journal.* 10:1 p. 14-31.

2. Epstein, M. 1996. *Thoughts without a Thinker. Psychotherapy from a Buddhist perspective.*
   Duckworth. London.

   Welwood, J. 2000. *Toward a Psychology of Awakening:. Buddhism, psychotherapy and the
   path of personal and spiritual transformation.* Shambala. Boston & London.

   Watson, G. 1998. *The Resonance of Emptiness. A Buddhist inspiration for a Contemporary
   Psychotherapy.* Curzon. London.

3. Batchelor. S 1997. *Buddhism without Beliefs. A contemporary guide to Awakening.*
   Bloomsbury. London.

   Batchelor, S. 1994. *The Awakening of the West. The encounter of Buddhism and Western
   Culture.* Parallax Press. Berkeley.

PART III

TUTORIALS FOR THE BUDDHA

This terror and darkness of the mind must be dispersed not by the sun's rays or the bright shafts of day but by the face of nature and her laws. We start then from her first great principle that nothing ever by divine power comes from nothing. Sure fear holds so much the minds of men because they see many things happen in earth and sky of which they by no means see the causes, thus think them done by power divine. So when we have seen that nothing can be created out of nothing, we shall at once discern more clearly the object of our search, both the source from which each thing can be created, and the manner in which things come into being without the aid of Gods.

– Lucretius.
'On the Nature of Things'.

13

THE BUDDHA IN SOHO

Let us suppose that the Buddha returns to Earth, parachuting as it were, into the busy streets of Soho, London, equipped miraculously with the English language, suitable clothes and cash for lodgings. Being the Buddha, he would counter a high level of culture shock by mind stabilising mantras and, after a few days of adjustment, set out to discover the nature of the social world in which he found himself.[1] Visiting the halls, bars and pubs of the city, talking with a multitude of people, he gradually begins to build up an understanding of place and people, the modern western world view.

At first the material aspects of this new world would grip him; the huge buildings of business overlooking revered inns, churches, museums and theatres of a past time; the dense and noisy traffic; the adventure of travelling on the tube; the extraordinary technologies, mobile phones, television, radio; the speed and volume of communication of all sorts, the internet; the miracle of flight by craft bigger than any ship he had known; the coherence of the planet almost as a single whole – a total world of humanity yet driven by strife of all kinds. Over the city hung a nervous intensity, hidden fears of further terrorist attacks.

Gradually he would sense the profound concern his companions had for self-rewarding experiences, their excessively ambitious workloads, their personal advertisement in conversation and their highly individualistic forms of dress or speech. He saw that this concern with self was very different from the type he had known and rejected in ancient India. Very few were concerned with personal salvation either through sacrifice or some form of merging with the ultimate nature of the cosmos, atman merging with Brahman. Most were busy enhancing material possessions and personal credentials to improve or sustain their status in the eyes of others right now in this material world of competitive buying, selling, acquiring possessions and sexual influence, all such things being markers of whom they felt themselves to be. Conversations, radio programmes, television all suggested this to be a major preoccupation of the time. Even trivial markers, the current craze for mobile phone ring tones, for example, were coming to be pointers to a young person's self-concerning individuality. He soon came to believe that behind this almost unconscious preoccupation lay a fear, a fear of being meaningless, a fear that rested upon an implicit absence of any awareness of ultimate personal value. Once upon a time, he realised, there had been a sense of security in the Christian faith and its loss seemed to evoke a curious blend of grief, anxiety and hedonism. Many were in complete denial of any such theme and found their compensation in money and what money could do for them. Seeing a profound and pervasive suffering, the Buddha felt sadness and compassion. He saw that at root mankind was still languishing in the deep ignorance he had come to understand and transcend through his enlightenment.

Yet, in some ways, people were much freer to 'be themselves' than in his time. Although there was no caste system such as he had known, and although there were many social differentials, yet people could represent their needs, wants and opinions through an electoral system underlying governance. In principle, it seemed as if the people had a strong say in government. This democratic principle lay at the root of social life and was often jealously defended. Yet, as he examined the daily news, he quickly saw how vested interest, power groups, huge wealthy institutions, the power of money and the contrivances of spin could distort and even corrupt such a naïve picture of political process. Furthermore, power groups behaved in many ways just as individuals did; carelessly maximising benefits to themselves in every possible way.

In returning to Earth, the Buddha had a purpose. He wanted to see how far his ancient teachings might be having an effect on the way people lived and experienced their world today. In order to make such an assessment, he soon realised that he would have to build up an understanding of the modern world into which he had introduced himself. The way things were clearly depended on a knowledge base vastly more developed and inclusive than in his time and also upon beliefs and attitudes that controlled the use to which that knowledge was being put. Yet he was also quick to see that the underlying structure of the human mind remained very much the same as he had known it; that expressions of 'good' and 'bad' reflected patterns with which he was not unfamiliar. The narratives by which people understood their lives were not difficult to reconcile with his prior-understanding and he saw that, as in ancient times, it was in the misleading depths of these narratives that the people of the world were getting lost.

After some weeks, he bumps into some local intellectuals, in particular one professor from nearby London University who, struck by his intelligence, openness and the seasoned maturity of his original insights, invites him around to his college where they could have more formal discussions. In effect, the Buddha was learning fast, not only in a manner conferring street wisdom, but also through private and mutually rewarding 'tutorials'.

He learns that great world religions, the 'religions of the book' – Christianity, Islam and Judaism – had immense influence on public opinion even though most scholarly academies had long ago abandoned them. The Christian idea that there was a God with personal attributes who created the universe and lay down the laws of human conduct through dogmas that had to be believed on pain of punishment in this life or another, was generally superseded in the academies by rational, this worldly, analyses of how the whole thing worked – material science. And it was science that had yielded the extraordinary technologies of the time while undermining any religious sense of transcendental value. In this perspective, mankind appeared to be a rare, possibly unique, phenomenon in a vast unfeeling, unknowing, cosmos ruled by laws that could be stated in mathematical form following intensive empirical investigation. The belief that humanity lay at the centre of a universe made meaningful by the will of a creator god who had mankind specifically in mind, had become increasingly rare, at least in the scholarly worlds. Individuals seeking the meaning of their existence could no longer call upon such myths to sustain themselves before the awareness of a life that seemed to have no ultimate, personal point and which terminated in death. Scientists, dedicated to uncovering the truths of the material world were mostly agnostic as to its ultimate value and lived by a form of stoicism affirming a humanism of authenticity that did not pretend that things were other than they were, or seemed to be.

The Buddha soon realises that at the root of science lay some of the same insights that he had come across in his pursuit of truth. He was amused to note that his Law of Co-dependent Arising expresses exactly the underlying root of the scientific endeavour – that phenomena are dependent upon causes and conditions and that causal dependency lies at the root of impermanence, the rising and falling of everything in the process of time. Things are far from being discrete independent entities, they relate in complex ways to other things in a mutual contextuality. Impermanence is far from being random. He would probably be too polite to insist that he was therefore the first scientist, for he would have seen that whereas he applied this law primarily to phenomena as experiences in mind (*i.e.* a subjective empiricism), these Western scientists saw it as basic to a material process to which the mind of the observer was pretty well irrelevant (*i.e.* objective empiricism.).[2] He would have been excited to discover, however, that both the continuity of form and the emergence of new phenomena could be understood by a fresh empirical law, which he had not thought of Charles Darwin's principle of natural selection.

Looking back to his own time, the Buddha recalled the vision of world and life creation that he had employed in teaching two young monks about the origin of morals. Based on then current ideas, he had argued that once upon a time there was a world of radiance in which self-luminous, sentient forms consisting solely of mind lived in rapture. Such forms took the shape of human beings that were as yet still luminous, traversed the air and were glorious in a world that yet lacked the light of moon and sun. Genders had not yet appeared. Gradually, as the earth took shape, its surface became a colourful, sweet scented crust, tasty like honey. One being began to eat it and, craving more, went on doing so. Others followed suit and soon all were involved in greedy feasting. As they did so, their luminosity faded and time began. Some of the solidifying bodies became beautiful in the eyes of others and some ugly. Discrimination and jealousy began and the earth began to loose its taste. The people began to grieve for what was happening. Plants appeared, feasts continued, greed grew, jealousy and competition led to the division of land and assets. Theft appeared, sex originated and disgust appeared. As evil acts increased so stealing, lying, killing and punishment emerged upon the scene and, in desperation, the people appointed a king who did his best to rule wisely. People resolved to live good lives, some became ascetics, and some scholarly intellectuals, some farmers and gradually the castes emerged. Those who lived good lives were reborn in happiness; those who did not lived in suffering. Anyone who was self restrained and followed a path of wisdom could attain freedom from evil in this life.

Looking back on this story the Buddha smiled. It seemed to him that it was not at all a bad metaphor for what he was observing. In its broad, imaginative brush strokes, it presented a moral viewpoint on this world. Other narratives of his time had seen the cosmic process as a cyclic one. The Universe rose and fell in cycles of innumerable millions of years. Chatting with physicists over the refectory lunch table, he found that they too were concerned with the role of time in cosmic understanding. After the Big Bang did the Universe go on expanding forever or was its mass sufficient to cause a gravitational return to point zero? Yet more mysterious was the notion from 'string theory' that there might be an incalculable number of universes all incommunicable with one another rising and falling in their own times. These mysteries were far from resolution; let alone what the meanings human beings might read in them. The stars, he noted, still twinkled in their mysteries. Taking his eyes off the heavens, he once more focussed his attention on the facts of suffering.

THE POINT OF IT ALL

It was well after midnight but the lights were still on in the small Islington restaurant where the Buddha sat engaged in conversation with a young waiter he had got to know in the recent weeks. Jim was Anglo-Greek, twenty-six years old, an unemployed Ph.D, filling in time before going wandering across the world with a rucksack. Jim had many questions and found the condition of the world unsettling. The Buddha began to think that Jim might be able to assist him with his enquiries and decided to explore his interests and cast of mind. After the other diners had gone, Jim often stayed up late talking with the Buddha who grew to enjoy his perceptive anxieties. Sometimes it was not until the early hours that they locked up, put out the lights and went home through the quietened streets. Pouring out yet another last cup of coffee, Jim was saying how worrying he found the world.

"You know, I was brought up in Greece and loved the Orthodox Church with its beautiful music, its icons and all those certainties. I felt safe then. Unfortunately, I read too much and studied science in the University here in London. I no longer know what to believe. Nowadays, I find myself anxious almost all of the time."

"Do you enjoy the work here?" asked the Buddha.

"Oh yes, I want to do this waiting job perfectly. There is real style to good waiting if you know how. The Greeks can be very good at it. Do you know there are only two places where you can find a waiter actually running between tables and not spilling anything? Yes – Piraeus and Dublin!"

"What's the root of your worry then?"

"Its a little strange. My world seems quite stable yet my reading disturbs me and indeed my life experience these days is one of complete uncertainty. I wake at night full of doubts. What is it all about?"

"Good question! Indeed, what is it all about?"

"I feel I know less and less the more I read and read. Especially nowadays with all this emphasis on deconstruction, I am only sure of one thing and that is uncertainty."

"Well," said the Buddha, "maybe that is exactly how it is!"

"How's that?" asked Jim. "Why shouldn't we have some certainties like those in which the old Fathers on Mount Athos believed?"

"You know," the Buddha said, recalling a refectory table conversation, "even science is rooted in uncertainty although today I suppose it is in

Science that we seem to see most certainty. Yet Bertrand Russell discovered that the language of mathematics by which Science relates to the cosmos was actually based in uncertainty."

"How come?" asked Jim.

"I've heard that early in the last century, Russell and Whitehead were investigating the basic principles of mathematical knowledge. They eventually wrote a great tome on the subject. One day Russell realised that there was a sort of irresolvable paradox underpinning all logical statements. Russell has tried to explain it simply. Imagine a great library. It is being catalogued according to subjects. And then a catalogue of catalogues is compiled. When it is done, someone asks 'Does this catalogue include itself in the library?' What's your answer?"

"Well – yes, I suppose it would. Yet it is also not the library so it should be outside it. It describes the library but is not actually part of it."

"Exactly," agreed the Buddha, "that's the paradox. Strictly speaking, it works like this. Some sets, or catalogues if you like, seem to be members of themselves, while some do not. The set of all sets is itself a set, within which it seems to include itself. Yet, an empty set cannot be a member of itself because of course it would not then be empty. Suppose we form a set of all sets that, like the empty set, are not included in themselves. The paradox arises from asking the question whether this set is in itself. It is if and only if it is not! Whitehead and Frege, the great German mathematician of the time, both of whom hoped to establish an irrefutable logic as the basis of thought, were most put out. Simply put, it means that our thought about classifying thoughts remains paradoxical. Is our understanding of thought within thought or apart from it? There is uncertainty right at the basis of thinking."

"Something like Heisenberg's principle then? You cannot tell whether an electron is best described as a wave or a particle, nor can you determine both its position and its movement at any given instant. It seems it has to be one or the other."

"As I think I understand it," said the Buddha, "this electron is actually neither a wave nor a particle. These are merely complementary and not alternative descriptions. This is only a paradox if you allow it to be one by adopting the stance "it has to be one or the other." The wave has no uncertainty associated with it, it just gives the probability at each position and time of the outcome of certain measurements relating to the electron. The 'Uncertainty Principle' between position and momentum or time and energy arises quite naturally from the mathematics of the wave."

Jim took up the argument, "It seems that so long as we deal with macrophysical entities, things in our sensible world, one can apply laws of straightforward causality, for example the Buddhist Law of Co-dependent Arising – that events have causes and causes produce events. At the microphysical level of the quanta there are no such certainties. I believe it is for this reason that although we are within touching distance, so to say, of the Big Bang we cannot actually get there. The original bang remains a mystery. It happened before either space or time existed. Only when time and space have emerged can we determine any regularity. At the singularity itself we do not even know what dimensions may have been in play."

"So far indeed, it seems so," replied the Buddha. "We encounter mystery."

"I will tell you what really scares me," said Jim. "One day the sun will expand till it reaches from horizon to horizon and the scorched earth will melt. It seems desperately tragic that all trace of humanity, the gorgeous palaces, the cathedral spires, libraries, works of art and literature will all simply disappear. Nothing will remain of us. Not even a memory. This thought makes my blood run cold. It really affects me. No joking. What is the point of anything if that is our fate in store?"

"At least that is some four billion years in the future."

" Maybe – but that thought doesn't help me."

"You know," said the Buddha, "there was one scientist who, when he was told all this was four billion years away, said 'What a relief, I thought it was four million!'"

Jim did not get the joke. He looked really distressed and sunk in himself. Time to get serious, thought the Buddha.

"Whatever we may feel about it, it is a huge distance away in time," he said "It seems plausible that life will have moved to other galaxies by then. Possibly some memory or trace of our time now will still be present among people of these distant futures."

"Seems unlikely," muttered Jim.

"We don't know how to measure such a likelihood over so long a period. Just think of the extraordinary advances in our understanding of the cosmos in the last two hundred years. Magnify that by millions of years and a very extensive and maybe very different comprehension of the cosmos will certainly arise."

"To leave our galaxy is a very different matter from a trip to Mars or even leaving our own solar system. It is very difficult to imagine it."

"Of course, but really no more of a problem than that of a man of the fourteenth century imagining radio or e-mail. In any case you are making an assumption."

"What's that?" asked Jim.

"You are supposing human beings of billions of years hence will be the same as we are today. Very unlikely, I should say. So many developments will have occurred: genetic control over our abilities, cloning, the creations of various kinds of cyborg and robotic machinery and the continuing evolution of scientific understanding, space travel, maybe time travel – who knows? My guess is that we would find it a big problem relating to and even understanding such future people. Their mindset would be incalculably different from our own."

"Certainly it would pose a bigger problem than talking with a Stone Age man" said Jim. "And again we may also have discovered we are not the only life forms in the universe."

"I agree. I feel pretty sure that in other galaxies there has been some parallel evolution of what we call life. Maybe science fiction will come true given the immensity of time we are discussing."

"I am wondering why I find all this so disturbing. I suppose it is because such thought undermines all my assumptions. It is as if I am assuming I will go on for ever, that humanity will also remain the same and that God is in his heaven and all's right with the world. Actually, it is obvious that any such permanence is impossible. A dim awareness becomes a sort of almost unconscious threat."

"Something like that, I expect," responded the Buddha, "but I am wondering why you do not find the mystery of things something to wonder at?"

"Oh, don't get me wrong! I do wonder at it. It is awesome. So awesome indeed I find it difficult to imagine how cosmologists can contemplate it without fainting! Whether I look through a big telescope or down a microscope, I am always filled with a sense of wonder. Yet, as a scientist I have had to suppress that wondering in favour of analysing what I was doing, what the stars were up to or what the little organisms were wriggling on about."

"Are you saying that attempting to be rational spoilt the fun?"

"Not quite. Thinking about such matters, puzzling over the results of experiments, for example, is fascinating. I recall pacing up and down a library in the excitement of some of my own research discoveries. At such times, however, I was not thinking or referring to myself; there was no threat. It is only when I ask what is the point of my being here that these panics start."

"So the mystery is over-whelming?"

"I guess so.

"What if you look inward rather than outward?"

"Well – I do know something about that. I have meditated, done some Zen and listened to the Dalai Lama. Its great stuff but soon my mind goes down and the depression looms again. Its difficult to hold onto what one has realised when the mind is calm."

"Indeed so," said the Buddha, "yet it may be that in meditation you are avoiding the mystery and then the threat inevitably returns. In meditation, one has to delve immediately into the current problem. What's this? – You need to say – and stare straight into your fear of the unknown."

"Indeed – and that is really scary. What if I have no point at all?"

"Well – what exactly would this 'point' you are talking about be?"

"I suppose it would amount to the meaning of my existence."

"And what is this existence?"

"Hmm – I get a glimpse of something when you ask that question. Perhaps meaning is something outside existence – just as the catalogue may be outside the library. If you look at it one way, meaning accounts for existence, if you look the other way existence is its own meaning."

"And if you look a third way?"

"Am I getting your drift? A third way might be to know that it is I who supplies the meaning – just as the librarian supplies the catalogue. The library just goes on meditating, as it were, on its own shelves just as existence remains whatever meaning I impute to it."

"Seems we are getting somewhere," said the Buddha, "So you are not supposing that meaning is supplied from outside - from the cosmos itself for example."

"Well – I don't see how that could be. The cosmos just is. The sun keeps shining without asking why. It's I who ask why? It is I who have a brain with intentionality – not the cosmos."

"So who are you?"

"That's the mystery!"

"Well then - how many mysteries are there? We seem to have found two. There's the universe and there's yourself."

"Yes- of course but that's just the way it seems because I have such a mind as I have. Actually these mysteries are just one big, total mystery."

"Is this big, total mystery still alarming?"

"Curiously not – it just sits there – like a cat purring in an armchair, which I want to sit in!"

"Why not do some sitting with the cat? It seems you need to learn how to purr!"

Jim's face was brightening. "I have always found cats inspiring – so self-contained – or rather so self-absent. Tail curled round, fur washed, just gazing over the garden – alert – alert."

"So, sometimes not knowing is marvellous!"

"Yes – you are beginning to sound just like the Buddha!"

"Everyone's a Buddha," said the Buddha. "Shall we go further into this another time?"

I'd really appreciate that!" replied Jim.

LATE NIGHT TALKING: THE LAW OF CO-DEPENDENT ARISING

The Buddha had taken to writing up his notes in the spacious cavern of the Reading Room in the British Museum. Here, in its stately calm, he reviewed his investigation. While he realised that his studies could only comprise a mere snapshot of Western culture, he also felt that he was beginning to spot the essential themes in play that were driving the culture of the time. He was focussing his investigation especially on contemporary practices and ideas relevant to his original themes of two thousand five hundred years ago in Iron Age India. He wanted to see how congruent these ancient themes might be with ideas in the modern world.

He knew that outside the scientific establishments and western universities, the long established world religions, particularly the Abrahamic trio with their anchorage in metaphysical absolutes perceived as ultimate realities, wielded enormous influence and were tragically at loggerheads with one another. Given the politics of religious and cultural conflict, there was little common ground between Christianity, Islam and Judaism although the wise men of each could still talk to one another. Unfortunately, wise men and women were few on the ground. The resentment and cruelty of fundamentalist Islam, the narrow mindedness of orthodox Jewry and the bigoted self-righteousness of evangelical Christianity in U.S.A. had little in common bar their spiritual poverty. None of these viewpoints had rational contact with the world of the academy in which science, positivism and capitalism dominated a very argumentative scene.

He also observed that Buddhist ideas were attractive to thoughtful people, especially those appalled by the sufferings of the world and with minds open enough to reflect on the broad conspectus of modernity. He wondered repeatedly whether there was anything he should do to widen their reach. He was already teaching ancient languages and giving meditation classes in London, and these were well attended, but there were other teachers at this level who knew the local culture better and who spoke better English. He foresaw that to announce his presence as a

Buddha in the world would simply cause confusion. He could see the tabloid headlines "Buddha Back!" "Schizo thinks he's Buddha!" The gossip and the confusion that would certainly arise did not seem helpful. Indeed, he felt that anyone who claimed to be a Buddha could not possibly be one. O, the Ironies of fate! He remembered his final words to Ananda – It's not the teacher but the teachings that count. He had never appointed a successor but allowed the drift of enlightenment within confusion to proceed in a natural way through the self-discoveries of his followers. Teaching in fact was going well, there were great living teachers as well as poor ones. He would trust in human nature to carry through the necessary exploration. Even so, he felt that a rapprochement between Buddhist ideas and the modern academy could exercise a beneficent influence on the future and here he felt he should set down his thoughts, but first he needed to understand the world-view of modernity with greater clarity.

The Buddha was discovering that Jim, the waiter in the Islington restaurant, was not only clearly intelligent but also very knowledgeable. His doctorate had focussed on the history of scientific ideas yet he was primarily interested in how ideas create the world we live in. He was a bit of an existentialist. To the Buddha, he seemed an ideal person with whom to pursue his enquiry, certainly more alert to current problems than his academic friends in the college who mostly viewed things through a screen of their own competitive theorising. One evening he put his project to Jim thereby starting a long walk through contemporary culture with a well-informed guide still enthused by a youthful urge to discover, explain and understand.

"OK!" said Jim, "Let us suppose you really are the Buddha wanting to see how his ancient ideas relate to modern thought. How far are we-of-today thinking along similar lines? Have we learnt anything from his – your – teachings? Do ideas today have anything in common with what he – you – originally taught? Does this have a bearing on the crisis our civilisation now faces? How should we proceed?"

"I think our starting point should be exactly where I, the Buddha that is, also began. After my time spent with several teachers, I realised that any assertion about an ultimate cause for everything could be no more than a projection of a personal belief. Their assertions about an absolute ground of being were purely metaphysical; they could not be anchored in the sensible, the sensual, and the actual experience of life. Further more, meditation showed they could not be anchored in the mind either. Those ideas were responses to needs for safety, desires for world and life transcendence, but they were essentially illusions born out of those needs and desires. It was as a result of such realisation that the Law of Co-dependent Arising seemed an obvious truth. It was the basis for my thinking once I had become convinced of it through personal experience."

"Remind me what your Law states," Jim asked.

"Actually to call it a Law is perhaps somewhat presumptuous. It is more a simple statement about how things are – both in experience and in observation. Yet, although it can be simply stated, it is in fact deep and subtle. Not to appreciate it amounts to ignorance in which attachments to words and concepts leads to strife. Fundamentally, it expresses an accepting experience of impermanence and its implications. Every compounded thing changes; nothing is permanent. Events arise through predetermining causes and become causes of something else themselves. Everything is in continuous flux. Chains of causation also interact so that everything keeps getting more complex, a process sometimes slowed by its compliment, we might call it co-dependent destruction. There is no unchanging root principle or fundamental, isolatable cause, no 'absolute' to use a term often used in the West. Of course, this means that we have no ultimate security to rely upon! Everything is in process. That's it!"

"I see," said Jim, "it is a statement about an easily overlooked fact of life. Kant would probably have said it expressed *a priori* knowledge of an irrefutable truth. Actually, it is more a statement about conditionality than about linear relations of cause and effect. It asserts that where something exists it is conditional upon something else. Where B exists it is conditional upon A. For example, suffering is the consequence of ignorance, of a personal past and mental awareness in the sense that it is conditioned by the presence of these factors. Without such factors suffering could not exist."

"You must not forget," added the Buddha, "that although ignorance is the first named in such series, these conditioning factors also feed back to shape the occurrence of ignorance itself. The law functions both objectively and subjectively.[3] The relativity apparent in the examination of mind also applies to the appearance of all things. Every thing is co-conditioned in a web or 'matrix' of relations and this realisation stands as the basis of the intellectual expression of awakening."

"What this means," interrupted Jim excitedly, "is that, essentially, the Law of Co-dependent Arising proposes a set of systemic relations that closely resembles the General Systems Theory of modern times.[4] And we only came up with that in the last century!"

"Indeed so," the Buddha continued, "the Law is opposed not only to the linear causality inherent in the Brahmin thought of my time but also to the linear causality apparent in the history of western thought and science itself. As I understand it, the usual endeavour in experimental science is to isolate a cause or a limited set of causes to examine the effects of removing or otherwise manipulating them."

"You are right." said Jim, "Such an approach is indeed the basis of the hypothetico-deductive system whereby most scientific discoveries have been made. A perspective viewing the systemic interdependence of all phenomena is still a relatively recent arrival in scientific thought and one often neglected in favour of short-cut analyses that work within their limited frames and without reference to a wider context. So many complex phenomena in biology and in cultural studies are the result of many interacting factors operating often at differing levels with feed back loops between them. General Systems Theory accepts this and works with such complexity. There is a consistent trend nowadays towards more inclusive thinking that belongs to such a holistic approach. Evolutionary thinking for example is very much on the move in this direction.[5] One of the great pioneers of General Systems Theory, Ludwig von Bertalanffy (1901-1972) indeed argued that such an approach would lie at the basis of a new world view based on holistic vision rather than reductionist reasoning."

"I believe that a number of other recent thinkers have followed through on that idea with versions of their own," said the Buddha.[6]

"Yes, indeed," said Jim, "it's an important contribution to modern theory, yet holism in Western thought is not new. Indeed one of its first proponents, you know, was Heraclitus in the fifth century bce and there were other Greeks including the Stoics who thought similarly.[7] Their views were largely set aside by the later prevalence of dualism in Greek thought. In the 20th century, Jan Smuts and Alfred North Whitehead put forward influential cases for a holistic approach.[8] Neither made great headway against the high tide of Cartesian dualism, positivism and behaviourism of the time yet their ideas have remained as alternative, controversial interpretations of knowledge. Holistic methods now contribute to research on many social projects.[9]

"Whitehead considered the universe to be one vast mesh of dynamic events taking account of each other in a complex holistic system. He thought the human organism had immediate access to this great mesh through a direct participative, emotional rapport. The French psychoanalytic genius, Merleau-Ponty, argued similarly that all language and discursive knowledge presupposes a consciousness – world union prior to thought, a totality which is anterior to every distinction including that of consciousness and nature."[10]

"We seem to be edging beyond the frontiers of scientific thinking here?" queried the Buddha.

"Indeed," continued Jim, "Holism is sometimes confused with Vitalism in which some purposive force beyond our knowledge is believed to direct the universe or drive evolution. Lovelock's Gaia Hypothesis is a case in point with some non-scientists seeing in it evidence for the planet Earth existing in some sense as a conscious being. Lovelock was actually drawing attention to the complex interrelationship of the geological, meteorological, biological and social systems of the planet within one whole system with homoeostatic properties; a proposal entirely within the field of science. Yet others, the 'panpsychists', believing the universe to be conscious; the 'mysterians' believing consciousness to be beyond understanding; and the supporters of Intelligent Design as a supposed alternative to Darwinian evolution, all go well beyond science in supposing metaphysical forces to be at work in giving meaning to our world. I take the view that they are confusing the ways of speaking that may be appropriate to subjectivity with those appropriate to objectivity and are basically seeking a replacement for the lost God of Christianity. That loss is very hard for some to take."

"I think I'll stay with the simplicity of the Law," concluded the Buddha, draining his cup, "Next time I want you to tell me about Darwin."

End Notes

1. American observers in the 50's were amazed by the psychological stability of Tibetan lamas encountering New York on arrival directly from Tibet. Puzzled by how they countered such dramatic change they noted that the recitation of mantras restoring the tranquillity of their minds was the means they employed.

2. Crook, J. H. 1980. *The Evolution of Human Consciousness.* Clarendon. Oxford.

3. For a precisely detailed description of the Law see; Nyantiloka. 1972. *Buddhist Dictionary. Manual of Buddhist terms and doctrines.* Frewin .Colombo

4. Macy, J. 1991. *Mutual Causality in Buddhism and General Systems Theory. The Dharma of Natural Systems.* SUNY. New York.

5. Sober, E. and D.S. Wilson. 1998. *Unto Others: the evolution and psychology of unselfish behavior.* Harvard University Press. Cambridge. Mass.

    Wilson, D.S. 2002. *Darwin's Cathedral. Evolution, religion and the nature of society.* University of Chicago Press. Chicago.

    Oyama, S. 2000. The *Ontogeny of Information: developmental system,s in Evolution.* Duke University Press. Durham NC.

    Richerson, P.J. and R. Boyd. 2005. *Not by Genes alone: How culture transformed Human evolution .* University of Chicago Press. Chicago.

6. For example: Bateson, G. 1979. *Mind and Nature: A Necessary Unity.* E.P. Dutton. New York.

Paul, L. 1961. *Persons and Perception.* Faber. London

Skolimowski, H. 1994. *The Participatory Mind.* Arkana. London. Also: Ash, M. 2001. *Where division ends: on feeling at home in Chaos.* Green Books Dartington.

7. McEvilley, T. 2002. *The Shape of Ancient Thought.* Allworth Press. New York.

8. Smuts, J. 1926. *Holism and Evolution.* Also an Encyclopaedia Britannica article of the same title in 1927.

Whitehead, A.N. 1929. *Process and Reality.* London.

9. Heron, J. & P. Reason (in preparation 2008). Co-operative inquiry and ways of knowing. In P. Reason & H. Bradbury (Eds.). *Handbook of Action Research.* (2nd ed.). Sage Publications. London

10. Merleau-Ponty, M. 1962. *Phenomenology of Perception* (C. Smith, Trans.). Routledge Kegan Paul. London.

14

CO-DEPENDENCY AND
EVOLUTIONARY HOLISM

"Now I must do my homework!" said the Buddha. "There are clearly some parallels between the Law of Co-dependent Arising and theories of evolution. What are the essential features of Darwin's theory that make it perhaps the most fundamental understanding of our time?"

"I'd better give a little lecture!" smiled Jim. "Biological evolution is of course an undoubted 'fact' demonstrable to all in an examination of fossil sequences in rock strata, yet the interpretation of the process by which this has occurred is still intensely debated. Evolutionary theory is no simple hypothesis but rather a body of inference; a 'paradigm' dependent on relating together evidence from experimental biology, genetics, anatomy, behavioural ecology and evolutionary psychology. Like all such paradigms, it is subject to development and change as emerging evidence and fresh insights shift the direction of inference and hypotheses. Indeed, the development of knowledge may itself be an evolutionary process involving the differential selection of ideas, a suggestion supported by Richard Dawkins' view of a 'universal Darwinism' concerned with the evolution through selection of any replicating entity or idea."

"So evolutionary theory goes beyond the study of genetic determinism?" queried the Buddha.

"Indeed so. The two major fields of genetics and evolutionary biology originally developed largely in isolation from one another and their relationship was for a long time difficult to establish. Thanks to the insights of great biologists,[1] these perspectives eventually became closely entwined in a new synthesis. This 'neo-Darwinian' approach of the mid 20th century[2] came to dominate evolutionary thought providing the roots that lead into the concerns of today. Yet, the fundamental evolutionary process of natural selection operates without necessarily involving genetics.

To understand modern evolutionary theory you need to appreciate the power of natural selection. Essentially variations in strategies determining survival and reproduction are positively selected when they yield improved reproductive success for individuals showing them. While the causal involvement of genetics and the natural selection of genes are undoubted, the argument for adaptation through natural selection does not depend on any specific genetic interpretation.[3] Darwin's theory was built from a relatively small set of five points and of course, he knew nothing about genes. They came much later.''

" OK. What then were his first principles?" asked the Buddha.

"Firstly," responded Jim, "the capacity of populations of animals and plants for very rapid increase; exponential growth.

"Secondly, the resources available to most populations are usually limited and therefore, in spite of their capacity for growth, most populations tend to show a relatively constant size.

"Thirdly, during reproduction a range of heritable variants appears in each generation. For example, in a group of sibling puppies each one shows some difference from the others.

"Then, fourthly, just as humans may select heritable variants of a dog breed to create new breeds, so a natural selection due to environmental pressures favours variants that are better adapted to the constraints of their environments. In each generation some variants are more fit than others both in terms of survival to reproductive age and in terms of their subsequent reproductive success. Where the characteristics of successful forms are inherited, the population continues to adapt to its circumstances through the selection of such fit individuals. The adaptation arises primarily through direct and indirect competition between individuals for limiting resources such as food, homes or mates.

"Lastly, it is worth noting that Darwin himself said explicitly that natural selection was probably only one of the causes for evolution although plausibly the most important. Darwin's theory and Mendel's laws of inheritance treat selection as focussing on individuals and their behaviour and do not argue for any particular biochemical theory of the mechanism whereby inheritance occurs."

The Buddha interrupted, "So you are saying that any anatomical or behavioural feature that replicates with variation may be subject to the influence of natural selection irrespective of its underlying causation. Learning and cultural change may thus be as significantly a process of evolution by selection as genetic elimination."

"Yes indeed that is so. What is required, as Richard Dawkins points out, is that an evolving trait should be a 'replicator' that varies.[4] It is this that allows adaptation through differential selection. By setting the question of the mechanism of inheritance to one side, one can see that evolutionary theory is not even implicitly reductionistic – reducing explanations to genes and biochemistry – but rather ultimately holistic.[5] The idea of natural selection emerges as an algorithm that can apply to many circumstances of change and on many levels of change."

The Buddha confirmed, "So, when theorists talk of the 'fitness' of behaviour that does not therefore imply that a behaviour is necessarily genetically determined but rather that, whatever its origin, the behaviour has consequences in terms of reproductive success, either positive or negative."

"That's right. A one to one relationship between a gene and behaviour is probably rare, particularly in higher animals. For example, genes apparently expressing a particular behaviour may have been selected because they control physiological mechanisms that make the behaviour possible rather than causing it directly. The fitness of behaviour is dependent on more than a genetic basis. Supportive cognitive and endocrinal machinery is also vitally important. Behavioural strategies are often quite flexible and responsive to variation in the environment and this indeed may be crucial, determining the adaptability of a species within a varying habitat."

"So, you are telling me," the Buddha suggested, "that in the end evolutionary explanations must be holistic in that they require an understanding not only of lower mechanisms but also of contextual aspects of habitat such as demographic and cultural processes. Such an understanding would indeed necessitate a systemic rather than a reductionist analysis. You are telling me that individuals live within complex evolutionary systems controlled at several levels; co-dependent arising indeed!"

"I'm sure that's right," interposed Jim, "but look its one-thirty! I'm on the lunch shift tomorrow and need some sleep. Lets go on with this when next you're in for dinner."

"Good Lord!" replied the Buddha, perhaps surprisingly, " I got quite carried away. Cheers till the next time!"

PROBLEMS FOR AN ADAPTATIONIST PROGRAMME

A few days later Jim met the Buddha again. This time they were strolling along the embankment in spring sunshine glorying in the light on the river, the movement of the barges and boats and the slow circling of the London Eye.

"I think we need some examples to fill out our discussion," remarked the Buddha, " if we are too abstract we loose touch with actual living creatures."

"I agree," said Jim, "but we do need to explore the background a little more because the systems approach to evolution operates today with several different levels on each of which change may occur. Way back in the fifties and sixties experimental work on evolution focussed on testing the functional significance of individual behaviours. If something had a clear function the argument for its selection could be strengthened. Much of this work concerned examination of single factors only."

"Yes," agreed the Buddha, "I have looked up some of that stuff. Niko Tinbergen was a genius at that kind of work. For example, he was puzzled by the behaviour of birds removing broken eggshells from near their nests after their young had hatched. It was a clear-cut behaviour precisely done. Why? What was its function? I recall he did experiments in which mock eggshells were placed near nests. The result was a clear increase in predation by predators. The birds were removing the eggshells to sustain camouflage. The simple implication was that selection favoured birds that protected their young from discovery in this way. By manipulating the bird's immediate environment, Tinbergen made many such useful tests of the survival value of various behaviours. Ultimately it was thought that the genes determining the behaviour were the entities selected. I think, however, that such a view was rather a one-dimensional conclusion."

"Indeed," said Jim, "actually Tinbergen was aware that to conclude that single genes were the ultimate causation of innate behaviours was too simple. He argued that to answer the question why an animal behaves in a certain way, several distinct types of investigation are needed. The ultimate cause may be said to have been natural selection and we need to understand the way in which behaviour under selection gains or loses fitness. Yet, in addition, we need to understand the developmental process that leads to an individual behaving in a certain way, the manner in which innate elements guide development and interact with processes of learning. Then again, we need to know how a stimulus evokes a particular behaviour–a question about cognitive mechanisms.[6] In neglecting these questions, theorists assuming direct genetic causation set aside factors that may be crucial to the manifestation of a trait or behaviour. Much of the debate still in progress concerns the role such factors play."

"So, 'selfish genes' are not always the answer?"

"Ha, I see you have indeed been doing some homework! There has long been a struggle between those explaining behaviour as controlled genetically and those who favour its acquisition by learning. Although Richard Dawkins and Edward Wilson, the leading, popular sociobiologists, have tended to overemphasise their case in favour of genetics, neither they nor any other biological scholar is in fact proposing that life can be reduced to genetics. The biologists' case has been for a more general recognition that genetic factors are inevitably involved in human behavioural evolution. Biologists argue that we need to take account of such research in areas where it may have a bearing on policy, on education and on the personal understanding of life. Yet the key players among biologists also recognise the powerful role of acquired behaviour in the fashioning of culture and personal character. A 'blank slate' on which learning may write is not the only plausible basis for a civilised society and to achieve one an understanding of our biological inheritance appears to be vital."[7]

"There is quite a debate going on here then," the Buddha commented.

Jim went on, "Actually biologists have not always been entirely circumspect in their presentation of evolutionary theory so that less informed readers or journalists commonly misunderstand or misuse their metaphors and tactical ploys. A vivid but one-sided evolutionary metaphor can seduce even a good, professional philosopher. Evolutionary thinkers are currently engaged in a dispute concerning how far the role of natural selection is supported or modified by other processes operating through time. I'm afraid the arguments are characteristically unfriendly.

"Many biologists assume that a gene or genes for a behaviour are being directly selected by the environment, a 'genetic gambit' one might say. This is an assumption because the developmental process whereby the behaviour appears has not been examined. Selection may actually be acting at any point along a developmental pathway rather than on specific genes and many genes may be involved. The advantage of the simplistic theoretical ploy is that it allows mathematical modelling and elegant theory construction based upon a precise if partly metaphysical 'entity', the 'gene'. This makes theorising simpler but researchers know that many aspects of behavioural causation are being neglected. Journalists who are unaware of such shorthand often conclude that there must be a general argument here for direct single gene determinism for complex human behaviours."

"As I see it," the Buddha interposed, "a similar problem arises from the now widespread use of Richard Dawkin's phrase 'selfish gene'. Although this is clearly a metaphor, dire implications have been read into it. Dawkins simply meant that genes would replicate whenever they can. I think philosophers might say that the word 'selfish' belongs to a vocabulary referring to intentional choice by self-conscious beings who may serve their own interests or not as the case may be. Genes of course are mere chemicals with no intentionality whatsoever. They do their chemical work and then equally non-intentional environmental forces either select or eliminate the outcome. Dawkin's borrowing of a term from common speech seems to imply a driving force in evolution, and a soulless, unpleasant one at that, for which there is no evidence. There is no Èlan vital with either a selfish or a non-selfish motive involved!"

"We are entering arguments of some complexity here," warned Jim. "Genes probably only rarely act on their own. They may team up with others in the production of a trait. There is increasing evidence that genes function together as complexes. Individual genes may move from one complex to another so that a range of compositions arises through an internal process not necessarily dependent upon environmental selection. Indeed internal selective processes may be at work sustaining constitutional stability. Gene complexes seem responsible for the coherence of the species plan in each individual organism. They may vary in composition during the lifetime of an individual and also from one generation to another in a manner distinct from the sorting out of genes through natural selection."

"So the implication is that internal factors and their expression are involved in the evolutionary process additionally to external ones," concluded the Buddha. "The interactivity of genes suggests that individual genes are rarely directly the units selected. The unit being selected emerges here as the individual organism itself. Of course the genetic constitution of individuals is indeed thereby selected but the process is hardly one in which single genes can necessarily always be related to explicit behavioural functions."

Jim went on, "Not only that but further difficulties for the idea that the environment is directly selecting genes also arise from ecology. A species exploits particular features of the physical and social world that constitute its habitat and which ecologists call its 'niche'. In communities of several species, competition between them ensures that each inhabits a different niche; overlap is limited. The niche is not an objective property of the environment but rather a consequence of the ways whereby the organisms move around, compete with one another and exploit their habitat. The relation, for example, between woodland birds and their habitat is an interactive one involving the whole community of species. Great tits, Blue tits, Coal tits, Robins and Nightingales each have their own niche, the patterning of which results from their competitive relations over many generations. Changes in habitat orientation by one species may lead to shifts in niche construction by others. Coal tits for example show preferences for conifers, Blue tits for deciduous trees."

"I can see how co-dependence is emerging as a very real aspect of a holistic process here," added the Buddha. "The community of species as a whole provides the environment in which the evolution of behaviour arises. While geographical processes in forest, mountain, tundra, etc ultimately call the tune as to what sort of a collection of species is living together; the actual community is an expression of relations between species evolving together. Happenstance in ecology, demography, or cognition may alter the balance of the community in unpredictable ways, even chaotically. The direction of evolution is in no way predetermined."

"Indeed – and what's more, some circumstantial shift in the distant past might have altered an existing direction of selection to produce a very different kind of human being from the two of us actually present and gazing up at the London Eye!"

'PUNCTUATED EQUILIBRIA' AND OTHER ISSUES

When the Buddha next dined in Islington, there were few diners present and, to the amusement of the manager, he invited Jim to eat with him. At once, they took up the question whether processes other than natural selection might be involved in evolution.

Jim provided the opening salvo. "A key challenge comes from the work of Stephen Jay Gould in which he focuses on the marked breaks in the sequence of evolution, which could only be the result of interrupted adaptation. The most sensational of these breaks concerns the extinction of the dinosaurs. It seems their disappearance was due to large changes in world climate following a major meteor strike. The fading of the dinosaurs gave small warm blooded mammals the opportunity to expand into vacated habitats gradually creating the complex communities of mammalian species that are now, thousands of years later, being driven to extinction by human activities."

"So," summed up the Buddha, "these dramatic shifts in the course of evolution were not caused simply by gradual natural selection alone but in response to a sudden imposition of change in their habitat. Species of dinosaurs were so firmly adapted by selection to their long stabilised world that they did not have the flexibility to respond under the conditions of so fierce an environmental shift."

Jim resumed, "Gould and others also point out that long-term evolutionary changes cannot be solely the result of slow and continuous adaptive change because new species commonly appear within relatively limited time periods in between long periods of stability. Once evolved, many species stay anatomically unchanged for very long periods suggesting that their genetic constitution protects them to a considerable degree from minor environmental shifts. These details form the basis for the idea that evolution shows 'punctuated equilibria', long periods of stability and sudden, environmentally driven changes in whole faunas; the emphasis being on the power of the environment in inducing change. The continuing significance of selection within this frame is however not denied.

"Another point from Gould is that many genes do not express adaptive characteristics but rather non-adaptive traits that are an indirect spin off from the selection of other features. These he calls 'spandrels' – an analogy to the triangular architectural feature between a curved arch and a flat roof that are of no structural significance but which are an indirect consequence of the main functional features. A biological example may be the inner tube of the snail shell's coil. Such features imply the existence of a reservoir of genes determining non-adaptive structures. Mutations among them might then induce shifts in the characteristics of a species without the involvement of external selection."[8]

" As I see it then," the Buddha continued, "the implication of all this is not that selection is unimportant but that its action in determining the direction and pace of evolution may be modified by other factors.[9] We have concluded that behaviour of the several species present in a given environment often arises from their interaction with one another so that they co-evolve as members in a system. For example, the colours of flowers have co-evolved in step with the perceptual mechanisms of bees that pollinate them and which they supply with nectar. In addition, a species may show considerable resistance to external pressures due to internal processes expressing the conservative genetic complexes we have discussed. These two points mean that direct selection by the environment is to a degree muted both by such internal resistance and by the coherence of co-adapting organisms.

" Some theorists argue that a species presents a range of characteristics to the communal system and whatever is sufficiently effective for survival and reproduction is retained. Selection is here seen as discarding what is not compatible with the system rather than driving adaptation to a fixed and independent environment.[10] Communities of organisms are self-organising systems and individual species are components within a process. The old dualism, whereby species and environment were seen as separate, linked together only through adaptive responses to selection pressures, is here replaced by a non-dualistic systemic account. Within such a viewpoint any definition of the 'unit' of selection becomes dubious – the whole scenario is co-determining."

"You know", said Jim. There is a nice example in an African forest-fringe monkey.[11] The animals take fruit out beyond the edge of the forest and sit on termite mounds to eat. Seeds fall on the ground and their germination sustains the forward advance of the woodland habitat. All other things being equal, the monkeys thereby extend their own world. "Natural drift" is plausibly a better term than "natural selection" in describing such systems."

BEHAVIOURAL COMPLEXITY AND ECOLOGICAL INHERITANCE IN SOCIAL PRIMATES

Talking is not allowed in the Reading Room of the British Museum but the excellent roof restaurant provides a quiet atmosphere in which to chat after a light lunch. Jim at once recalled one of the Buddha's requests.

"You wanted rather less theory and more facts," he said. "There are so many good stories of field studies that we could talk about them for months. For our purpose I think I will describe just one investigation, which illustrates so much of what we have been discussing."

The Buddha poured out a postprandial coffee and prepared to listen, a notebook to hand.

"The biological programmes that underlie the social behaviours of higher animals are generally 'open'." began Jim, "I mean that relatively fixed, innate behavioural components may manifest within a wider, flexible responsiveness to contexts. The more complex the social life the more open these programmes tend to be. In particular, trial and error and exploratory learning may operate to create elementary cultures well before the evolution of language.[12] On meeting others, individuals make decisions that depend on moment-to-moment variation in motivation that relates to memory of past situations. The animal makes a decision on a cognitive basis appraising the motivational state of the other and who s/he is. Such choices are clearly the result of choosing between options on a basis of past memories and analysing appropriate cues from moment to moment. Cognitively based decisions of this type are clearly not coded in the genes as such, although the capacity to 'read' the social situation may well be based in the genome of the species. An animal's decision making is made not only within the confines of its biology and habitat but also by moment to moment appraisals of the motivation of the individuals with whom it relates."

" Can we have an example? " asked the Buddha.

" Sure!" said Jim, "Lets look at the social world of the Gelada baboon. We can see here some very clear relations of complexity between group dynamics, demography and climate. Geladas live in the high mountains of Ethiopia.[13] Their herds are composed of one – male groups or 'harems' together with 'all-male' groups of unmated males.

"The reproductive units consist of one male with a group of females, commonly sisters, although, as we shall see, occasionally two males work together in maintaining a harem held in common. Such groups move in herds together with the 'all-male groups' of non-reproductive males. The longer a harem lives together the more babies are born into it and the larger it gets. As group size increases, the bonding between the male and adult females gradually lessens due to the decreasing frequency of interactions between the male and each individual female. Basically, there are too many for him to service. In addition, the male shows little sexual interest in his adult daughters who increasingly comprise the female contingent. The dominant, older females mate most with the male and have most young and their daughters seek to mate with other younger males. Indeed they may assist such a one to take over the harem from their Dad!

"Young males employ several tactics to take over a harem and commence breeding. They regularly challenge harem owners who respond to their approaches with noisy chases and encounters. A weakening older male is easily detected. A young male that repeatedly harasses a fit owner may eventually tire him out so that he allows the intruder to become a member of the group. The older male stops resenting the sexual relations between the newcomer and his daughters and eventually the young male leads them out of the harem to form a separate reproductive unit. The process is often quite slow because the daughters remain very attached to their mothers.

"Sometimes a male opts for a frontal attack to gain the whole harem and fighting may go on intermittently for days. The daughters may begin to transfer their attention to the newcomer through grooming him and, in response to this, the older male makes renewed attempts to satisfy his females by increasing the amount of grooming he himself gives. Never the less, once several females have begun relating to the newcomer the older male must lose. He becomes peripheral to the group now dominated by the sexually active newcomer."

The Buddha added, "I have read that in many harem-forming mammals, when a newcomer has triumphed in this way, he may kill all the remaining offsprings of the defeated male in order to get females into oestrous quickly and establish his own young. Does that happen here?"

"Interestingly not," replied Jim. "Among geladas the old male may not be driven out but remains in the group assisting the newcomer in defence of their common group. He is no longer sexually active but his latest infants are not killed. It is as if the newcomer trades his forbearance for their continuing presence against the collaboration of the old male in defence. Indeed, after a long engagement, both animals may be exhausted, and a third opportunist may then attack and obtain the harem.

"Male Geladas attempt to obtain a harem in ways that differ with their age. Young ones enter by harassment and acquire the group's daughters. A harem may loose several sets of daughters in this way. Older non-reproductive males have little time left to reproduce and tend to stake all in a fight to obtain the whole unit. However there may be a price to pay, as large harems are unstable and most easily taken over by others. Over time, Gelada herds show cycles of harem creation and break down. As harems increase in size, so too do the numbers of non-breeding males. The harems become unstable as the number of young females in them increases and, when young males take them over, they create a larger number of smaller units of younger animals. Small numbers of large unstable harems thus alternate with larger number of smaller harems little threatened now by the low number of unoccupied males."

"That's an intriguing story," said the Buddha. "It shows how tactical behaviour based in subtle cognitive awareness can vary with changes in demography, individual need and group control. It demonstrates how many factors need to be taken into account in explaining any complex social structure."

"What I need to share with you now," said Jim, "are some studies that conclusively demonstrate the importance of analysing the co-dependence of factors operating on different levels in determining social behaviour. I think you will find clear demonstrations of your law operating here."

"Sounds exciting!" smiled the Buddha.

"A good many years ago the great geneticist C.H.Waddington pointed out that the behaviour shown by individuals often perturbs their environments producing changes which subsequently become continuing aspects of the habitat in successive generations.[14] Burrows, excavations, pathways, consumed resources, rubbish generation, scent marks, and so on may alter the humidity, cover, food and shelter availability, soil and soil moisture in a habitat. When organisms do change their environments in such ways, it follows that they also shift the balance of selection pressures that their offspring, kin or partners subsequently confront. If this is so, it shows that behavioural adaptation plays a role in altering the environment of evolutionary adaptation through time. We cannot therefore consider the environment as a static feature and a stable source of selection since it is modified by the lives of animals that inhabit it. Surprise, surprise – organisms are involved in their own future evolution! The great biologist Ernst Mayr and geneticist R.C. Lewontin have both supported these ideas.

"Evolutionist John Odling-Smee has rightly complained that most evolutionary analyses omit from consideration the effects of organisms upon their environment that act to change the environmental selection pressures in successive generations.[15] Behaviour leads to niche re-construction so that an untouched habitat necessarily changes through time. The 'ecological inheritance' of succeeding generations comprises not only the original environmental features but also those that have been created by the previous generations' activities. Evolution occurs not only because of genetic selection but also as a result of a changing ecological inheritance. The process becomes a cyclic interaction between organism and organism – influenced ecology, organisms becoming both the cause and effect of their own evolution. Environments respond to the activities of organisms inhabiting them, they are no longer fixed features in evolutionary equations. We have to explore the feedback cycles that occur between environment-modifying organisms and organism-modifying environments."

The Buddha interrupted, "In complex mammals such a viewpoint will have to include the relations between culture and genetic evolution and this of course leads us to the problem of how learning and imitation, nurture and nature, are related in understanding human life."[16]

"Indeed so!" Jim confirmed, "Some detailed modelling has recently attempted to describe the co-evolution of psychological and physical mechanisms in the social evolution of higher animals. Animals store information about the environment in a number of different ways. Adaptive behaviour involves the retrieval of that information from differing processes. Four such systems may be in play: the genetic constitution, information acquired within open programmes, accumulative individual learning, and the cultural pool of information acquired through imitation and education. Each system sets some constraints upon the others. Each level tracks the environment independently and does this by scanning for mismatches between environment and previous adaptation, the process running on different time scales and utilising differing mechanisms at each level.[17] When some contrast between the present and the past is detected information at the appropriate level is used in response.

"Where the features of the social environment change rapidly, such scanning involves the cognitive mechanisms involved in learning and imitation and the retrieval of possible tactics from the cultural store. Changes over a longer period of time lead to the variation in behavioural traditions. Even longer-term change leads to the differential selection of genetic processes between generations. The overall relationship between these processes tracks contrasting aspects of the environment. We have here a multi-level process involving biological, psychological and cultural transmission correlating in one process of co-adaptive change."

"That's quite wonderful," said the Buddha.

"And now I really must be off!" said Jim, "Who's paying today?"

"After all your hard work, certainly it's on me!" laughed the Buddha.

The Question of Altruism

" It's becoming pretty clear that a holistic approach to the evolutionary process is essential, but I have a question," said the Buddha over coffee one evening. "Everything we have discussed suggests that natural selection results solely in the selfish promotion of an individual's own survival and reproduction. As a Buddhist, you will understand I am concerned with compassion. Does evolutionary theory explain those undoubted cases of compassionate or selfless behaviour in both ourselves and some other species?"

" After what we have been discussing, you may be surprised to know that a lot of thought has been put into the question of the evolution of altruism," Jim told him. "Early in the last century a Russian biologist, Kropotkin, had described numerous examples of altruism among animals and pointed out that Darwin's theory would have problems with them.[18] Evolutionists had avoided the topic because it was difficult to see how behaviour seemingly disadvantageous to an individual's prospects for reproduction could evolve. Any altruistic animal would seem to be at a severe disadvantage in relation to reproductive success if not survival. Everything seemed based on effectiveness in competition. Yet, eventually, in a now famous paper, William Hamilton saw that benefits in fitness might none the less accrue to individuals who assist relatives – that is individuals also sharing some of the altruists genes."[19]

"How would that work?" asked the Buddha.

"Hamilton realised that fitness in terms of producing descendants depends on how many copies of a gene are passed to subsequent generations and not merely on the number of offsprings directly produced by an individual. If an individual, say a brother, helps a relative, a sister say, then the genes they share in common (50%) will continue into the next generation even though there may be a cost to the brother. He might have passed on more by himself had he not participated in helping, but, suppose his wife had died, he then continues to push genes to the next generation by helping his relative. So long as the benefit in terms of gene frequencies of transmission exceeds the cost, the brother's behaviour will be selected. For example, even if I find helping my brother expensive in terms of my lost gene transmission, if the number of our shared genes transmitted to the next generation is larger than my personal genetic loss incurred by the expense, my 'altruistic gene' will be selected. An organism's fitness is thus made up from two sources, direct fitness from its own reproduction and indirect fitness from the improved reproduction of a relative resulting from altruism, the two being known together as 'inclusive fitness'. A gene promoting such altruism would evolve if it had a positive inclusive fitness."

"Am I to suppose then," asked the Buddha, "that altruism would function in relation to inclusive fitness more effectively when altruistic acts were directed at close rather than distant relatives? If I share with a close relative we have more genes in common that I have with a distant one?"

"Yes indeed," replied Jim, "research shows that this prediction is indeed the case. This process of 'kin selection' has been demonstrated in many animals. For example, lionesses may suckle their sisters offspring as well as their own. Prairie dogs may give alarm calls more frequently when relatives are nearby than when a neighbour is unrelated. Among humans the intensity of childcare varies with differing categories of relatives: own children generally receiving more benefits and less harm than step children for example."

"But can altruism also develop between unrelated individuals?"

"Ah, yes, but by a rather different process. Robert Trivers realised that altruism did sometimes occur between unrelated individuals. Could this also be explained? The answer is yes – but it depends on the benefit received being in some way returned. Reciprocal altruism, 'you scratch my back and I'll scratch yours', occurs when both participants in an activity gain a net benefit from their participation in terms of frequencies of gene transmission to the next generation."[20]

"Yet, if an individual recipient cheats by not responding, a donor would surely be put at a serious disadvantage?"

"Of course. Giving assistance to an unrelated other does carry this risk. The question is how likely is cheating to occur? Computer modelling suggests that if the frequency with which individuals meet is common, then the continuance of helping may be mutually sustained. Since no one can be sure when the frequency of helping will diminish, there will be an advantage in choosing to continue. A policy of 'tit for tat' emerges as the best solution. Individuals follow two rules – cooperate on the first opportunity and thereafter do what the 'friend' does. If the friend cooperates, one also cooperates, if he does not then one withdraws support but if he resumes helping, one does the same. In this way, it is assumed that the fitness of this helping behaviour will be sustained. Two aspects are particularly important, an ability to recognise the individuals with whom one interacts and an ability to detect cheating."

"All this computer modelling feels very abstract to me," objected the Buddha.

"Indeed this is an issue," agreed Jim. "Mathematical modelling looks very sophisticated and indeed often is so: it has become quite an addictive pastime for biologists imitating research on engineering design, and, furthermore, it can be done in the armchair; no more muddy boots or climbing trees! But the intention always is to seek confirmation in empirical field studies. In the end only those models confirmed in the field survive. A natural selection of ideas, you see!"

"This leaves me wondering," the Buddha said, "whether in evolutionary thinking humans are ever 'truly' altruistic as most religions recommend?"

" Attempts to answer this question are often convoluted," replied Jim. "Disinterested altruism certainly seems rare. Acts of altruism may lead to large biological benefits to an altruist if reproductively successful individuals are then more willing to mate with it. Arabian babblers, sociable birds of the desert fringe, live in groups with many helpers at the nest. The helpers provide nestlings with food and actively compete with one another to do so.[21] Cooperating individuals are effectively rivalling one another in a demonstrable avoidance of cheating. When a potential mate chooses the best altruist for mating, a reputation for altruism may prove greatly beneficial reproductively. A kind of market place emerges in which the purveyors of altruistic acts compete to achieve reputations ultimately to their reproductive benefit.

"This story shows some resemblance to human food sharing where skilled hunters 'show off' by sharing their capture with others. This turns out not to be solely a matter of improving supply to relatives but also a means of gaining sexual favours from others.[22] By extension, one may argue that in advanced civilisations the gaining of a reputation through sharing of either commodities or information could lead to a return of favours going well beyond the sexual to include commercial contracts and further forms of market partnering which may of course be highly beneficial to the family concerned in terms of higher standards of living, good health and reproductive success. Such social incentives may indeed have become prime drivers in the complexities of human behaviour and reveal how various forms of behaviour, foraging, mating, grooming, sharing, inter-relate in complex ways that ultimately constitute patterns of culture. The concepts of the 'cheat', the 'altruist' and the 'saint' are applied to individuals within a system of mutual advantages."

The Buddha took up the theme. "In traditional Tibetan monasteries of the Gelugpa order young monks from poor farming families are celibate and may become famed for compassionate altruism and goodness. While lacking any personal reproductive fitness, they are among the few who receive an education, and traditionally this may lead to power and privilege. Their families inevitably benefit from the success of the celibate son.''

"That's fascinating!" said Jim. "It reminds me that in the practice of science a balanced relation between competition and cooperation is essential to the common purpose of using information in the process of discovery. Cheating, plagiarism, false results and failures to quote others' relevant work are profoundly condemned and careful reference to others' ideas and achievements essential to cooperative relations that are by no means always sustained."

"I am afraid all this means that disinterested altruism seems an unlikely proposition in human affairs." the Buddha pondered.

"Ah, but by your own account nothing is independent! Compassion must also have its precipitating conditions. Maybe we are simply discovering what those may be."

"Indeed it looks like it. Yet if we all came to think of one another as kin, a more widespread compassion might arise."

GAIA THEORY

When they next met, the Buddha suggested that they summarise their discussion so far. He felt that enough had been said to demonstrate quite clearly that the Law of Co-dependent Arising might legitimately be said to lie at the root of modern evolutionary theory, a basic source upon which the idea of natural selection depends.

"OK," Jim responded, "Lets see what we have done. The problem has commonly been that in evolutionary thinking only two interactants, the organism and the environment, have been considered thereby producing a highly dualistic argument: genes or environment, nature or nurture. The criticisms and suggestions that we have been exploring stem from a realisation that evolution occurs within systems wherein co-evolution of various types occurs at differing levels. This is where the comparison with your ancient Law becomes valid because it seems that everything interacts with everything else and the various levels of interaction evolve together. Actually we have not discussed what must be the most fruitful validation of your law – the evolution of our planet itself."

"Well then – tell me more!" said the Buddha.

"Some years ago, biologist turned climatologist James Lovelock proposed that the planet Earth was itself a self determining system capable of sustaining itself against the increasing heat of the sun. He proposed that it was itself therefore a product of evolutionary emergence that could even be likened to the evolution of a sentient being. There was quite an outcry. Most evolutionary biologists were working with a reductionist approach that had descended from Descartes. Sentience and mind stood on one side of a great divide beyond which lay inanimate matter. Life had indeed emerged on Earth but the planet itself was essentially inert matter. In any case, it seemed the evolution of a system as complex as that of a Planet could hardly be accounted for in Darwinian terms.

"Lovelock persisted. The Earth, he felt, evolved along with life. It had become known from the analysis of air bubbles retrieved from deep in Antarctic glaciers that the temperature of the planet had only varied within quite strict limits through enormous periods of geological time even though the heat arriving from the sun had got steadily much hotter. Clearly some sort of regulatory process was going on and such a process implied an evolutionary development through time whereby some process had emerged to limit overheating. To overcome his critics Lovelock needed a model that could reasonably realistically demonstrate how this could be. He came up with a brilliant idea – the Daisyworld.

"His computer model depicts a planet upon which grow two kinds of daisies, one dark and the other light. The dark one absorbs heat from the Sun but the light coloured one reflects it back to outer space, thereby cooling the planet. He ran the model through a time sequence of slowly increasing incident heat. The results showed that at the beginning, when the earth was cool and the incident heat only warm, the dark coloured daisies grew well absorbing the heat needed for their life processes and thereby adding to the planetary temperature; a positive feedback situation. They gradually covered much of the planet. Yet, as the sun's heat increased, the temperature eventually became too much for them. By contrast, the white flowers reflected back the heat and continued to metabolise well by reducing the incident heat affecting them; a negative feedback situation. The cooling planet gradually became covered with pale daisies. The pattern was reversible; by lowering the solar heat on his computer, Lovelock showed the advantage returning to the warmth collectors. Although simplicity itself, the model revealed how a complex self-regulatory system could arise through a process of differential daisy selection, which also had the consequence of keeping the planets temperature within limits. He renamed the self-regulatory planet Gaia after the ancient Greek goddess of the Earth.

"Such a demonstration led to intensive work culminating in the present day understanding of the extraordinary self regulatory systems involving key planetary chemicals that have the effect of sustaining the planetary system as a whole

"There are many such homeostatic cycles correlating in a massive system of planetary protection against increasing solar radiation.[23] The most significant of these is the carbon-calcium cycle. In brief, Carbon dioxide from heated rock in the Earth's depths is blown out into the atmosphere from volcanoes. This greenhouse gas prevents incident solar heart escaping back to space and so the global temperature rises. Yet, one effect of this is increasing evaporation from the oceans yielding rain and accompanying storms. Forests grow in the damp hot climate and the photosynthetic activity of plants eats up CO_2 in making sugars. The roots break up the granitic rocks releasing calcium that ends up in rivers and accumulates in the ocean. Photosynthesising algae use CO_2 to interact with the calcium that ends up as cellular chalky deposits used in making various protective organs, shells, carapaces, spicules etc. When these marine organisms die, they sink to the ocean floor with the CO_2 entrapped in the calcium compounds. This removal of CO_2 from the atmosphere cools the planet down. Sedimentary rocks, chalk and limestone, build up as enormous deposits of calcium trapped CO_2. Yet, tectonic plate movements of the earth's surface over vast spans of time push these rocks up against harder continental bodies. They descend to great depths where the intense heat and pressure breaks the chemical bonds thereby releasing CO_2 again. It rises in basaltic lava flows onto the ocean floor and blows up to the atmosphere again in volcanic explosions."

"What an extraordinary mechanism!" exclaimed the Buddha. "It is quite wonderful to think of all these processes mutually depending upon one another and indeed defining the possibility for life on Earth. But that is indeed not quite what Darwin meant by evolution is it?"

"Darwin never said that his principle of natural selection was the only process whereby life evolved and changed in adaptation to the environment!" replied Jim. "Yet he did believe it was the key to evolutionary understanding. We have seen how contemporary theory shows how natural selection occurs within systems of environmental change in a holistic manner. This Gaia theory still relies on natural selection. Its self-regulation occurs because of living processes and the micro-organisms and other creatures are all undergoing selection as the process proceeds. The holistic vision emphasises the importance of Darwinian change within a greater whole. Physical and biological changes work in tandem. Indeed without the evolution of living processes the homeostatic mechanism as a whole could not work. There is however, a great deal more work to be done on the whole question. Indeed, as you know, understanding the way we can control our own CO_2 emissions has become a critical issue right now."

"I can see no reason why the social sciences should not also be involved here too," argued the Buddha.

"I think so too," agreed Jim. "Regrettably, some social scientists, in spite of compelling evidence, have been adamant in their Cartesian insistence that the soul, self, culture, or mind was a totally different phenomenon from the material world. Supporters of this schizoid view are essentially arguing that things are what they want them to be rather than what the evidence tells us. In this assertion, they abandon the basic understanding in science that Edward Wilson emphasises in his book Consilience that there is an implicit connection between all phenomena from quanta to the stars.

"I agree with you that it seems right to argue that the picture of evolution as a set of systemic relations recalls the basic principle of the old Law of Co-dependent Arising. As we have already seen, the close similarity between this law and General Systems Theory is remarkable. We have here not so much an analysis of causation in the sense of a direct cause and effect relationship but rather a broader statement of contingency within which further studies of causation are implied. This also appears to be the case with current evolutionary thought. Learning is contingent upon behavioural constraints themselves contingent upon rules stemming from the interactions of genes. The parallel is exact."

Jim turned to the Buddha smiling and asked, "What then do you make

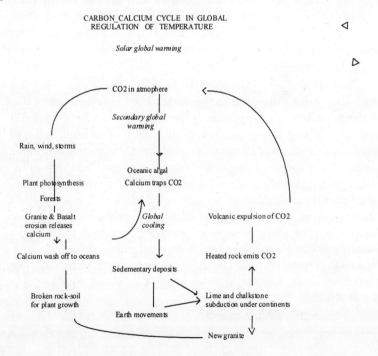

CARBON_CALCIUM CYCLE IN GLOBAL
REGULATION OF TEMPERATURE

of all this?"

"Well," said the Buddha, "It is not that the old Law in its profound simplicity can contribute anything to evolutionary theory as such but that the conformity between evolutionary theory, particularly in the holistic form we have been discussing, and the Law is a matter of interest, not merely in historical terms, but because within the contemporary search for personal 'meaning' the coincidence has an important relevance. Buddhist thinkers developed the law as the root for a morality no longer requiring external coercion from priestly or other hierarchies. In understanding this law as being in conformity with evolutionary theory we can also see that the Buddhist argument is in agreement with a fundamental scientific perspective. Within Buddhism, there is no breach between science and an ontological basis for ethics.

"All this is important because at the present time it seems that personal values in the modern West, wherever they extend beyond wealth and having a 'good time', remain dependent either upon god-given doctrines and dogmas of an Abrahamic religion, which have no relation to the scientific understanding of the cosmos, or on a stoical 'authenticity' within agnosticism. Such perspectives sustain the split condition of the western mind, which is the prime root of our 'not listening to the world' (Chapter 1). Perhaps now we can see that when we turn to examine the Buddhist interpretation of personal meaning we have something that may be quite remarkably related to the general perspective of evolutionary science - and indeed may be said almost to have predicated it."

"I like it!" said Jim.

"And yet and yet," cautioned the Buddha, "merely knowing this will not make much difference to the world. The existential use of the Law depends on directly experiencing the mutuality of all things and this is unlikely without a deep practice of spirituality. The implication of the interconnectedness of all phenomena is that any apparent one of them is empty of any specific thing-ness-it has no existence inherent in its own isolated being. Insight is needed to perceive that this means that emotional attachments to things, ideas, prejudices, beliefs resting in mere assertion, as objects to rely upon as sources of safety within impermanence is mistaken for not one of them possesses constancy, and that to defend such attachments through vicious argument, resentment, strife and terror is to base a life on total illusion. The only true course must be through sharing and mutual understanding and that means the cultivation of love. There's the problem."

"Yes indeed!" said Jim quietly.

End Notes

1. Plotkin, H. 1994. *The Nature of Knowledge concerning Adaptations, Instinct and the evolution of intellegence.* Allen Lane. Penguin. London

2. J.B.S. Haldane, R.A. Fisher, Sewell Wright and Julian Huxley in the 1930's.

3. Huxley, J. 1942. *Evolution: the Modern Synthesis.* Allen and Unwin. London.

4. Barrett, L., R. Dunbar and J. Lycett. 2002. *Human Evolutionary Ecology.* Palgrave. London.

5. Dawkins, R. 1989. *The Selfish Gene.* Oxford University Press. Oxford.

6. Dunbar, R. 1995. *The Trouble with Science.* Harvard University Press. Cambridge (Mass).

7. Tinbergen, N. 1951. *The Study of Instnct.* Oxford.

8. Pinker, S. 2003. *The Blank Slate.*Penguin

9. Gould, S.J. and R.C. Lewontin. 1979. The spandrels of San Marco and the panglossian paradigm. A critique of the adaptationist programme. *Proc. Roy. soc. Lond. Series b.* 205:581-598.

10. Varela, F.J., E. Thompson and E. Rosch. 2000 The *Embodied Mind: Cognitive science and Human experience.* MIT Press. Cambridge. Mass.

11. Varela et al. *loc cit.*

12. Gartlan, S. 1966. Ecology and behaviour of the Vervet Monkey. Uganda. Ph.D Thesis. Bristol University Library

13. Crook, J.H. 1980. *The Evolution of Human Consciousness.* Clarendon Press. Oxford.

14. Dunbar, R. 1984.*Reproductive decisions: an economic analysis of gelada baboon social strategies.* Princeton University Press. Princeton.

15. Waddington, C.H. 1957.*The Strategy of the Genes.* Allen and 'Unwin. London.

16. Odling-Smee, F.J., Laland, K.N. & M.W. Feldman. 2003. *Niche Construction. The neglected process in evolution.* Princeton University Press. Princeton.

17. Crook, J.H. 1995. Psychological processes in cultural and genetiuc co-evolution. In Jones, E. and V. Reynolds. *Survival and Religion: Biological evolution and cultutral change.* Wiley. London.

18. Plotkin, H.C. and J. Odling-Smee 1981. A multiple level model of evolution and its implications for Sociobiology. *Behavioural and Brain Sciences* 4: 225-268.

19. Kropotkin, P. 1902. *Mutual aid: a factor of evolution.* Heinemann. London.

20. Hamilton, W.D. 1964. Genetic evolution of Social behaviour. I, II. *Journal of Theoretical Biology.* 7:1-52.

21. Trivers, R. 1971. The evolution of reciprocal altruism. *Q.Rev.Biol.* 46:35-57.

22. Zahavi, A. 1974. Communal nesting by the Arabian Babler; a case of individual selection. *Ibis:* 116 84-87.

23. Daisy world; Lovelock, J. 1982. *Gaia: a new look at Life on Earth.* Oxford University Press.

15

THE NATURE OF PERSONS

PERSON AS THING OR PROCESS?

In his wanderings around Soho the Buddha had observed that most people he spoke with seemed to have very clear views concerning who and what they were, took pride indeed in affirming an essential solidity in themselves and evinced some alarm if their picture of themselves as a certain kind of being was challenged. People seemed to see themselves very much as 'things' or 'agents' in a given social world. Indeed, whenever he met a committed Christian, this view was strengthened not only by an affirmation that they possessed 'souls' of a certain moral character but that good souls could expect a happy life after death whereas evil souls were condemned to painful downfall. This soul 'thing' was perceived as transcending death. When he investigated academic opinions, he found too that some philosophers likewise stressed a certain thing-ness at the root of their conception of self. The philosopher Galen Strawson opines that the mental self is ordinarily experienced as a mental 'thing' in some usually undefined way. This entity is felt to be undivided, shows continuity through time and is distinct from all other 'things'. It is a subject of experience in the sense of having both ideas and feelings. It acts within the world as an agent and has a certain character or personality distinct from those of other humans. He argues against the view that a person is a 'process' rather than a thing on the grounds that all things are also processes when viewed in a universal perspective. Yet, in common parlance, thinking of a person as a 'thing' emphasises a certain fixity, stability and coherence. The idea of 'process' seems to allow a degree of impermanence and a greater possibility of change. The Buddha had taken a 'process' point of view, denying any fixed entity as a basis for the self. He had based his view on careful introspection utilising methods of meditation giving insight into the mind's deepest activities. What sort of a thing or process had he been investigating here? The Buddha began to ask himself how contemporary psychologists viewed the nature of the mind. He soon discovered an enormous literature on this theme.

Human beings are distinguished from other sentient beings by their massively superior capacity for learning, imitation and innovation that has allowed the progressive development of culture. Culture entails understanding the skills of others, the properties of materials and their uses. Enquiry and exploration has allowed people to continually refashion and innovate technologies: the use of fire; the domestication of animals; the creation of tools; nuclear energy and the internet.

The vehicle for the runaway emergence of material culture was language whereby innovation could be described, conveyed and spread across whole populations. Such skills did not replace the older mechanisms of instinctive responding or trial and error learning but were intercalated with and superimposed upon them in systems of information management enabled by the progressive evolution of the brain. An essential aspect of the development of personal skills was the ability to distinguish between the self as actor and others with whom one interacted.

A person has 'metacognition': the ability to be aware of and cognise oneself. Quite early in life the infant realises that s/he is distinct as a sentient being from the carer who attends to its needs. This initial insight develops into the emergence of a distinctive 'self' characterised by behaviour shaped by early and subsequent experiences. As the person grows so s/he acquires new layers of understanding both of self and others and assimilates the social world of a particular culture. In many ways, a person is the product of the environing culture, particularly as expressed by parents and later by peers. He or she continually grows and changes through education, just as culture itself does. Indeed, in recent centuries, culture, especially technological culture, has changed so rapidly that the enculturation of the young changes significantly in successive generations. The young people of today differ in important respects from their grandparents and great grandparents to an extent probably never experienced before.

Understanding of self and other rests on mental capacities far greater than those of any other animal. These all go under the heading of 'intentionality': that is the capacity to understand the beliefs, intentions and purposes of others, to have a 'theory of mind.' We all have a certain capacity for 'mind reading.' First order intentionality is simply knowing one's personal state – "I am hungry, angry, or feel upset." Second order intentionality is the capacity to infer, correctly or not, the state of mind of another, "I believe she is cross with me because I failed to meet her yesterday." Third order intentionality is a belief that someone has a belief about another, "I believe that he believes that she thinks I am naughty." "There seems to be a limit to intentionality at about six levels although not everyone may be capable of all of them" – "I believe (i) that my wife thinks (ii) that our son wishes (iii) me to think (iv) that she will allow (v) his sister to think vi) she may go out at night." These levels of intentionality form a hierarchical series constituting our capacity for theorising about other people's minds. Clearly there is great potential for misunderstanding. Cues from facial expression or gesture may be misinterpreted. One may project one's own hopes or fears into the inferences one may be making.[1]

Intentionality allows individuals to assess the motivations of others and to infer others' beliefs about their companion's intentions or purposes. Without these evolutionary pre-adaptations, culture based in the communal holding of world views simply could not exist. This must be especially true when the higher levels of intentionality are used in the context of elaborate metaphorical symbolism. Such symbolism is made possible through the human ability to fantasise emotional relating. We may imagine that the gods believe that we are avoiding our responsibilities and are angry with us. So they punish us with an avalanche. Such thinking is not only an effect of imaginative ability but also due to unconscious processes operating to create representations of every day events, both present and derived from memory, that come to symbolise social process. This seems to be the reason why dreams are often sufficiently interpretable to make personal and social sense. Such abilities underlying communally shared beliefs probably only emerged well after the evolution of language and underpin inner worlds of hopes, fears, fantasies of all sorts.

When we look around the world and observe the great differences between the structures of human languages and cultures we are necessarily led to wonder how far peoples of differing world-views can understand one another. What exactly may they have in common? How far can an Eskimo understand a Bushman?

CULTURAL CONTRASTS AND IDEAS OF SELF

The Buddha began pondering this question. The relativity of person and culture led him to ask how far human persons share general characteristics worldwide and what is currently known about this. If the differences are great how do human beings come to understand one another? Can people in highly divergent cultures ever understand one another? He decided to engage Jim in another exploration.

This time he arranged for them to take a long weekend holiday together so that they could go into the matter with few interruptions. They travelled down to the isolated Beaulieu Road railway station in the middle of the New Forest. There was a comfortable small hotel there set among heathland and deep woods. Jim was keen to do some bird watching and the Buddha thought this might be very enjoyable. Sure enough on a bright day in early summer they soon listed Green and Greater Spotted Woodpeckers, Stonechats, Wheatears, Curlews and Buzzards and then, excitement indeed, a pair of rare Dartford Warblers foraging about among closely set gorse bushes on the heath above Matley Bog.

That evening Jim took up the Buddha's challenge. "The complexity in this question is revealed when we realise the number of mental properties that are involved. First of all there is consciousness, the basis of being aware both of self and of others. Then there is language, the basis not only of concepts concerning things and events to be described and communicated but also of internal talk – thought. Contrasting languages structure thought in different ways and this may influence the way in which one thinks about oneself. Persons feel emotions that are often of great complexity, shame or guilt for example, and express them in self-description and in making comparisons with others. Persons' needs and wants are expressed in verbal description and emotional expression. Individuals feel that all these elements comprise an essential unity, which can be given a name – the name commonly assigned by parents – John or Maria. Yet this unity can be threatened not only by the world and other people, their words and attitudes, but more insidiously by those within oneself."

The Buddha joined in, "I suppose the basis of human personhood lies in genetically based, universal, traits common to the whole human species. After all, there is much in common between the emotional vocalisations and facial expressions of human kind worldwide. These must be based in a species-specific mentality within which certain universal rules of behaviour, thought and expression manifest. Certain psychological traits may have a universal distribution and may be based in the genome of the species, as evolutionary psychologists have suggested. Yet, there is also evidence for marked differences in the organisation of self between one culture and another. The linkage between culture and the way in which an identity is attributed to a person's self is extremely close."

Jim took up the theme, "Cultural norms are the basis for attributing properties to oneself just as the collective representations of persons come to constitute important components of culture. There is mutuality, a reflexive relationship, between culture and the way in which one perceives oneself. Individuals attribute an 'identity' to the self through reference to the culture or cultures in which they live and this goes on throughout life. This identity is what a person considers himself or herself to be. Identity is therefore an attribution; an individual's personal construction of self as an expression of what he thinks and feels him or her-self to be. Indeed this is what is meant by a 'mental' representation. While a person is undoubtedly biologically embodied, he or she understands himself or herself through the cognitive manipulation of relevant information. Indeed self is nowadays often viewed as neither less nor more than a narrative."

"I have been doing some reading," the Buddha continued. "Differences in the styles of self-expression between cultures can be large indeed and are often related to the social contexts of competitive communication. There are for example considerable differences between European and particularly US styles of 'selfing' and those of peoples of East Asia.[2] Research on personal behaviour in the United States reveals an emphasis on individualism, on promoting one's 'identity' as positive. The individual experiences his or her self as distinctive, integrated, meaningfully expressive of socially acceptable values that gain approval, yet which are unique. The individual is competitive in comparing self with others and constructs self around attributes, possessions and achievements that contrast in a self-promoting way with those of others. While such characteristics undoubtedly owe their origin very much to the 'frontier' spirit of white America and a protestant orientation to life, in today's U.S.A. these characteristics relate clearly to the consumer culture in which individuals are now raised. Choice is openly available in the market economy and one can choose how to distinguish self from others, keeping up with the Bernsteins, discretely or sometimes indiscreetly showing off a new car, house, hairstyle, or qualification. Life, like commerce, is essentially competitive and maximising. Just as a consumer economy needs to generate novelty to sustain sales, so too does the self seek renewal as fresh means for self-manifestation. Self-expression in this culture is very much linked to money."

"Psychological testing suggests that white Americans in the U.S.A. habitually tend to overate their abilities as they attempt to preserve a highly positive and often exaggerated self-esteem," Jim added. "It may be that expensive mistakes in national foreign policy are in part an expression of this overweening tendency! It is, however, not the case that Americans ignore relationships but that relationships are often used as means for self-promotion or for the maintenance of self-esteem rather than as part of a mode of interdependent living. There is a strong focus on individual rights that is often expressed in expensive litigation. In the US and in Europe also, such marked individualism tends to conflict with moves towards communal values and the creation of community."

"In the US," went on the Buddha, "it seems that children tend to be praised for their distinctiveness, positive reinforcement being given more to encourage a child to feel good about herself than as a marker of achievement. In the US, tests have shown that when a friend succeeds in a task unrelated to an individual's interest he tends to be supported and given admiration, yet, when success is in an area similar to that of one's own interest, signs of jealousy or resentment may appear. Self reports and evaluations are rarely critical or self-aware but rather emphasise one's own good points and feelings."

"When we look at the Japanese," said Jim, "a very different picture emerges. In Japan, social studies show that customs favour expressions of mutuality, interdependence, self-effacement and an appreciation for communality at many levels. Education emphasises not the cultivation of distinctiveness but rather participation in communal activity to the extent of favouring an ability to read others' minds while maintaining critical self-reflection. Japanese people tend to feel a sense of connectedness with others, a need to fit in and a tendency towards seeking to promote social harmony that contrasts markedly with the Euro-American sense of separate identity, boundedness and a need of being in control of social situations even within contexts of interdependence. Japanese tend to present different aspects of self in contrasting social situations, fitting into the norms of a particular gathering rather than standing out within it. Japanese language also employs different expressions in relation to social rank with a high frequency of varying 'honorific' forms of politeness to those treated as higher in some hierarchy."

"In China too," the Buddha picked up the story, "a study of poetry and philosophy suggests an awareness of a distinctive self that parallels that of Europeans.[3] Yet Taoist, Buddhist and particularly Confucian themes of mutuality are commonly significant and, in contemporary testing, an awareness of a need for community is expressed. In the Confucian tradition, virtue is achieved as an individual develops into a social being. The social order is constructed in terms of paired relationships that express difference within asymmetries: father-son, emperor-subject, husband-wife, elder-younger. Appropriate behaviour and manners are believed to create harmony and effective social functioning when they are correctly cultivated. There is an implicit assumption that what is good for a group will also be good for the self. Ideas of individual 'rights' in such a context will clearly differ from those in America. Self-definitions in China are often less individualistic and more expressive of a role in relation to others than is the case for Euro-Americans."

"In business dealings," Jim went on, "and even in close friendship, the Chinese show a phenomenon often described as 'face'. A Chinese friend will be cautious about sharing personal feelings until a respectful intimacy has been established. This is not so much a matter of risking a loss of esteem in self's or another's eyes but rather part of an overall need not to stand out distinctively from the norm of a group. Chinese in business interactions will tend to protect each other's face as well as their own. Negotiations are cautious, filled in with invitations to social events, involve extensive behind the scenes discussions with superiors and take a long time. In politics and administration, Chinese mistakes often arise through the covering over of the errors of others. Excessive confidence rather than caution is unlikely to be a root of political mistakes. Again, in another East Asian country, Korea, there is a marked emphasis on what we may call 'we-ness' expressing a sense of corporate or communal intimacy, mutual comfort or acceptance. Members of a group are felt to embody some fundamental feeling of relationship rather than as being a simple collection of individuals."

"You know," continued Jim, "even greater differences from the Euro-American norms become visible when we consider societies, commonly tribal in nature, in Africa or Papua for example. In Africa there are many contrasting groups of people living under conditions as varied as the dry savannah of the Bushmen or the dense forests of the Pygmies. Research will doubtless show contrasts in self-processes between such varying groups. Some generalisations have already been made. Africans in their traditional worlds are said to have little conception of a person separate from community. Community and person are so closely related that in a legal conflict in Lower Congo senior members of the matrilineage will argue for the defendant yet it is the clan as a whole that wins or loses a case. Jurally all members of the group are equal so far as an outsider's opinion is concerned and no one therefore has an individual identity so far as such legal matters are concerned. Differences between individuals are identified in terms of hierarchical ranking within the group. The self as experience is without the boundaries a Western world person would conceive but rather extends through the group and back into the ancestral realm.

"Membership of an African community may depend on the presence of certain individual characteristics based in position in society. Parent-hood is often a vital necessity because an individual who is not reproductive is not connected to the past or future and therefore not a 'member' of the group. Personhood is conferred as a result of participation in the collective world. Anthropologist La Fontaine has noted that not every individual is fully a person, or even a person at all, in societies that define human beings by their place in a social chain linking past with present.[4] Such a manner of perceiving self may have close connections to the kinship system but this does not seem to have been investigated as yet."

"Another common feature in such worlds is a failure to distinguish clearly between the spiritual and the material, the mind and body," contributed the Buddha. "Communal feeling may extend even to dead ancestors who are perceived as playing active parts in the life of the group and to whom various obligations are due. Good ancestors act to sustain group integrity while bad ones tend to cause dissension. Ancestors are felt to play a role in the maintenance of communal welfare. The person exists within a world of spirits. In the Congo, tribal people may take care not to step on someone's shadow or have their own stepped upon. Personal power is lost to the other under such circumstances. Parts of the body may also participate in selfhood so that injury to a limb or other organ is also damaging to the personality. The spirituality of a person may extend beyond the apparent self."

"Yes, indeed that may seem to be the case," said Jim. "For example, the divinities or 'totems' of Dinka tribes of the Sudan are inherited from ancestral fathers and considered to be spiritual beings, living members of a tribe. While tribal individuals are in some settings distinct persons, in others they are seen collectively as participants in the manifestation of an ancestral spirit. Invocations in ritual invoke this quality. When engaged in sacrificing, the tribal spirit possesses the individual Dinka. The possessed may run around in a staggering manner or verbalise in glossolalia but otherwise they appear sunk into themselves, eyes unseeing, muscles twitching. At such times they are said to be 'not themselves' but rather the divinity itself. As anthropologist Lienhardt remarks, "The individual I, both public and private, is temporally submitted to and replaced by the clan 'we'."[5]

"I think we can overdo that argument," said the Buddha. "Africans must also be aware of individual idiosyncrasies that are described in folk tales and appear in self-expression, for example in dance."

"Well," said Jim, "Lienhardt argues that although degrees of individuality are indeed appreciated, the self of a person is traditionally seen as hidden or undiscoverable. In the Congo the root of being is seen as a sort of undifferentiated awareness upon which the discourse of relationships is superimposed – like writing on blank paper. Being is not alive until named, just as a written page acquires meaning from the words.[6] The self of a person is ultimately elusive and this is perhaps related to the fact that self and body are not as precisely distinguished as is the case in Europe or America. Perhaps we may suggest that the notions characterising a person in a society are closely linked to the structure of authority and kinship as well as to the way in which spirituality, the ancestor, say, is conceived in its economic functioning. Above all, self-understanding and self-conceptualisation arise within the social representations by which an individual's world is constructed.[7] These comparative researches need extensive development but enough is now known to demonstrate that world civilisations support people whose sense of self and its expression can show marked differences. An understanding of these contrasts is of vital importance in the context of global politics today."

"An understanding rarely shown in western politics, I am afraid," added the Buddha.

SELF IN SOCIETY

"So, how do psychologists think of the self in modern society?" Asked the Buddha.

Jim leaned back in his chair after an evening meal that well rewarded their walk through the woods. "Modern psychological theories of self emphasise the close connection between the concepts by which person-hood is created and the social environment," he replied. "Self and culture are viewed as each participating in the other. The first, and one of the foremost, theoretical interpretations, comes from the work of George Herbert Mead who worked at a time when most of psychology was sunk in behaviourist reductionism and rejected concepts seeking an under-standing of self or consciousness. Mead was interested in the means whereby self-conceptualisation could have evolved and he anchored his theory in the signalling behaviour of animals using gesture. He argued that animal signals functioned as stimuli for eliciting appropriate behaviour in social situations. Such gestures are 'signs' indicating an individual's intention to behave in a certain way, aggressively, sexually or whatever. The respondent reacts innately to such signals in a manner that is adapted to the other's behaviour in ensuring survival or reproductive success. A threat signal may lead to an avoidant response, for example. Such interactions are however not conscious in the human sense. Mead did not suppose animals to be aware of self.

"Mead thought that the perception of other selves emerged from a more basic understanding of objects. The appearance of an object in its context is 'read' through the interpretation of past occasions in which it appeared. Persons likewise interpret the social world through recalling the meanings of gestures operating in the field of social relations. Awareness of self, Mead argued, requires understanding the meaning of another's intention as if one was oneself performing it. One interprets the meaning of one's own behaviour through understanding the meaning of another's action in making the same movements. According to Mead therefore it is the 'introjection' of another's intention that allows a comprehension of the meaning of one's own social behaviour and hence of the self performing it."

"Hm, how complicated!" observed the Buddha.

"I'm afraid so!" Jim went on," Once the capacity for this reading of signs is established, Mead argued, visual or verbal gestures become symbolic of mutual understandings between persons. Symbols are no longer mere signs. Abstract percepts, such as a phoneme in language or a written set of letters, can symbolise complex psychological states or intentions. Words in languages come to indicate contrasts in time, past or present, location here or there, and the various tenses in the conjugation of verbs comprise an imperative mode, subjunctive possibility or conditionality. An understanding of symbols requires participation in conventional norms mutually learnt or agreed upon within a culture. Indeed this is what culture is."

"Vocal stimulation must be of an especial importance here," added the Buddha. "In addition to the one spoken to, the speaker can hear his or her own utterance. Communication involves not only responding to one another's talk but also the monitoring of what oneself has said. The same is true of emotional sounds whether linguistic tones or simply moans, shrieks or shouts. Vocalisation allows one to overhear one's own thought and, if there are doubts, two internal voices can dispute together either aloud or in the head as thought. In this way self-awareness arises in the taking of roles initially defined through observing others' behaviours."

"This has further implications," said Jim. "An individual can now engage with himself internally through observing his own thoughts just as two separate individuals can experience each other's words. Within such an internalised conversation one can modify a future course of actions without others knowing. Within each person there is an internal social world that is private and does not have to be expressed to another. The operations of this internal world give the person a degree of independence from the external, social realm in which she is situated. The person is not a passive respondent to the social world but a reflective one. Responses can be determined in thought prior to any action. Such a capacity of course also allows for deviousness and indeed deceit.

"Taking his cue from William James,[9] Mead distinguishes between two aspects of the self, the 'I' and the 'me'. The 'I' is the basic motivation arising as a desire, while the 'me' is the socialised self, which incorporates norms derived from observations of others. As Mead put it, the 'I' propels action while the 'me' directs it. The 'I' may innovate while the 'me' controls. The mutuality of individual and society is regulated by the interaction of these two aspects of self."

The Buddha was leaning forward reflectively. "Yet the very fact that the mind derives its understanding of the world though internalising it, raises the question as to whether a mind can perceive 'reality' or merely its own representation of it, which may be to varying degrees erroneous. Jesting Pilate's question "What is truth?" has a basis in our psychological ambiguity."

"Social psychologists, Peter Berger and Thomas Luckmann, have investigated this issue in depth."[10] Jim responded. "They argue that consciousness is always intentional, it has an object. Objects arise in differing contexts, not only in the outer world but also the inner. Imagination, poetry and dreaming present objects to the mind in very different modes. Such contrasting forms of experience create differing realities and the relations between them may often be far from clear. Dreaming about someone may have a different meaning from actually meeting her, yet the two versions are likely to have connections that are open to interpretations biased by other factors; past childhood experiences, effects of drugs, the ambience of an occasion. Multiple meanings create multiple realities and the mind may be said to objectivise the subjective while also subjectivising the objective."

"That's nicely put!" smiled the Buddha.

"The title of their book," continued Jim, " '*The Social Construction of Reality*', emphasises how the everyday world presents itself as a realm of interpretable objects that seem solid, present and appearing in ways considered normal. Social structure gives me a world in which I can create a self that is related to apparent regularities that exist outside me. Yet institutional realities established by convention, such as the rules of a dining club, the imposed moralities or prejudices of religion, differ from physical objects in that they are based only in social usage. Their reality, although collective, is subjective. One cannot find a dining club rule sitting at the table where it is none the less expressed.

"Berger and Luckmann emphasise that human beings 'reify' aspects of the conventional world, viewing accepted social standards as if they had the status of physical things – as if they were touchable objects or cosmic laws, rather than being simply agreements about conduct and the interpretations of affairs. Reification implies that we are capable of forgetting our own authorship of the human world. Our engagement in dialectic between our purely mental products and ourselves is lost to consciousness when a thought is made into a thing. The reified world risks loosing its humanity when we reify ideas about society as if they exist outside ourselves: operating with controlling force instead of being known as the products of a personal and social process."

"It's a compelling argument with great import," the Buddha contributed. "Reification is a consequence of treating aspects of social convention as if they were really existing objects. Human beings then see themselves as products of this reified order rather than being its creator. Such thinking objectifies the social world as a fixity in which we deny ourselves our intrinsic freedom. We invent Gods and then allow our characterisation of them to order us about."

"Unfortunately reification occurs not only in everyday thinking but also in theory construction," added Jim. "Theological or philosophical ideas may be given the force of external truths that constrict the mind within merely mentally created channels. Reification is especially strong in religious or political thought where concepts that yield an illusion of security, or suggest a transcendental reality that can be experienced after death, may gain great power. Such assumptions can then be coupled to obligatory moral codes imposing norms whereby the powerful, priesthoods or presidents, can exercise control. Berger and Luckmann argue that personal understanding of the process of reification and the entrapment it can entail is relatively rare and requires a 'de-reification' of the mind. They argue that such a capacity is a late development both in history and in individual lives. Even so it is at least 2500 years old. The Buddha's message concerned itself precisely with the de-reification of concepts, did it not?"

"Completely so!" murmured the Buddha. "It is the only way to freedom!"

EXPERIMENTS ON THE EXPERIENCE OF SELF

The Buddha and Jim were sitting by a mossy bank in a beech wood glade near a murmuring stream. They had sat there in meditation for an hour in the dappling sunlight. Refreshed, they began opening their packages of sandwiches for lunch.

The Buddha returned to their topic of discussion. "You know, what we have been discussing remains very much in the realm of theory, an advocacy of a particular, sociological view of the human condition. Although these ideas express insightful understanding of human life, they are not experimentally based and subject to empirical testing. Do you know of some experimental studies that can add flesh to these suggestions?"

"Yes indeed," replied Jim. "Psychologists have extended such perspectives with experimental examinations of testable hypotheses. Lets look at what they have to say. Psychologists Duval and Wicklund,[11] for example, argue that the self operates in either one of two modes of awareness they term subjective and objective self-consciousness – terms they derive from William James notions of 'I' and 'me'. They have designed experimental situations to demonstrate these distinctions. 'Objective self-consciousness' or 'me' is present, they tell us, when one's attention is focussed upon one's own body, person or mind as if it were an object. One's self is then the focus of attention and this usually involves explicit or implicit comparison with others. By contrast, when one's attention is directed away from self, at others, the scenery, the passing of time, then the subject, 'I', is the source, not the object, of the attention – so called 'subjective self-consciousness', an awareness looking out from rather than at the self. Duval and Wicklund argue that these two modes are exclusive. One cannot be simultaneously in both modes. It is either the one or the other. They say that when a person's attention is directed towards a consideration of his personal virtues, it is impossible at the same time to focus attention towards driving nails into a board.

"The 'me', that is Objective self-consciousness, operates comparatively. One compares oneself continuously with others using a set of culturally established standards. In this way, we attempt to regulate our self-esteem and a sense of well-being. We live in a world where standards of social correctness commonly demand compliance. Our deviations from 'normality' lead us to bring ourselves back into conformity with socially accepted conduct. One has previously learnt what is approved socially and what is not and these values have become internalised as ratings on scales of self-approval. When one's attention is drawn to oneself, a momentary evaluation of one's personal desirability begins, the measure of it being derived from the views of others whose approval is desired. The process occurs along a multiplicity of dimensions created within the culture of which one is a member."

"OK, but where's the experiment?" interrupted the Buddha.

Jim nodded, "Here it comes! It is unlikely that all one's covert comparisons with others will support one's self-esteem so Duval and Wicklund suggested that sustained focus on 'me' becomes uncomfortable. They based their experimentation on seeing whether this was actually so. In contrived situations where there is a discrepancy between an ideal and one's actual, perceived state, a painful feeling is commonly experienced. When an individual is so self concerned that he continuously evaluates 'me' on one dimension after another, he will inevitably discover inadequacies that promote anxiety or concern and prefer to revert to an awareness looking out on the world without self-reference.

"The condition that gives rise to a 'me' or an 'I' is the presence or absence of stimuli in the environment that call for attention to self. The experimenters therefore arranged tests in which subjects were exposed to these differing conditions. Even the presence of a mirror during the performance of a task can induce anxieties without the person understanding the source. By manipulating experimental subjects into differing degrees of objective self-awareness, the experimenters showed that the lack of comfort had a number of consequences. Someone in a group expressing opinions opposed to those of the group often seeks to adjust his 'error' even when he is correct in his opinion. In a small group where an individual has no way of determining correctness, he will tend to adopt the opinion of the group willy nilly. Some startling experiments have shown that the norms of an experimental group may influence a test subject towards actions he would normally not even contemplate, even committing acts of cruelty of a potentially criminal nature of which he would not normally dream."[12]

After a bite at his sandwich, Jim continued. "Surprising as it may seem, when people are interacting socially, they are usually rating themselves unconsciously on scales of relative superiority or inferiority. They base their evaluations on ratings such as attractive or not, intelligent or not, deserving or not, class origins, race etc. Such dimensions have widespread influence in human life. One quite normally experiences oneself as subtly one-up or one-down in relation to another. People judge themselves according to whether they feel themselves to be in control of a social situation or not.

"Some psychologists argue that people respond to social situations in ways that may be either 'externalist' or 'internalist' with respect to their so called 'locus of control.'[13] An 'externalist' is a 'me' focussed person most of the time and feels judged and controlled by others. Her locus of control lies outside herself. Such a condition leads to lack of confidence, a feeling of being unwanted, unattractive or inadequate. The 'internalist', by contrast, shows a purposeful focus, involvement and commitment to an 'I' based activity irrespective of the views of others. The release from ego-concern creates for such a person a basis for a sense of fulfilment unattainable through the worried introspective discriminations of objective self-awareness. If you can just "be yourself" in social situations you will generally feel socially comfortable. Not surprisingly such common advice has experimental confirmations!"

"I'm glad to hear it! Yet these experiments seem to differ from Mead's ideas in an important respect," the Buddha pointed out. "As we have seen, Mead saw 'taking the role of another' as the psychological basis from which an individual's self originates. What you are now saying suggests that individuals are not necessarily dependent on the views of others but may construct self-awareness out of their own initiatives towards others. Indeed, research on the development of infants shows that from the very beginning young children set up transactions with mother. A young child's sense of self arises from these interactions, which may generate both 'I' and 'me'."

"Yes, that's a valid point," Jim agreed. "Furthermore, I must tell you that the subjective component of self awareness, when we are focussed outwards from the 'I', has a number of implications that will delight you. Psychologist Mihaly Csikszentmihaly[14] noted that involvement in games and in certain types of highly absorbing activity in work result in enjoyment and a positive evaluation of the self. These are the conditions, you recall, that Duval and Wicklund called "subjective self consciousness". Such conditions appear to be important components of happiness. How do they arise?

"Certain sports that provide their practitioners with rich enjoyment have not been easy to understand. Why rock climbers should climb or mountaineers struggle to the peaks of dangerous mountains, sometimes engaging with a very real possibility of death, is a classic question. Climbers report that it is not so much the ascent of a peak that is important but the activity in itself. In research with people as diverse as chess players, rock dancers, and surgeons, Csikszentmihalyi found much the same principle at work; the activities themselves were self-fulfilling. Rewards came from the doing them rather than from an particular achievement and were described again and again in terms of creative discovery, exploration, testing of competence though praxis, competitive matching of skills against others, or against a rock face or in working through a surgical problem. The need for total attention in such pursuits gives rise to a strange joy that is perhaps the most characteristic feature of such engagement."

" Did he not call that 'flow'?" asked the Buddha. "There is much that excites me here."

Jim went on, "You are right. This work is of especial interest to Buddhists. Perhaps the clearest sign of flow is the merging of action and awareness. The person in flow has no dualistic perspective: he is aware of his actions but not of himself. Based on extensive interviews, Csikszentmihaly found that if a skilled person believes a task is too demanding on his capabilities the resulting anxiety precludes flow. Conversely, when a task is too easy, opportunities for boredom arise followed by anxiety stemming perhaps from a need for a more demanding and hence more rewarding performance.

"He describes modes of action in which total involvement excludes self-judgement and in which the end, purpose or meaning lies in the action itself. Wherever such total involvement in a skill develops, the 'flow' experience may arise. I myself remember states of flow in highly competitive rugby matches at school where, for the duration of a hard fought game, there was an almost trance like state of absorption in which toleration of exhaustion was a prime feature. Such states also arise in combat in warfare, as in an infantry platoon in attack. Soldiers in WW2 who were dropped behind enemy lines to join resistance forces have often reported these days of extreme danger as the most fulfilling moments in their lives. Adjustment to normal life was sometimes difficult for them once the war ended."

The Buddha interrupted, "So you are telling me that the main features of flow which differ from everyday life include one-pointedness of mind, absorption in the timeless moment, integration of body and mind, sharing with companions, oneness with nature and a sense of contact with an ultimate reality. I believe this has been called 'deep play'! It seems that such states resemble spontaneous experiences accessible through certain religious practices and which have been discussed throughout the history of Buddhist meditation."

"I am sure you are right," said Jim. Csikzentmihalyi also investigated less extreme experiences that occur more commonly in everyday life. These he called 'microflow'. Daydreaming, talking to oneself, to plants or pets, humming or singing, watching events, hearing radio, smoking, walking or jogging, dining out or sex could give rise to similar but less intense experiences of satisfaction. In experiments in which such activities were suppressed, individuals described themselves as tense or irritable, listless, defensive, unfriendly and lacking in energy or purpose. Where the activities are solitary rather than social, the subjects rate themselves more positively, perhaps because of an absence of associated self-awareness in company. These findings suggest that 'idling' may be an important means of balancing forms of awareness in daily life. The meaningfulness of life may be related to achieving such a balance and Csikszentmihaly is of the opinion that excessive, implicitly competitive, interaction inducing too much self-awareness, as for example in the business world, may be related to the prevalence of depression and escapism in Western society. Alienation may be due to the absence of a sense of intrinsic reward in life's activities in the modern world."

"I am thinking," said the Buddha, "that the significance of the two contrasting modes of experience which we have been discussing, whether we call them 'I' and 'me', objective and subjective, internalist or externalist, or action versus receptive, has very wide implications. They may be anchored in the contrasting functions of the cerebral hemispheres, the left being concerned with logical analysis, language, speech, symbolic thought while the right is concerned with spatial organisation, synthesis, image management, music and so on. A person experiences social life through positioning herself in relation to these modes. The distinction between them may be especially important because of its relation to the moods associated with self-appraisal. Ego concern, if too intense, can become destructive, depressive, while ego release leads to focussed awareness, bare attention, openness and flow. Many Buddhist practices aim to achieve exactly this."

" I thought you would say so," said Jim gathering up the sandwich papers. The evening was growing cool as they strolled back to the little hotel.

THE SUFFERING SELF

Jim and the Buddha had seen that in the emergence of a mature self the mind seeks to balance differing modes of experience, modes that may be opposed to one another and which may thereby produce emotional stress or discord. We now know that suffering is by no means a simple reaction to physical pain nor to a sudden trauma, although both may be involved in distress, but caused particularly by re-emergent, habitual attitudes towards events, especially social events, that originate in the earliest days and months of life and which persist as hidden determinants of experience and motivation into adult life. Suffering is intimately conditioned by the process whereby an infant succeeds or fails to emerge from parental care as a person in his or her own right. Such unconscious factors determine for example whether one tends habitually towards an 'I' or a 'me' perspective on social events. It has been said that deep suffering is always a result of distorted love. Such a view squares very well with the Buddha's approach to suffering as a consequence of 'ignorance'.

After dinner that night, the two of them took up the problem of the causation of habitual suffering. The Western literature that deals with the origins and cure of mental ill health is necessarily a part of social psychology. They were not discussing here mental suffering that is the result of biological causation, defects of the brain, neurology or endocrine activity for which modern medication is often an effective response, but, rather, with suffering that, originating in the earliest mother-infant interactions, has an essentially social causation. Not only is the self a social product but the suffering a self may experience also has a social origin.

During coffee, Jim was saying, "We have to start here with one of the greatest doctors of mental life. Sigmund Freud was the pioneering explorer who sought to understand mental suffering through an approach that started in biology but became increasingly social as his understanding developed. Freud's approach, psychoanalysis, became the basis for a treatment that is itself social; a search for understanding between analyst and patient in which the analyst plays an interpretive role. Since Freud, many differing modes of interpersonal and group action have developed to aid those suffering from mental distress. While many are derived from the concepts of psychoanalysis, some, while sharing a common origin, take a very different line. This field as a whole has been called 'Psychodynamics' and includes a range of psychotherapeutic theories and methods. We cannot discuss them all, and some indeed are pretty wild. Lets stick to the main themes."

"I have heard that these approaches have often been criticised as being unscientific and indeed the experimental methods characteristic of physics or chemistry and common in biology are not applied here," commented the Buddha. "The material for psychodynamic enquiry is the narrative through which a patient or client describes himself and his dilemmas. The roots of these personal stories are however hidden and a prime task of a therapist is to uncover the hidden origins, a process known as 'the recovery of the repressed', and to share these findings in such a way that the patient can accept them and return to health. Even before Freud, it was realised that much of the rationale behind a persons' attitude was 'unconscious'. Here are themes, unknown to the person, that motivate attitudes to events in adult life and, so long as these are not understood or worked through, happier states of mind are unlikely to arise."

"Indeed the approach here is very different from more standard scientific enquiry," added Jim. "It is participatory through and through. Working with clients is a very intimate process and a therapist requires extensive training to resist falling for the many ploys and emotional demands that a client can transfer onto him or her. The work is tentative, not a matter of delivering opinions, but a mutual exploration of origins and the way they determine a client's distress. It is very much a process of decoding the client's secret life, so secret she does not know it herself. As such it can be called 'hermeneutic' resembling the decoding of ancient texts rather than being objective in the usual scientific sense. The personality of the therapist plays a major role both in interpretation and in the outcome. Indeed, as psychotherapist Lavonia Gomez makes clear in her description of the theories of master analysts in the 'object relations' tradition, a therapist's theory is often very clearly influenced by who he or she is - as much as by their work with clients."[15]

After a sip from his cup, Jim continued. "In spite of the highly subjective nature of the process, a body of opinion has developed that has considerable consistency. The patterns underlying mental distress are

quite largely understood and the relations between client and therapist
that tend towards success are increasingly well known. This is then a body
of knowledge that provides valuable if tentative explanations of human
life and which is just as worthy of respect as other more experimental or
'objective' methods. As is perhaps inevitable, however, the whole tradition
is a product of Western culture and its value for people in other cultures
remains open to exploration."

At this point, a young lady at the adjacent table surprisingly interrupted
them. "Do excuse me!" she said with considerable charm, "I cannot help
overhearing what you have been discussing and it intrigues me. You see,
I am a psychotherapist working in a Southampton practice myself."

"Well then," said the Buddha, "you must certainly come and join us.
Waiter! Do bring us some more coffee – or would you prefer some tea?"

"Coffee will do fine," she replied, moving her chair to join them. "I
hope you don't mind my interrupting. My name is Eleanor."

"Not at all," said Jim. "If I may put it this way – now we can hear something
from the horse's mouth. Can you outline for us some of the history of
psychotherapy?"

"I'll give it a go," said the young therapist, "but first lets sit more
comfortably in the lounge."

"The mainstream of thought in psychodynamics is known as 'object
relations'," Eleanor began. "The word 'object' here means a social theme
appearing in the inner world of the self, which produces habitual
orientations to others in the 'real' world. Although Freud did not use this
term, his thoughts started the ball rolling."

"I understand," said the Buddha, "that Sigmund Freud (1856-1939),
together with Karl Marx, Albert Einstein and Charles Darwin, has been a
great originator of grand ideas that became a major preoccupation in
Western culture in the twentieth century. Indeed Western culture can be
described as essentially Einsteinian, Freudian and Darwinian in many of
its key concerns while Marx is still important in political theory."

"Indeed," said Eleanor, "these cultural patterns distinguish the Western
world from other contemporary cultures in India, China or the Islamic
world where they are less a focus of interest if indeed understood at all. In
the West, these themes provide a basis for contemporary humanism and a
counterpoint to Christianity. Their opposition to orthodox religion
accounts in large measure for the schizoid, intellectual patterns so vivid
in the West today."

"Freud has of course been criticised," she went on, "and more than
that, rejected, rebutted and generally mauled, yet his key concepts,

sometimes restated or used in ways that differ from his own orientation, remain a part of every educated person's vocabulary and the basis of theory and practice within the mass industry of mental health. The relations between the *id* and the ego, the oral, anal and phallic states of development, the Oedipus conflict, transference and counter transference remain at the root of much psychodynamic discussion.

"Freud believed mental life began at birth through the expression of biological drives of an innate nature. Only gradually did the need to relate to others socially begin to play a role in personal development. These innate drives were unconstrained demands for satisfaction in relation to the nutritional, eliminative and sexual urges of the baby. Often hotly disputed, these ideas perhaps gain more support today as a result of the work of Evolutionary Psychologists emphasising genetic origins. However, Freud's own ideas in his later work together with their development by object relations theorists stress biological origins much less. The emerging relationship between self and significant others in the mind of the developing child has moved to the forefront of attention in theory, where it indeed remains."[16]

"Lets see if I understood Freud's' fundamental terms rightly," requested Jim. "The *Id* refers to a world of innate urges and the concept has some resemblance to the 'I' of Mead's formulation. It lies at the foundation of experience. The 'Ego' arises in the mental work whereby the baby attunes to the behaviour of carers who are by no means in the business of satisfying its every whim. The ego embodies a 'reality principle' whereby the infant begins to comprehend its immediate world of rewards and rejections and to adjust to it. The 'super-ego' is the world of others' ideas that the infant has to take on in order to become a social being in conformity with the expectations of society. In Freudian thought much of this comes through the father."

"You've got it," Eleanor confirmed. "The so-called oral and anal stages arise from a struggle between the babies innate feeding and eliminative demands and the wishes of the carer. When the experience of this struggle involves too much rejection, punishment or too little discipline, the infant suppresses its pain in denial and may repress it completely. Such repressed material does not however disappear. It remains in the 'unconscious' as a dynamic root of subsequent distortions in attempts to relate with others. The 'unconscious' is thus a world of hidden forces, a mental reality but one unknown to the growing child. The 'Oedipus conflict' in the boy marks the emergence of sexual orientation towards the mother and a realisation of father's overbearing role in this regard. Of course, none of this is objectively understood, it operates in a world of mental shadows, suppression and repressions. Eventually the child incorporates the father's behaviour, but with residual, repressed resentments. The young person may remain deeply split and antagonistic to any authority.

"Such experiences in childhood, Freud argued, become the hidden roots of distorted projections onto to significant adults as the child grows up. Since we all suffer through this developmental process, everyone is to some extent affected. We all endure suffering of this origin but most of us come though without too much distortion. When painfully unadjusted to reality, an individual may seek the aid of a psychoanalyst. Freud's method was to listen closely to what the analysand said and then interpret it in such a way that the patient could recover the repressed material and incorporate it in an understanding that allowed a less distressed relationship with the world of others. Understanding one's self, in this view, does the trick."

"Sounds like an admirable procedure," commented the Buddha.

"Yes, but there are problems," continued Eleanor. "One of Freud's discoveries was that the patient would project onto the analyst the very distortions he or she had acquired in a painful development – as if the analyst was himself the father or mother of the ancient story. Furthermore, this 'transference' could lead the unwary analyst into a 'counter-transference' projecting his own hidden themes onto the patient. Out of careful consideration of such themes with a range of people, including much self-analysis, the analyst may develop considerable skill in assisting a patient towards recovery. The work may however take years and is by no means necessarily successful. Much of the search for better forms of therapy has involved attempts at methods that work more speedily."

'That brings us to Klein, I imagine," said Jim.

"Indeed so. Melanie Klein (1882-1960) herself had a tragic life that undoubtedly accounts for the dark tone of much of her interpretation of mental illness. Her work focussed directly on very young children. Whereas Freud inferred the child in the adult from therapy with adults, Klien observed the child mind of infants themselves. Kleinian theory emphasises subjective experience and its meanings rather than biological origins in the development of mental structure. In particular she saw how infants related at first not so much to a carer as a whole person but rather to 'part objects', breasts, penises etc, and her descriptions are often very colourful utilising the vocabulary of young children to illustrate her discoveries. Klein developed a method of observing the play of children whereby she could observe their preoccupations directly."

"As I recall it," Jim contributed, "Klein saw mental life developing around oppositions between rewarding and unrewarding experiences with the same 'part object'. In particular, she saw the opposition between the 'good breast', that is a fruitful one, and the 'bad breast', a denying one, as fundamental to the growing relationship with mother and a key focus of early discrimination. Unlike Freud, however, she saw early conflicts rooted in anxiety arising from the stresses generated by these oppositions rather than in the frustration of early sexuality. She saw children as splitting their mental worlds between 'good ' and 'bad' in an extreme way. The fairy godmother and the wicked witch inhabit virtually distinct mental universes. In order to trust and love, the bad aspect of life has to be split off, yet it remains potent, present in the unconscious. The problem then is that when the 'bad' is unavoidably re-experienced, the child faces an undiluted negativity of its unreconstructed projection upon another. To Klein, the oral phase of Freud becomes the 'paranoid-schizoid position', a self-persecutory split, to which, in later life, serious regression may occur."

"Yes, that can be very tragic," said Eleanor. "In normal development a child gradually realises that 'mother' expresses herself as a whole. There actually are no two positions because mother turns out to be both good and bad. According to Klein, this emerging understanding leads to a 'depressive position' wherein the child seeks to come to terms with the problematic and opposed themes in its mental life. The problems this entails may lead to the many forms of illusion whereby neurosis develops. All individuals go through this process whereby eventually a balanced understanding of self in relation to others hopefully emerges. Maturity, in this view, is the capacity to cope with inevitable depression, ambivalence, sadness and guilt.

"Klein's approach emphasises the emergence of fantasy as the field of 'object relations' within which development occurs. Psychological health lies in the extent to which we develop a capacity to see beyond the projections of good and bad and to appreciate the balance between them that is social reality. Ill health returns when a relapse into the paranoid-schizoid position occurs. In adult life, events can easily produce such a relapse and any ultimate security from inner torment is not easily achieved.

"From these beginnings, later Object Relations practitioners and theorists focussed on particular aspects of mental life and provided yet further interpretations. Ronald Fairbairn believed that the child is mentally undivided at birth but that early experience creates a schizoid state. The baby translates occasional and inevitable incidents of carer indifference into feelings of abandonment that become unbearable. The only way that the baby can sustain the relationship, Fairbairn argues, is to hive off the painful experience as a repressed inner state. Whenever this experience emerges from repression, feelings of dependency coupled with intolerable yearnings arise. The repressed image of the carer is seen as rejecting – thereby giving rise to resentment. The ensuing anger is then split off and disowned as dangerous and it becomes a hidden source of both hostility and guilt."[17]

"Complicated!" said the Buddha.

"Indeed so," continued Eleanor, "One realisation derived from Fairbairn's work is Donald Winnicot's concern with the significance of what he called 'transitional objects'. He meant devices or ideas that help the child bridge the gap between it's wants and its disappointments.[18] The best-known example is the teddy bear. Teddy is always good even when Mummy is bad! Teddy is a receiver of projection, usually of the good aspects of the ideal object. Relating to Teddy becomes a source of transitional security whereby the difficulties with the bad can become managed as the self gradually matures. In most cases, Teddy is eventually left in a cupboard and is no longer needed.

"Sometimes, however, the issue becomes far more complex as when various ways of behaving, thought systems or philosophies, become transitional in a similar way but are then mistakenly taken to be solutions to life's problems – so that maturity fails to emerge. Conversion to a religious or philosophical view may be one example. The selfless communist, Christian or fascist fundamentalist locked onto a 'transitional' belief becomes unable to relate to actual persons as a mature adult. Such a person may then do either a lot of generalised good or sometimes great evil. On achieving political power yet stuck in believing a viewpoint to be the ultimate good, such a person in tragic delusion may defend it with indifference to cruelty and barbarism, the hallmarks of 19th century idealisms, whether of the left or right, and from which we are not yet free.

"Michael Balint's concept of the 'basic fault' sums up a prevailing perspective in these various analyses[19] "As we have seen, in all these theories birth is perceived as the beginning of a process of psychological disruption whereby an untrammelled state of union with mother is broken. As the baby experiences the ambivalence present in all relating, so a splitting process develops whereby the psychological pain of acute anxiety is repressed in complex ways. Such repression, Balint argues, constitutes a 'basic fault' in human nature When this is boosted by actual abuse or negligence on the part of mother or significant others then the repression involved becomes malignant, rather than relatively benign. It has the potential to erupt destructively in adult life. Balint's term is derived not only from 'fault' as in 'mistake' but more generally from the notion of a geological 'fault' lying undetected beneath a peaceful landscape until it moves. Psychological earthquakes may likewise be extraordinarily and surprisingly destructive."

"It seems that many of the oddities of adult human behaviour arise from the 'defences' we develop to offset the potency of the basic fault." said the Buddha. "What has occurred here is a breakdown in fundamental trust. Other people are dangerous! This is not something that troubles only a few of us. It is almost certainly common to all members of our species although the manner of its expression in cultures other than the Western world is as yet barely understood."

Eleanor agreed. "Balint views the therapeutic relationship as an adventure in trusting. When the earth moves people often seek psychotherapeutic help. The experience may be little more than a sense of alienation, worthlessness, or simply a not knowing of oneself. There may be repeated tendencies to wreck relationships through increasingly predictable but neurotic behaviour. The feelings expressed are actually the surface appearances of defences against internal splits. Through seeking to understand such defences in the company of the therapist the client takes a risk in facing powerful negative feelings that inevitably emerge"

"Indeed such work demands a sort of courage," Jim added for he seemed to have some experience of these things. "Letting go of defence is a new beginning. It may occur in brief discoveries, or progressively as a sustained awakening in which the risk is gradually seen to be purely illusory, or at least quite different in nature from what the repression supposed. The outcome is an emergence into self-trust within relating to others, who are now always understood as potentially ambivalent persons - like oneself. What has arisen here is a trust in a self that is independent from others and no longer dependent on the transitional relationship with the therapist."

"You probably know," went on Eleanor, "that the process is often fraught because the client makes numerous demands on the therapist that arise from the neurosis. The therapist has to steer a very delicate course. It is essential not to fall in with demands that stem from the client's illusions. The good therapist continually frustrates the client but in such a way that the client comes to understand his own distorting demands and to perceive the precise role the therapist is playing in the transitional process. Yet, sometimes a client becomes so angry he will abandon therapy. The therapist has then failed. But if the therapist begins to allow appointments at unusual times, or attempts to meet neurotic demands, then he also fails because the client is learning nothing and various kinds of mutual co-dependence may be arising. The skills of a gifted therapist are hard won.

"Balint was quick to point out that therapists who sustain a stance of superiority or remoteness, perhaps as a result of counter-transference, or who allow clients to see them as powerful even saintly healers, are unlikely to be successful. In such work, the therapist needs to keep the hierarchical aspect of the work in a very low key, to be open and trusting within a quietly intimate rapport allowing the client simply to be there in his or her vulnerability. In a setting of unbiased care, broken trust can be repaired. While a personal history cannot be gainsaid, new beginnings can then arise. There is a certain optimism in Balint's perspective for it seems that something like happiness may at last be attained."

"These are all very social theories and practices. Has anyone had a further look at the biological basis for such problems?" asked the Buddha.

This was more in the field of Jim's interest so he took up the point. "The work of John Bowlby indeed returns us to a consideration of biology. He felt that the object relations approach in psychoanalysis was becoming too subjective, too involved with the analysis of fantasy and the decoding of inner experience.[20] He sought ways to return to the integration of biology and psychology inherent in Freud's original work so that psychoanalysis in general could be more open to empirical examination as a contribution to psychological science. He was able to achieve this through an interest in ethology, the zoological study of animal behaviour, which was exploring behavioural development in young birds and primates and developing an extensive experimental literature. The work of Konrad Lorenz on 'imprinting' suggested that many animals were innately primed to fixate on parental figures in attachments that became the basis of social organisation. Research by ethologists Bill Thorpe and Robert Hinde in Cambridge and Harry Harlow in the US offered Bowlby the ideas he needed to create his 'attachment theory' for humans. His approach, leading to experiments with young children and their carers, allowed the emergence of an empirical literature, which, none the less, supports the basic ideas in the interpretive work of object relations theorists to a considerable extent.

"Harlow's pioneering experiments with infant monkeys initiated research that is today finely tuned. He found that young monkeys deprived of the presence of their mothers became so distorted in their behaviour that once adult they could neither mate nor parent young. Distorted mothers raised distorted young. Infants separated from their mothers clung to wire models of caring figures that were covered with cloth and therefore seemingly 'caring', rather than to wire models that only supplied milk. This suggested that Freud and Klein were wrong in suggesting that attachment derived from feeding requirements. Instead, it appeared that the satisfaction of innate needs for maternal support and comfort was essential for emotional maturation; a position supporting the view that babies' behaviour originates in seeking loving care rather than pleasure.

"Bowlby argued that human relationship arises through the expression of behaviour selected naturally in evolution and which appears in an orderly sequence to ensure bonding as the basis for social life. These behaviours interact all the time with environmental conditions to lead to the formation of the self and to relating between adults. Separation from significant others constitutes a crisis whenever it occurs in human life. It leads to processes of mourning similar to distress shown by other primate species. Separation in babyhood has seriously deleterious effects on psychological development in humans too. Mothers also have innately based systems of responding to babies, intense involvement, the speaking of baby talk and sensitive responsiveness to stimuli from the baby."

"Thank you for that," said Eleanor, "Bowlby's work led on to some very interesting experiments with human mothers and babies. Mary Ainsworth, a colleague of Bowlby at the Tavistock Clinic in London, developed the 'strange situation' test as an experimental method to investigate the effects that different styles of mothering had on young children. The approach has been found to be broadly repeatable in a range of cultures. Such work in U.S.A. by Mary Main and Eric Hesse has been especially significant in recent years.

"The test is constructed as follows. Mother, baby and a stranger (to the baby) settle into a playroom equipped with toys. After some minutes, the mother leaves and the infant's behaviour is noted for a set period in the presence of the passive stranger. When the mother returns the response of the infant is recorded. The whole process is videotaped and analysed in great detail. The results portray the baby's orientation to his/her mother that can then be shown to correlate with the mother's preceding behaviour and responsiveness as a carer. Secure infants, although distressed by the mother's departure, demand and receive care from her on her return and then continue to play happily with toys. Less secure infants show avoidance or ambivalence to the returning mother while the most insecure do not appear unduly upset by her departure but ignore her on her return, watching her closely and unable to play at ease. Some showed panic on separation and simultaneously clung to and fought mother when she returned. A fourth group, diagnosed later, was confused and showed chaotic behaviour on mother's return and appeared dissociated.

"These behaviours were shown to correlate with the quality of care shown by the mothers to the babies during their first year. Mothers of secure babies had interacted with them freely and warmly and were accurately empathetic. Insecure-avoidant babies had mothers who behaved rigidly in their caring behaviour while avoidant babies had unresponsive mothers who were unpredictable and insensitive in their caring. The fourth group had disturbed mothers who came from backgrounds characterised by abuse, psychosis or neglect. Bowlby's emphasis on the caring environment has been repeatedly confirmed in such research, which now encompasses a large literature. His lifetime concern with child welfare stems from his academic work and is of great significance in childcare and understanding today."

The Buddha recalled, "John Bowlby also became interested in the whole process of mourning personal loss whether in a child or an adult. When children between the ages of six months and three years are unavoidably separated from mother or primary carer for long periods, their distress develops through three phases. The first is violent distressful 'protest'. A separation longer than a week leads to 'despair' in a withdrawn state with tears or apathy. Even longer separation leads to 'detachment' whereby the infant appears to adjust to loss. However, if the parent now returns the child may fail to respond, remain aloof or even not recognise her. Such cases are heart-rending for those who experience the family situation. Repeated separations are followed by an inability to create relationships. Fostering such children is often accompanied by extreme difficulty. Such children may be angry and destructive."

"Yes," said Eleanor, "and furthermore, Bowlby's work with forty juvenile thieves showed a correlation between delinquency and separations in childhood. In the worst cases, a psychopathic inability to feel or show affection becomes the root of criminal behaviour. Grief has led such children into a defensive repression of all feeling as too painful to experience. Needless to say, therapeutic work with such adolescents can be extremely demanding and success difficult to achieve."

Time was getting on and the effects of coffee wearing off. The Buddha suggested that they convened again after breakfast the following morning.

A POSSIBLE CURE FOR SELF MAY BE?

The Buddha, Jim and Eleanor were strolling in the garden. Eleanor said to the Buddha, "Jim has been telling me that you are interested in the way the ideas we discussed last night might be related to Buddhist thought in ancient times. Have you come to any conclusions?"

"I am certainly amazed at the depth and detail in which these enquiries have been made and at their profound concern with healing mental illness," replied the Buddha. "We have seen together that the psychodynamic approach shows the attainment of a mature self experiencing a degree of happiness in the world to be a process fraught with difficulties. 'Selfing' is a complex developmental process that continues throughout life. The initial causes of difficulty lie in the unavoidably ambivalent behaviour shown by carers to infants who, in comparison with other mammals, are born in a condition necessitating total dependence on the mother. Carers have their own concerns that may not mesh well with the needs of very young children for total support. Children have to come to terms with what to them is an always a less than totally satisfactory love. While it may be 'good enough' in most cases, the work to undo deep and unintentional distortion may go on throughout life. Suffering is indeed a condition inseparable from human life."

Jim added, " Few infant mammals are so dependent on the care of others as are human babies: many species are free-living soon after birth. It is in the context of an unavoidable dependency that carer and cared for have to find a mutuality that works through a balancing of the conflicting needs of both parties. The whole process is a major theme in the sustaining of effective social life in which the rearing of children is the ultimate biological objective."

"You know the Buddha's first Noble Truth stated that 'Life is suffering'," said the Buddha. "It seems as if these modern ideas amply confirm those words of the sage in the Deer Park at Sarnath all those centuries ago. Buddhist models of mind are much simpler than those we have been considering but maybe go to the root of the problem more directly. Yet I think their purpose is slightly different."

"I was once in Kyoto and met a Zen master," interposed Jim. "We discussed psychotherapy and he agreed a number of his monks certainly required it! But I remember something he said especially vividly: 'Zen is total therapy!' He clearly thought that Western methods of healing the mind only went so far. They lacked the radical *coup de grace* he clearly felt Zen could supply."

"Maybe," the Buddha took it up, "that's because psychotherapy is primarily seeking to return a patient or a client to a normal life riddled with tensions that only too easily re-activate all sorts of personal problems. One has to see the interdependence of all this. Society reflects individual development and development occurs within society. If society too is sick, there seems to be little hope for an ultimate solution. Yet suffering is not necessarily sickness. It may simply arise from an error in understanding. Zen confronts the self immediately and leads to an analysis of oneself in the context of emptying the mind through meditation. As the mind repeatedly empties itself of its engrained concerns, someone may discover he is not so bad after all. If a self-acceptance arises, the mind turns to others and that allows happiness to emerge from the shades.

"Yet to say 'Zen is Total therapy' is possibly a little dangerous for beginners. It may set up all sorts of expectations. A Zen practitioner has a lot of preliminary work to do: calming the mind to allow meditative experiences to arise, re-orienting awareness towards deliberate compassion, thinking through a life story. If he or she launches into Buddhist practice without doing these preliminaries, mistakes are easily made. I think the psychodynamic approach would be a valuable preliminary practice for many people. [21] One should not hurry into Buddhism. The seeker has to be prepared."

End Notes

1. Dunbar, R.I.M. 2004. *The Human Story.* Faber and Faber. London. p. 48.

2. Markus, H.R. Mullally, P.R. and S. Kitiyama. 1997. Selfways: diversity in modes of cultural participation. In: *The Conceptual Self in Context.* Neisser, U. and D.A. Jopling (Eds.). Cambridge University Press.

3. Elvin, M. 1985. Between the earth and heaven: conceptions of self in China. In: M. Carrithers, S. Collins & S, Lukes (Eds.). *The Category of the Person: anthropology, philosophy, history.* Cambridge University Press.

4. La Fontaine, J.S. 1985. Person and individual: some anthropological reflections. In M. Carrithers, S. Collins & S. Lukes. (Eds.). *The Category of the Person: anthropology, philosophy, history.* Cambridge University Press.

5. Lienhardt, G. 1985. Self: public, private. Some African representations. In M. Carrithers, S. Collins & S. Lukes. (Eds.). *The Category of the Person: anthropology, philosophy, history.* Cambridge University Press.

6. The complexity of Congolese conceptions of awareness and being are well explored in Barbara Kingsolver's remarkable novel *The Poisonwood Bible.* Faber and Faber. 1999. See especially p. 238.

7. La Fontaine. *loc cit.*

8. James, W. 1890. *The Principles of Psychology.* MacMillan. London.

9. Berger, P. L. and T. Luckmann. 1966. *The Social Construction of Reality.* Penguin.

10. Mead, G.H. 1934. *Mind, Self, and Society.* University of Chicago Press. Chicago.

11. Duval, S. & R.A. Wicklund. 1972. *A Theory of Objective Self-awareness.* Academic Press. New York.

12. Milgram, S. 1974. *Obedience to Authority.* Tavistock. London.

13. Phares, E.J. 1976. *Locus of control in personality.* General Learning Press. New Jersey.

14. Czikszentmihalyi, M. 1975. *Beyond boredom and anxiety: the experience of play in work and games.* Jossey-Bass. San Francisco.

    Czikszentmihalyi, M. & I.S. Czikszentmihaly. 1988. *Optimal experience: psychological studies of flow in consciousness.* Cambridge University Press.

15. Gomez, L. 1997. *An introduction to object relations.* Free Association Books. London.

16. Guntrip, H. 1983. *Schizoid phenomena, object relations and the self.* Hogarth Press. London.

17. Working with these emergent attitudes in therapy is the root of several therapeutic approaches including Eric Berne's (1961) well-known 'transactional analysis'.

18.   Winnicot, D.W. 1988. *Human Nature.* Free Association Books. London. 1990.
        Wininicot, D.W. 1965. *The Maturational process and the Facilitating Environment.*
        Hogarth Press. London.

19.   Balint, M. 1968. *The Basic Fault. Therapeutic aspects of regression.* Tavistock.
        London.

20.   Bowlby, J. 1969 and 1973. *Attachment and Loss.* Vols. 1 and 2. Hogarth. London.

21.   Epstein, M. 1996. *Thoughts without a Thinker.* Psychotherapy from a Buddhist
        perspective. Duckworth. London.

16

SELF, CONSCIOUSNESS
AND CULTURE

What actually is the self? So long as we discuss it in terms of the roles or identities that people adopt in society, we seem to be on firm ground. I am John the writer, you are Esmeralda the lawyer, and she is Bertha the politician. No apparent problem. Are we then the performances of names in role? If so what exactly is this performance and to what is the name attached? Then again, as we saw in the last chapter, we can speak of experiences of self under different conditions, in contrasting cultures, in performing tasks or climbing mountains or perhaps undergoing forms of therapy. We can indeed describe our experiences as manifestations of ourselves. But what exactly is experience? How has it evolved? Why is so much of it an immersion in suffering? Is there such a thing as evil? As we begin to ask the more searching questions, we become aware of paradox.

THE HARD PROBLEM

The Buddha and Jim were back in London but to continue their investigations into Western psychology they thought it would be a good idea to invite Eleanor up for the weekend to continue their discussions together. They met in the Buddha's rather poky rooms in Soho. He had tidied them up carefully, bought some flowers, got in some cakes, food for the evening and fresh fruit juice. After tea, they settled down to talk.

Eleanor posed the problem. "What am I? Am I a biological entity, an experiencing subject, a social role, a name or a narrative, or perhaps all of these? Yet there is one undeniable fact – I normally experience myself as a conscious entity and I am assuming you are one too. At least that is my common sense belief. There would be little point in talking with you if I thought you were unaware of the meaning of words or indeed the experience of reading texts. You don't point out a flying bird to a blind man."

Jim took up the question. "Yet there is no way I can be sure you are conscious. I am making an assumption. You may tell me so, but should I believe you? I watch the sheep dogs rounding up sheep. It's a brilliant performance but is it conscious? And if so, of what? It seems I can never know. Philosopher Thomas Nagel has asked, 'What is it like to be a bat?'[1] One can imagine hanging upside down or flying around squeaking and spotting insects on the wing by sonar but that is only me imagining myself to be a bat. To experience the bat's world as 'the thing in itself' I would have to be a bat. Since that is impossible, I will never really know. In any case, I cannot even know whether the bat actually has a subjective world or *innenwelt* as the German biologist Jacob von Uexküll called it.[2] Maybe my own experience of an apparent world misleads me into supposing other sentient creatures have somewhat similar worlds too. On the other hand, similarities between my brain and that of a collie dog suggests that there may be some experiences more or less in common at least between man and dog. Close parallels between human and ape behaviour suggest the same here too. Jacob von Uexküll (ie a u) believed that a study of sensory mechanisms could go some way to understanding the experience of other animal species. Is he right?"

The Buddha joined in, commenting, "We are running into philosophical problems here. There can be no 'scientific' answers because consciousness itself is not a 'thing' which one can examine or test, rather it is an 'appearance'. It always escapes our grasp and indeed there is no readily accepted definition of it in what I feel to be an increasingly verbose field of 'consciousness studies'. Answers to these questions go beyond the physical. They will necessarily be based in 'metaphysical' assumptions, some of which may be materialist, others spiritualist, with every other possibility in between. While there are a number of approaches that clear the way to a greater understanding of the phenomenon, to actually grasp the nature and meaning of consciousness itself has become more not less problematical as thinkers probe the issue – and probe they certainly do. An understanding of human life may seem to depend on it."

"Yet," said Eleanor, "there are number of questions we can reasonably ask. What are the conditions under which consciousness is present? And what are the conditions when it is not? How far do certain activities seem to require consciousness? What brain regions are active when consciousness is present? – And so on. All such work describes the circumstances and conditions under which consciousness in a human being arises. But what it is and why do we have it – the questions slip from our grasp."

"Philosopher David Chalmers has described the difficulty as the 'Hard Problem', Jim said. "How do the physical processes in the brain give rise to personal experience – the subjective world? The relatively 'easy' problems concern information processing, perception, cognition, the physiology of attention or anxiety, causes of sleep. Most of us would also say that we know what it is like to be conscious but as to how and why we should be so appears to lie beyond us. Why should the brain be conscious at all – it seems it could do all its calculations without that. Indeed the more we seek to describe personal consciousness, the more it seems to recede, becoming something like space – perhaps. Metaphors and poetry loom as the only way of expression."

"The 'hard problem' may seem absurd – after all we just are conscious," rejoined Eleanor, "but it does seem conceivable that human beings could do everything they do totally without consciousness. Consciousness does not seem to have a function; it doesn't seem to do anything! We can account for most of our behaviour and much of our cognitive ability in terms of the functions of brain mechanisms and their evolution. Furthermore, the remaining problems of this nature seem quite open to future research in brain chemistry, neurology, artificial intelligence, robotics and so on – but how and why consciousness arises remains unanswered. Yet, we give accounts of ourselves in terms of experience, consciousness. It is the way we operate."

"Much of the riddle lies in the difference between the verbs 'to have' and 'to be," commented Jim. "I can say I have a brain with certain properties; I have habits; I have a headache; and I have intelligence, sadness or a stomach-ache. Or, indeed, I have consciousness. In such statements the possessor, the observer, myself, is distinguished from the property that I have. I can view the matter 'objectively'. There are two things here – two conceptual fields – dualism as it is called. Descartes, in proposing a complete separation between mind and matter except at one point of contact, the pineal gland, started this ball rolling. Science largely depends upon this way of thinking coupled with mathematical modelling of observed results in experiments or other forms of observation. The world is described through observation in objectivity, the observer in relation to the observed. It is one form of knowledge. The other is 'being' itself. When I say 'I am', what is that?"

The Buddha added. "If I say I am good, bad, happy, fat, alive, dying, such a statement may perhaps be agreed upon by others – yes he is fat – but the 'is ness', the feeling that constitutes being, remains known only to myself. The experience is mine alone; consciousness is private. This is another form of knowledge – direct rather than indirect, a presence rather than a description. As you know, the field of study concerned with this is called Phenomenology. It is full of problems circling around the ultimate paradox of the 'hard problem'."

"The great Victorian psychologist William James was well aware of this problem. His extensive work pivoted upon it in many ways."[3] commented Jim. "On the one hand, consciousness and matter seem to be completely separate, but, on the other hand, the mental is completely dependent upon the physical. James disallowed both the idea that the human being was a mere automaton and the idea that there was some special Cartesian mind stuff interacting with the brain through some special connection. He urged the study of the linkage between physiology and mental life and his work remains deeply influential today.

"The 'automaton' perspective crystallises around the question whether a Zombie could replicate human life. The theoretical Zombie can do everything a human can do but it is not conscious. What would being consciousness add to this? Is subjectivity needed? But if a zombie could do absolutely everything you or I could do then logically we would not be able to infer whether it was conscious or not. Everything it did might look conscious but whether it was indeed having private experiences we could never tell. The problem would then be no different from whether I can ever know for sure that you are conscious."

"Perhaps the problem seems absurdly academic," said Eleanor, "but the advances in computing have created robots with extraordinarily human like behaviour. Rodney Brooks at MIT has created a robot called Cog, which is so built as to be able to learn about its environment and develop some adaptive behaviour. This machine is constructed by embedding devices that connect its perceptions to its actions directly without the need for internal built-in models of the habitat or the construction of representations of the environment. The devices are layered and programme one another progressively, the higher functions based upon the development of the lower. It thus acquires behaviour in much the way a child might. Cog can focus on faces and eyes, attend to a caregiver, follow gestures and give nods of agreement. Such skills enable it to learn from humans around it in a progressive manner, its behaviour arising from the functioning of numerous information processors for perception and movement. In addition, it has feedback sensors that give information on the state of all moveable parts. Currently Cog has no memory, no sense of time and no linguistic ability but Brooks' design allows for the incorporation of more devices that may enable these abilities to develop. If he achieves this, would we expect the machine to be conscious? It would certainly look as if it was. What would we say when Cog starts to talk to us about its feelings? But I am very far from sure that the four or five levels of social intentionality of which humans are capable could be replicated in this way."

Jim took up the point. "Another advanced robot called Kismet is the brainchild of Cynthia Breazel. Unlike Cog, it can take turns in interaction with humans. Kismet is just a head with large eyes, an elementary face, ears with microphones inside and lips. Eyes, ears and lips all move. It runs on fifteen computers using differing operating systems and no one computer is in charge. It can hear and make sounds and has no language but it can respond to pitch patterns of the human voice detecting the differences between approving, forbidding, attention requesting and calming tones. It responds accordingly. It can create facial expressions and make sounds relating to mood. When people are introduced to Kismet, many of them interact with it exactly as if it was a person. They behave as if it was alive and as if it was as conscious as they. It has been argued that in such interactions people are not actually relating to Kismet but rather to the whole collection of people who created the devices that run it. None the less the attribution of consciousness to Kismet is felt to be very compelling."

The Buddha joined in. "Many will say that the computing mechanisms in these robots are acting as if they were conscious. The machines 'pretend' to be conscious but, actually, they have no clue about what is going on. They are simulators. But then the question emerges as to when and how one could tell whether the apparent conscious awareness is really present or simply an 'as if' performance. It is here that metaphysical arguments step in, often clearly based in purely ideological concerns of the contributing thinkers. Some will argue that only biological machines can be really conscious. Others will say that if a machine has the right properties then consciousness will automatically emerge. Machines showing intentionality would be strong candidates here. Some have argued that the cosmos itself might be conscious, the 'Panpsychist' position. The use of the word 'conscious', normally referring to personal experience, is perhaps merely confusing in such a universal context. In any case, we could never know if inorganic matter was itself conscious because, if so, it would not be different from ourselves.[4] We would be like fish that swim in water but do not know it because they partake of it. David Chalmers argues that if the computational machinery were appropriate then conscious states will appear, but he does not say what would be the extra property required making this happen.[5] Dan Dennett, by contrast, takes the view that the whole issue of consciousness is an illusion.[6] We may think we are conscious but actually, beings, other complex computers and ourselves are all behaving 'as if' so far as being conscious is concerned. Yet, even was he to be right in this assumption, since we think we are conscious, the question emerges as to how that illusion happens and why."

"Rodney Brooks [7] takes the view," said Eleanor, "that the involvement of computers and cyberspace in human lives will alter the way in which we think of consciousness. Already we can replace or enhance many activities by the use of electronic devices implanted in the body. Disabled people can already control their wheelchairs and such like by thinking. Implanted electrodes pick up brain signals and control an external device. Susan Blackmore[8] asks what will happen should miniature mobile phones with access to the World Wide Web be implanted in the brain. We might then be conscious of a whole vast world beyond ourselves in which we would be participants. Consciousness might seem to have expanded to something like infinity of knowledge. The questions "What is real?" and "Is it me?" then become an ultimate paradox."

"The literature attempting to resolve the hard problem is already vast." said Jim. "Individual books are correspondingly bulky. Dan Dennett's tome 'Consciousness explained' has 511 pages and fails. David Chalmer's book runs to 414 proposing a perspective entirely at odds with Dennett's. Sue Blackmore's recent textbook runs to 459 pages in an attempt to cover the ground for students. As we have suggested, the main contrasts between these points of view depend neither on experiment, nor on evidence or objectivity, although appeals to all of these may be made, but rather on the personal world-view of an author. The fact is that consciousness conceived as a thing or a property remains a mystery and none of these stances have even begun to solve the problem. We are left, as Blackmore informs her students, in even greater perplexity that when we began. Nick Humphrey even suggests that the apparent mystery of consciousness might have a function; to provoke us into thinking we are special and thus to work hard in preserving ourselves."[9]

Summing up the field, the Buddha said, "Francisco Varela has distinguished four approaches to explaining consciousness: reductionism; functionalism; phenomenology; and 'mysterianism'. The reductionist argument seeks to solve the problem in the study of the brain, cognitive mechanisms, or hypothetical determinants. The approach is primarily focussed on experiments and uses traditional scientific inference. In some of these approaches consciousness is believed to be based in phenomena at the quantum level – which takes the discussion out of psychology altogether and merely deepens the mystery through placing the term in an entirely unfamiliar context, thereby changing its meaning. Functionalist approaches look for what consciousness does, can do or might do. It is essentially an evolutionary perspective since, if a function can be proposed, one may also argue that it has evolved through selection. Biological, social psychological and anthropological approaches are all in play here. Phenomenology focuses on the accounts people give of their experiences and the way in which these relate to objective experiments. It includes what may be called 'subjective empiricism'[10] investigating what happens in experience when phenomenological variables are changed as in studies of prolonged attention, sensory deprivation, altered states, Husserl's methods of introspection, gestalt psychology or Asian meditation systems. This has also been called 'first person science'. 'Mysterianism' claims that the whole thing is a mystery and that we may never be able to solve the Hard Problem."

"Phew!" said Jim. "It really is a bizarre field of investigation. One of the big battles is between what philosopher Daniel Dennett calls the A team, of which he is captain, and the B team is headed by David Chalmers. The B team includes the philosopher John Searle, Thomas Nagel and the psychologist Steven Pinker among others. They insist that consciousness necessarily involves 'first person enquiry'. There is a subjective ontology, they say, the study of personal being that cannot be reduced to objective, third person explanation. Chalmers accepts as fact that we do have subjective experiences and that these vary under differing conditions. Our knowledge about them comes from immediate first person, private experience. We have to study them as such because they comprise the central material we ask a science of consciousness to explain."

"By contrast the A team, which includes Quine, Hofstadter and others besides Dennett, considers subjective phenomena irrelevant or illusory. They focus on what people say and do, arguing that there is no other way to get at the problem. When this 'third person data' is thoroughly understood they believe there will be nothing else to explain. They argue that when we have inner experiences we are actually creating illusions that seem to be states of experience. We seem to be conscious and it is this very 'seeming' that needs to be explained. Dennett argues for what he calls 'Heterophenomenology' by which he means the study of what other people say of their experiences."

"Oh dear!" said the Buddha. "Do we really need such words?"

"Well," said Jim, "they don't help much. Dennett is trying to avoid 'first person science' entirely. He believes a coordinated approach using physical sciences in relation to what people say of their experiences can eventually provide an account of private experience however seemingly ineffable. This approach uses peoples' accounts of themselves to gain insight into their lives. It leaves aside such questions as to whether the described fictional worlds are actually experienced. There is no room here for subjective empiricism apart from the gathering of descriptive data. The question as to whether consciousness is 'as if' or 'real' is not addressed. Dennett's approach seems to be basically a form of cognitive or linguistic reductionism. As with all reductionisms the colour fades from the screen."

"What are we to make of all this argumentation?" asked Eleanor. "Where the confusion is as considerable as these disputes suggest, we may suspect a profound philosophical muddle; one indeed we are hardly likely to resolve here. Yet, there are one or two pointers that may be useful. We have already noted that Berger and Luckmann in their book 'The Social Construction of Reality' discuss the human tendency to reify the abstract and then to attach value to that abstraction as if it were a thing or a possession. For an example, we may take the word 'Spring'. The word points to a condition that appears once a year after winter and before summer. I love Spring – you may say. Yet, if we go looking for 'Spring' we won't find 'it' apart from the blooming of snowdrops and daffodils and the appearance of green buds and leaves. 'Spring' 'is an abstraction indicating a period of time, yet the way we use the word is the same as if we were talking about a table or a chair. Everyone knows what Spring means but we do not expect to go out and locate it under a bush. The rules for its meaningful use make that absurd.

"Similarly, in most of the theories we are discussing, we find 'consciousness' very much reified as a thing or a locatable process. The differing stances try to explain why this thing appears, or what capacity leads to its manifestation. Quite plausibly, 'consciousness' is inappropriately treated in this reifying way. The word denotes a condition in a manner akin to 'Spring', 'Health' or 'Time' – a descriptive abstraction without location. What kind of meaning then has 'consciousness'?"

"It seems to me", said the Buddha, "that 'consciousness' is a summarising abstraction referring to the facts of personal experience. Indeed 'experience' may be a more useful word here because it has been less rigidly reified. Experience, like spring or time, runs along, defines a quality with many themes, images, symbols, and thoughts. Spring appears with flowers, birds and trees without itself being anywhere to be found. The birds, leaves and flowers are spring. Thoughts, images, feelings, the so-called *qualia*, are experience. In English we call it 'conscious' to distinguish the experienced and remembered from events that have happened without being experienced or remembered – under hospital anaesthesia for example. We find 'consciousness' as 'experience' and neither of them is a 'thing'."

"We *are* experiencing machines rather than machines that *have* consciousness," contributed Jim. "By setting aside the dualistic reification we have perhaps a simpler problem to handle. Whatever the brain may be doing, some of its processes appear as experience. That is the nature of the beast. Whether experience is conscious, or just seems to be so, no longer matters; either way, there it is. You and I could not be engaged in this discussion without the experience of reading or if we lacked brains. It seems the investigation can only proceed, as William James suggested, through observing the concurrence of experience and the circumstances that give rise to it: the warmth of early summer, bird song, green leaves, memories are themselves experience. How they relate to whatever gives rise to them may appear by studying the physical processes that mediate them. There is something out there that the cognitive activity of the brain makes sense of, more or less. Language creates the contexts within which these items are felt as meaningful and it is highly involved in the process. We may say that experience is brain physiology manifest and certain states of brain physiology create awareness. Each side may surrender to the other. The plan of study becomes monistic rather than dualistic. Adopting this stance may eventually help us to discuss where the machinery might be found. Can we by-pass the Hard Problem in this way?"

Eleanor took it up, "Part of the difficulty in exploring this problem may lie with the contrasting 'language games' we use. We 'play' with ideas in varying ways inferring contrasting meanings according to the rules of differing word 'games'. Philosopher Rom Harré has pointed out that one side of the Hard Problem is expressed through one 'game', the other side by another.[11] As Ludwig Wittgenstein has argued, we need to understand the use of words, like 'consciousness' or 'experience', within the particular games in which they are used. Harré argued that the games used in giving accounts of the subjective have different contextualising rules from those used in accounting for the subjective in some objectivising manner. One may use concepts meaningfully in one game, which one cannot do in another. This is like taking someone to see a game of football and not saying whether it is soccer or rugby. The ball is played in different ways in each game although it has the same name in both. Talking of consciousness in the context of phenomenology is a very different 'game' from discussing its significance as a property of some unknown brain process. We need to explore the contrasting rules in these differing games. The Hard Problem itself may be illusory after all."

"It looks as if the Hard Problem poses a paradox not a question." The Buddha said. "We need to understand what a paradox is. Consider, for example, a Zen koan. Koans are paradoxes gaining their power and interest from the perplexity they induce. This power derives from the fact that a koan brings together expressions from contrasting language games in such a way that terms appear in a novel usage in which their meaning is disallowed. There is a sudden short circuit as the mind flounders in meaninglessness. 'What is the sound of one hand clapping?' is one such koan. Only two hands can clap so a basic understanding has been discarded here and hence with it the normal meaning. The task then is to find a 'game' that heals the split and restores, discovers or transcends meaning."

"We may take this koan further," added Jim. "The rule says one clap involves two hands yet claps may also arise quite appropriately from two people clapping their hands together with one another. Clapping games may emerge with four children doing complex rounds of mutual claps. A theatre is filled with clapping at the end of a performance. Someone may say – Listen to the 'clappage'. Struck by this odd word, in which 'clapping' has been reified by a grammatical shift and a verbal invention, one might enter the theatre, stupidly of course, looking for the 'clappage'. Even while clapping, continued one might start searching for the 'clappage' under the seats or above the chandeliers. One may soon be reading articles in the philosophical journals asking where 'clappage' is to be found. There is no 'clappage' apart from the clapping but the linguistic twist makes it seem so."

Mechanisms of Awareness

It was a Sunday morning, bright and fresh, so the three discussants went down to Hampton Court, becoming not inappropriately lost in the maze. Afterwards in the café they went on with their discussion.

The Buddha began " There is no consciousness apart from experience. Maybe we should look where experience arises."

" Few would disagree that the brain is involved," said Jim. "Horace Barlow argues however that consciousness can only arise in the context of communication with another.[12] Social experience leads to the incorporation of others' ideas and experiences and the recall of these in inner reflection allows insight into one's own world. These then are realisations leading to functional social behaviour, an idea going back to Mead. Consciousness requires a remembered partner for reflection: it becomes a forum, he says, not of a single mind, but of the social group with whom the individual interacts. Consciousness becomes fundamental to the evolution of culture."

Eleanor added, "John Searle[13] and Jeffery Gray[14] both espouse versions of a mind-brain identity theory arguing that the mind is fully an expression of brain activity evolved through time by Darwinian processes of selection."

"Yes," said Jim, "most such versions of this perspective argue that there are two kinds of event, mental and neurological that correlate in space and time. Searle bases his argument on the difference between macro and micro descriptions of a system. He illustrates his account by pointing out that a glass of water may be described either in terms of its macro-properties of fluidity contained in solidity or by its micro-properties, the molecules and atomic physics of the constituents of water and glass. He argues that a similar relationship exists between descriptions of mental activity and brain processes. The surface phenomena of experience are underpinned and explained by the micro processes that determine them. Macro and micro elements are aspects of the same phenomenon. He argues that just as the liquidity of the water is caused by the behaviour of elements at the micro-level, and yet at the same time is a feature realised at the macro level, so in exactly that sense of 'caused by' and 'realised in', mental phenomena are caused by processes at the neuronal level and realised in the very system constructed by neurones. That's a quote!"

"But Jeffery Gray points out that the parallel is not symmetrical," continued Jim. "In a scientific hypothesis, the macro level is arguably based in elements described at a micro level, which are then explored through experimentation. The hypothesis is constructed precisely so that the micro level explains the macro features of a system. In the mind-brain case, however, this is hardly so because none of the micro-elements have been considered capable of explaining the macro-level of experience. It is precisely the problem of relating experience and brain that remains the central issue. Gray points out that bottom-up modelling, explaining a process by examining its determination at the micro -level, should not be at the expense of top-down modelling in which the macro properties are seen as equally causal with those at the micro level. He points out that while the molecules determine the liquidity of water it is this very property of liquidity that determines the location of the molecules, water runs downhill for example. We can see a set of relationships emerging here that the ancient Chinese have already discussed in their Hua-yan philosophising." (See Chapter 8).

"To make some sort of progress here we are going to have to hazard a guess at the nature of the connection that may exist between these two levels of description," argued the Buddha. "We have seen that experiences occur in particularly clear form when we are engaged in various forms of problem solving or task completion, with the quality of experience varying according to the capability of the individual. Anxiety arises where one has doubts about one's capacities. (See Chapter 15) At the root of such experiences must be a mental 'model' of capacity based in judgements made according to certain criteria. Feelings or estimations of one's capacity are continuously rated against the difficulty of the task. In proposing such a 'model' a neuronal system rather than the neurones themselves, is hypothesised to be responsible for an outcome.

"We know for example that sensory input to the brain goes to numerous dispersed locations but we have no knowledge of any 'place' where their integration and comparison may occur. We may infer a comparator but this is a hypothetical construct derived from description of behaviour and experience and not a neurophysiologic fact. How and where the evaluations are being made we do not know. May be there is no location. The whole cerebral structure may be implicated holistically. Since we know nothing of how experience may actually arise in the brain, we are forced to talk in terms of 'models' of this kind in trust that someday we may be able to establish their actual neural basis."

"Indeed," said Eleanor, "it seems that experiences arise in correlation with a continuous modelling of the outer circumstances and inner condition of the body. The experience of a stream of awareness may be rooted in a repetitive scanning or monitoring of several sets of models associated with the arousal system in the brain.[15] The repeated scanning of inner states provides in some unknown way the experience of time, the apparent passage of which varies according to the novelty or intensity of the engagement. The scanning detects changes that indicate novelty against a continuing background. Novelties are then evaluated against some criteria of importance and, if judged to be significant, may be brought to attention through awareness. Such detection of 'dissonance' is known to be important in a number of physiological processes and seems likely to underpin consciousness. Boring, unvarying continuity of input attracts little attention. In walking to the office, the banker may have no recall of the events along the way because his attention is firmly locked onto the remembered problems lying on his desk. The familiar condition of the traffic need not receive attention. Should the untoward happen however he is at once 'there'."

"Conversely," said the Buddha, "in some meditation states wherein little or no novelty arises, time appears to cease."

"I think," said Jim, "the most basic system of this kind is bodily awareness – the feedback from receptors in muscles, tendons, joints and skin that record movements and report back to the brain. The brain has previously copied its instructions to the body and the novel feedback is compared to this copy and deviations from it noted. This can be combined, of course, with direct observation of physical movements. The body is continuously sending innumerable signals back to the brain for monitoring but only a few of them stimulate attention. The massive quantity of background information is unconsciously processed and matched to an established norm, the 'body schema', deviation from which is brought to attention. Thus, a painful pinprick is instantly recognised as a deviation that needs attention.

"There is also top-down observation. One may deliberately place attention on one's big toe so as to become aware of it yet, normally, sensation arising in one's big toe is not given attention in consciousness. When does a stimulus evoke attention? One must suppose that innate mechanisms evaluate deviations within the 'body schema' that suggest danger and that criteria for evaluating risk operate in deciding what comes to awareness. What the nature of this awareness is remains the mystery. Rather lamely, all one can say is that it is the subjective quality of the macro level induced by the underlying micro-level activity!"

"I imagine," said Eleanor, "that there are other systems operating in parallel with your bodily modelling – for example, a model to monitor how you are situated or placed in a room or under a tree, and another to evaluate the social context of your activity. We can think that all three, the bodily, situational and social models, are cooperating to produce an embracing, composite model of what appears to us as 'reality'.[16] Where we experience ourselves to be is a function of the current focus of attention arising in relation to biological needs, situational challenges and social complexity. The system evaluates any new issue that arises according to criteria, which may be either innate or acquired through cultural experience. The system operates as a whole providing us with the integrated 'reality' within which we live – which we can now see is necessarily a virtual one. Much of the monitoring process remains unconscious since only input relevant to an ongoing issue need be 'observed', a process that allows for the repression of painful thoughts and the neglect of unused memory."

"The stability of our experience of reality may however not be derived solely from our immediate perceptions but also constructed through the re-creation of memories to fill in the picture," said Jim. " In ill health or under drugs a distorted reality may be repaired, as Susan Blackmore has suggested,[17] by recourse to memories that help reconstitute the appearance of a normal world. Our reality models are essentially hypotheses, which are tested by actual experience in the world and in society. The most effective in engaging the 'outer' world become the assumed background within which we live. Furthermore, they provide the basis for our sense of ourselves as unitary beings in the world. Such an integrated model becomes the basis for being; we experience ourselves directly as being that model not as having it. This can only mean that the model itself is the experiencer – is consciousness."

"Yet there is more," added the Buddha. "Human consciousness is usually self aware; there is an awareness of awareness, 'meta-cognition' as it is called, that underlies what enables me to say, 'I am me'. There seems to be an observer of 'my 'being' and this mental division is presumably the great difference between most higher mammals that lack language and ourselves. The capacity to be 'reflexive' in this way seems to be the basis for mental reification – the seeing of self and things as objects in a world. We may argue plausibly that objectifying experience preceded self-awareness and that, once the recognition of self had arisen, the capacity to share one's own experiences with others became possible. The biological and social value of being able to do so has been immense."

"If the reality model is the basis for 'being', we have some sort of purchase on exploring its biological roots." said Jim. "What exactly is the process that supports this cognition? Is it holistic or otherwise? While the hard problem remains, at least we have some sort of a road map with which to explore it."

BRAIN, FRONT ENDS, BEHAVIOUR AND
SOCIETY: ORIGINS OF SELF-AWARENESS

After supper, the three friends took up their discussion again.

The Buddha began, "Most investigators agree that the fundamental context of human experience is undeniably the sense of self. Self, culture and society are all mutually co-determining. We are seeking therefore to understand the bases upon which this co-determination rests and need to show how it arose. Recently, a set of evolutionary stories have emerged that throw increasing light on this theme. All of them assume that the cognitive processes of the brain underpin these phenomena. We must therefore begin our exploration with the brain and have another look at its evolution. Where did it come from?"

Jim replied, "Cephalisation, as Sir Arthur Sherrington called it, is the start of the answer. [18] It means the formation of a head at the front end of a mobile body. In the early days of evolution, single celled organisms began to live together eventually creating animals of many cells, multicellular organisms. As they became more efficient in controlling both their internal processes and their exploitation of an environment, cell assemblies formed tissues specialising in differing functions: ingestion of food; digestion; elimination of waste; respiration; reproduction through the production of germ cells; and information processing. These are the characteristic means whereby an animal processes its world, survives and reproduces.

"Many early animals such as starfish, sea anemones, jellyfish, were 'radially symmetrical'. They had nerve nets around the body providing integrated behaviour focussed around a centrally located mouth where food was ingested. Other animals became 'bilaterally symmetrical', movers with front and rear ends, sides, back and underside. These animals developed sense organs at the front end where food was captured or otherwise ingested. The simple sense organs near the mouth linked to nerve 'ganglia' where the sensory information about the outside world was integrated with inputs from internal sources to produce behaviour efficient in feeding, attack, escape and reproduction. Natural selection moulded both sense organs and the nervous system to function appropriately in behaviour in whatever the environment of adaptation might be."

Eleanor took up the account. "So the brain developed at the front end of mobile animals as an information processor relating bodily movement to circumstances. Naturally enough, as life became more complex, so the brain developed to cope with new needs. Genetically based programmes controlling behaviour became organised as neuronal 'modules' in the brain achieving the marvels of instinctive behaviour ethologists study today. Later in evolution, it became essential to respond to circumstances that changed frequently within the lifetime of an organism. Genetic selection became too slow a means of responding since it only happened between generations. The innate, genetically controlled programmes became increasingly open and filled in by learning, which could bring about behaviour changes within the lifetime of an individual. These 'evolutionarily flexible strategies' remained restricted by their innate basis but, as lifetime complexity, particularly of a social nature, developed, so the acquired behaviour became predominant in the control of tactics.[19] Animals living complex lives became more and more programmed through their immediate lifetime experiences. In social animals, the collective behaviour of groups began to yield simple forms of culture found in many mammalian and some bird species but only finally emerging fully as culture underpinned by language in humans. The study of the emergence of culture has been a key focus in Behavioural Ecology for the last forty years, while the main aim of a research group calling themselves Evolutionary Psychologists has been to determine the extent of genetically determined universals that control behavioural expression."

"We have already discussed," Jim said, "how human experience, including mental suffering, is formed within social relationships. (Chapter 15). We need not be surprised to find that the main selection pressures shaping culture and mental life occur within group living. A key question concerns the origin of the especially large size of the human brain; not only for its own interest but also in relation to the consequences its evolution has had on other aspects of human behaviour and culture. The brain is essentially a computer and it is particularly the enlargement of the cerebral cortex concerned with computation that is of that is of interest here. So what was the enlarging brain computing?"

Eleanor joined in, "You know, Alison Jolly, a primatologist studying the relatively primitive lemurs of Madagascar, wondered why they did badly in laboratory intelligence tests when compared with monkeys.[20] She guessed the answer might lie in the greater complexity of the social lives of the monkeys requiring greater computing power and hence greater intelligence, which could then generalise to laboratory tasks. The more complex the social life – the larger the brain perhaps?"

"It seems so," said Jim. "There are many complexities in social life that need continuous monitoring and assessment. Primates, like other animals, form groups largely because being in a group lessens the probability that a predator will catch any one individual. Relationships develop within such groups and alliances between individuals may support their fitness through forms of altruism. Yet, since cheating may occur, individuals must be able to recognise friend from con-man or rival. Indeed, the function of intellect may have originally been the manipulation of social relations to an individual's advantage.[21] Increasing intellect requires more computer power; larger brains capable of 'mind reading' computing the likely results of varying types of encounters with others. This idea is the basis of the 'social brain' hypothesis underlying much of the current evolutionary theory of human mentality."[22]

"Primate brains are indeed significantly larger than would be expected by comparison with other mammals of similar size," added Eleanor. "Recent studies have suggested that it was indeed an improved ability to solve complex social problems that was the impetus for increased brain size in Primates. Monkeys, baboons and apes live in social groups of varied and complex organisation within which many forms of coalition develop and change through time. As group size enlarges, an individual has to keep track of its relatives, relate to dominance hierarchies of perhaps several kinds, recognise grooming companions, sustain alliances in reciprocal altruism with other individuals and to be on the look out for social cheating. In groups, individuals spend much time building and servicing relationships, creating coalitions with important consequences for the reproductive success of individuals. Cheating and manipulative strategies lead to the emergence of counter measures to avoid being deceived or cheated. Outwitting others, either in cheating or in the emergence of counter measures, becomes an important activity for which intelligence and big brains are needed."

"The theory goes as follows," said Jim addressing himself to the Buddha. "Among Primates, the mean group size correlates with the size of the cerebral hemispheres – suggesting that the bigger the group the greater the complexity of social relations. Social complexity correlates with social tension and primates reduce tension by grooming one another. Increasing group size seems indeed to correlate with increased time spent grooming – at the expense of other activities. Now, while grooming may have originated in the removal of ectoparasites, its high frequency and duration necessitate a further explanation. Being groomed does seem positively pleasurable to a primate and this may be due to the release of endogenous opiates that alter mood and engender relaxation. Individuals in larger groups spending more time grooming may be releasing more opiates over a longer period, getting time out to relax from the competitive business of social life. Yet so much time is spent in doing this that the time available for other essential activities becomes reduced to a limiting degree.[23]

" In the case of early human ancestors, group size appears to have risen so high that this conflict between spending time enjoying tension – reducing grooming and the performance of other essential activities may have become acute. The result would have been a necessary restriction of grooming, which in turn would then have restricted the group size to an emotionally tolerable level. Calculations have suggested that this should limit human group size to about 70 individuals. How then can humans sustain their actually much larger basic groups of around 150? In theory at least, the stress engendered by groups of such a size should lead to their fragmentation. One idea suggests that language evolved from grooming behaviour because it allowed easier negotiation of social tension in large groups!"

"Oh yes, I remember," said Eleanor, "during his field studies, Robin Dunbar noticed that grooming Gelada baboons kept up a constant muttering. The tones of the muttering by animals in close contact expressed mood and emotional state so that information about an animal's intention or state was becoming available to near-by companions. Dunbar realised that, in very early humans, similar muttering could have developed into signifying sounds and hence become the origin of language. Calls containing information would allow meaningful communication at a distance and could reach more than one individual at a time. This means that social information within a group could be broadcast around in a more extensive way than any one-to one intimacy of grooming could ever allow."

"Plausibly therefore," Jim broke in, "language would have evolved in stages from group communication in contact calling to the spreading of mood, attitude and intention and finally to the communication of emotion and finally ideas through signifying sounds. Actually, fossil evidence suggests helpfully that the anatomical features required for the control of breath and tongue needed in speech appeared not earlier than the earliest *Homo sapiens* communities, thus coinciding with the great enlargement of the human neo-cortex of the brain."

"What's more," added Eleanor excitedly, "there is suggestive, albeit indirect, evidence for these ideas coming from the pattern of conversations in human groups right here and now, among students for example. Gossipy conversation is supported by laughter, a unique human feature, which has an effect on the production of endogenous opiates important in generating good mood and which also has a positive effect on the immune system. Chatting together is good for you. Yet, men talk differently when in the company of females than when talking together in single – sex groups. Why? Could conversation also facilitate behaviours associated with increasing genetic fitness in competition with others?

"Arguably, the relative sizes of the human sexes suggest that humans were originally mildly polygamous and that rules regarding monogamy are later cultural impositions. In polygamous mammals, the males display to attract females who look out for the most impressive males bearing signs of high fitness – so called sexual selection. It happens that in observed conversations women talk together mainly about their personal relations while men speak with one another more factually about tasks and processes. In groups containing men and women, men usually talk more and women listen more. Indeed, in some such groups it is quite difficult to get women unaware of this fact to participate to the same extent as men. Furthermore, when such student groups are discussing academic subjects it tends to be the men who show off what knowledge they have in disputation with one another. Some will be clearly better at this than others; perhaps those that best imitate a favoured teacher! Dunbar suggests humans may have developed 'conversational lekking' comparable to the lekking behaviour of birds or mammals in which highly coloured males show off to females who quietly choose which ones they prefer as mates! Conversation may thus not only be a substitution for grooming but also a context for human sexual selection."[24]

"My goodness," said the Buddha, "that's a fascinating idea! But what about any understanding of one's own behaviour in such situations?"

"Indeed," responded Eleanor, "in social life it would be important for an individual to distinguish between feelings expressing a response to another's motivations and those arising from one's own.[25] This would only be possible if individuals were aware of a distinction between feelings arising from their own motivations and those evoked by others. Self-awareness would be the way to do this. Nick Humphrey has argued that such an 'inner eye' observing the processes of its own brain would allow an individual to understand by analogy the feelings and hence intentions of others, a notion which he tells us the philosopher Thomas Hobbes had had long before.[26] The sense of self as an inner representation could have evolved because of its utility in this way."

Jim took up the point. "Communication would then be occurring between individuals each of whom would be capable of understanding each other's self-understanding mutually. As speech became a prime mode of communication, the words signifying I, me, you, they, would have soon appeared as useful reifications to facilitate communications – whether as intended truth statements or false ones. Either way they would function effectively in the social games upon which personal 'fitness' now depended.

"In language, sounds have meaning – they refer to something. Within the speech of a community they allow very effective communications about things, intentions, doubts, policies – the stuff that social competition and collaboration within culture is made of. The 'self' represents the body's strategies at a newly emerged level of social interaction – culture. Dunbar has pointed out that once human beings had evolved the mental processes that allowed the imputation of self, concern for one's own welfare became focussed through this cognitive attribution rather than directly through responses to hunger, satiation, sexual need or fear. With the development of language, the concepts of 'I' or 'me' could be verbalised and their concerns opened to public discussion. On the one hand, the evolution of such a device has enabled self-identifying humans to adapt and adjust collectively to complex environmental and social situations with extraordinary skill and speed. On the other hand, the self is subject to delusions in which the relation between the inner world and outer circumstances becomes tenuous. Where such delusions are collective and heritable the potential for the emergence of maladaptation is greater than for any other animal. Language threw human cognition into an entirely new and often highly problematical arena wherein illusion could function as the 'basic fault' in human adaptation to the world."

"Exactly so," murmured the Buddha.

REPLICATORS IN LANGUAGE AND CULTURAL CHANGE

In 1975, F.T Cloak pointed out that in behavioural development neural mechanisms provide 'instructions' moving an individual's condition from one state or stage to another. Such instructions may not only be genetic, they can be cultural. Could there be cultural evolution as well as biological? Innate programmes of behaviour in higher mammals are flexible in that they are sufficiently open to include information derived from present experience. Such a capacity promotes adaptability through the speedy tracking of both environmental and social changes. Once a species became capable of culture, instructions take the form of ideas of which there were two kinds, concepts in the mind and the social or physical products, written laws, institutions, buildings, monuments that they create. This is an important distinction in that physical structures have long endurance and can, as it were, bring the past into the present. Ideas, Cloak thought, could infect the mind somewhat like viruses and some could provoke behaviour that might not be beneficial but actually harmful to an individual or to its genetic fitness.[27]

Richard Dawkins took up this theme, pointing out that such cultural instructions or 'memes' as he called them, would be subject to evolution through selection just as genes were. Any population of replicating things showing variability, fecundity and differential viability would be subject to selection and this was certainly true of memes. In 'The Extended Phenotype', he showed that a universal Darwinism included cultural evolution through the selective elimination and promotion of memes. Memes were the second replicators additional to the genes. Dawkins' contribution has had immense significance in drawing the realm of culture within the fold of evolutionary theory. A key issue at once became the manner in which cultural evolution through the selection of replicating memes was related to genetic selection in the determination of behaviour.[28]

In 1989 Richerson and Boyd provided a formal analysis of the way in which the differential transmission of memes through learning and education could occur.[29] In any cultured population, they argue, there is a range of ideas responsible for variations in behaviour. In each generation, young people choose a variant by exhibiting a preference for it. This may arise through the imitation of a performer, guidance through education or other forms of personal influence or fashion. There are three forms of preference:

Firstly, in what they call 'direct bias', choice is based upon an individual judgement.

Secondly, choice may depend on the frequency of a variant and a tendency to adopt the ideas of the majority through conformity: This may be one reason for the maintenance of regional differences in culture.

Thirdly, a variant may be favoured because some influential people, classes or institutions have adopted it. Richerson and Boyd call this 'indirect bias'. In such a case, choice is based on imitation arising from social influence and not due to some perceived intrinsic value to the individual. This is the case for what is known as 'fashion' but may also include choice based on social coercion. Thus, state propaganda for a just war, or through the demonisation of an 'enemy', may alter the frequency with which individuals perceive peace as essential policy.

Their analysis shows that some cultural traits are of greater significance to biology than others. The adoption of a meme may or may not support an individual's fitness. Memes may be either anti-natal or pro-natal, limiting birth rates or increasing them. For example, in cases of indirect bias, people whose ideas may not support parents' concern with optimum reproduction may exert an influence on them. A non-reproductive priesthood keen on celibacy may promote imitation by others to bring about substantial decreases in family size. Such an influence may occur irrespective of family economics or welfare. Indirect bias through the fashionable influence of others may effect many social variables including the behaviour of men and women in marriage or other forms of partnership, family structure, personal fecundity, gender preferences among offspring, birth interval, rearing techniques, and inheritance rules. Male chauvinism, excessive feminism (the 'Society for Cutting up Men'!),[30] sexual orientation, militarism and educational, nutritional or medical fashions all have effects on the demography of a population and the 'fitness' of its participants. Sometimes, indeed, an anti-natal fashion may go into runaway mode so that the actual survival of a population may be at risk. Where such occurs, Richerson and Boyd suppose that constraints on such behaviour would soon be selected, certainly at the genetic level, but the outcome would depend on time scales. Genetic selection is a slow process; cultural selection can act extremely fast. The vast casualties incurred by recent wars or ethnic cleansing are a case in point. Populations may think themselves out of existence through sheer stupidity or failures to adopt appropriate means of exploiting the environment–as in the case of the Viking settlements in Greenland. There is no reason to suppose that human beings are not capable of such actions for even recent history demonstrates a capacity for it.

The three friends had become so absorbed in their discussion that they agreed to meet again the following weekend. The Sunday morning bloomed beautifully and the Buddha and his young companions went for a long walk though the parks enjoying the charm that London can exert on such a day. Pausing on a park bench near the sparkling waters of the Serpentine, they resumed their discussion.

"You know," said Eleanor, "there is a lot of controversy about these 'memes'. In her book, 'The Meme Machine' Susan Blackmore has promoted their study to the level of a new science – 'memetics'.[31] In a brilliant set of deductions she uses meme theory to account for a great many phenomena. Blackmore is nothing if not ambitious 'My aim' she tells us, 'is to show that many aspects of human nature are explained far better by a theory of memetics than by any rival theory yet available' – and she includes brain size, origins of language, talking and thinking, altruism and the Internet. Each chapter indeed provides an exciting and provocative read and as a contribution to 'universal Darwinism' her book is important, yet a number of important criticisms have been directed at this perspective."[32]

Jim took up the account. "Blackmore bases her account in the suggestion that imitation is the root of culture. Imitation provides the replicability of memes. Culture consists in those themes that are optimally imitated. Imitation is indeed especially well developed in humans, being found in elementary form right from the babies' first few weeks. What we imitate, Blackmore argues, is the memes and through this process, instructions to behave are passed down from generation to generation and subject to selection through preferential copying. An exploration of the history of ideas or the spread of idiosyncrasies such as the reversed baseball cap reveals much about how memes become popular and increase/decrease in frequency. Humans find them of interest for one reason or another, and talk and think about them. Some memes come to dominate our lives so much that they influence our choice of lesser memes. If you are a Nazi, it becomes easy to believe in the elimination of inferior beings such as gypsies or Jews. If you are a Christian you seek to alleviate poverty and be kind to people. Memes combine in meme-plexes, which appear to drive our lives – they seem like viruses that infect us with seeming good or ill.

"Blackmore argues that once imitation evolved, the meme, a second replicator additional to the gene, was born. As people began to copy one another, she says, the highest quality memes, those with high fidelity, fecundity and longevity, did the best. A spoken language would then emerge from the success of copyable sounds that were high in all three. The early speakers not only copied the best speakers in their society but also mated with them, creating natural selection pressures on the genes to produce brains that were even better at spreading new memes. Memes and genes would then have co-evolved to produce our species with its extraordinary properties of a large brain and language."[33]

Eleanor interrupted, "Memes are certainly not 'just a meaningless metaphor', as one critic has argued, but do they really provide 'the grand unifying theory we need to understand human nature' that Blackmore believes memetics to be?

"What exactly counts as a meme?" asked the Buddha.

"Yes – there's the problem," said Jim. "Various authors have included rules, tunes, ideas, clothes, fashion, pottery skills, knowing how to use a computer, the Odyssey, Beethoven's symphonies, philosophical systems and many more. Blackmore argues that anything passed on through imitation is a meme; in which case they are a remarkably disparate lot. Blackmore treats the meme in a manner that parallels Dawkins' thinking on the selfish gene. The 'meme' like the 'gene' is an abstract term that allows theorising based on a unifying concept, a unit. But can the same theory apply to Kant's philosophy as it does to reversed baseball caps? Such ideas function at very different levels of meaning and have very different functional effects in human life. To lump them altogether under a common term is equivalent to bracketing an ecosystem together with a worm because both in differing senses are alive. Memetics proposes an analysis based on an extreme abstraction – and here we begin to encounter problems."

Eleanor joined in, "Blackmore adopts what she calls 'the memes eye view'. What must a meme do to get itself copied? One possibility is that it will encourage the growth of a bigger and better vehicle – brain size. Language increases the flow of memes and the probability of their being copied, the Internet likewise. These developments are therefore driven by the memes. Memes cause their evolution. The argument here parallels the "genetic gambit" in which, although no analysis of it's actual mode of expression has been made, the gene is considered causal in an adaptationist argument. But, whereas genes have more or less identifiable properties, memes might be anything.

"The memetic gambit"seems to be based on air. First of all – can a meme have a 'meme's eye view'? Does it have intentionality? Of course not – and Blackmore actually says so. Just as genes are chemicals that get selected so memes are signifiers that are imitated. They themselves are totally neutral. If a gene or meme is selected it passes on and replicates. It was in this neutral sense that Dawkins used the term 'selfish'. Yet, Blackmore, with her 'memes eye' hat on, insists – 'Memes spread themselves around indiscriminately without regard to whether they are useful, neutral or positively harmful to us' – or again – 'Genes fight it out to get into the next generation and in the process biological design comes about. Memes fight it out to get passed into another brain or book or object.' In many such expressions, Blackmore appears to be talking not at all about neutral signifiers but rather, succumbing to the intentionality implicit in the 'selfish' metaphor, she writes as if memes had intentions. The language is teleological. She adds purposiveness to what she has described as inert and then speaks of 'meme driving' rather than meme selection and ignores whatever it is in human nature that drives choice in imitating anything. The chosen is put in the place of the chooser; the cart is driving the horse. What we need here is an analysis of how, when and why imitation occurs and that depends on human nature and by no means only on the flux of ideas."

"Agreed," said Jim. "Meme talk, like much of gene talk, treats memes like genes as discrete units, sometimes combining as in 'meme plexes', but units none the less. Yet, in discussing current evolutionary theory (Chapter 14), we have concluded that a much more systemic or holistic thinking is needed. Similarly, in all this meme talk, there is a failure to understand that words and concepts actually work systemically – and this failure undermines the argument.

"The father of linguistics, Ferdinand de Saussure, had the vital insight that words could not be understood merely by their reference but primarily by their difference. The word 'table' has meaning not so much by referring to this object in the centre of the room but by the fact that the word differentiates that object from other items in the same class, chairs, stools, beds, carpets, bureaus, and such like. Words are always related systemically within sets of other words and the sets of words relate to one another in the same way. By extension, philosophers see that the same is true of the meanings of words, meanings relate to other meanings through their difference rather than any discrete identification. Words are signs comprising two aspects – the signifier – the pronounced sound- and the signified. If you hear the word 'table' alone you might think of an item of furniture, a mountain in South Africa, a summary of train arrivals and departures, or the data presented for a statistical analysis. Without context, meaning cannot be given. In addition, as Julia Kristeva has argued, conversation between speakers involves a sharing of the contexts of thought that differ for each speaker. A word may mean something different in each. The creation of meaning is worked out between them. The acknowledgement of meaning is thus 'deferred' until this negotiation reaches an agreed conclusion through deferral, or 'deferance', as philosopher Derrida puts it in French, punningly."

Eleanor took up the argument. "This must be the basis for Mary Midgely's critical point that 'thought and culture are not the sort of thing that can have distinct units at all. They do not have a granular structure for the same reason that ocean currents do not have one – namely because they are not stuffs but patterns'. [34] While, as Ed Wilson stresses, [35] the careful creation of appropriate terminology is vital in all science and especially in the defining of units fundamental for analysis – particularly mathematical analysis, mistakes are made when abstract terms are used to reify a phenomenon in a way to which they are not suited. An analysis that splits patterns of movement within difference and deferral up into abstract, ultimately metaphysical units can only be misleading. The hiving off of memes from motivations neglects the humanity underlining choice and imitation and this requires a much more precise examination."

"Perhaps the way out of these dilemmas is to consider the way in which ideas actually move in society," suggested the Buddha.

"Yes indeed," said Eleanor. "Serge Moscovici in Paris has provided such a study. He examined the way in which the key ideas of psychoanalysis had filtered into ordinary Parisian conversations, women's magazines and church publications.[36] He found a replication of 'memes' with a vengeance. Psychoanalytical ideas were selected by people who found them useful in expressing new thoughts about social relations, and this in spite of the fact that the actual theory of Freud was little or not at all understood by the users of such terms as 'unconscious', 'repressed', 'Oedipus complex' and so on. People were thinking with borrowed terms, the origins of which they mostly did not understand. Furthermore, some Freudian terms had been selected in this way and others not. Why? Probably it became fashionable to speak of one's motivations in a classy way enhancing self-esteem and status through 'being with it' – an example of 'indirect bias'. A similar story comes from California with the spread in conversation of 'psychobabble' emanating originally from psychotherapists consulting rooms. Such new modes of self-expression were not so much 'meme driven' as selected by their users for a range of social rewards."

"Moscovici went on to develop a theory of 'social representation'," said Jim. "A social representation comprises ideas, images and metaphors constructed by people in the course of understanding some event. It expresses an attitude and is used in discourse to present a case. An attitude towards something, immigration, say, is shaped by the way the movement of peoples is conceived, being affected by images, memories and hearsay concerning class, colour, unemployment, and political stances of left or right. The offering of a specific opinion, and hence the taking of a stand, is more dependent on how a topic is socially represented than upon any 'objective' knowledge of the phenomenon.

"Social representations arise in the constant exchange of views in all sorts of social and media events and provide a common currency for discussion and communication. They are of course the meat of the advertising world. Where coherent views arise, they may form the roots of collective prejudice or conversely, liberality. By contrast, when people with divergent representations interact, disputes are likely to arise and participants may quickly turn to mutual rejection, discrimination or violence.

"You know, for example, as organic farming has become popular, so the products are vividly advertised with rural images of sunshine and green fields bursting with crops often irrespective of any detailed examination of benefits to health. Similarly, new experiences are anchored by linking them to the way similar experiences are represented or, alternatively, split off as divergent from them. The whole process is continuously dynamic and one in which the difference in shades of meaning of words and terms and their deferral during communication play major roles. Ideas are not fixed, like words they may mutate or slide in meaning. Indeed they are often not so much selected as transformed in the course of social interactions and shifting contexts."

"Another way of understanding ideas," Eleanor went on, "is through 'discourse analysis' or 'discursive psychology'. Here conversational or political speech is dissected to perceive what the intention behind various forms of address might be. People have 'stakes' in projects and use words and phrases in complex ways to achieve ends or sustain positions whether rhetorical or social. Again, here the choice of ideas used in such expressions is guided by strategies to achieve either stated or disguised goals. The ideas do not drive the process, they are manipulated for very human reasons, rank, esteem, forms of advantage, some of which may indeed result in shifts in personal 'fitness', others may not, or may even have negative effects at the biological level. These research programmes reveal how ideas actually function in human communication, attitude formation and stake holding. Where ideas may appear to be in the driving seat is where they are used to promote or coerce others into certain forms of behaviour. The ideas may seem to be driving the historical process, as in the growth of capitalism or communism, or the conservatism of religions, but closer examination reveals the all too human motivations that lie behind such changes. If we want to uncover the prime movers in social change, empirical research such as this is of greater use than metaphysical assertions concerning the possible value of a new fangled abstraction."

Jim responded, "Another example of the way in which cultural changes may arise comes from work on group membership. Positive or negative representations of one's own in relation to others' groups can affect well being and reproductive success. Immediately after World War II, Henri Tajfel worked to help restore young Jews to normal life in France, a process necessitating an understanding of racial prejudice and guilt. [37] Moving to

Britain he continued his research as Professor of Social Psychology in Bristol University combining an experimental, laboratory approach with fieldwork that led to theoretical insights."

Eleanor followed on. "Tajfel argued that social representations and other forms of categorisation form the basis for ascribing identity to oneself through membership of a particular race, group, faction or class in society. Physical markers or ways of speech may be used to differentiate between groups and these are incorporated as parts of a member's identity. There is an arbitrariness about this. Brown skin, for example, is a noticeable boundary marker while brown eyes are not. Quite small criteria come to differentiate between 'us' and 'them'. Individuals express themselves in society by recognising identity in socially defined and variously biased ways. Encounter group facilitators, for example, know that powerful inter-group effects can be created simply by dividing a group into two for as little as an hour even when such a division is not done in any way to arouse antagonism. When antagonism between groups is deliberately aroused, as in famous experiments in boy's camps, the effects in the community are deep and far reaching.[38]

"Tajfel showed that individuals evaluate the groups into which they categorise themselves in either positive or in negative terms. Where participation in a group does not contribute positively to a person's sense of identity, he or she will tend to seek membership of a different group that will confer a more positive value to self. If however, due to prejudice, such a move is not possible that same person may fight strongly for the rights of the group to which they are confined.

The main point is that the perception of a relative deprivation between groups will start someone either on a course that changes his own social identity or which will engage him in activities that shift the social situation of his group as a whole in the direction of increasing its perceived value in society at large. In the first case, he shows 'social mobility', in the second he provokes 'social change'. In cases where barriers to changing identity are high, as when social mobility is prevented by racial prejudice or political reasons, then the perception of deprivation increases and desire for social action to change the situation is generated. By contrast, where few barriers to mobility exist, dissatisfied individuals tend to move into new worlds wherever possible. Generally speaking, members of minorities tend to move towards the majority when positive valuation may seem to lie there. Such actions and such mobility may have major effects on personal well-being and ultimately perhaps also on genetic fitness."

The Buddha joined in. "So feelings of deprivation are feelings of failure which may arise irrespective of the actual material or economic base. Both positive and negative expectancies can arise from comparisons that may be based on almost any distinguishable attribute of one group compared with another. Feelings of deprivation will continue so long as unfulfilled expectancies are supported by a sense of grievance or a feeling for their legitimacy. Indeed the process of history must consist largely in mobility and change occurring in response to social comparisons of this kind and the factors that generate it. In the case of 'inferior' groups, a perception of grievance legitimates the sense of deprivation and the urge to action; in groups already undergoing change, it justifies the moves under weigh; and in 'superior' or dominant groups, it legitimates the defence of the status quo seen to be under threat: – think of Northern Ireland, South Africa or Israel.

"One cannot split ideology, including of course its distorted forms, from the basics of social perception. Current problems arising from Islamic terrorism need to be examined in these terms and are unlikely to change until better understanding emerges. Ideas arising from deprivation undoubtedly drive action in such situations but these in turn arise from the basic urges of human nature for status, esteem and conditions fit for reproduction and the manner in which these are socially conceived."

"And the story is not complete yet," added Jim addressing the Buddha. "We can understand that all this complexity arose with the need of our ancestors to compute advantages and disadvantages within social life but we need to know also that the changes arising from bigger brains did not have merely social effects among adults. They initiated a whole set of integrated biological developments connected with human birth and the suffering that arises in connection with parenthood. 'Life is Suffering' began very early."

Problems with Big Brains

The development of the bigger skull produced problems that necessitated further evolutionary adaptation. Compared with other primates, human babies are very under-developed at birth. Whereas Great Ape babies' brains are half grown at birth, humans are only one quarter developed. Human babies thus need to complete their brain growth outside the womb over a long period. Indeed, it takes a year for brain growth to be completed and in the meantime, the baby is totally vulnerable and dependent on the mother.

The reason for this exceptionally early birth lies in the shape and size of the woman's pelvis. Bipedal walking evolved early in the hominid line and for this a rather bowl shaped pelvis shorter than the longer pelvis of apes was required. The dramatic increase in brain size at a point long after humans had become fully adapted to bipedal locomotion created something of a problem. Some sort of evolutionary compromise was required to deal with "the eye watering prospect of trying to squeeze an ever larger head through an ever smaller hole."[39]

Compromise was achieved in two ways. Women's hips are wider than men's and in fact, women's locomotor capacity, especially in running, is less. But the main compromise lay in giving birth to the baby while its head was still small and flexible. This meant birth when the baby was otherwise incapable of independent life. From a primate perspective, human babies are born prematurely, indeed only just at the point when they can survive outside the womb. This early birth, with total dependency of baby on mother, necessarily has major effects on the mother's behaviour because the obligatory care of babies, toddlers and children imposes limits on the mother's alternative behavioural possibilities. The conflict is not only in terms of time available for other 'professional' activities such as we see in modern culture, but poses fundamental problems in conflicts over biological fitness.

Eleanor was discussing the consequences of all this "According to the evolutionary paradigm, any behaviour by mothers that promotes the biological fitness of children should be progressively selected. Even so, the value of a mother's investment in any one child is related to the probability that it will survive to reproductive age and itself produce children. In theory, if the conditions for bearing or rearing a child do not support this probability, the mother may well abandon a pregnancy or even a born child. Yet, theory also argues that, from the child's point of view – and in opposition to the mother's – the baby will seek to maximise its own chances of survival and reproduction. There is thus an inevitable, underlying conflict of interest in the relationship between mother and baby and this begins in the womb. Do you know that between 30-75% of pregnancies are spontaneously aborted during the first fortnight of life?[40] This appears to be due to the selective elimination by the woman's body of low quality foetuses: the mother is however not personally aware of the process.

"For a pregnancy to be sustained, high levels of the hormone progesterone produced by the *corpus luteum* of the mother are needed. Progesterone production from this source decreases two weeks after the release of the egg and to sustain the pregnancy the embryo must itself produce a hormone to stop the regression of the *corpus luteum* and thereby sustain progesterone levels. If the released egg has not been fertilised, the *corpus luteum* naturally degenerates, reducing progesterone until the lining of the uterus is shed in menstruation. If, after fertilisation, the growing embryo fails to sustain the supportive womb, it is itself lost. An endocrine failure by the embryo probably signals its poor biological quality predicting a poor chance of survival or poor postnatal health. The mother's body consequently ejects it. Additionally, if the mother's health is poor, the embryo may be unable to sustain its uterine support so that the mother, by losing the baby, recovers her health; the condition of which may of course have been due to economic and other family circumstances."[41]

"That's a remarkable set of safeguards," remarked the Buddha.

Eleanor continued, "Furthermore, a child born into a family is immediately faced by the fact that a mother has to distribute her care among her children. We have already seen that maternal styles of attention and care deeply effect intimacy and trust between the mother and child with consequent effects on the child's mental development. A woman can enhance her genetic fitness by adjusting the level of her investments in her several children thereby increasing the likely survival and reproductive success of a favoured, healthy child. In opposition to this, each child may be expected to seek to maximise the care they receive from mother even at the expense of their siblings. By ensuring its own reproduction, a child would pass on more of its genes to the next generation than would be the case through the reproduction of its brothers or sisters, each of whom carries only half of its genes. There is an inevitable conflict between the fitness interests of mother and child and between siblings."

" Is this really so?" asked the Buddha.

"Surprisingly," continued Eleanor, "research shows that children brought up within the same family are more dissimilar to each other than they are to any two unrelated children selected at random. This counter-intuitive finding suggests that within the family there are conflicts between siblings causing different styles of behaviour to emerge. Some works suggest that parents treat each offspring differently, thereby pushing them into contrasting developmental trajectories.[42] Initial differences in ability will favour one child over another so that the less able in one respect has to find its own focus of ability in order to attract a share of parental investment. First-born children tend to be more conforming, responsible and antagonistic than later born children who are more imaginative, flexible and rebellious.[43] Older children behave in a manner that retains their advantages over later born siblings by emphasising family stability in support of parents. Younger children adopt more diverse and imaginative ways of coping with family tension and retaining parental support. It seems likely that this differentiation may reduce sibling rivalry by giving each child its own parent – attracting realm of competence. Family life encourages divergent developmental trajectories by which children may find success in life. There are also indications[44] that suggest younger children seek support outside of the family through friendships more than elder ones do. There is little doubt that as children grow, the peer group becomes as important to their development and differentiation as does parental care."

Jim added, "Parents indeed commonly encourage high levels of achievement in their children. Plausibly the way parents bias their encouragement of their children to achieve educational success varies according to the family context.[45] Where the future is uncertain, parents may opt to have children more quickly. Evolutionarily speaking, the amount of effort invested in any particular offspring is likely to depend on how probable it is that such effort will be translated into grandchildren. Under circumstances of tragic poverty this may mean that an optimal parental strategy is to invest nothing at all in a particular offspring once it is born."

"Seems extraordinary!" The Buddha remarked.

"Well," said Jim, "infanticide is actually an extremely widespread phenomenon found in almost all human societies.[46] This seems odd when the basic Darwinian argument emphasises parental care in achieving reproductive success; indeed love of children is a prime characteristic of human life. The widespread occurrence of infanticide suggests there is more to this than the mere carelessness of leaving a baby in a handbag on the Brighton line!

"Infanticide has three main causes: male doubts about paternity, poor offspring quality and poor economic resources. Whereas a woman can always be sure that a baby is her own, this is not the case for a man. All other things being equal, men seem less willing to invest in the care of a child fathered by someone else. Men need reassurance that a child is theirs before being willing to invest in its care. Guaranteeing paternal certainty is a main theme in many traditional societies. The insistence that women should be virgins on marriage, arranged marriage before puberty, the confinement of women as in the harems of the wealthy, unattractive clothing for married women and other crueller practices such as Chinese foot binding preventing a woman walking more than a few yards and clitoridectomy to reduce a woman's interest in sex, are all devices whereby a husband can be more secure in the belief that a child will be or has been fathered by him."

Eleanor added, "It is interesting that mothers in Western maternity wards often say the baby's features resemble the father's whereas neutral observers are more likely to see the mother in the child. Mothers suggest a baby resembles Dad especially when he is present – perhaps in order to reassure the father of his paternity and thus to encourage his emotional and economic investment in its well-being. Whether this is conscious on the mother's part or not has not been researched."

"In some cultures," said Jim, "failures of virginity tests at marriage can lead to abandonment of the marriage, disgrace for a girl's family and make it unlikely that the girl will ever find a husband. Illegitimate pregnancies may also cause disgrace not only to a woman but also to her family and relatives. In some cultures, women disgraced in this way may be in danger of their lives. Of course, the difficulty of rearing a child under any of these circumstances encourages abandonment of an unwanted baby. Infanticide may also occur when a baby is deformed in some way or had an unusual birth or when events of ill omen occur around the time of birth; all circumstances that would lead a mother to assume consciously or unconsciously that raising the child to adulthood with any possibility of it reproducing was unlikely or impossible."

"Unusually low birth weight or the arrival of twins may put a strain on a woman's capacity to lactate," added Eleanor, "and there are figures in the medical literature showing that one of a twin often dies young, plausibly sacrificed in some way by maltreatment or neglect so that the other may survive. Poverty or crisis situations may make it better to terminate investment, conserve resources and await conditions when offspring survival would be more likely. Both eighteenth century and contemporary abortion rates suggest women may suspend reproduction pending the arrival of better circumstances. The loss of a baby following the death of a husband and prior to courting another man may increase a woman's attraction, as she would be unburdened from responsibilities the man may not wish to share. And of course her child would be carrying none of his genes."

Jim continued the story. "A contrasting situation develops when family circumstances can support many children and there is pressure on wives to produce them. In such strongly 'pronatal' families, rapid serial conceptions put pressure on the woman's physical capabilities in rearing and lactating and wet nurses may then be employed. While the parents remain solicitous for the welfare of such children, employing wet nurses does the work needed to raise them and governesses or tutors are employed, as the children get older. Aristocratic families were often strongly pronatal in this way to ensure the succession of wealth. One Duchess of Leicester, for example, gave birth to her first child at the age of sixteen and her twenty first and last at the age of forty-six!"

"Furthermore," added Eleanor, "as competition for good wet nurses developed between wealthy families, the quality of care became less and late born children suffered. Once an heir and a spare son had arrived, later boys might be sent to wet nurses elsewhere on the estate or further a-field, their care then being unmonitored by the parents. In Germany, in the eighteenth and nineteenth centuries, the mortality of infant sons who had three or more elder brothers was double that of earlier born sons! Wet nursing evidently increases reproductive success but also leads to reduced investment in children seen as surplus to family requirement."[47]

Sources of Suffering and Evil

The Buddha reflected that these studies show quite clearly that conflicts of interest rooted in the contrasting means whereby parents and children consciously or unconsciously endeavour to maximise their inclusive fitness through reproductive success play a major role underpinning the circumstances of child rearing. He had also learnt that much adult mental suffering is rooted in mental conflict arising primarily in the earliest years of relationship with mother and that father's attitudes play a further complicating role. It seemed to him that we might soon be in a position to assemble a more general theory whereby the human experience of suffering is seen to have a biological basis in the conflicts of interest they had been discussing. Many of these conflicts, he realised, are expressed in the holding of attitudes and the adoption of ideas or ideologies that mediate between social and biological levels. He began to see why the self has to go through such a stressful process before it can reach a more or less balanced adult life. Suffering was not so much a maladaptation as a consequence of compromises forced upon mother and child in biological evolution.

As they took a break, the Buddha looked out of the window pondering what they had been discussing. Suffering, as he had long ago known, was clearly an intrinsic part of human life but a specific form of human suffering was mental rather than merely physical. The mental aspect arises in relation to the self, perceived as a unitary being – the subject of experience. As a growing child begins to conceive its 'self', it is subjected to all the situational pressures arising from the necessities of rearing. No wonder the self is often distorted into bizarre forms of self-protection through repression, defence and denial. Consciousness of self is to varying degrees always painful. Not to suffer is thought of as 'good', he contemplated, and we humans spend much time, money, intellectual endeavour and philosophical speculation in avoiding hurtful or psychologically damaging experiences. Suffering in itself cannot however reasonably be called 'evil' – it is simply unavoidable.

The Buddha returned to his companions. "What then is evil?" he asked.

Jim responded, "Perhaps the most open definition would be to say that any action deliberately undertaken to cause another suffering is the root of evil. For example, the down treading of rivals to an extent that is not merely the resolution of competition but intended to eliminate them in shame, disgrace, suicide or murder involves the suspension of empathy to a degree that merits the term. Empathy is the positive side of childcare and fellow feeling, which allows cooperative endeavour, joy and a feel for the worth-whileness of life. To deny such experience totally to another is in all cultures considered an evil thing."

"Yet, you know there is more!" added Eleanor. "The extraordinary willingness of some humans to inflict cruelty, the terrible cases of serial killers and their methods of torture. We must consider the institution of cruelty in circumstances of ethnic or political 'cleansing' and the forms of military inquisition in Nazi Germany, Cambodia, Serbia, Dhafur and prisons in Iraq."

Jim said, "Most mammals have means whereby competition is regulated so that an opponent lives to tell the tale. Dogs in particular can stop a punishing fight by rolling on their backs in surrender. The victor simply stops fighting and lets the fallen go. Even where males of certain mammalian species take over harems and destroy the offspring of the preceding owner, the killing is direct and not practiced as cruelty. It has therefore been with surprise and some horror that male chimpanzees have been found capable of cruelty in the mutilation of rivals and that this has once been extended to the murder of a human child that happened to get in the way."

"How so?" asked the Buddha.

"Chimpanzees live in groups of males and females in which dominance hierarchies and alliances determine mating success. Chimps are not primarily predators but some populations do hunt monkeys for meat and share it between them. With increases in population density, rivalries develop between neighbouring groups of males – mainly in relation to territory but also in relation to access to females. Recently a gang of males has been found attacking and mutilating to death a defeated rival male, tearing its flesh and beating it in clear attempts to inflict pain. Many such cases have occurred in the community of apes living in the Gombe Stream Reserve made famous by the pioneering studies of Jane Goodall.[48] She had found that one way of acclimatising the chimps to her presence was to feed them. Regular banana feeding became the means to important discoveries through direct observations of animals habituated to human presence. However, the feeding stations became places of violent competition and it has been suggested that the provision of locatable food in this way has been the cause of social disruption based on severe fighting in food competition. At first, it seemed that other groups without such provisioning showed far fewer incidents of this sort but new research suggests the problem to be quite general. It may therefore not be the case that the killing of rivals relates solely to human interference but to be more generally related to the density of a population. Research continues."

Eleanor pointed out, "Some primatologists[49] have been struck by the willingness of some chimps to torture another. They point out that fighting of this kind need not involve cruelty, so why does it occur? In his 'demonic male' hypothesis, Richard Wrangham suggests that it is the chimps' advanced abilities in being able to know themselves through a degree of self consciousness that is responsible for such behaviour. An animal that can empathise with the feelings of another through the projection of a knowledge of its own feelings, can also know what another feels in situations of both affinity and enmity. It seems that over many years in intensified situations of food or territorial competition, Chimpanzees may develop an emotion of hate for their rivals encouraging them to indulge in a satisfaction of knowingly inflicting pain when a rival had been defeated.

"It is far from certain how far this hypothesis can be generalised to apes in general or attributed only to males but a disturbing insight has arisen. Our very human ability to empathise and understand the feelings of others may be the root of hate-filled behaviour that deliberately inflicts cruelty in the destruction of another. Where this arises there is no doubt about the dangers of 'evil' – because we do not know the horizon beyond which this dehumanising tendency may lead. So far, we have had the Nazi genocides, Cambodia, 9/11, Beslan and Bali.

No doubt there is much more to come, as horror and its emotional effect becomes a weapon of terrorists and defending governments forget their human responsibilities in reprisals."

"There is an extraordinary paradox here," remarked Jim. " It is precisely the capacity for empathy that psychologists believe allows the expression of vicarious altruism. The 'empathy-altruism' hypothesis states that observation of another's suffering stimulates feelings of sympathy, compassion and tenderness as an empathic emotion. Tests suggest that these responses are not based in some selfish motivation. We have then the extraordinary proposal that our capacity to empathise with the feelings of others underpins both cruelty and kindness Rooted in our human nature is a profound ambivalence. We need to understand what it is that tilts our behaviour one way or the other.[50]

"We are indeed tragic beings," said the Buddha.

CONCLUSION

The Buddha lay in bed reflecting on the day's long conversations. In his First and Second Noble Truths, all those centuries ago, he had argued that life was suffering and that suffering was due to desire. These stories of contemporary discoveries concerning the development of the human mind through infancy with all its struggles seemed to him to fill out the picture in an extraordinary way. The origins of the mind in developing a self involved motivations ensuring survival and also success in reproduction. The story of how these motivations had evolved seemed remarkably clear. These were indeed the roots of desire. Together with the fear of loosing itself, either because of social abandonment or finally through death, these experiences of self constructed the patterns of human suffering. Yet how complex was human society! Warfare and competition were endemic and arose always from the need to gain wealth or superiority in one form or another. Value was placed on money because of what it could buy – eventually survival and reproductive security. Religion with its illusions of ultimate safety was dangerous to oppose. Anger arises out of fear that a faith may die and with it the meaning given to oneself. These social fears and ambitions were rooted in the values humans held. The very capacity for empathy with others seems to lie at the root of both cruelty and kindness. Was wealth a good thing? Was Jesus or Mohammed the greater prophet? When was a freedom fighter a terrorist? The holding of contrasting values lies at the root of such disputes. And the deepest of these concerns the argument about how to run the world.

End Notes

1.   Nagel, T. 1974. What is it like to be a bat? *Philosophical Review*: 435-450.
2.   Uexküll, J. von. 1909. *Umwelt und Innenwelt der Tiere.* Berlin.
3.   James, W. 1890. *The Principles of Psychology.* Macmillan. London.
4.   McGinn, C. 1999. *The mysterious flame: Conscious minds in a material world.* Basic Books. New York.
5.   Chalmers, D. 1996. *The Conscious mind. In search of a fundamental theory.* Oxford University Press.
6.   Dennett, D. 1991. *Consciousness explained.* Little, Brown and Co. Boston Mass and London.
7.   Brooks, R.A. 1991. Intellegence without representation. *Artificial Intellegence.* 47:139-159.
     Brooks, R.A. 2002. *Robot: the future of Flesh and Machines.* Penguin. London.
8.   Blackmore, S. 2003. *Consciousness – an introduction.* Hodder and Stoughton. London.

9. Humphrey, N. 2006. *Seeing Red: a Study in Consciousness.* Belknap Press.

10. Crook. J.H. 1980. *The Evolution of Human Consciousness.* Clarendon. Oxford.

11. Harré, R. 1996. *Methodologies for the study of Consciousness: a new synthesis.* Proceedings of an International Symposium. Fetzer Institute. Kalamazoo. 1996. Ed.: Janet Richardson & M. Velmans. p.186. (Private distribution. Contact: Max Velmans. Goldsmith's College. University of London.)

12. Barlow, H. 1987. The biological role of consciousness. In: *Mindwaves.* Eds. C. Blakemore and S. Greenfield. Blackwell. Oxford.

13. Searle, J. 1987. Minds and brains without programmes. In: *Mindwaves.* Eds. C. Blakemore and S. Greenfield. Blackwell. Oxford.

14. Gray, J. 1987. The mind-brain identity as a scientific hypothesis: A second look. In: *Mindwaves.* Eds. C. Blakemore and S. Greenfield. Blackwell. Oxford.

15. Crook, J.H. 1987. The Nature of Conscious Awareness. In: *Mindwaves.* Eds C. Blakemore and S. Greenfield. Blackwell. Oxford.

16. See Crook, *loc cit* above.

17. Blackmore, S.J. 1984. A psychological theory of out of body experience. *J. Parapsychology.* 48:201-218.

18. Sherrington, C.S. 1947. *The Integrative Action of the Nervous System.* Cambridge University press.

19. Crook, *loc cit.,* above.

20. Jolly, A. 1966. Lemur social behaviour and primate intelligence. *Science.* N.Y. 153:501-506.

21. Humphrey, N.K. 1976. The social function of intellect. In: P.P.G. Bateson and R.A. Hinde (Eds.). *Growing points in Ethology.* Cambridge University Press.

22. For a recent critical survey of this perspective see: Barrett, L. and P. Henzi. 2005. The Social Nature of Primate Cognition. *Proc. R. Soc. B.* 232, 1865-1875. Also: Mithen, S. 2006. Ethnobiology and the evolution of the human Mind. *J. Roy. Anthrop Inst.* (N.S.): 45-61.

23. Dunbar, R.I.M. 1996. *Grooming, Gossip and the Evolution of Language.* Faber and Faber. London.

24. However – casual observations suggest that when the topic of conversation concerns intimate experiences women contribute far more than men. Superior feminine skills at interpreting the emotional behaviour of men may facilitate this but research seems wanting.

25. Crook, J.H. 1980. *The Evolution of Human Consciousness.* Clarendon. Oxford.

26. Humphrey, N. 1983. *Consciousness regained.* Oxford University Press.
    Humphrey, N. 1987. The inner eye of consciousness. In: *Mindwaves.* Eds. C. Blakemore and S. Greenfield Blakewell. Oxford.

27. Cloak, F.T. 1975. Is a cultural ethology possible? *Hum. Ecol.* 3:161-182.

28. Dawkins, R. 1982. *The Extended Phenotype.* Freeman. Oxford

29. Richerson, P.J. and R. Boyd. 1989. A Darwinian theory for the evolution of symbolic cultural traits. In: Freilich. M. and Hadley, S. (Eds.) *The Relevance of Culture.* Bergen and Garvey. New York.

30. Solanas, V. 1971. *SCUM Manifesto.* Olympia Press. London.

31. Blackmore, S. 1999. *The Meme Machine.* Oxford University Press.

32. Corning, P. 2003. *Nature's magic. Synergy in evolution and the Fate of Humankind.* Cambridge University Press. See also chapters in Haldane, J. (Ed.). 2004. *Values, Education and the Human World.* Imprint Academic. Exeter.

33. See a critical assessment by Robert Aunger. Chapter 41 in: *The Oxford Handbook of Evolutionary Psychology*. (Eds.) R.I.M. Dunbar and L. Barrett. OUP. 2007.

34. Midgely, M. 2001. Why memes? In: *Alas poor Darwin. Arguments against Evolutionary Psychology*. H. Rose and S. Rose (Eds.). Vintage. London.

35. Wilson. E.O. 1998. *Consilience: The Unity of Knowledge*. Abacus. London.

36. Moscovici, S. 1984. The phenomenon of social representations. In: Farr, R.M. & S. Moscovici (Eds.). *Social Representations*. Cambridge University Press.

37. Tajfel, H. (Ed.). 1978. *Differentiation between Social Groups*. Academic Press. London

38. Sherif, M. and C.W. Sherif 1953. *Groups in harmony and tension*. Harper. New York.

39. Barrett, L., Dunbar, R. & J. Lycett. 2002. *Human Evolutionary Psychology*. Palgrave. London.

40. Haig, D. 1998. Genetic conflicts of pregnancy and childhood. In: S.C. Stearns (Ed.). *Evolution in Health and Desease*. Oxford University Press.

41. Maternal changes in blood pressure during pregnancy relating to the supply of nutrients to the placenta and the occurrence of pregnancy sickness have also been accounted for by similar arguments (See Barret et al. 2002 for review. p. 172-3).

42. Lalumiere, M.L. et al. 1996. Why are the children from the same family so different from one another: a Darwinian note. *Human Nature* 7:281-290.

43. Sulloway, F. 1996. *Born to Rebel*. Pantheon. New York.

44. Salmon, C. A. and M. Daly. 1998. Birth order and family sentiment: middleborns are different. *Evolution and human behavior*. 19:299-312.

45. Perusse, D. 1993. Cultural and reproductive success in industrial societies: testing the relationship of proximate and ultimate levels. *Behavioral and Brain Sciences*. 16:267-322.

46. Daly, M. and M. Wilson. 1981. Abuse and neglect of children in evolutionary perspective. In: *Natural selection and Social Behavior*. R.D. Alexander & D.W. Tinkle (Eds.). Chiron. New York.

47. See review of studies and the Trivers-Willard Effect reviewed by Barrett et al. 2002. p.184-188.

48. Goodall, J. 1986. *The Chimpanzees of Gombe. Patterns of behavior*. Belknap. Harvard University Press. Cambridge Mass & London.

49. Wrangham, R. & D. Peterson, 1996. *Demonic Males: Apes and the Origins of Human Violence*. Houghton Mifflin.

50. Fultz, J. & R.B. Cialdini. 1991. Situational and personality determinants of the quantity and quality of helping. In: Hinde, R.A. and J. Groebel. *Cooperation and Prosocial behaviour*. Cambridge University Press.

17

ECONOMICS AND ETHICS

The Buddha was becoming restless. He was gaining a clear picture of the extraordinary results of scientific investigation in the modern world but it was giving him an uneasy feeling that he had slipped off the road of his initial enquiry. Why was this? He pondered. He came to realise that his prime interest now lay in finding out what were the values people held and by which they led their lives. It was here that he felt a great difference from his own time. There was little spiritual orientation such as he had known in ancient India. Such religions as there were, he thought, hardly reached the level of spirituality already developed in India before his time. While science and psychological enquiry were providing an amazingly detailed map of human origins, behaviour and experience, none of it told people how best to live. There were few value judgements within the modern stoicism of scholars upon which to base a path of wisdom – although the truthful authenticity of many was certainly a start. Description and analysis, however penetrating, show people what they are but not how it would be wise to be. Many of the causes of suffering were known but a root insight concerning what to do about it appeared lacking or confused.

The Buddha remembered that in his Third Noble Truth he had argued that the suffering inherent in life arose through desires and attachments and that these might be relieved through abandoning such attractions. He remembered sitting under a tree in the Subhaga Grove near Ukkattha in northern India giving a sermon to his monks.[1] He had argued that the holding of all sorts of opinions about gods, one's own being, experiences of the everyday and spiritual practices as personal properties led to a self-centred delight that would inevitably lead to defence of views, strife and therefore suffering. This was all due to a failure in understanding, he had told his hearers. The wise had discovered that when this sense of selfish possession was abandoned an awakening to freedom occurred, and the suffering from such causes could be set aside. He smiled when he remembered that those present had not been delighted. Could it be that they had understood. He had taught that the way to let go of self-concerning opinion was through no killing, no stealing, no lying, no harsh speech, and for monks he had included no sex and no intoxicants. If someone's ethics were based upon such constraints and upon their further application to daily affairs much happiness would result.

He saw that the holding of views and opinions as 'mine' or 'yours' lay at the root of much strife and hate. If that had been true of his time, no doubt it was still true today. But what exactly were the views that people now held. Knowledge, he saw, was providing the world with powerful technologies for both creation and destruction but little wisdom concerning how to apply them and this seemed to be yielding more harm than good. In his heart, he felt the alienation stalking the streets in the escapism of so many people: their search for sensation; drug addiction; alcoholic fantasy; anxiety from provoking news bulletins; false identifications and endless tourism. People seemed to be living in some sort of drugged denial. A quest for origins was all very well, but to what action could it lead? He decided to look more closely at the more recent history of our times, the values that control current society and the life of citizens.

In his own life he had had experience of politics, had indeed acted as consultant to rulers of his time, and had observed the transitions in government from small quasi 'republican' systems with rudimentary democracy to authoritarian monarchies that were eventually to became vast empires. The motive for the growth and expansion of states had been control of resources for the production of commodities and trade. Economics and the ambition of kings lay at the root of such historical changes, at the very root of political action. The values of people had moved away from those of pastoralism with spiritual security towards conquest, gain and expansion. So what of the present era? He set to work to find out.

When Jim heard of the direction the Buddha's enquiry was taking, he doubted his own competence in this area and decided to invite an old friend to join them. Professor Jeremy Humberger was a colleague of his old supervisor in university; an economist by training, he was also a bit of a philosopher. When they next met, Jim brought him along. The Buddha observed this rather wizened little man with an untidy goatee beard and sharp gaze with interest. He suspected a critical intellegence and a polished scepticism that he sensed would be helpful. He offered coffee and asked him to tell them about the movement of ideas in the recent history of values.

"You must know for a start", began Professor Humberger, "there are several ways of describing history. One is to prepare an account in terms of the values and actions of leading personalities, the sequence of emperors, kings, queens or prime ministers, presidents of great powers, generals, statesmen, philosophers, divines or writers. Here we see portrayed the outcome of skill, wisdom or folly as deployed by individuals in their time. We may call such an approach, which focuses on individual singularities, an 'action' theory. An alternative approach is to examine history in the light of changes in economics, social systems, culture, ethics or technology, that is to say in terms of processes not persons. Many processes relate together and co-determine one another so that such an analysis tends to become increasingly holistic. Examination may uncover underlying or hidden themes often needing a quite abstract analysis. This approach may be termed 'motion' theory.[2]

"These two approaches are essentially contrasting perspectives for clearly the one need not antagonise the other. In some periods of history great personalities have stamped their imprint on their times to an outstanding degree whether for good or ill, others have had long term influences for many years after their short lives have come to a premature close, but always the condition of the times, economic and technological, belief systems and psychology have also played critical roles in determining historical outcomes. Since the industrial revolution, the complexities of economics, the geography of supply and demand and the power of regional ideologies have played a particularly predominant role. Individual actors seem caged and their influence more predetermined by circumstance than before. Recent history indeed suggests that the significance of individuals is being steadily eroded by the role of abstractions deriving from machine intelligence within huge, multi-national industrial complexes. Even now however the person may exert a critical influence in institutional change: Ford in the development of American capitalism; Gorbachov in the last years of the Soviet Union; Thatcher in shifting the attitudes of a nation; George W Bush in unwisely invading Iraq without an exit strategy."

The professor was getting into his stride: he sipped his coffee. "Anyone who has lived through the last fifty years," he went on, having re-captured his audience, "has been aware of accelerating socio-cultural change on a global scale, much of it profoundly unsettling to established values. No longer are the world's regions largely independent from one another, all are increasingly tied together by an ever expanding and ramifying system of finance which, beginning in the West, has spawned powerful interconnected yet competitive variants in other regions. Old stabilities, values and assumptions are being undermined at an ever-increasing rate. Major political shifts involving changes in regional ideologies have tilted the threat to civilisation away from an atomic war between superpowers to the increasing threat from international terrorism, ecological contamination, over-exploitation of non-renewable resources and a failure to manage world poverty. National identity itself becomes increasingly meaningless in a world of regional unifications financed by trans-national capital. People are often confused as to where they belong, to what do they owe loyalty; Britain or Europe say."

THE EMERGENCE OF POST MODERNITY

Jim felt they needed to explore economics as a useful approach to ideology. "A major theme preoccupying a number of contemporary thinkers," he interrupted, "is the shift from 'modern' to 'post-modern' culture; a turn that has moved us from one style of economic determinism to another with concomitant cultural and philosophical changes. Can we have a look at the processes of culture change in terms of underlying economic determinants? That would surely be a motion theory approach of considerable power and persuasiveness?"[3]

"Yes, indeed," said Humberger. "We are living through profound changes in the nature of Western capitalism, which, since the industrial revolution, has become the predominant culture of the entire globe. These dynamic, financial and commercial processes drive the cultural shifts through which we are living and also lead to the increasingly severe environmental problems still lacking resolution and becoming ever more menacing. In spite of the triumphant success of the capitalist mode of production, the fundamental contradictions inherent within it, as first analysed by Karl Marx, are still untamed and exert profoundly destructive effects on may aspects of human life.[4] Whether contemporary capitalism also has a latent potential for overcoming the very problems it creates is the greatest issue of our time."

"What are these contradictions?" asked the Buddha.

"Well," said the Professor, "the three prime characteristics of capitalism interfere with one another. Lets have a look at them and gain a basic understanding. The first we call 'Growth orientation'. Capitalist production requires growth to function. This is because the capital accumulation upon which further investment is based depends upon profit. Within the commercial world, company shareholders, from whom the capital for an enterprise comes, are required to provide continuing investment upon which further growth-oriented production depends. Shareholders are encouraged to do this by being provided with a dividend that comes from profit on their investments. It follows that the monetary value of the labour used to produce commodities must be less than the sale value of the product. Furthermore, since welfare provision by modern states is based in the taxation of profit, the very existence of social services of all kinds is rooted in the success of the capitalist endeavour.

"Then there is 'Labour exploitation'. The successful sale of commodities depends on their being attractive to customers and this is sustained by development and novelty. Growth is vital if the system is to be self-sustaining and this necessitates a difference between wages to workers and the value creation of the process. Since the spin off from profit goes to the ownership of companies, a class differential between labour and ownership is inevitable. There will always be a struggle between the maximisation of wages by labour and the company seeking to maximise profit through the control of labour.

"Thirdly, there is 'Competition'. Companies compete in commodity markets. Any company that can produce a cheaper commodity of comparable utility than others will achieve the higher turnover upon which profit depends. Technological advances and organisational changes in production aim not only at products that are more effective but also cheaper prices, a process necessarily focussing on the reduction of labour costs. Conversely, of course, labour, traditionally led by union activity, seeks to maintain its standard of living by resisting both technological innovation and organisational changes because these may lower income and reduce the size of a work force – and hence union strength.

"The contradictions within the process arise because the interaction of these three factors tends to produce an alternation between periods of successful capital accumulation through the successful sale of products with labour demands under control, and periods when poor selling products accumulate unsold, both capital and labour lie idle and unemployment reigns. If the cost of a commodity rises, sales fall, production exceeds demand and eventually drops, labour is laid off and companies move to introduce further technological and organisational fixes. When unsold products accumulate excessively throughout a market, a major recession develops as happened around 1930 on a more or less worldwide scale."

"All this began with the Industrial Revolution, I suppose," said Jim. "The development of industrial manufacturing in Britain in the nineteenth century coincided with the enclosure of public lands by private property. Large numbers of country folk lost rights to common pasturage and were forced off their land and into poverty. These people formed a large resource for industrial labour recruited to the emerging factories. In time they formed a whole class unknown before; a distinctive stratum in the body politic – the 'working class'."

"Yes," continued the Professor. "The economic system of the industrial revolution spawned a culture based on class divisions quite unknown previously. New ways of life and social consciousness emerged in the early twentieth century based upon the new class relations. One could say the capitalist captains of industry were ruthless in their quest for gain while the workers on whom they relied sought a fair share of the pie. The production system known as Fordism, after Henry Ford's giant automobile works at Detroit, yielded a 'modern' culture characterised by a marked simplification of architectural style to suit the functionalism of the system, huge factories emerged, vast assembly lines with individuals performing robotic tasks. Huge financial institutions developed, magisterial bank and office buildings, skyscrapers, high-rise blocks and formal estates. The countryside, now regimented by railway lines, motorways and system agriculture became increasingly a dormitory land for the cities. The underlying concern with ever more comfortable styles of life was satisfied through a science delighting in nuclear power, chemical fertilisers and fixes of all kinds. The rationalist values of the humanist 'enlightenment' generally held an optimistic sway with hopes for a changed world, removal of poverty and new styles of living. All this generated a rationality cleaning up the untidiness of old regional ways of doing things through rigidifying codes deriving from capital necessity. Inevitably a reaction set in with resistance to the machine-like mould into which culture was falling, identical airports world wide, city centres increasingly interchangeable and global class problems.

"Triggered by periodic financial crises the early reaction to 'modern' capitalism was essentially romantic whether fascist or communist. Fascism emphasised the place, the *volk*, the locality, and negated the universalism of the enlighten- ment thrust. Communism, emphasising the class struggle, the inherent exploitation of labour and the critique of monopolism, failed, as did fascism, to create a democratic system of government and, lacking popular legitimacy, degenerated into proletarian dictatorships which meant, Stalin, Mao and others even worse. Soviet gigantism paralleled that of the capitalist world but lacked the dynamism to sustain it. Yet, in spite of the immensity of the struggle between orthodox market capitalism and these alternatives, the conflict may in retrospect be seen to have been a sideshow in comparison to the playing out within capitalism of its own contradictions between competitive growth and over-accumulation."

"So how effective was this capitalist system, then?" asked the Buddha.

"In spite of periodic setbacks, some of them serious such as World War II, the capitalist system between the ending of the 1930's depression and the 1970s was generally expansive and recessions were controlled by careful state-organised balancing of capital accumulation and labour needs rooted in the ideas of John Maynard Keynes. For most of the period, vast potential markets existed within expanding economies at home and abroad and the low cost of raw materials under global colonialism greatly assisted the industrial powers. Ways out of recession have been traditionally associated with devaluation, debt rescheduling, retooling of the production mechanisms and the placing of excess capital in other parts of the world where new foci of capitalist expansion could be kick started and pump primed from outside, the hoped-for benefits pushed into the future. As new crises loomed in the 1970's, the Fordist and Keynesian solutions no longer seemed to work as before. The conditions which brought about changes at this time were very complex and are perhaps still not completely understood."

"The triggering circumstances," said Jim, "included the exhausting expenditure of U.S.A. in the demoralising and unsuccessful Vietnam conflict, dollar devaluation and the OPEC inspired rise in the price of oil but a major underlying factor must have been the very success of capitalism in becoming totally global with the consequence that spatial expansion as a solution to over-accumulation ceased to be an effective response to crisis – especially since old colonial territories were now independent states. The response took the form of 'flexible accumulation' in many shapes and guises that recall to mind some biological responses to density dependence (Chapter 2). All these changes underpinned the cultural shifts known as 'post modernity'."

"What do you mean by a more flexible accumulation?" asked the Buddha.

Humberger took up the thread, " Flexible accumulation is a change within the system whereby the gigantism and mechanistic structuring of old capitalism gives way to smaller scale networking in production, sub-contracting, diversification of products and processes, multiple company goals rather than single ones and looser more democratic, even idiosyncratic, organisational control with more participative and less authoritarian leadership. Labour becomes associated with profit taking through new forms of company ownership and management through a more flexible and enforceable relation with unions. Economics wider in scope than in scale becomes the norm, standardisation gives place to smaller batch production, which is driven by demand rather than resource availability. Labour focuses on learning multiple tasks, less robotic work and the payment of wages is made more personal and anchored less in fixed rates for invariant jobs. On-the-job learning becomes typical as industries adapt more easily to new demands and situations."

"The cultural spin off parallels these flexibilities," said Jim. "As the economic scene became more diverse and complex, so did culture. Old rigidities of class, ethnicity and gender opened up as diversification proceeded and as teenagers and women became increasingly part of the network of commerce especially in the media, entertainment and service industries. Art picked up on the break down of rigidities and reflected it in chaos of varying styles. All ideological assumptions became questioned and ephemeral personal values were often adopted through identification with briefly noteworthy celebrities, short-lived fads and fantasies. A myriad of life styles and gender variants emerged as 'permissive' culture becomes increasingly on line with the new economics."

"Furthermore," went on Humberger, "philosophy itself 'deconstructs' to the extent that no certainties remain other than the fun of criticising texts. When the only resources for thought are found to be the fallible texts of outdated certainties, the consequence is a rampant relativism wherein any belief, religion, ideology or idea is as good as any other. No basis for value remains since all values have the same value, doing one's own thing. Science, in spite of remaining the mainstay of the entire structure, gets a bad name since the values of scientists remain largely those of an outdated modernism. Vaguely defined 'new paradigms' are in, their exponents usually quite ignorant of their origins in orthodox laboratories, cybernetics, holism and participative enquiry. In the superficial religiosity of our time, romantic evangelism and New Age spirituality spawn old superstitions in new guises."

"Sounds like chaos!" remarked the Buddha.

" Not far off it!" said Jim. "All this ferment, anchored in changing economic practices, has led to a great increase in personal liberty and expression for many, yet such freedom is also associated with profound uncertainty. Old role models and institutions, church, school, royalty, seem increasingly irrelevant in a churning world of high personal mobility, reduced communal values, image making, the attempt to fix oneself somewhere if only for a moment. Heavy investments in the image industries, advertisement, news selection, soap opera creation and media promotion have led to a distortion of culture through an increasing monetisation. Mini-cultures spawn around the elaborate, empty intellectualisms of clique members talking to one another and selling their chat. Culture becomes something to buy rather than something created by the cultured. Statistical surveys of public opinion influence the way political ideas are presented and trust is lost as 'spin' prevails. The gutter press undermines values by catering to the literally vulgar tastes of a semi-literate majority making the sophisticated appear fools or fuddy duddy. Young fogies are in and just as quickly out, and false consciousness of all sorts appears together with imitation antiquity, every local bar becoming an Elizabethan inn with plastic oak beams and inglenooks filled with gas-fired logs. In Britain, a fashion for excessive boozing has lead to violent street encounters when the pubs empty at closing time. Young males resenting the successes of hard working, bright young women and a social climate favouring feminism, act out gross, often violent behaviour, in a crude, self-defeating culture of 'ladism', which some of their crudely dressed mols seem to appreciate. Virtual reality blossoming on new television technology provides a dreamtime in which image-identifying persons float in a maze of projections ultimately controlled by commercial monitors."

"And in the background," Jim continued, "with looming menace, are the results of continued planetary denudation due to the unrestricted exploitation of non-renewable resources and the accumulation of planetary waste. Coupled with the ecological crisis in some areas is permanent, politically tolerated, unemployment. The technological complexity of electronic commerce has meant that the employed earn excellent wages and a wealth driven lifestyle while the demand for complex skills has meant that the unskilled become the unwanted. The result has been the rapid emergence of an underclass, the poverty-blighted, street-sleeping, cardboard-box housed population of disaffected individuals who, failing to make it in the system, have nowhere to go, nothing to identify with and no money for comfort: a situation naturally at its worst when the market goes down. Furthermore, while many of the unemployed are well educated, often with fine degrees from universities that remain excellent if under-funded, many belong to ethnic communities resulting from immigrations of questionable wisdom in earlier times of economic prosperity. Look at me – I suppose I should still be hob-nobbing with the mangkas in Piraeus!"

Humberger added, mournfully, "We have watched the imagined, nightmare cities of a not distant future shape up on television screens where vast buildings of international corporations, paying fat salaries to jet setting computer skilled executives, overlook burgeoning street scenes where small scale entrepreneurs come and go. Back of the streets drift the unemployed, the criminals, the addicts, in an ever increasingly resentful mass bursting out in joy riding and police bashing expeditions. It's us or it's them and one day may be them if only they could find out how. And that is only one of the new nightmares. Islamic terrorists riding in on immigration become a permanent worry. At least they have some values!"

"So what are politicians doing to stop this rot?" asked the Buddha.

"Sadly," replied Humberger, "many, perhaps the majority, are in thrall to the demands of trans-national capital or the military-industrial complexes of great nations. Others are trapped in short-term administrations subject to periodic elections in which they have to satisfy poorly educated voters subject to all sorts of whims and prejudices. Yet there are some, along with the liberal intelligentsia in general, who are deeply concerned with these tragedies. Some fine politicians are trying but mostly failing. At least the newspapers often do a good job in keeping opinion on the boil and effectively exposing corporate corruption."

GLOBALIZATION

The social phenomena the friends had been discussing relate particularly to the developed nation states, U.S.A., Europe, Japan, but the effects of change are felt world wide. The world seems to be shrinking; an event in New York rapidly has effects in Kuala Lumpur or Tokyo. This experience of global shrinkage is known as 'globalization', a phenomenon with many aspects. In particular, the development of methods of global transportation and communication have been so transformed that monetary transactions can occur through the internet almost as soon as thought about and the delivery of goods and materials achieved within time periods never imagined in previous ages. More than anything else, these effects of technology have speeded up economic and financial affairs so that changes in these domains influence social life with an increasing rapidity. The mobility of people increases as they respond to new opportunities in places distant from home. Far-away places talk to one another within minutes. A few hours flying takes one across the planet. Components of products can be produced in far-apart locations on different continents and transported quickly to an assembly point. Money can flood a market one day and drain it the next. Manfred Steger sums it up as 'a multidimensional set of social processes that create, multiply, stretch and intensify worldwide interdependencies and exchanges while at the same time fostering a growing awareness of deepening connections between the local and the distant.'

Humberger was saying, "We should not however consider globalization to be a new phenomenon. Ever since mankind emerged from Africa, one kind of global spread or another has been going on. It seems to be an inevitable consequence of human biological and technological success in taming the original planetary wilderness. The growth of vast medieval empires created regions of unified control containing safe routes for trade and exchange. Relative stability in Central Asia allowed the appearance of the Silk Roads connecting China with Persia, India, Rome and medieval Europe. Safer shipping and navigational aids, together with spectacular naval victories over Holland and France, allowed the maritime empire of the British to link the furthest points of the globe across the oceans. The development of air travel made maritime dominance irrelevant. The aeroplane fuses the nations of today's world into one great interdependency. It is the speed of change that makes the post-modern globalization into a historically unique phenomenon. The prime effect is financial, making some unbelievably rich but the poor even poorer."

"Yet the powers that comprise the new world order do remain nation states." said Jim. "Historically, these states are a relatively new phenomena replacing the archaic patterning of loosely defined empires. In 1648, the Treaty of Westphalia brought to an end the disastrous Thirty Years War that ravaged the European continent in the names of Roman Catholicism and Protestantism. Underpinning the treaty was the acknowledgement that Europe was divided into sovereign, territorial states over which no superior authority or convention ruled. Each state made its own laws and methods of settling disputes. Newly created international law aimed to establish enduring relations between states but only in so far as to allow each to continue on its own way. Cross border conflict was a matter for the contestants to sort out and were usually settled by force not at all regulated by external agreement. It was understood that some states were bigger than others but again no authority regarding the balancing of their transactions was established. In other words, states could do as they liked but were expected to minimise conflict. Not surprisingly, the system broke down with the increasing competition between European states seeking to establish empires outside Europe that would ensure resources and control markets in an ever-growing industrialised competition. In addition, there was the gradual merger of nations into rivalling blocks of treaty states. After the two world wars, the League of Nations and the United Nations have sought to create a system of agreed international law that would provide a super-ordinate, conventional authority within the rules of which nations would conduct their affairs peaceably with one another."

"Unfortunately," Humberger joined in, "in the early 1930s great economic depressions in Europe and America brought down the entire capitalist dominated world. At the same time, the vengeful terms of the Versailles treaty concluding World War I produced a severe social and economic crisis in Germany, which, together with deep resentment, was one of the causes for the rise of Nazi Germany and World War II. The victorious powers in 1945 took it upon themselves to create a worldwide economic system that would balance the world's economies so that such a catastrophe could not occur again. Under the leadership of the United States and Great Britain, national representatives met in the small New England town of Bretton Woods in 1944 and drew up the agreement intended to regulate international economic relations and commerce for the future. The International Monetary Fund (IMF) and the World Bank were charged to carry out this task.

"The newly created IMF believed there was a need for collective effort by states at a global level to ensure that a worldwide depression did not develop. Depressions originate when there is insufficient demand for the products of economic activity. Over accumulation follows with resultant cut back in the work force, unemployment and the rest. John Maynard Keynes, the Cambridge economist, had seen that to offset a drop in demand a government could stimulate an economy by itself instituting new and original projects. This could be done in many ways including the cutting of taxes, lowering interest rates and increasing government expenditure. Keynes' detailed arguments were not simple and have undergone revision to account for the delays in response that may occur – but essentially his basic formula holds. The IMF therefore initially drew up policies whereby nation states showing downturns would stimulate their economies to prevent a collapse that would have inevitably affected their trading partners and potentially spread world wide. The IMF itself could provide funds to enable an upturn to be generated."

"The problem was that in the 1980's a shift in economic theory became influential in response to accumulating world problems," added Jim. "The new theory argued that markets were best left to themselves and would automatically recover. For example, it was supposed that when cars over-accumulate and workers are laid off, distress undoubtedly arises, but, once the market has fallen sufficiently, sales of new and cheaper cars will get going again and all will be well."

The professor broke in, "This of course assumes that the manufacturer has funds to do the necessary research and development – which may not be the case. Reaganite and Thatcherite policies were based on such themes and the IMF was converted to such a view. Funds would now only be given to countries if they raised taxes or interest rates, which had the effect of accelerating a downturn that should in theory hopefully lead to a rapid recovery. Essentially this meant that when a poor country dearly needed finance to boost its local economy it could only do so once it had bottomed out. The effects socially and financially have commonly been disastrous."

Humberger continued, "These shifts in economic policy were associated with two other innovations strongly supported by the IMF; market and financial liberalisation. Market liberalisation means that all countries open their borders to trade and cease maintaining tariffs to protect their own products. While this has permitted many companies to invest abroad and produce products more cheaply in areas where labour costs are low–and so boost employment there at least for a time, it has also meant that big producers can sell their products in small countries at lower prices than local producers who therefore go out of business while the prime earnings go abroad.

"Financial liberalisation means that a country's currency market is opened in a similar way. An investor can then buy units of, say, a South Asian currency at one price and sell it at a profit if its value rises. When the currency value is low, money pours in and, as it rises, pours out again. A South Asian investor, say, can keep his money in dollars until his currency falls when he can perhaps buy a lot of it in risky expectation of an upturn. The result, given electronic communication, can mean almost instantaneous flows of great sums of money around the world and contingent instability. An example: on the strength of the market huge development projects arose in South Asia, mammoth buildings etc. When the money drained away, the market fell, properties remained unfinished or unoccupied and the firms that built them, together with the smaller banks that had loaned to them, went bankrupt. The social consequences, especially for the middle classes and those they employ, can in such cases be disastrous. The wily investors meanwhile, in far off New York, London, Tokyo or Frankfurt, may make millions."

"A book I have found especially helpful here," said Jim, "is Joseph Stiglitz' *Globalisation and its discontents.* Of all people, he ought to know what he is talking about. He is a Nobel Laureate in economics, one time chief economist to the World Bank, its senior vice president till January 2000 and a member of President Clinton's Council of Economic Advisors. He describes in admirably clear detail the alarming march of economic misapplications throughout the globe since the 1980s that lie at the root of widespread distress and resentment."[5]

"Of course," intruded Humberger, "you must understand that globalization in itself is not bad. Opening up international trade has helped many countries grow far more quickly than they would otherwise have done. International trade helps economic development when a country's exports drive its growth. Export led growth was the centre piece of industrial policy that enriched much of Asia and left millions of people there better off. Because of globalization many people in the world now live longer than before and their standard of living is far better."

"Indeed," replied Jim, "globalization has in some respects done much good and retains its promise but, as Stiglitz argues, the policies followed, both by developed states and by the IMF since the abandonment of a basically Keynesian philosophy, have been deeply flawed and the current lack of trust world wide, as demonstrated in the mass protests at the Seattle meeting of the World Trade Organisation (WTO) and again in Genoa in 2001, is fully justified."

"I agree," said the Professor. "You see the chief beneficiaries of global economics in recent decades have not been nation states but the huge trans-national corporations (TNCs). These vast companies of limited liability compete in world markets through takes-over of lesser competitors, their collections of titles covering many types of commerce and their chief executives and directors earning astronomically vast salaries. The liberalisation of trade and finance serves their interests perfectly, allowing them to move whole industries around the globe following geographical shifts in financial circumstances. It is extraordinary how vast these TNCs have become. The biggest 500 of them account for 70% of world trade. Mitsubishi is larger financially than Indonesia, General Motors than Denmark and Wal* Mart than Israel. Salaries of high officials of these vast commercial empires commonly exceed the incomes of small nations.

"In common with all capitalist enterprises, these mega-firms must grow through profits and set out to shape the market so as to exclude or reduce the impact of competitors. This means not only controlling or influencing the media in their favour but also pressurising and maybe bribing small governments to allow legislation, contracts and ecological policies that favour their interests. In addition, through the trade and financial liberalisation policies of the IMF, they can enforce the entry of their products onto small states whose own producers thereby fall by the wayside. Furthermore and again grossly unfairly, their influence on the governments of the developed nations leads them to support tariffs and controls that exclude products of developing nations from finding a competitive market in precisely those regions where money could be made. Unfair, discriminatory trade laws and a failure, so far, of plans for debt relief, underpin the continuing poverty of much of the not-very-well developing world."

"So who controls a TNC and who is responsible for the effects of their business operations and economic policies?" asked the Buddha.

"In a sense, the answer has to be no one," responded Humberger. "A TNC is an economic machine within which the management is totally embedded. A TNC exists to pay dividends to its shareholders. These people mostly invest indirectly through their stockbrokers and unit trust managers; many probably do not even know where their shares are held. Unless they make a critical investigation into the ethics of their investment policy they leave the whole vast machine to run along on its own – maximising, competing, controlling exploiting, virtually automatically in response to shifts in world financing. Reading their newspapers, shareholders may tut tut with distress but they have no power to slow the advance of the steamroller in which they hold a tiny share. The IMF is actually paid for by the global taxpayer but the controlling authority is the United States. Stiglitz's book reveals a band of ideologues in charge committed to faulty opinions and seemingly ignorant of the best understandings of economic theory. Furthermore, there are court cases in process attempting to deal with extraordinary corruption in high places – most seriously but not exclusively in U.S.A. An unresolved question is whether the IMF and the TNCs could operate in a different, more socially conscious and globally responsible manner. The answer must of course be Yes, but how?

"For example, IMF advice and the hypocrisy of TNCs led to the wilful imposition of market policy on Russia leading to a massive failure in that country's recovery from the collapse of the Soviet system. By contrast, comparative study shows that states that refused to follow IMF-advised policies emerged more strongly from their crises than those states that did so. While the Czechs followed IMF advice, Poland did not and benefited the most. India and China both had their own capital controls and escaped the ravages of the global economic crisis. Stiglitz tells us that while developing countries with 'liberalised' capital markets actually saw their incomes decline, India grew at a rate in excess of 5 per cent and China at close to 8 per cent. This is remarkable given the overall slowdown in world growth, and trade in particular, during this period. China achieved this by following the prescriptions of economic orthodoxy–that–is when faced with an economic downturn respond with expansionary macroeconomic policy. The judgement is damning."

Jim continued the discussion, "Joseph Stiglitz points up a number of trends that would make a positive difference and which need to be incorporated in a more Keynesian approach to the support of state economies. Given the dangers of capital market liberalisation, interventions through the banking and taxation systems are important to limit short-term capital flows. Provisions for rapid restructuring after bankruptcies would allow a quicker recovery. Big bailouts should be avoided since they are so often used to pay back creditors rather than financing recovery. Banking regulation to prevent excessive or unwise loans is essential. Developing countries need to develop means of insurance against fluctuations in the international capital markets and to improve safety nets of all sorts. Financial policy needs to be related much more closely to social and cultural processes at stake and here local understanding is likely to be of greater import than that of bureaucrats in a Washington office."

"Indeed!" confirmed Humberger, "there needs to be a return to basic economic principles. The IMF needs to return to its original mandate of providing funds to restore demand in countries facing an economic re-cession. Countries in the developing world repeatedly ask why, when the United States faces a downturn, does the IMF argue for expansionary fiscal and monetary policy, and yet when they themselves face a downturn, just the opposite is demanded. The smell of hypocrisy is not easily dispersed."[6]

"These economic issues are compounded by the changing power struc-ture of the world," said Jim. "For a time, we saw the emergence of vibrant economies in SE Asia, the retreat of an economically unbalanced United States exhausted by military competition with the USSR and overspent in the Vietnam War, and the slow and problematic re-awakening of Europe beset by renewed ethnic problems. The Western World seemed to have lost its hegemony of influence, even if it retained a very expensive military strength often poorly deployed as in Vietnam, Afghanistan, Bosnia and Somalia. Local problems were subtle and did not respond to Western pressure, as they tended to do in the days of the Cold War. Meanwhile China grew and grew. And then came Saddam Hussein's invasion of Kuwait and the onset of the Iraq saga. In spite of internal economic problems, U.S.A. had built up an unrivalled military technology and emerged as the sole global 'super power. The world began to depend on the wisdom of this giant which, given its history of democracy, freedom of opportunity and so on, might have been expected to be positive. Sadly, this was not so. The dubious election of George W. Bush showed that, far from being a democracy, U.S.A has become a form of plutocracy where the exhorbitantly rich backed by industrial interest groups can raise huge sums virtually controlling the media to buy the presidency. And in U.S.A., the governing party of the President has enormous powers. The Republicans, a party boosted by self-interested business institutions, some of them highly corrupt, included so called 'neo-conservative' elements believing that the whole world could now become the play space for American wealth. Decisions to go to war with Iraq unsupported by the United Nations were falsely based on the supposed intellegence firstly that Saddam supported terrorism and secondly, that Saddam held stocks of Weapons of Mass Destruction that could threaten the Western world. The whole justification for war made by Blair in Britain to a resistant public and House of Commons seems clearly based in cleverly disguised lies, not errors. Horrible as Saddam's regime was, it was no actual threat to the West, indeed to a degree it provided a shield from the much more dangerous terrorism emanating from Islamic fundamentalists."

"So why the war?" asked the Buddha. "Was it the Bush family's revenge, was it oil, or was it simply a stage in a developing American economic imperialism?"

Jim replied, "Theories, especially conspiracy theories, abound for historians to sort out. Claiming the right to make a pre-emptive strike outside the authority of the United Nations, the USA is now shown to have done so without even the intellegence to support the case. The prime result is the picture of an overweening superpower ignoring the world forum of the United Nations, going it almost alone, making a fool of itself in the eyes of shrewder old hands in the diplomatic game, bedding itself down with no exit strategy in the unending strife of civic terrorism in Iraq itself and making little progress in controlling the global terrorism of the Wahabists. The British are right to enquire why their Prime Minister, tagging on to Bush's coat-tails, also led them down this muddy track."

"Meanwhile," added the professor, "the terrorism responsible for the 9.11 catastrophe in New York continues, only partially subdued by the unfinished conflict in Afghanistan. While the fundamentalism of the Wahabist minority within Islam is the root source of this suicidal destructiveness, the whole Islamic world remains disturbed. A prime cause, apart from its older memories of European imperialism, lies in the Western, particularly American, failure to do anything about Palestine. While the Israeli state has a right to its existence, the Israelis have to realise that Israel is essentially the last Western colonial project in an Arab land. Careful and empathetic negotiation between Israelis and Palestinians is the only way out of this problem but neither the Israeli government nor its American supporters know how to act or remain unwilling to respond appropriately to suggestions on offer. Faced by Israeli power and dominance, the Palestinians remain understandably defiant and intransigent. The continuing chaos, the underlying ignorance and suspicion of the Muslim world by the West, the Arabs own failure to develop democratic institutions and the rumbling competition for control of oil, all sustain a political scenario within which terrorism will continue to thrive and the traditional freedoms of Western citizenry reduced. There will soon be no place that US tourists can safely go!"

"It seems," the Buddha said, "that at the heart of the matter also lies the increasingly self-critical suspicion within the thinking public that Western ways are in some sense wicked. What could be more wicked than the destruction of the precious rain forests, the ozone layer, the dumping of vicious pollutants in the third world, and the existence of vast food reserves only a few hours flying time from desperate starvation? What could be more selfish than the policies of the TNC's and the concern of the IMF that international loans be paid back even before an economy has righted itself. There are those who can see that Islamic fundamentalism has gained strength precisely on the back of Western prejudice. The failure to meet these challenges suggests a profound lack of appropriate values in the Western world, an awareness that creates deep unease: cheating; lying; theft; gross hypocrisy; ethnic cleansing; and sexual fantasy appear institutionalised increasingly in our habitual forms of thought and presented in the Western media almost as norms. Yet, in the wings, remain the old moral injunctions awaiting some new expression. How do you think a new world ethic can come into being?"

"There is much in what you say," rejoined Humberger, "Yet we should not give way to too much doom and gloom. There are many departments of government and Non-Governmental Organisations (NGOs) that are struggling to meet major world challenges of poverty, hunger and famine, slavery, sexual exploitation, terrorism, conflict and environmental, destruction all over the world.[7] Some of them operate with a self-denying idealism that I am sure you would only praise. The *Médecins sans Frontiérs* charity, in particular, does exceptional work under dire conditions employing selfless doctors of great courage. Even so, I have to agree that the underlining philosophy for most such works is an instrumentalism, a search for practical solutions that leaves underlying issues of the conflicting values of the varying worldviews untouched. The world is too small to continue to support such endless conflict. We are indeed in need of an overarching perspective with which all those capable of influence can agree."

SOURCES FOR ETHICS

The Buddha was dining once again at the Islington restaurant. It was late night coffee time and Jim joined him at table as the last customers were departing.

"Speaking of ethics, we might ask how our great ethical systems developed in the first place," Jim began. "The appearance of ethical systems in the conduct of social behaviour is without doubt a hallmark of humanity. Almost all higher animals show rules whereby social organisation is maintained but these ethological rules lack self-reflective and mutually discussed controls. The origin of consciously deliberated systems and indeed of human morality in general, has become an important topic of recent discussion – much of it necessarily speculative[8]. A recent compilation of essays[9] provides a new view on the origins of cultural restraint. Morality and ethics depend on the holding of values and any escape from contemporary dilemmas depends very much on how human values are created and from what base."

" What can we say about the evolutionary origin of morality that may show whether we have some innate basis for the creation of ethics or not?" asked the Buddha.

"There are some fresh ideas coming up," replied Jim. "Christopher Boehm is director of the Jane Goodall Research Centre in the University of Southern California. He has worked with chimpanzees both in the wild at the Gombe Stream Reserve and with the detailed behavioural records and film kept at the centre. He has also conducted field research with Navajo Indians and Serbs. Throughout, his interest has focussed on conflict resolution and moral evolution. He looks for plausible origins in the theoretical ancestor common to Chimpanzees, Bonobos and Human. These three species are very closely related and he infers their traits in common have been present in their imagined Ape ancestor.

"Each of the three species forages for a living within territorially bounded communities that are subject to splitting and mixing as individuals move around. Status rivalry, particularly between males, occurs in all three and during a dispute an individual either dominates or submits. Individuals may club together to form coalitions, not entirely based in kinship, which support an individual member and which may drive away territorial rivals and provide assistance in joint hunting or collaboration in suppression of conflicts. Among captive Chimpanzees, a very large coalition of females has been seen to control the aggressive behaviour of a male of whom they disapproved – in spite of his great size and strength. All three species show high levels of intelligence in deceit and detecting deceit, evidence of mind reading and a capacity for mutual aid that extends beyond kin and seems based in mutual empathy.

"Chimps and Bonobos live in ranked hierarchies of dominance in which an alpha male comes to be the chief and whose sexual access and reproductive success is dependent on his aggressively asserted rank Humans, by contrast, form sexual bonds in either polygynous or monogamous sub-units within a community. These human behaviours plausibly began when violence from would-be dominant individuals became socially controlled during the formation of marital units. Indeed Stone Age bands probably consisted of broad coalitions, which would have severely limited the capacity of any particular individual, whether male or female, to attain overall sexual dominance. An egalitarian band facilitates the emergence of natural but not despotic leaders and supports them in acting to reduce the aspirations of any would-be despot. In this way, the clever but possibly physically weak tracker of game, a dotty shamanic genius and the heroically strong could each be an effective group member, the contrasting expertise of each being equally valued. Social approval, control of deviance and the maintenance of self-esteem would have come to replace dominance and force in social control."

"Are there living societies that suggest this to be correct?" asked the Buddha.

"Contemporary Hunter Gatherers do show comprehensive social controls," replied Jim. "Whenever a dispute arises, it is perceived as a group problem requiring collective management. Sometimes a deviant individual is judged but in many an instance, it is the problem itself that is socially examined and resolved. The dispute fades away without penalties being imposed. Egalitarianism seems to form part of the social skill needed in living nomadic life, especially if it is in a hunter-gathering style. High levels of collaboration in both hunting and gathering, in defence against predation, in the joint use of varying skills, are facilitated by control of disputation, especially in any dispute that predicts the rise of a socially disruptive bully.

"Does this include marital problems?" the Buddha asked.

"Actually," replied Jim, "Boehm does point out that there is one area of conflict where social control is poor – adultery. Sexual access is no longer determined by rank so any threat to exclusivity in sexual bonding is especially threatening to males and raises complex group issues. The strength of the impulse that leads to adultery and the violence with which it may be met are not very well controlled in such a community. An individual guilty of such behaviour or a respondent who may have reacted with murder, usually has to leave the community either for ever or until feelings have quietened down."

"It is certainly instructive," the Buddha commented, "that the Biblical ten commandments given by Yahweh to Moses for the well being of the wandering Israelites focuses on just such points as do the precepts of Buddhism, controlling killing, cheating, lying, shirking, theft and sexual crimes. Such values become political; infringements becoming a source of gossip, judgement and social exclusion or admiration. The Iroquois, for example, formed large multi-tribal republics with political institutions subtly controlling authoritarian tendencies. Indeed theirs was a form of representative government that was not ignored during the framing of the American constitution."

Jim returned to his theme, "Although the discovery of agriculture may not always have led to less egalitarian behaviour, it seems certain the emergence of large scale farming, marketing of surplus and trading did so. The production of surplus allowed some families to become wealthy and others poorer, leading to competition between land owners and the sexual selection of wealthy men for daughters of the poor to marry, both associated with all the ploys that Machiavellian intelligence could bring to the achievement of power. The original tribal rules could be expanded into institutions of social regulation through formal religions that maintained privilege and social position and which often lasted for centuries. Today, with the advent of the vast and impersonal world of monetised industrial capitalism, many of the original ethical controls have broken down under the impact of individualism. Money is now the ultimate value and controls on financial dominance seem almost non-existent."

"So how did the great ethical systems of religion come about?" asked the Buddha.

"In his book, *The Ethical Crises of Civilization*, Leslie Lipson asks whether there is evidence for ethical evolution," Jim replied. "Ethical advances have come in fits and starts and the conditions for improvement are not easily understood. The philosopher Karl Jaspers pointed out that there have been periods when dramatic shifts in the ordering of society and the values attributed to life have burst upon the scene. He called these 'axial ages' upon which pivot major socio-economic and ideological changes. These periods alternate with centuries during which conservatism reigns and society becomes increasingly static. Sometimes these sudden changes affect quite differing regions of the globe within the same few centuries. This pulsation in history may perhaps be compared with the 'punctuated equilibria' observed in biological evolution. Sometimes a breakthrough follows a breakdown but this is not always the case. Often an exceptionally gifted individual offers new ideas that alter the values people hold and hence the way they live. It seems likely that social changes induced either by increasing population, settlement in new habitats, new materials such as iron coming on stream, or density dependent shifts in economics, have produced situations that became increasingly unstable and during which the imagination of gifted individuals created new ideas that came to replace older ways of being. Lipson argues that there have been two especially great revolutionary periods in the cultural history of humanity during which the root values of the contemporary world were established."[10]

"OK, when were they?" asked the Buddha.

"In the first, we find great figures living widely apart within the same few centuries, Zoroaster, Confucius, Lao Tzu, Gautama Buddha, Mahavira the Jain, Hebrew Prophets and Greek philosophers whose influence has set the tone of the ethical evaluation of conduct ever since. In spite of significant differences, the basic commandments for living which they recommend have a core in common to do with tolerance rather than killing and warfare, honesty rather than deceit, respect for property, care in sexual relations and for family integrity and generosity rather than meanness toward others. It is easy to see how such values became important as tribal structures became complex, populations increased and urbanisation with commerce began: any trend in an opposed direction always led to social and economic chaos or tyranny with misery. Societies full of murder, dishonesty, lying, stealing and adultery do not make for happy people and do not seem to last long.

"The second axial age, you may be surprised to hear, occurred in Europe after the Renaissance when the soporific power of the Church was at last broken and inventive genius flowered with the expanding commerce of the middle classes. There was a return to many of the values of the classical Greco-Roman world with key emphases on the value and importance of the individual standing for himself before God and the world, the rights of all human beings for respect to their persons and for minimum standards of health, accommodation, opportunities and freedom from exploitation. These humanistic values rapidly began replacing the other-worldly focus of the Church with its intolerance of change, moralistic prescriptions on sex and marriage, and refusal to explore the nature of the world through science."

Jim put a lump of sugar in his cooling coffee and continued, "This movement, known as the European 'Enlightenment', has been at the root of 'progress' ever since: progress in understanding nature and utilising the resources of the planet; in health care; in removing gross exploitation of other races, children and women; in slavery and work; and above all, after the French and American revolutions, in promoting the rights of human beings everywhere. Changes in ideas clearly lead to changes in action."

"I imagine," the Buddha interrupted, "that several factors are needed for such great advances to occur. The first may be a situation of economic and technological change that poses severe problems for an existing social order, the second, a cultural structure sufficiently flexible to accommodate social change and the third must be the presence of outstandingly creative individuals who perceive a way forward to a breakthrough."

"Indeed, a breakthrough often seems to have followed a breakdown but history is far from unanimous in this regard. We may hazard perhaps that the first two conditions are present right now and that the last may be imminent." Jim agreed. "The current Western dilemma stems from the deeply schizoid nature of Western culture in which the humanistic tradition of the Enlightenment is superimposed upon a powerful, other-worldly tradition seeking the transcendental solutions offered by the Churches. Somehow, the rejection of transcendentalism is associated with guilty doubt. The absence of a settlement with 'God' remains supremely unsettling. Someone may come up with a solution and it may not be a Westerner!"

The Buddha went on, "The paradox seems to be that the altruistic values of Christianity remain rooted in an other-worldly religion while the forward march of humanism has come to lack values of any strength other than individual 'freedom' based in self concern. The Christian, altruistic requirement to care for others as for oneself has weakened, while the capitalist thrust founded through the protestant work ethic has led to the handing over of nature to human exploitation through rampant self-promotion in business.[11] Indeed, in Britain, you have seen how the harsh effects of Thatcherite economics, allowing the rich to get richer while the poorer pay, have been resisted only by the divines of a Church with its own social values and finances in deep chaos."

"No doubt," Jim said, "we need a new axial age. The conditions would appear to be right but the pressure from individuals has not yet developed to a take off point. Clearly the search is on for many Westerners are in quest of an ethic for a better world, exploring, for examples, the relevance of ideas found in North American Indian religion, ancient Astrology, Celtic mysteries, Arthurian legend, the fragile guruism of New Age spirituality and the more orthodox traditions of mystical Christianity, Sufism, Jainism and Buddhism."

"Yet what exactly are 'values'?" the Buddha asked. "To find out we have to withdraw our gaze from the outer swirl of economic and political turmoil and consider the lives and experiences of those enduring these changes. Values are personal and to the personal we must now return."

Jim replied. "To me, it seems that root values are about our use of time, space and people. How are we to find worth-whileness in an active life? What is self-actualisation? How should we spend our time? What should we do about our environment? How should we relate to others? Is there meaning in the cosmos or do we have to create it? Are we victims of forces beyond our control or are we responsible for our fate and that of generations to come? We need to consider our awareness of time, space and relationship."

TIME, SPACE AND COMMERCE

On the following Sunday the two investigators went down to Southampton joining Eleanor on a windy, shower bespattered trip on a Red Funnel ship to Cowes and back. The weather kept them in most of the time so they renewed their discussions in the cafeteria watching the landscape of the Solent float by.

Eleanor took up the issue of ethics in the use of space and time. "We live within our personal ecologies of meaning construing our relations with the 'outer' world on the dimensions of space and time. In everyday experiencing, place and time often seem separate modes of being rather than inseparably related. Standing in front of a fine landscape painting, we seem to witness a timeless space. The landscape is static, frozen in time; it is all space. Contrariwise, when we gaze from a window witnessing the movement of the boats on the Solent everything is change and change is time."

"Yet," said Jim, "reflection tells us there is just one continuing 'arrow of time' pushing us relentlessly to our personal deaths and, in whatever way we experience space, time never ceases. In slowing down time before a painting, we experience space while being pushed by time increases our awareness of mortality. The millennial shifts in culture are happening so fast that feelings of personal irrelevance and an unrooted anxiety have become endemic, especially in urban life. This is the 'future shock' of Toffler[12] and what David Harvey terms 'space time compression' or the ' annihilation of space by time'.[13] Such changes are driven by the endless capitalist demand for growth through innovation."

"Even in medieval Europe, time involved money," Eleanor added. "The cost of transporting raw materials, goods or products increased with time spent in travel. Likewise, time spent in office tasks of administration and management, time consuming indeed with quill and parchment, cost merchants large sums they desired to reduce. Time measurement, the ubiquity of clocks, came to express the non-agricultural concern with hours and minutes on the job rather than the opportunities of changing seasons.

"A prime mode of increasing turnover and hence profit lies in the reduction of transportation time and a speeding up of administration. As new technologies, canals, railways and air transport came on stream so the restrictions of space and distance in the economies of scale became reduced. So it is too with the typewriter, telephone, radio, television, word-processing and so on. Work can often now be done from the home using word processors, internet, broadband, fax and cash cards so that the old divisions between work and home life, town and country become abolished. Dormitory villages are more continuously occupied and the disappearance of the older agricultural communities continues apace. Seasonality loses significance, coffee breaks, tele-programmes, and baby sittings rule the timing of the ex-commuters lives."

Jim agreed, "Space-time compression has reached the point where satellite images from anywhere in the world can appear on personal screens all within a few moments news bulletin. Time zone differentials are overcome leading to a 24 hours market in shares. Only hours separate the openings of financial markets in New York, Tokyo, Frankfurt or London. The global uniformity of high speed transactional processing annuls constraints rooted in the old spatial dimension. Art forms, dance, expressions of life ways and religions formally cultures apart flash on and off our screens becoming mixed in an extraordinary barely digestible collage. An averaging out of values occurs, for nothing from anywhere is more valuable than anything else. Everything is merely relative while the fear of uncertainty driven by the pressure for change is never appeased."

The Buddha summed up. "This is a world of stimulation, of sensation not of reflection, for there is no time to reflect. It is as if the qualities of becoming are paramount while those of being are neglected. Being requires the opposite of space-time compression. To 'be' implies a dominance of space over time, a relative cessation of psychological movement within which to savour the relative constancy of a period. A concern with place does in fact give this need some expression. Within a place, locational constancy reduces the anxiety of change. One has the temporary illusion of stability."

"That's so indeed," said Eleanor. "Of course, given the world we live in, the relief that this brings then becomes itself a commodity. Great cities with monumental buildings and a relaxed atmosphere from past culture have an air of permanence. Value is added to doing business there. Tourism focuses on the uniqueness of place. Places themselves may be falsified or even manufactured to stop time by the creation of the imitation old. Belonging to some illusory but seemingly underlying continuity becomes a marketable commodity, a resting place between birth and death where the flight of the arrow of time seems for a moment to have paused in some reflective space."

"Sadly," added Jim, "the churches of traditional Western religion seem often as much concerned with the rush of becoming as our culture in general. It is precisely in this general context that many have turned to the East in sad ignorance that a deeper Christian tradition remains extant in tucked away monasteries where the practices established by the ancient desert Fathers still provide a contemplative atmosphere that may yet say much to our time."

The Buddha took it on, "We may well argue that it is in the use of time and in our understanding of time that one root of contemporary psychological alienation lies. The headlong rush into change may produce only more and worse addictive hedonism. Rather than space-time compression, we need periods for space-time expansion and it is precisely in this area that the age-old message of the Fathers has something to say. Yet the same or very similar message is conveyed in Buddhism with a philosophical power uncluttered by the confusions of Christian theology and with a methodology of meditation honed by yoga."

"Look who's talking!" joked Jim as the disembarkation began.

VALUES AND THE FUTURE

That evening Eleanor thought through the conversations of the day and began to write in her diary.

"In the post-modern world with its extraordinary diversity of modes of life, overlapping ethnicities, uncertain class boundaries, travel channelled for comfort in tourist managed lands, televisual experience, we are faced with virtual realities of many kinds. An inconsistent schooling, focussed more on training for modern jobs than on enriching personal life, leads to the development of a fractured personal identity. We have our face for the work place, another for the home: we are pressured by the common values of the media into the specious conformities of a fashionable individualism. Unconsciously subscribing to a collectivism of isolated selves we hoodwink ourselves into the belief we are becoming 'somebody'.

The development of a personal self image is not often assisted today by the provision of role models that can give stability in any of the places and times within which we function. The breakdown of marriage and the family home means that figures on the television screen, mere shadows, often become the only exemplars for the young, parents no longer having qualities that command attention. Single parent families without fathers can rarely provide boys with masculine models worthy of respect, itinerant males being hardly likely to provide the relationship a boy seeking a positive identity needs. Furthermore, the quality of the images purveyed by the media is determined by the popular demand for reality-forgetting sensation: soap operatic, cardboard persons living life styles unobtainable for the majority produce merely a modern 'dreamtime' unrelated to socio-political realities.

We need to inject into this social confusion some set of ethically related ideas that link the traditions of humanism to those of a spiritual quest that is not a mere nonsense in the withering gaze of the scientifically educated. A founding consideration here may be that not all forms of capitalism lack the inhumanity of Thatcherism. In continental Europe there is a much greater respect for society. In Germany, the relations between labour and business have been carefully nurtured to yield policies of socially related public financing which have had considerable economic success but have not withstood the downturn of recession. The short lived but brilliant success of the Japanese economy has been likewise based not only on much governmental initiative in the support of industry but on a business ethic that focussed on the social aspects of company life and the national community. These are perhaps signs of a possible middle way between a gross capitalism capable of destroying humanity and some sort of social vision. We need to create an economic system based on values that benefit all. Capitalism as an evolved relationship between commerce and the wider society need not necessarily be evil. It is quite possible to create a social capitalism not based in some discredited ideology but in a renewal of strategic planning that can manage the Worlds ills. Such may however depend on a worldwide change of heart as well as new forms of pension provision. Can politics change values or must a change in values determine a politics that can bring about change?"

Meanwhile, back in his Soho flat, the Buddha was also turning over the day's events. He came to think that those who have now become the technological elite of post-modern capitalism, the so-called 'captains of industry', have not only great opportunities but also major responsibilities. Far less duped than most by the cults of our time, perhaps they may already be seeing beyond the limited materialism of Thatcherism, and the weasel words of a 'New Labour' engaged in subordinating traditional values of the left to a commercial ethic. The age of complete relativism in which all creeds and customs have the same value, simply doing one's thing, might be passing into a search not this time for some overarching ideology but for a flexible way within which none the less universal values could be expressed. After deconstruction, perhaps we could turn to reconstruction. Yet the deep issue is unconscious, institutionalised greed. How then in this decadent time to reconfigure our obsession with our selves, he wondered, sleepily.

End Notes

1.   See the Mulapariyaya Sutta in Nanamoli and Bodhi. 1995. The Middle Length Discourses of the Buddha. Wisdom. Somerville. Mass.

2.   Bailey, W. 1986. Consciousness and action/motion theories of communication. *Western Journal of Speech Communication.* 50.1.74-86. See also: Burke, K. 1969 *A Grammar of Motives.* U. California Press. Berkeley. Also: Matson, F. 1966. *The Broken Image, Man, Science and Society.* Doubleday. New York.

3.   This chapter relies heavily and gratefully on the instructive text of David Harvey, 1990. *The Condition of Postmodernity. An enquiry into the origins of cultural change.* Blackwell. Oxford

4.   The importance of Marx here lies not at all with the later emergence of communism as ideology but with the profundity of his insight into the capitalist process, so great a contribution to contemporary thought that to ignore it amounts virtually to an option of ignorance.

5.   Stiglitz, J. 2002. *Globalisation and its discontents.* Penguin.

6.   See Stiglitz, p. 240.

7.   For examples see: *Departmental Report.2006*. Department for International
        Development. The Stationary Office. London. Also: Shambaugh, J. J,
        Oglethorpe. R, Ham and S, Toghnetti. 2001. *The Trampled Grass: mitigating
        the impacts of armed conflict on the environment.* Biodiversity Support Program.
        Washington. DC.

8.   Broom, D.M. 2003. *The Evolution of Morality and Religion.* Cambridge University
        Press.

9.   Boehm, C. 2000.The origin of morality as Social Control. In: Katz, L .D. (Ed)
        Evolutionary Origins of Morality. Imprint Academic. Thorverton

10.   Lipson, L. 1993.*The Ethical Crises of Civilization. Moral Meltdown or Advance.*
        Sage. London

11.   Tawney, R.H. 1926. *Religion and the Rise of Capitalism..* Harcourt, Brace and
        Company. New York

12.   Toffler, A.1970. *Future Shock.* New York.

13.   Harvey, D. 1990. *The Condition of post modernity.* An enquiry into the origins
        of cultural change. Blackwell Oxford.

18

THE DIVIDED MIND OF
WESTERN PHILOSOPHY

The Buddha continued to eat most evenings in the small restaurant in Islington. It was out of the way, discrete, warm and comfortable and served a wide range of dishes. He was enjoying sampling the various menus from all over the world available in multicultural London. One of his favourites was Turkish food with its hints of Greece as well as the distant orient. He had become well known to the owner and usually sat at a reserved table near the back of the dining hall from where he could observe the clientele and sometimes overhear their conversations. He kept pretty much to himself because he had found that, for some unfathomable reason, people were drawn to him and wanted to talk. He often relished this but there were evenings when he just wished to sit alone, read a book or watch the passing scene. Jim continued to join him most evenings for a late night coffee.

THE CONTEXT OF THE CARTESIAN REVOLUTION

One evening Jim approached him. A guest who also ate from time to time at the restaurant would be very happy if they could meet. The Buddha said he would be delighted and a short man with vivacious eyebrows, sharp, dark eyes and an odd accent joined him over coffee. Soon the Buddha found that his companion had a style to his conversation that was refreshing, even challenging. The man was acutely observant, enjoyed the nuances of words, disagreed with most arguments, scorned both politicians and intellectuals, and, although obviously one of the latter, appeared to love the world through hating it and shone with a delight in conversation itself. He was French.

"Ah Monsieur!" he was saying, "You won't discover anyone discussing values here in London! Even if you found a philosopher worth talking to, he would only be interested in Truth – la Verité. Ah-la Verité – an obsession ici! The English and the Americans seem never to ask what is the use of knowing truth – even if that were possible. And perhaps they have a case after all. What indeed can you do with truth?"

And the Buddha was reminded of his 'tutorials' with University professors at which the hard sciences or psychology gave an account of the world that certainly took a pride of place in their arguments. Values were relative, culturally determined, idiosyncratic maybe. You could believe what you want. Here was a man who was questioning all that. He was intrigued.

"You see, Monsieur, ici à Londres, there are no philosophers, only empiricists. The only true philosopher they had was an Austrian–ce Monsieur Wittgenstein. He was a student friend of that Bertrand, how do you say it, Russell. Well, alors, I have to admit Russell was a character even if as dry as dust in his thinking. Do you know that when he was about to receive a Chair in an American university some conservatives took exception to his liberal views on sex and his atheism? They cooked up a lawsuit accusing him of being lecherous, libidinous, aphrodisiac, narrow minded, a liar lacking in moral fibre quite unsuited to a college evidently dripping with holiness. And, of course, perhaps they were right! He was un peu méchant peut être de temps en temps. But that would have earned him a chair in the Collége de France! Monsieur, if you want to understand European thought, you must come to Paris!"

And so it was that the Buddha, beguiled by this style of irreverent, critical discourse, found himself in a small hotel in Le Quartier Latin enjoying the street life, sitting outdoors in the cafes of Paris in the springtime. As in London, people seemed to want to talk with him but what they seemed to love best was an argument.

He asked one young woman who had joined him after a light lunch, as attractive in her manner as in her vigorous debating skills, whether she agreed with anything.

"Ah, mais non! We must disagree about everything."

"Everything?"

"Oui, monsieur, for that is how we can change the world."

"Do French people never agree about anything?"

"Ah, but of course!" replied Dominique. "The English are – 'ow do you say it – perfide – perfidious. The Americans, – hypocritical and stupid – as well as having too much money. They want to buy the whole world. French is the only language really worth speaking and if you want to eat well, you must never leave this place! But, of course, Monsieur, we will never admit we agree about such prejudices! If someone puts such a view forward – everyone else will suggest an alternative!"

The discussion turned to the holding of values and the Buddha discovered that it was indeed the meaning attributable to life that seemed to make the French tick: Wisdom not Truth. He set to work to understand what this difference could mean. To his surprise, he learnt that the Germans, or some of them, evidently had thought the same way too – and indeed had set this whole ball rolling.

The young, feminist philosopher was in full spate. "In London, Cambridge and Harvard they talk about something they call 'continental philosophy' – as if the British did not belong to our European continent! And indeed, I sometimes fear they do not. And the Americans like to begin philosophy with some local pragmatist or other. They do not have long memories – our transatlantic cousins. What they call 'continental philosophy' lies at the root of Anglo-Saxon thought, just as it does of ours, the Germans', the Poles' or the Russians'. But it is true that whereas most of the Anglo-Saxon thinkers in this last century came to revere objectivity so called, and empiricism, we on this mainland of Europe, persisted in trying to find out how we should live and not merely what life was. To the empiricist, this seems like a waste of time, but over here, we speculate about how to live a good life. It's not easy since 'God is dead'! Who can tell us what to do? That is what we keep thinking about. Of course, we are scientists too, and 'continental philosophy 'indeed intrigues some Anglo-Saxons, but if you want to learn about it, just see how we talk, how we argue. Both ways of thinking, truth and value, make up philosophy. We feminists, in particular, try to find a different viewpoint–less dominated by the egoistic assertions of all you men!"

"Do you think there is a middle way?" asked the Buddha.

"Maybe so – if we are to survive, we need to find it."

"Why do you think philosophy is in such a mess?" The Buddha asked.

"It's a long story," replied Dominique. "We used to be taught that the emergence of science and progress was the result of the European 'Enlightenment', whereby the rediscovery of Greek humanism during the Italian renaissance spread to northern Europe. As the superstitions and the dominance of the Church receded, so a new age of enlightened reason gave rise to new modes of personal freedom, democracy, technological progress and the spread of trade around the world. In his book *Cosmopolis*, Steven Toulmin shows how simplistic had been this understanding of history.[1] The enlightenment of Europe had actually entailed a backing away from the freedoms of a renewed humanism in favour of the establishment of a rigorously abstract philosophy, which, while it allowed the march of science, came to omit much of the free discourse and openness that the Renaissance had at first engendered. Science on the one hand, God on the other. Not much in between. This was the result of war. Thirty years of it."

"A long time for a war!" remarked the Buddha, "How come?"

"The Thirty Years War grew out of the collapse of the huge European empire of Spain, which linked the Netherlands to Italy and to Spain itself. Germany was a mass of small states. Only France and Britain were of a size similar to that of today. Religious disputes between Catholicism and Protestantism raged, the contrasting interpretations of Christianity becoming more entrenched and irreconcilable. Henry of Navarre, King Henry IV of France, sought to bring about a greater tolerance that would allow less strife within his kingdom. He pronounced the Edict of Nantes giving the protestant Huguenots rights in catholic France and he endeavoured to negotiate between the catholic and the protestant positions. When he was assassinated in 1610, all Europe recognised that the last hope for tolerance was dead. The rulers of the small, central European states backed one or another religious position and employed large mercenary armies to fight each other. The horrors multiplied, vast swathes of countryside were laid desolate, cities ruined, murder and mayhem reigned. To all thinking people the inability of the rulers, bishops and politicians of the numerous states to bring about a settlement was a source of great distress and fear.[2] The need for security through regulation was paramount in their minds when at last, at the Peace of Westphalia (1648), the states stabilised their boundaries and their religions around the concept of 'nations'."

" So how did this result affect philosophy?" persisted the Buddha.

"You see," resumed Dominique, "before these disasters had struck, European thinkers of the late Renaissance, Francis Bacon (1561-1626) and Michel de Montaigne (1533-1592) for example, thought and wrote in an open sceptical style that engaged every topic of interest, great or small, relationships, odd far-off customs, dress, manners. The everyday life as they found it was the realm of their discourse. These thinkers were religious in the open, easy fashion of the times, they were church-goers, and their writings did not harp on theological justifications. Their humanism was therefore not anti-religious; they were not troubled by their personal salvation. Montaigne discusses his personal habits engagingly, his greediness, his sexuality, but without self-reproach or any need to justify himself. Their religious affiliations did little to constrain their cool, open discussion. They were non judgemental.

"After the terrors of the war, Descartes was, by contrast, deeply concerned about whether his views were acceptable to the Catholic Church. He made them so by arguing that the only thing he could be certain about was his own thought. 'I think therefore I am' – the famous 'cogito'. For Descartes the uncertain, material world could be the subject of reasoned investigation while the character of the mind remained under the authority of the church. Montaigne had vigorously rejected any separation of mind and body. He had seen them as intimately related, rejected prudery in sexual matters, enjoyed sex and wrote openly about it – even to the extent of expressing his embarrassment before a lady when he failed to produce a satisfactory erection! Descartes, by contrast, only discusses the passions in the abstract. Feelings and passions are the actions of the body not the mind. They are what the body does to us, rather than our deepest experiences. To Descartes the mind calculates, it reasons. Feelings come as it were from outside. As Toulmin says 'Taken at its face value, Descartes' position implies that a philosopher can disclaim all responsibility for his erections, unless he has good reason for deciding to have one!' There is not only a philosophical difference here: profound changes in social morality and self-expression have taken place. Yet there is only fifty years between them."

"I can see Descartes' position was not a very happy one!" mused the Buddha.

"Even so, in those scary years Descartes' mind-body dichotomy became deeply influential," continued Dominique. "The deep divide depends on a number of his determining beliefs:

– Fixed laws set up at creation govern nature. Objects are inert. God ordered things into higher and lower. The higher determine the lower. Humans of course are higher.

– Humanity is capable of rational thought that follows different rules from merely natural causality. Humans establish systems of reason to live by that are not determined by nature. Thought and action are likewise not determined by natural, psychological causes.

– The separation of reason from causation, thought from nature, means that human beings are themselves divided, being part natural and part creatures of reason. Human lives are, on the one hand, intellectual or spiritual; on the other, they are carnal and bodily. Emotions and reason are thus perpetually at odds with one another. And reason has to be in control if order is to be maintained."

"Toulmin's reasonable thesis is that this extraordinary shift in the valuing of personal and bodily experience was a consequence of the traumatic insecurity engendered by the long years of horrific warfare. In a search for security, ideas that provided a kind of clarity and certainty in the resolution of doubt and which also allowed the investigation of nature and the growth of business without the interference of the church became attractive. The divorce between Cartesian science and an open exploration of feeling, consciousness and value began at this time. The outcome of such a split meant that reasoning Christian souls in their growing business undertakings worldwide could freely exploit an inert natural world. Such was not the business of the church and morality was not put in question by such action. Indeed successful exploitation and money making was to the Calvinists a sign of God's approval.

'The language of nature was mathematics and by its use an increasing penetration into the causality of the universe developed, Isaac Newton eventually producing his extraordinary insight into the laws of gravity. Yet, Newton also was not at ease in his world. Like Descartes, he pondered the relation between science and religion and was in certain respects a religious alchemist. While the abstractions of his theory produced an outstanding mechanical model of the universe, feeling, emotion and selfhood were once again kept outside. While Newton may have believed mathematical cosmology was the language of God, the universe was not speaking theology nor did it provide a reason for human life."

"A sort of philosophical schizophrenia, it seems," remarked the Buddha.

"Indeed so – and the root of many of our troubles," Dominique told him.

Back in London, the Buddha conferred with Jim. He felt he needed some account of how Western philosophy had moved in recent centuries. He wanted to know how western thinking had got itself into such a split condition and whether it contained any hints for reunion. Jim thought that Western philosophy was so complex and detailed that they would easily get lost in innumerable sidelines if they were to discuss it only casually. He offered to write up a brief summary that the Buddha could peruse before they discussed it. The Buddha felt this to be a useful idea. A month later Jim handed him a document. That night the Buddha began to read. We will start with Kant, Jim had told him.

KANT'S PERPLEXITY

The Konigsburg philosopher, Immanuel Kant (1724-1804), published a book *Universal natural history and theory of the heavens* in 1755 using Newton's theory of gravitation to demonstrate how the entire universe might have developed from a distribution of particles that had been initially random. Kant was certainly up to speed in his acquaintance with the science of his time. But it was not science as such that perplexed him. It was the question whether human reason alone could determine the nature of things or whether an analysis of causality required experiential proof: indeed was such proof obtainable?

Kant was a meticulous philosopher whose works remain among the most important and also most difficult within the European tradition. He was so precise and disciplined that people were said to set their clocks by his passing through the town. Seemingly remote, a hypochondriac who was not un-affected by the charms of women but remained unmarried, Kant lived simply and often solitarily, yet he was none the less a delightful host entertaining friends and fellow thinkers to luncheons to which philosophers ever since must wish they had been invited. His lectures were evidently enthralling, discoursing on the whole range of history, science and philosophy with wit, humour and satire. Without bias, he sought for the truth of how things could be understood. Konigsburg (Kalininburg), in what is now a western province of Russia languishing in poverty, is no longer the charming small port it once was. The town was reduced to rubble by modern war and Kant's corpse removed by vandals from his tomb in 1950 and lost. There remains, none the less, a monument to him attached to the castle wall on which appears a quotation from his works:

"Two things fill the heart with ever renewed and increasing reverence, the more often and the more steadily we meditate upon them: the starry firmament and the moral law within."[3]

Prior to Kant, most philosophers had worked by constructing systems of thought based on propositions that were then developed purely through reason. In Kant's time, the foremost of such thinkers was Gottfried Wilhelm Leibniz (1646-1716) who believed that the mind contains certain innate principles, intuitively true, with which it constructs a valid description of the world. Since these initial principles of thought were innate and true, there was no need for them to be confirmed in experience. The mere experiences of mind give rise to our ideas about the world but do not reveal its fundamental nature yet, by virtue of the application of these unmistaken principles of thought, our capacity for reasoning gives rise to truth. Reality can only be reached though reason because only reason can rise above the phenomenal to perceive 'the vision of ultimate necessities, which is also God's'. Leibniz ends by arguing that the universe consists of 'monads', singularities of experience, existing in neither time nor space but eternally.

Kant, by his own account, was awoken from these 'dogmatic slumbers' by a reading of the Scottish thinker David Hume (1711-1776) who proposed a very different interpretation of the nature of thought. Reason operates with ideas yet ideas are acquired only through the operation of the senses. The content of every thought must therefore ultimately refer to experiences that form its basis. Belief can only be established as true when guaranteed though confirmations in sensory knowledge: reason alone without an experiential basis cannot yield true understanding, by itself it provides no more than metaphysical waffle. Yet, experientially based ideas only provide a picture of the world as it seems. All such views remain contingent on the viewer, they depend on a point of view and no perspective independent from that of the viewer is available, nor can one be made so. The relating of experiences merely provides a picture of a seeming continuity of causal necessities. Reason cannot go beyond such viewing independently because it works only with the meaning of words rather than with matters of fact. Even the existence of a self, can be doubted.

Kant, as scientist, felt that science rested on a view that understood real necessities. Hume's scepticism was to him therefore dumbfounding, for, while it demolished such a merely rational system as that of Leibniz, Kant felt there must be some truthful relationship between philosophical propositions and objective science. His greatest masterpiece, the *Critique of Pure Reason* (1781) is an attempt to resolve this contradiction.

Knowledge cannot be dependent, Kant argued, on either reason or experience alone. Both are required. Experience provides the content of a reasoned position but reason creates its form. Without reason there can be no formal argument: without content, there can be no thought. Knowledge depends on the synthesis of both. Yet, although such knowledge can transcend the merely individual view of the knower and can amount to a collective claim concerning the nature of the world, it is still not possible to know the world in itself – as the '*ding an sich*'- the thing in itself.

Knowledge can be built up independently of whatever may be merely my contribution to it. It is not solipsistic. Yet, my perceptions (*i.e.* observations, experiments) and those of others who may agree with me, necessarily preclude independent, trans-human knowledge. Although such an 'absolute' perspective is unobtainable, experience does yield an objective understanding because it utilises awareness of time, space and causality in such a way as to present an ordered view on an independent world. This is the view obtainable through science. It is also the reason why science proceeds through the verification of standard positions (agreed theory, paradigms) that change when found not longer to be adequate.

Kant made use of an important classification of philosophical propositions. True ideas or propositions may be either *a priori* (true beforehand) or *a posteriori* (true after checking). A priori propositions are statements that are true independent of experience – such as 'two and two make four' and mathematical equations generally. *A posteriori* propositions need to be affirmed in experience – and would be untrue if not so confirmed.

Kant thought *a priori* truths were of two kinds: (i) / analytic – where the truth is guaranteed by the intrinsic meaning (*i.e.* 2+2=4); and (ii) / synthetic – where they predicate something not implicit in the subject. This is puzzling since, to an empiricist in the Humean tradition, there cannot be any synthetic *a priori* knowledge, synthetic truths can only be known through experience (*i.e. a posteriori*). "All wives are married" or "tigers are cats" are analytic statements and are shown to be so in merely analysing the words. By contrast, the statements "tigers are always ferocious" or "dead toads on motorways are killed by cars (not foxes)" are not tautological and merely analytic but synthetic and testable in experience, therefore they can only be *a posteriori*. The implications of these distinctions, at least to empiricists, are that any ideas proffered as true yet independent of experience – such as references to God's will or monads, are merely 'metaphysical' and their use must be meaningless because they cannot be confirmed. Yet, to rationalists, metaphysics becomes essential in argument if we are to have any complete, objective knowledge standing outside experience. Without metaphysics, there is no way to avoid the scepticism of Hume. So – is it possible to have true knowledge by rational reflection outside experience?

Kant said no. Knowledge can only be of the world we experience. Propositions only make sense if they obey this view. Beyond that, we may suppose, metaphysically, there remains the world in itself, but of that we can have no true knowledge.

Yet – and yet – Kant insists there is synthetic *a priori* knowledge! Kant argues that since mathematical statements are true by pure reasoning rather than merely by analysing the terms, there must be some basis for the *a priori* nature of mathematics (by which we understand the cosmos), which must be itself *a priori*. He goes on to uncover other importantly indubitable statements of a similar kind – "Things persist independently of me." "Objects exist in space and time"; "Every event has a cause." Such statements seem true by pure reasoning and do not need experiential confirmation.

Kant's exploration of these pure reasonings consists of complex argumentation of a subtle and often elaborated nature. The problem is whether "the subjective conditions of thought can give objective validity." Kant observed that all statements derive from certain fundamental categories of thought, which he deduced by tracing ideas to their conceptual roots functioning independently of the environment. He found twelve of them. Two of them are 'form' and 'force'.[4] A pen is an artefact, an artefact is a material object, and an object appears as a form – the final root of the deduction being 'form'. Likewise writing is an action, a movement, which is rooted in 'force'. The use of such categories in

reasoning allows us to map experience in a way that 'reflects' the underlying nature of the world. Furthermore, there are two even more fundamental 'intuitions', namely space and time, which differ from the categories in that they do not arise in numerous examples but are always just
there as themselves. Everything appears in space and time.

By using these categories and intuitions, Kant came to the view he
calls the 'transcendental deduction', that is a deduction as to an objective
world transcending mere dependence on experience. The categories
and intuitions provide an image of the world that amounts to a picture of
the world in itself; one which can be relied upon as objective. This picture
is not made up of platonic forms or Leibnizian monads but simply of the
things around us. It is they that provide us with the intuitions and categories
by which we understand them. Kant saw a relationship between sensibility
and understanding and therefore between world and mind, that allows
an objective deduction which is reliable – even though we have not touched
the 'thing in itself'.

Transcendental deduction is not a deduction from experience but
presupposed by the nature of thought as it examines experience. Kant
uses an expression "the transcendental unity of apperception" to mean
the oneness whereby self-consciousness relates to the world in a manner
that transcends the limitations of mere experiences. Such transcendence
can only occur however where the subject lives within the world that the
categories of mind describe; a world that provides an objective
understanding yet one in which things in themselves may still be other
than they seem.

We need to note the great difference from Descartes here. Descartes
found as indubitable the proposition "I think therefore I am." and split
this thinking mind off from the material world around it. Strictly speaking,
Kant has revised this view to say merely "I think therefore I think." The
subject is not a predicate but simply an instance. What this 'I', of which
thinking is the predicate, may be is not explored and maybe cannot be
explored within thinking itself for thinking cannot transcend it. Kant no
longer separates the mind from matter. He argues for the role the
existence of things has in the way the self-mind apperceives them. He has
established the objectivity of a world as no more than the observers' own
categorical relationship to it. Any philosophical question can only be
asked from within such a perspective.

Within such a world how should one live? Having wormed his way to a
third position that, while saving science, did not subscribe to mere
empiricism, Kant realised that there was nothing in his analysis that
answered this question. He proceeded to try and resolve this issue, the

question of values and ethics. While his answer is far less persuasive than his account of understanding, it remains important and gave rise to intense discussion subsequently, indeed into our own time. Kant argues that understanding cannot give us truthful access to the realms of spirituality or ethics, yet we have a capacity for faith rooted in intuitions towards ultimate meaning. Even though faith gives no grounds for certainty or indeed objective knowledge, none the less we can come to trust it. Kant has not only 'saved' science from sceptical empiricism, he seeks to save religion too (Critique of Practical Reason 1788).

Roger Scruton interprets Kant's difficult argumentation in the following way.[5] We have seen that the unity of the self, the "transcendental unity of apperception", arises from the use of the categories and intuitions of the mind that presuppose the structures of experience. This is an assertion of the nature of the mind that goes beyond a need for experiential proof. It is synthetic *a priori*, rather than something given *a posteriori*. The mind in this sense lies at the very boundary of what can be known for, while it cannot transcend the boundary of experience yet it can, as it were, look beyond it. In this, there is freedom to speculate without constraint and to choose when faced by a choice of action. This 'transcendental freedom', as Kant called it, lies therefore at the base of ethics. The freedom to judge is practical reason not pure reason and the roots of such judgement are 'synthetic a priori principles of action', practical laws about what to do.

Reasoning persons are not only self-conscious centres of knowledge, they are also agents that act in the world. A choice of action depends on a reason not on a cause. Actions are justified by reasons not by explanations as to causes, they depend on a will to ends and means. Reason prompts us to act and thus gives rise to the will for action. Judgements to act in one way or another do not depend on knowledge of causes but rather on reasons that Kant interprets as 'imperatives', properties of the mind much as he believes the categories and intuitions of knowledge to be. Here we encounter Kant's famous 'categorical imperative' lying at the root of choice and defined by him once more by abstracting back from choices to an underlying root. The categorical imperative demands one to act only by a maxim by which 'I can at the same time will to be an universal law', essentially 'Do as you would be done by'. Kant's assertion that this imperative is innate in the mind points to the root whereby we will action, the root of morality and, by extension, the root for a belief in God as the source of such morality even though, once again, we can never know that source 'in itself'.

Kant argued that particular axioms of practical reason give rise to an intuitive morality that regarded all people as equal before the law, a respect for self and others, and hence a forbidding of murder, rape, theft, fraud, dishonesty and coercion. It allows an individual to abstract a position from a personal situation whereby he or she can evaluate the actions of others. Here then is the root of justice as well as of personal ethics, judgement being directed not on circumstances but as to whether a good or bad intention is present. People act not merely because they may be caused to do so (by the brain for example or by social coercion) but from reasons. Based on his or her reasons a person may be regarded with respect, affection or love. It is the will to the good that lies at the root of social approval.

Kant believed that underlying all action is some apprehension of the moral law. Even when that law may have been disobeyed, the individual will have some sense of self-betrayal. The emotions may cause diversions from the good yet conscience works to reinstate the presence of the abstract law that underpins all values.

PHILOSOPHY AFTER KANT

Kant's philosophy did not escape criticism even during his lifetime. If reason was the hallmark of the Germanic 'enlightenment' then it had to be allowed to criticise itself. Johan Georg Hamann (1730-1788) took the view that you cannot separate reason and experience in the dualistic manner of Kant. Thought depends on language in which form and content, reason and experience, are inextricably mixed. In the practice of language, you cannot distinguish between experiential concepts and grounding intuitions – they run together. Hamann's friend, Friedrich Heinrich Jacobi (1743-1819), argued further to the effect that reason alone, even on Kant's terms, could only lead to the undermining of any basis for spiritual belief or morality. One either has to opt for the rational agnosticism of the scientific enlightenment or adopt an irrational leap of faith. Much of human life is based in such irrationality and controversies about the relative status of reason and faith lie at the root of the divisiveness of subsequent European thought.

Jacobi opted for faith and attacked Johann Gotleib Fichte (1762-1814) for his Kantian ideas, which Jacobi considered to be leading to what he termed a nihilism based purely on the properties of the ego. Fichte was booted from his chair in Jena as a result and Jena became a seat of German romanticism.

We have to understand the power of Christianity at this point in time, the accusation of nihilism becoming the trumpet call of Christians defending their world view against a secularising tide of rationalism. It was either nothingness or God.[6] The problem of nihilism caught on in a big way leading to a diversity of positions. The suggestion that nihilists were replacing God with their own egoism perhaps led Mary Shelly to the fear of the monstrous in her novel *Frankenstein* (1819). Dostoevsky worked the theme of logical suicide – without God what reason for living? The ultimate freedom would be to take one's own life. Yet, others saw in nihilism a great release, a shocking burst of creative freedom.

The great problem now became the search for some way of unifying what Kant had divided. Kant's attempt to go beyond Descartes had not convinced. How to reconnect thought and the freedom of moral choice? Schelling opted for a life force in nature, Fichte for self reflection leading to freedom, Hegel for transcendent spirit, Schopenhauer – the will, Nietzsche – power, Marx – social praxis, Freud – the id and the unconscious. All these movements arose out of the criticism of Kant. Kant remains in many ways the pivot on which European thought about value turns: philosophy driven by the fear of nihilism.

What happened from this point on is the story of the great divide. As a broad generalisation we can say that in Britain and subsequently in America the scepticism of Hume and the associationism of Locke supported a basically Cartesian stance within which scientific empiricism flourished The extreme logical positivism of Rudolf Carnap (1891-1970) and the Vienna circle caught on, so that British philosophy in the twentieth century under Russell, Ayer and Ryle sustained a basically reductionist position favourable to behaviourism in psychology and the rejection of any determination of behaviour by internal forces, consciousness itself being viewed as a mere epiphenomenon. The American version was well argued in the work of the pragmatists, William James, George Dewey and the contemporary Richard Rorty. By contrast, on the European continent, while there was of course outstanding work being done in science especially in Germany, a much broader set of philosophical controversies raged within which questions of value, morality and its basis were in the forefront. These positions were far less homogenous than those of the Anglophone empiricists and agonistic debating in the lively and sometimes excessive Gallic mode played a creative role. In the following sections, we will outline some of these positions and disputes that lead up to the contemporary situation.

ROMANTICISM AND RESISTANCE

It is perhaps surprising that Kant's immediate successors in Germany, J.G. Fichte, F.W.J. von Schelling (1775-1854) and George Wilhelm Hegel (1770-1831), attempted to heal the rift by creating an idealistic perspective that essentially turned Kant's mental intuitions and imperatives into visions of an absolute truth accessible through philosophy. The unifying principles by which mind realised a seemingly objective world now became mentally inherent aspects of reality itself, thereby giving direct access to the transcendental. This turned Kant's arguments inside out. Universal mind, now spelt as it were with a capital M, was the determinant of both experience and reason. Human beings were instances of Mind in a participatory relationship with the cosmos rather than in dualistic separation merely seeming to have knowledge of it. The human mind now appeared to be the vehicle for the self-revelation of the universe.

Richard Tarnas[7] expresses this vision well: "*nature pervades everything, and the human mind in all its fullness is itself an expression of nature's essential being. And it is only when the human mind actively brings forth from within itself the full powers of a disciplined imagination and saturates its empirical observation with archetypical insight that the deeper reality of the world emerges. – The human imagination is itself part of the world's intrinsic truth.*" The key prophet of this movement was Hegel who saw philosophy as a dialectical progression to a final vision of the 'absolute'.

Hegel's soaring vision proved deeply attractive to many and crossed the Channel to inspire British poets, especially Samuel Taylor Coleridge (1772-1834); and also to provide an underpinning for a concern with the 'sublime' in nature, meaning not merely beauty but rather awe, mystery and wonder (Burke) as personally, even mystically, experienced, for example, by William Wordsworth in the Lake District. Coleridge himself was more involved with the meaning of things, with what could be read from nature and experience. He was no naturalist interested in facts and their relationships.

John Stuart Mill (1806-1873) wrote essays comparing the visions of Coleridge with the practical perspectives of Jeremy Bentham who stood on the far side of the emerging divide.[8] Bentham was a sceptic in the tradition of Hume, always probing and doubting the truth of traditional statements and undermining convention. He used his critical gifts to propose social reforms in a radical manner and looked towards scientific progress as a means to better ends. By contrast, Coleridge wanted to look into the origins of ideas and examine their meanings. In this, he foreshadowed an emerging hermeneutic tradition, looking for hidden and not so hidden meanings in convention and tradition. He was thus mainly conservative in outlook reconstructing ideas from uncovered perspectives. Bentham was 'analytical', Coleridge was – well – 'continental'.

Mill observed that in the contrast between Coleridge and Bentham the whole dilemma of philosophy in Britain in his time could be read. The opposing positions of Hegelians and the Cartesian supporters of Hobbes and Locke resembled sectarian disputes in religion, the views of one party being beyond the pale for the other. Yet, Mill himself welcomed the presence of antagonism in philosophy. He regarded speculative opposition as essential for gaining clear insight, whether in philosophy or in democratic, parliamentary government. His appeal for tolerance within dispute has however been little heeded.

LOGICAL POSITIVISM VERSUS PHENOMENOLOGY

The whole story was to be repeated again with rather greater venom in the mutual antagonism between the exponents of the 'logical positivism' of the Vienna Circle headed by Rudolf Carnap (1891-1970), and the philosophy of Martin Heidegger (1889-1976). The Vienna circle consisted of a group of analytically inclined philosophers, Hans Hahn, Otto Neurath, Moritz Schlick, Rudolf Carnap and others. The group took a radical stance rejecting metaphysics as nonsense and asserting that all philosophy concerned either analytical statements, tautologies that were necessarily true, or empirical statements ultimately verifiable against 'facts'. To Carnap, any statement that was not verifiable lay outside philosophy, which meant, of course, that most of philosophy could be tossed in the rubbish bin. The task of philosophy, said Carnap, is the logical analysis of statements. Logical positivism is thus the analysis of meaning through verification. All metaphysical statements are bad art, because at least art does not theorise but simply gives expression to our feelings. Logical positivism became closely associated with a rigorous philosophical scientism favouring reductionism, behaviourism and the rejection of anything untestable.

Carnap's extremely dogmatic position could not be maintained for long and for reasons Kant would have appreciated. Karl Popper (1902-1994) pointed out that many if not all scientific theories contain highly speculative components. Einstein's theory was, for example, untestable and primarily speculative conjecture and, like much of Newton's work, was largely accepted because of its great power of explanation rather than confirmation in experiments. Theories according to Popper are scientific if they can withstand refutation, and if they cannot be refuted, even in principle, they are metaphysical. The key problem was the verification of the principle of verification. It is neither an empirical statement nor is it a tautology so how can it be verified? How can the verification principle verify itself? If it cannot do so, it is itself metaphysical. Furthermore, study of language was leading to a realisation that words and sentences do not necessarily have a direct relationship with some immediate factual reality, rather there is a fabric or net of meanings that need holistic interpretation.

The analytical – synthetic distinction breaks down – much as Jacobi had argued – and the dogmatics of logical positivism collapse into pragmatism.

All this, however, was after the fight with Heidegger – or rather his denunciation by Carnap. Arguing that metaphysical statements, that is those that are neither tautologies nor verifiable, are merely meaningless, he dismissed Heidegger's thought as arrant nonsense. To the Vienna circle such a philosophy was a return to the merely speculative and was furthermore, linked to resurgent Germanic aspirations after World War I. If philosophy was to be analytical in the logicians' sense then Heidegger's examination of 'being' lay outside philosophy. Heidegger did not make a formal reply to these charges. Probably he believed that the force of his thought as expressed in his magnum opus 'Being and Time' would take care of that and he was content to remain rather loftily above the debate.

Heidegger argued that prior to the study of knowledge (epistemology) there must be an understanding of 'being' (ontology) – *i.e.* that which exhibits and uses knowledge. His whole philosophy thus focuses on or around the question 'What is being? In adopting this focus he was influenced by Franz Brentano (1838-1917) and the 'phenomenologist' Edmund Husserl (1859-1938), his own teacher, whom he eventually succeeded on the chair at Freiburg: to encounter Heidegger we need first to meet these two philosophers briefly.

Brentano had emphasised the difference between mind and matter, mind having 'intentionality' – a term meaning that minds were always 'on about' something as an act of consciousness referring to some object. A stone or a tree cannot be said to be concerned with anything – it just gets on being itself. Minds however engage with their environments, strategically, and this puts them into a unique category of being. Husserl endeavoured to determine the nature of this intentional subject of consciousness, which Kant had termed the 'transcendental unity of apperception'.

We may view a table from many angles and, although each sighting is different, yet we manage to have a unified sense of the table there in the room. According to Husserl, it is the synthesising action of consciousness that bestows this unified meaning on sensory experiences. One recognises the unity underlying manifold representations of an object, a unity he referred to as the 'essence' of the thing. Husserl developed a distinctive subjective empiricism not unlike that of Indian yoga and Buddhism. To observe the action of consciousness he required a subject to 'bracket' out all assumptions about the exterior character of a thing, setting aside any dogma regarding external existence. The subject then examined the thing as it appears in consciousness alone – more or less as a sort of platonic form. This results in no mere sense of object constancy as in an after image, but an intuitive sense of something as a singularity prior to conceptualisation.

In further 'reductive' analysis, Husserl looks solely at the subject rather than the object of consciousness. Unlike the contents of awareness that vary, the subject remains one and the same. The observer sees a flow of consciousness in which nothing particular is registered. It appears that the subject the observer intends to observe cannot actually be seen because to see itself it would have to become an object to itself, which would then no longer be that subject which one was attempting to see! Meaningful consciousness seems to depend on having an object. Without an object, the investigation passes beyond language.

Although Husserl made use of several other practices of 'reduction', he was not able to press this "transcendental reductionism" further. None the less, he had exposed the nature of awareness in a radically new way. He also believed that this understanding was a true 'objectivity' in which the nature of the subject was included. He rejected the sciences of his time as a false 'objectivism', over concerned with the subject-object split to the extent that the subjective was being cut out of the lived relation between mind and its life-world. Life in his time, he believed, was taking place increasingly within a field of unlived abstractions creating a crisis in which the rootedness of life in a lived relation to history and society was becoming lost. If true 'objectivity', in Husserl's sense, was to be established he believed a proper understanding of the subjective arising of phenomena was essential. Objectivity would then be seen as an intentional consequence of the activity of consciousness. Husserl's work was to have a great influence in the emergence of 'phenomenology' and Gestalt psychology as well as in much subsequent existentialist philosophy. The bells are still ringing today.

Returning to Heidegger – a prime difficulty in reading him is his creation of neologisms; compound terms that are often difficult to lift from German into English. His key word is Dasein – a compound expression meaning to be or being (sein) and here (da)– hence 'being here'. Dasein then is not an abstraction – it is on about something, it is intentional. Dasein appears in sentient beings among which the most important is human being. Dasein must naturally precede and pervade its activities, it's 'knowing'. It is primordial and therefore must be an essential focus of philosophy. Being (Dasein) is inevitably always personal – an I or a you, and it is primarily a possibility – the what it may become. Circumstance may constrain what it may become but there is always an element of choice, a possibility to become X. If that possibility is something that has been freely chosen, then it can be said to be authentic.

For the most part, however, being is sadly inauthentic, a response to those others who coerce or otherwise persuade or influence a choice. If Dasein does things merely because 'they' do it or believe it, or if one is following a convention without choice then one is inauthentic, unreal. Yet, if I have intentionally chosen to conform to what 'they' do, there is still authenticity. Authenticity depends on making up ones own mind, being one's own person – and this does not mean some mere eccentric whim but a whole way of self-expression.

Dasein is itself embodied and will die. It is however not something like an immortal soul that lives in a body. Death is final, one lives in awareness of death, in a knowledge of time that runs forward in imagination to one's death and then back again to one's birth and so back up to the present where one is. Dasein is being in such awareness of time. Although time is momentary, Dasein knows time as it's being. Dasein is always alongside others; it is present in a world and never separate from that world. It exists therefore within a quite everyday understanding of being. Things around it are not mere things, they exist in relation to their potential uses, their past employment, their future potential. A hammer in a tool shed is not just a tool with a metal head; it has potential, has been used before, can be used again, and is not the same as a screwdriver. Space and time are intimately involved in the mutual connectivity of everything in Dasein.

Being and the world are therefore complementary to one another, not reactive in mere engagement. Dasein comes into being with the world not as separate from it, it is therefore a priori, space and time are innate in its awareness and so is its knowing of a world of others. One may suffer from moods, of states of mind that derive from a situation, but Dasein itself is prior to all that. Moods can give insight; the moon among pines may induce a reflective mood that amounts to an understanding that one lives within, at least for a time. Such an understanding calls up interpretation, but that is not something added, it is already presupposed in the circumstance, in the involvement with things and others. Involvement discloses an interpretation from within understanding. It is important to be resolute in authenticity and, in this sense; history is an account of Dasein and the presence or absence of resolution in the time of the world.

Heidegger's involvement with the Nazi's in the 1930's has called forth much comment but had he been more of a commoner it is doubtful whether his minor involvement would have attracted much attention. One must remember that, in its earliest manifestation, Nazism seemed to bring hope to a despairing Germany, and a way out of communism. Heidegger was always a conservative patriot but never anti-Semitic. There is nothing in 'Being and Time' that indicates commitment to Nazism and after Hitler's ruthless murder of Ernst Rohm and his followers in 1934 it seems Heidegger became disillusioned and took little further part in politics. Indeed, it seems he was under surveillance by the Gestapo near the end of the war since his lectures could be interpreted as containing covert criticisms of the regime. Yet, a bad smell remains; after all other thinkers had shown a different response.[9]

Heidegger's influence has been considerable especially among thinkers such as Jean Paul Sartre, Maurice Merleau – Ponty and Jacques Derrida in France and the theologian Paul Tillich in Germany. Steven Batchelor has compared Heidegger's thought to some aspects of Buddhism.[10] In the end, whatever his lack of political insight may imply, the quality and intensity of his ideas will continue to inspire both approval and criticism.

THE CAMBRIDGE ORACLE: LUDWIG WITTGENSTEIN

Anyone coming up to Cambridge with even a slight interest in philosophy in the 1950s would soon have realised that a great presence had recently passed from the scene. Going through the courts of Trinity College, one would be shown where Wittgenstein had had his rooms and held court from a deck chair in a sparsely furnished chamber in which he did his philosophy freely before the eyes and ears of his students. One would hear strange stories of his friendship with Bertrand Russell, climbing a tree and arguing with Russell far below. And indeed, watching the expansive gestures of philosopher John Wisdom thinking on his feet before a blackboard, one realised the style was still in vogue.

Ludwig Wittgenstein (1889-1951) was indeed a remarkable and in many ways quite a strange man. The son of an Austrian industrialist and a banker's daughter Wittgenstein came from an exceptionally wealthy and cultured Viennese family at a time when Vienna rivalled Paris as the culture capital of Europe.[11] Wittgenstein's mother was Roman Catholic and, although his father was a protestant of Jewish family origins, he was brought up in the Church of Rome. Indeed, although he left the practice of a formal religion far behind, he remained concerned with spiritual matters throughout his life and even contemplated becoming a monk. As a teenager and young man, Wittgenstein was not happy and settled nowhere until he came to England and studied aeronautical engineering at Manchester University designing an unique propeller and becoming interested first in the mathematics of design and then in the study of mathematics itself. It was this that led him into the philosophy of mathematics and the discovery of Bertrand Russell's (1872-1970) work on the subject. He met Gottlob Frege (1848-1925) at Jena University who advised him to study with Russell. Characteristically, he rushed to Cambridge and, as it were, bearded the lion in his den. Russell was immensely impressed and, even though Wittgenstein only stayed five terms at Cambridge at that time, the two of them became much more than master and pupil. They clearly sparked ideas off one another in a remarkable philosophical friendship, each in due course owing much to the other. On leaving Cambridge, Wittgenstein travelled, lived for a time in a remote hut in Norway, and was then caught up in World War I where he served in the Austrian army as an engineer and artillery officer. He was captured by the Italians with a philosophical manuscript in his rucksack and ended the war in a POW camp near Monte Casino where he wrote much of the first draft of what would become his first great contribution to philosophy. During those years, he remained much concerned by religious ideas and his solitary, perhaps self-mortifying, tendency may have been a consequence of his homosexual orientation.

Regaining freedom, he tried his hand at school mastering, at which he was a disaster, built a modern house for his sister and got to know philosophers at Vienna University – in particular Moritz Schlick of the Vienna Circle. At last, he sensed his true profession and returned to Cambridge, obtained a doctorate and gained a Fellowship at Trinity College succeeding G.E. Moore as Professor of Philosophy in 1939. As a British subject, he avoided internment during World War II and worked in hospitals in London and Newcastle.

Back in Cambridge after the war, he gave lectures but loathed the collegiate style of life, especially high table conversations, so much that he hardly ever turned up in hall for dinner. Eventually he resigned his chair, lived once more in a remote cabin, this time in Ireland, and completed his second great contribution to philosophy. So striking was his character, his vivid gestures when teaching and the intensity of his gaze that many people have left memoirs of him. A powerful, dominant character, intense, restless and complex, he could be ruthless in responding to less bright students. But many fell under his spell "as if mesmerised by the intensity of his expression."[12]

Wittgenstein's philosophical career falls into two parts. The first culminated in the *Tractatus Logico – Philosophicus* published in English in *1961* but available in various forms for many years before that. The second culminated in *Philosophical Investigations* published in *1953* after his death from cancer.[13] This work is remarkable in being very largely a complete refutation of his earlier thought.

Wittgenstein's early interest in the logic of mathematics had led to investigations into the logic of propositions that could be expressed in the notation of formal logic. Work in this subject was often exceedingly abstract and the question at its root was how could the propositions of logic be meaningful. Wittgenstein argued that language mirrors the world in that the structure of language is a reflection of that of the world. The world is made up of (i) simple objects that combine in (ii) states of affairs, to create (iii) facts. The world is the totality of facts. Corresponding to this and, as it were, mirroring it, language is based in (i) names that build into (ii) elementary propositions that comprise (iii) propositions that picture the facts of the world. The totality of propositions comprises language. Propositions built from elementary constituents have meaning because they picture or mirror the facts of the world. The general idea has been called the 'picture theory of meaning'.

In the Tractatus, propositions are basically pictures of worldly form. The limits to what can be meaningfully said or thought is imposed by the picturing relationship of language and world. Reality depends both on what is the case and also what is not the case, so we need to know which propositions are logically true and which false. There are however non-factual propositions such as tautologies and correct mathematical statements that are logically true but do not say anything about the world because they would be consistent whatever forms the world might take. It follows, Wittgenstein argued, that nearly all propositions of philosophy that do not picture the world simply have no meaning. Ethical statements or the metaphysical theses of religion do not have a picturing relationship with the facts of the world and are therefore, logically, simply meaningless. A large part of philosophy actually says nothing – at least nothing that can be said to be true or false.

Meaningful statements must concern matters of fact: statements about right or wrong or the existence of God go beyond matters of fact and have no factual meaning – however this does not mean they are unimportant. Indeed, however strange it may at first seem, Wittgenstein held the view that such matters were of a 'higher' order and that the silence of the Tractatus concerning them should reveal this to be so. This is because the Tractatus is not concerned with what the objects of the world actually are. No proposition in it concerning states of affairs can reveal their ultimate nature. Logical propositions merely elucidate a picturing relationship and beyond that nothing can be said: "Wovon man nicht sprechen kan darüber muss man schweigen." [14] The religious and the ethical 'show' themselves outside language.

It has been argued that Wittgenstein may have taken this view, in a manner not unlike that of Kant, to protect the ethical and the religious from materialist reductionism in science and this is indeed suggested by his relationship with the Vienna Circle. The Circle had drawn a line between what was science and open to analysis through 'logical positivism' and metaphysics, which was nonsense and therefore considered worthless. Only factually based propositions could be scientific and meaningful, other statements were either emotional noises or exhortations of various kinds. The purpose of philosophy, the positivists argued, was to clarify propositions of empirical science through logical analysis. This of course reduces philosophy to an aspect of science, a position far from Wittgenstein's; his engagement with the Circle faded out. While Wittgenstein showed a respect for religious and ethical statements, the Vienna Circle was mostly totally rejecting of them as mere superstitions.

Wittgenstein's work was totally formal. Nowhere does he relate his ideas to actual conditions in the world. This is where he differed from Russell, who based his similar arguments not in abstract objects and names but rather in sense data and judgements of this or that. Russell positions his arguments in relation to our sensory information concerning the world: he relates to the world itself rather than merely to the logic of propositions mirroring the world. It may be that this difference, together with the contrast between the ideas of the Vienna Circle and his own, gradually shifted Wittgenstein towards a refutation of the Tractatus and towards the work that culminated in the Philosophical Investigations.

Wittgenstein gradually realised that misunderstandings in language cannot be solved through the construction of an explanatory system, especially a formal system. The Tractatus turns out to be merely one form of language itself. The essential thing therefore is to discover how language actually works in the everyday. There are many different forms of language in each of which the 'grammar' differs. When one employs language, one uses words in a certain way conforming to a set of rules governing its application. We need therefore to describe these forms of language and the differing rules that govern statements in different contexts. There can be no single explanation of language as such, what is needed is the exploration of forms. Since these are many, there is no single theoretical model that can be applied to the whole of language. This means the Tractatus and its formal approach had to be totally abandoned.

Language may be used to tell stories, to make a report, to affirm or deny, to speculate or ask questions, to present riddles or tell jokes, to thank, pray, curse, philosophise and so on. Each of these comprises a 'language game' in which speaking is an engagement with a form of life. In the same way as there are board games, card games, soccer and rugby football, Olympic games, Chess or Draughts so there are various forms of language, some of which share features or rule structures and some of which do not. Some language games have family resemblances, just as soccer and rugby are both field games for teams but one game is played with a ball using feet and in the other case the hands. One has 'goals' and the other 'tries' in the scoring of points. These field games differ greatly from Chess or Draughts played by two persons where pieces move across a checker board – the rules for the movements of pieces being different in the two cases. Language is a collection of language games.

Naming is no longer, as in the Tractatus, a basis of meaning; rather names enter discourse in ways that depend on the rules of the game. Mastery of language depends on being able to use many expressions in a variety of ways, each way having its own form or rule structure. It is the way a word or expression is used that becomes important to its understanding. The slogan "Do not ask for the meaning – ask for the use!' expresses this simply and directly. The word 'blue' can suggest a colour, a mood, a type of song, a Cambridge athlete; while 'red' can be a person, a political view, a colour or a trade name. If we know the use, we understand what is being said. Some expressions deal with comprehending an object's use, others with how another person feels or how one is oneself feeling. Furthermore, different people may use the same word in different ways; 'up north' the word 'brass' may be used differently from 'down south.' Again similar words, perhaps of common origin in differing languages, may have quite distinct usages. Understanding depends therefore on mastering a technique in the speaking of a language. It means knowing how to say something, or do something or use something. The psychology is of little interest, what is important is a skill. Where there is confusion in language, it is commonly due to an erroneous understanding of the rules in play. In resolving these mistakes, philosophy takes on a therapeutic role.

There is no rigid calculus here that predetermines usage; language is negotiated as one penetrates the sense with which another is using a word, expression or a joke. It does not therefore have a fixed form but drifts with shifts in usage. Rule following is not therefore always the best guide to understanding because the interlocutor may be using a rule with which one is unfamiliar. One has then to interpret what the difference may be. For example, Tibetan lamas who have received little training in English often present the words of a sentence in English in a totally backwards fashion. House your faraway is. Yet, once one has listened to this for an hour or so, one hears it quite normally as comprehension catches up with a shift in rule. In German, verbs famously end sentences, they do not necessarily do so in English – and so on.

Rules must not be seen as coercive, rather they indicate a form of expression that is or has been collectively negotiated. One enters a collective understanding to varying, negotiable degrees and with varying degrees of skill. One's French may be grammatically appalling but vigorous, confident usage may lead to partial success. Usage comes about by agreement, through custom. Meaning is an understanding of use across a whole range of local and national language games, which are entirely public. The skill involves rule following and rule adjustment: one has to know what rule following is.

Language and constituent language games express 'forms of life' – a consensus that includes not only speech norms, but also non-linguistic behaviour, expectations, moral assumptions, traditions which human beings share in varying degrees depending on location, origin, age etc. This implies that the 'truth' of a statement is simply the accepted form within a given culture or community. Truth is relative to its frame of reference. There is no ultimate beyond the local – justifications and explanations are relative to context. Meaning is thus public rather than private and Descartes "I think therefore I am" – the 'Cogito' – cannot be an absolute – rather, as we have seen above, it emerges from an historical context as well as a personal life.

The question of whether a private language could be meaningful arises here. For example, 'pain' is a private experience but we learn it's meaning, Wittgenstein argues, as a substitute for groaning or other expressions of hurt. A child picks this usage up from adults who talk to him. "Where is the pain–darling?" The private languages of children gradually conform to that of adults unless there are especial reasons for a child's secrecy. There will however be criteria for determining, for example, whether the child is pretending, perhaps to avoid going to school. Criteria once again depend on rules to check meanings.

These thoughts lead us to downgrade the importance of private states of mind or affirmations of self or ego, or indeed 'memes' in isolation, and look rather towards the public usage and the skills of representation and misrepresentation. Statements about pain or self are learnt expressions regarding immediate or remembered events rather than doors into mysterious inner worlds. Similarly, knowledge itself is better understood in relation to the forms of life in which it is found, rather than as some seemingly occult inner process. Reasoning and justifying come to an end in the form of life to which they relate. The foundations of belief, however strong, do not transcend this. Even so, we need to recall that 'inner' processes of experience are not always easily expressed in language.

Perhaps we are left with the question that evolutionary biologists may want to answer – is there some innate basis for knowing, for the ability to understand rule following. But here we are leaving the game within which Wittgenstein has been speaking. It remains somewhat strange that

Wittgenstein, working in Cambridge, is far better known in the Anglophone world than he has been appreciated in continental Europe even though there are many parallels between his philosophical development and what was happening on the continent in the same period.

PARISIAN INSIGHTS

During the 1930s and again after World War II there can be little doubt that Paris was the intellectual capital of Europe. For many years a number of thinkers of the highest calibre lived and worked there showering the world with ideas, some profound, some offering great insights, some rather foolish and one or two quite crazy, but all in an inimitable Gallic style. The names of Sartre, Merleau – Ponty, Lacan, Julia Kresteva, Levinas, Simone de Beauvoir. Lyotard, Foucault, and Derrida increasingly ring bells outside the often rather closed and elitist realm of French culture and generate Internet hits of ever – greater frequency worldwide. The reason seems to lie in the coming together in one period and place of a number of European trends all focussed primarily on problems of being and value rather than on logical analysis and science. And the reason for this is perhaps not far to seek – once again – war. Two World Wars with their widespread horrors on the Somme and over Dresden and the coming into being of the most sophisticated mass cruelty the world has even known, Auschwitz and Belsen, right in the heart of a country that had been one of the most profound contributors to European philosophy and music, amount to an ethical challenge by no means yet fully met. Compared with France, the world of the Anglophone victors, without entirely neglecting such themes, has had much less to say about them and with nothing like the same argumentative creativity.

The central pivot of all this activity was the problem bequeathed to European philosophy by Kant and taken up repeatedly down the centuries. How can we find truth in knowledge and how should we live? The medieval Christian certitude that God was in his heaven and all's right with the world had begun to collapse when the Polish astronomer Nikolaus Copernicus (1473-1543) demonstrated that the Earth was not the centre of the Universe. This was the start of the grand demolition whereby Man, supposedly the focus of God's attention and intention, dwindled in significance to become an unique organism on a small planet in one of a myriad galaxies of an ever changing Universe of which we have no sure understanding. By degrees the realisation that God was dead led to many attempts to replace him. Hegel, Schopenhauer, Marx all created idealised pivots for the discussion of value yet the omnipresence of a corrosive nihilism underlying philosophy and indeed Western culture as a whole became increasingly inescapable.

Nietzsche, Heidegger, Freud, Marx, Saussure, provided fundamental themes and set the stage for a creativity only matched by Parisian theatre and art driven likewise by similar themes. It is in the challenge of Nihilism, Existentialism, Psychoanalysis, Marxism and Linguistic theory that we find the seedbed for the philosophies we now have to discuss. The complex relations between these themes were taken up in differing ways by the Parisian thinkers and the favouring of one approach over another and the varying ways in which they were developed provide the sources for the agreements and the disputes between them. Although the disputes run back through Heidegger, Husserl and Hegel to Kant, perhaps the most immediate starting point was Nietzsche.

SOURCES IN NIETZSCHE

Unable to deny nihilism, Friedrich Nietzsche (1844-1900) faced head on the fact that the very basis of values that had sustained not only Christianity but also the whole Western philosophical understanding for so long, had fallen apart. His life was a continuous struggle to find new values, a new orientation, and a new humanity that could cope with such an unnerving realisation.

The brilliant son of a village pastor in Saxony, young Friedrich so excelled in Classics that he became a full professor in his mid twenties. Soon however he abandoned an academic career and became a philosopher working often in isolation for some sixteen years, pouring out an extraordinary range of ideas based in an almost total rejection of the worldview of his time. To understand Nietzsche, his biographer, Walter Kaufmann, tells us we have to think of him as an utterly lonely man. A description survives from a visitor who discovered a shy, extremely polite person of about five feet eight in height, somewhat stooped, reserved, unaffected and suffering from extremely poor sight. "He was living in modest boarding houses in Italy in bare, cold rooms. His sensitive stomach meant he had to watch his food very carefully for an upset disturbed his nerves seriously. There was no wine or beer, coffee or cigarettes at his place but on a tray lay innumerable bottles, pills and potions with which he fought his insomnia, his migraines and his stomach cramps. His only possession, apart from books and papers, was a heavy wooden trunk, a few clothes and a spare suit. Wrapped in an overcoat, his dim eyes assisted by double glasses, he would sit for hours, writing, writing, and writing. His loneliness is expressed occasionally in outbursts in his letters and underpins again and again the thrust of his writing. His books were at first hardly noticed by anyone, which, for man of his profound pride and lonesomeness, must have been a deep source of hurt. He told a visitor that he felt himself to have a task or mission that he had to complete; to empty himself of it until it was done."[15] His output was prodigious and was brought to an end only by an insanity that crippled his mind in 1886 and lasted until his death in 1900.

Nietzsche has inspired and influenced an extraordinary range of writers, poets and playwrights as well as philosophers but has often been misunderstood, the early translations into English being particularly disastrous. Neglected in the Anglophone world until relatively recently, his main impact was in France. Totally averse to any philosophical systematisation, his literary style was difficult, often aphoristic using complex but striking metaphors but commonly lacking any thought – through development of ideas. He was constantly modifying his thought in work after work; later commentators often failing to understand that what they were reading was a mere way station on his journey. His greatest work 'Thus spake Zarathrustra' was written as a strange parody of the prophetic books in the Bible, yet it is a major attempt to create a possible morality for a world acknowledging the death of God.

Nietzsche saw that if there was no God or transcendental realm then there could be no outside authority for human values, rationality, standards or truth. All these have to be created within human culture itself. Although humans may create their values collectively and personally by their own choice, such freedom has been subordinate to authoritarian ethics almost throughout Western history. The later Greek philosophers subordinated the natural expression of the tragicomedy of life to reason. Nietzsche attacks Christianity but not Christ. Christianity attempted to state the truth and was undone by its own honest courage – Christian culture in finding no certainty has had to accept an unacceptable truth. Yet, the Christ life in its honesty was admirable. The Church undid Christ, says Nietzsche, through creating a system that denigrated the poor through pity, thereby aiding their failure. By encouraging dependency, he argued, such values perpetuate inauthentic living, a life lacking in will.

Although we have long lived by such conventions, Nietzsche argued, the original premises in a supposedly divine law now no longer hold. Conventional values have become systematised, made rational for the 'common herd' and constrain freedom. Minimally, one must break out from such a position through a personal exercise of will. All ways of construing ethics have therefore to be re-evaluated in the light of honest attempts to create a new order in a godless world, a way of being that honours authenticity.

Nietzsche valued the individuality of persons so that generalised psychologising was anathema to him even though he was an accurate interpreter of persons and understood the importance of the unconscious. Morality was to him an individual matter not something of universal significance. Knowledge is not absolute; it is relative to differing civilisations and persons. He felt however, prophetically, that an excess of knowledge could be dangerous and would be better suppressed if it had no social value.

Nietzsche believed one had to grow through an authenticity of personal choice and the exercise of will requiring an absolute acceptance of everything that happens, good or bad. Here is a reason why pity for others as well as oneself should be abandoned while yet maintaining the feeling of compassion for those who struggle. The aim is to create a higher type of human person (*Übermensch*, often translated as 'superman') who accepts and understands all, not as some system of belief but as a heartfelt relating to the world, a form of aesthetic being. To do this the *Übermensch* has to conquer all tendencies to self-indulgence, the desire for comfort, pity for the world, and strike out with all that is adventurous. Life itself is the only true value and his assertion of life becomes an evolutionary strength allowing the emergence of a new way of being.

Nietzsche feared that the way the world was going, its hesitancy, its decay of culture, its deadening residues of faith, would prevent such a renewal happening and it is perhaps this fear that drives his passionate style of writing, his hurried moving on, his failure to work through the meaning of many metaphors and wild hopes. His strange notion of the 'eternal return', that the world repeats time in endless cycles, each one exactly as before, is perhaps a metaphor for a longed-for security in which the acceptance of the present has become permanent; an attitude only possible for one possessing the grandeur of mind of a *Übermensch*. "It is only as an aesthetic phenomenon that the being of man and the world are eternally justified."

From this brief account,[16] we can see that the adoption of Nietzsche as a sort of in-house philosopher by the Nazis was a very cruel act of fate. While his ideas of power, individualism and the *Übermensch* were easily distorted in support of fascism, Nietzsche's intention was towards individual freedom not some form of totalitarianism ruled by gangsters. Yet, the failure to think through the implications of his poetic and metaphoric style of argument left him open to many interpretations and it must be said that he never worked out how *Übermenschen* could live with one another. He was not concerned with a democracy of the herd; perhaps this was an inevitable result of so lonesome yet so dedicated a life.

SARTRE AND BEYOND: BAD FAITH AND FREEDOM

The nature of being and the dilemma of how to live a life of value in a world devoid of transcendental authority provide the bases for existentialism, the exploration of the nature of human existence as such. In particular, Jean-Paul Sartre (1905-1980) stared into his bleak assessment of the nature of human freedom yet, in a life of considerable self-promotion, he remained devoted to the Marxist concern with the down trodden, a position that was however to earn him considerable obloquy when he refused to condemn the Soviet version.

Following the early death of his father, Sartre was raised in the household of his domineering grandfather, an author in his own right and an uncle to Albert Schweitzer. At first, Jean-Paul received a very private education and was generally expected to be brilliant. An ugly boy, he considered himself a genius and spent his life attempting to prove it. Although in some ways hardly an attractive character, Sartre's energy, enthusiasm and undoubted brilliance, his enjoyment of public display, Gauloise cigarettes and conversation in heavily smoke-filled rooms, bars and cafes, his womanising yet also his long and profound relationship with Simone de Beauvoir, his support of the working class and student revolt, generated a trendy movement towards highly individual self expression and radicalism among the young of which the 'beat generation' were the ultimate inheritors.

Sartre expressed his ideas in a number of striking plays and novels but his chief work was the philosophy described in his major work *Being and Nothingness*. (L'Etre et le Neant 1943). Here we find the worked out expression of his analysis of self and consciousness rooted in a phenomenology derived from Husserl. From the complexities of this work, we can extract the following as a hopefully, workable summary.

Sartre's first move is to focus on the intentionality of consciousness as its prime characteristic; consciousness is on about things, it is a consciousness of matters outside itself. 'Things' are beyond consciousness and never limited by their presentations to it. In their apartness, they comprise a realm of being Sartre calls 'in itself' (*en soi*). Consciousness is neither part of the 'in-itself' nor has it any characteristic other than to intend. It is thus in a sense quite vacuous. Since no object of consciousness can itself be conscious there is a sort of void at the centre of our existence: awarenesses of ego, body, memory all pivot on vacuity in this way and the result is an implicit awareness of lack at the root of human being. Consciousness is essentially a negation; everything it can be conscious of is not it. Yet, in relation to the 'facticity' of it's being, consciousness, while knowing it is nothing, is entirely free and 'for itself' (*pour soi*). In being aware of oneself as being directed outwards towards the 'in itself' while being nothing in one's-self there is great distress. This is ultimately intolerable and, in fleeing from this appalling vision, consciousness creates projects to conceal its nothingness from itself. This flight Sartre calls 'bad faith'.

Within the endeavour of conscious 'for-itself' to become 'in itself', there is no escape from the awareness of empty freedom, yet, in the discovery of others, one discovers oneself to be an object in the worlds of others. One is then a 'being for others' because the look of another creates of oneself an object in the world much as shame arises from the accusing gaze of a judge. Relating to others inevitably creates self-defeating projects involving a conflict between various freedoms in bad faith. Love is the wish to possess another's freedom just as sex aims for an identification with the body of the partner. Neither can overcome the fundamental nothingness of being. Life, as in Sartre's novels, is thus a conflictful path of search and loss, of courage, nausea and despair in an attempt to come to terms authentically with voidness as the root nature of one's mind. Good faith would be an awareness of the relationship between freedom and the facticity of this voidness in undistorted acceptance. Strange as it may seem, Sartre's followers often found romance in the sheer horror of a life behind blank windows, in the desolation of an attractive despair and the struggle to be one's own authenticity. Existentialism had a strong appeal among those who believed in the attempt at overcoming bad faith. What seems to be unclear is whether Sartre himself believed this to be possible.

Michel Foucault (1926-1984) and Roland Barthes (1915-1980) in their distinctive ways have extended Sartrean thought to show how the individual is rendered a pawn of social discourse. Foucault used the term 'subject' (where others might use the word identity) not only to indicate the subject of a statement or a thought but also to emphasise, cunningly, the subjection of the individual as being subject to conventions established to sustain relations of power. Unexamined social discourse commonly defines what is believed to be knowledge, truth or the nature of self, but which is actually a part of the power play of its originators. Words that establish convention are the roots of sustained power – hence, with growing public sophistication, the growing suspicion of government and the contemporary resistance to spin.

Foucault often begins his writings with a vivid account of an individual history. He researched the sad story of Adelaide Barbin who was brought up as a girl, fell in love with a woman teacher with whom she slept but eventually, as a result of others' suspicions, consulted first a priest and then a doctor who found she had rudimentary male genitalia and no womb. She was thereafter considered to be male and endeavoured to live as a man named Abel. Her diaries show that, as a girl, she had had a relatively well-integrated social life but, as Abel, she could not create a workable identity. She became incoherent, unable to sustain her former relationships, aware of sexual affection but no longer able to fulfil it, she eventually committed suicide. Foucault shows how social convention regarding sexual identity failed to provide a loophole for an exceptional case and lead to her death. Similarly, he points out that in ancient Greece, although homosexual relations were common, there was no such thing as a defined homosexual identity. It was simply not that important. Today, when at last the law no longer makes homosexual orientation a crime, there is still pressure to define oneself according to a fixed notion of gender affiliation by 'coming out', visiting 'gay' pubs or bars or, conversely, by being 'straight'. The possibility of a wider range of gender activity is thereby diminished because social convention, here of recent origin, coerces gender identity within narrow channels. Elsewhere, Foucault points out that the grim cruelty of medieval punishments oddly allowed an individual to resist social coercion more easily than in a modern prison where, under constant observation, a prisoner is subjected to a daily regime intended to bring him into subordination as a conforming citizen. By contrast, a bold medieval resister at a public execution could by acts of courage perhaps persuade the crowd to release him.[17]

Yet, power never exists without its bipolar companion- resistance, a word very meaningful in France following the Nazi occupation during World War II. Parents and teachers, the law whether good or bad, moral conventions, all subject the child or young person to the authority of power, Foucault argues, and this is in due course resisted. The conventional good life 'subjects' individuals seemingly for their benefit, and, through discourse, persuades them to a belief in their own subjection. Every moral code, argued Foucault is a form of subjectification, which in one way or another entails its resistance. Resistance is however often bought at a price. Contemporary whistle blowers who reveal state or business corruption may face the law or accusations of libel – they certainly lose their jobs. Convention, resistance and conscience are linked together. Individuals most usually come to define themselves and their choices according to convention, and, invaded by a discourse, they, as it were, become nothing other than the discourse – like speaking clocks telling the time as required. Here we have a version of the meaning of 'bad faith', an authentic subject replaced by the reflexes of words.

A reading of Foucault makes it very clear how the moral discourse of a communism or a liberal humanism can support the power of leaders through encouraging social approval for those saying the right things and who are thereby 'subjected'. If one examines such discourse one becomes aware of the use of terms such a 'democracy', 'tyrant, 'weapons of mass destruction '(etc) to persuade and hence subject citizens, initially resistant, to a policy supporting a particular use of power. The speeches of George W Bush and Tony Blair's spinful equivocation in his use of politically controlled public enquiries are cases in point. As subjects increasingly resist, the ploys of the power holders are revealed.

Louis Althuser (1918-1990) also attempted to show how capitalist society is maintained through ideological discourse. Marx and Engels had argued that ideology was the means whereby a ruling class, whatever its nature, sustained itself. In medieval or feudal times, for example, appeals were made to loyalty or honour while, under contemporary capitalism ' freedom of choice', to observe any one of fifty channels of TV for example, is the current buzzword sustaining consumerism. During the period of high European imperialism, social Darwinism was popular among some advocates of the social selection of the fittest – and even today, the 'market' is often assumed to be 'natural'. Such ways of presenting the world may keep the citizenry in a state of agreement with their masters. Ideology sustains its appeal through suggesting the inevitability or the natural character of its claims.

Arguing from a Marxist basis, Althuser showed how a 'Repressive State Apparatus' could maintain a mode of production by way of an 'Ideological State Apparatus' broadcasting the meanings and values by which a citizenry imagines it lives in an inevitable mode of existence. A police state is not then needed. Ideological State Apparatuses may be religious, witness the power of the Roman Catholic clergy in Poland or Ireland, may be based in union activity, or expressed in policies regarding schools, drugs or immigrants. In fact, the main ISA, argued ALTHUSSER, is education. Schooling and higher education inculcate obedience, deference, naive psychologisms, gender behaviour, unexamined ideals of liberalism and what it means to 'serve the community'. The ideological system secures consent through an implied common sense so that the very idea of an alternative becomes unreasonable. Even so, and contrary to ALTHUSSER, education can also inculcate criticism and resistance among those taught to be socially aware – studying Althusser, for example!

Roland Barthes argues that conventional bourgeois ideology sustains itself through communal values whereby a standardised person acquiesces in a way of life within which hints at a darker underside are conveniently ignored.[18] To the bourgeoisie, a conventional set of values, being 'one of us', comes so naturally that prevailing standards of wealth, taste and good common sense are rarely questioned. We no longer own a discourse, we are it, subordinated to the symbolic world it presents.

Fortunately, in recent years, the investigative press has been doing a good job in holding up mirrors to dark corners and asking questions that eat away at the roots of naive obedience. The understanding of oppression, however benevolent and convincing, is perhaps becoming clearer today than in the years immediately following World War II and we owe much of that clarity to the provocative work of these thinkers.

STRUCTURALISM AND DECONSTRUCTION

The liberal-humanist conception of the self as a real entity interacting meaningfully with real things in order to produce progressive effects or to sustain a value system is severely challenged in the approaches we are discussing. The humanist assumes a real world out there which reason can comprehend and which language depicts. Language to the humanist conveys the uniqueness of a person, the self or 'I' expressing 'my' personal truth of experience in the world. All this is set-aside in the perspectives we are now considering. The mind has become no more than a receptacle for a discourse by which social power controls the personal and wherein language itself becomes the pivotal figure. If God has been replaced by Absolute in Hegel, by Will in Schopenhauer, by Being in Heidegger, in Lacan we have symbolic language itself. The structure of language emerges therefore as a supremely important focus of attention.

Ferdinand de Saussure, (1857-1913) was professor of linguistics in Paris and then in Geneva. His pupils put his lectures together after his death so we have no account of his sources directly from him. It seems however that the ideas of a family friend Adolphe Pictet 1799-1875), who wrote on language in the context of studying the aesthetics of poetry[19], were his initial inspiration. Saussure argued that in language the sign (*i.e.* the word) is divided into two components, the signifier (sound) and the signified (its meaning) but that there was no constant relation between them. A word for something differs between languages, may have different grammatical gender, and may shift in precise meaning: as *mouton* in French stands for both 'sheep' and 'mutton' in English. The meaning of a signifier is found not in its reference to something but in its difference from words that could stand in for it (see also Chapter 16). To understand a sentence, one needs to know a whole language implicitly. *Langue* (language) is a system in which *parole* (word) has meaning therefore only by differentiation. Understanding meaning necessarily requires a holistic approach. Languages provide patterns or structures and in 'structuralism' it is this patterning that is examined rather than the person originating the talk or text. The author is of little importance compared with the inevitable citations from the past that in varying compositions make up a text. Ideological pronouncements, such as we have just discussed above, are sets of citations that can be analysed through a deconstruction of what is written or said. The personal, authorial voice consists in no more than a citation of themes. Authors, as it were, inhabit pre-existing structures that they reproduce in the composition of any sentence. It follows that for you and I our apparent originality is an illusion, for we are simply recombining the 'already said'. Our cherished identities are the products of whatever linguistic system occupies us. Yet, by focussing on the system itself, the structuralist approach sets aside historical aspects. Levi-Strauss, for example, in studying the forms of cultures using a structuralist approach, thought he had established universal themes valid throughout time. He was not interested in how such forms may change with shifting conditions.[20]

Jacques Derrida has taken this approach much further becoming the leading philosopher of linguistic deconstruction that may be extended to the analysis of any cultural theme. In many ways, he characterises the philosophical aspect of postmodernism. Together with Foucault and Lyotard he challenges the entire system of modern politics and economics as a means to social justice. Derrida does this by questioning the language of self-evident 'truths' based in conventional dichotomies between the various expressions of 'good' and 'bad'. His work has been found to be highly controversial not to say subversive and, furthermore, being presented in various experimental ways with numerous learned cross-references, it is neither easy to read nor to understand. The intensity of the philosophical conflicts he has created has matched those between politicians with a mutual distaste of opposing ideologies. It was extraordinary that the normally well-mannered and sophisticated University of Cambridge fell apart in dispute over a suggested award of an honorary degree to Derrida in 1992. For the first time in some thirty years, the dons had to put the matter to a vote. Derrida won his degree by 336 votes to 204 but opponents remain vocal. As an Algerian born Frenchman, Derrida has also been much involved in activism on behalf of a number of political causes including the rights of Algerian immigrants in France. He expresses his views in actions.

Derrida's perspective begins with the recognition that Western metaphysics from the Greeks down (or up?) has taken the form of systems positing a central focus upon which the argumentation depends. As we have seen, in the Christian era God took this pivotal position, but philosophers since the Enlightenment have placed other concepts in his place in efforts to resist a central nihilism. Such systems, Derrida argues, are always built up from dichotomies - bipolar units in which one term is positive (good) and the other negative (bad) with the negative one subordinated to the positive – as in light-dark, male-female, above-below, right-wrong. In linguistic theories, speech has been seen as more important than writing and this is because, Derrida, says, speech involves the presence of the speaker and thus guarantees the existence of a self. Presence is one side of the bipolar opposition between presence-absence with presence (speech) privileged over absence (writing), a perspective called 'logocentrism'. All philosophical centres imply a presence from which the rest of the argument follows in dependency.

Derrida's argument generalises to cultural concerns and in particular to the self. The idea of 'I' takes the pivotal role, the central position in the 'language' (*langue*) of my self-system and all acts or thoughts are the 'words' (*parole*) of my self-system. The central positioning of 'I' acts as a guarantor of 'my' being. In Western thought systems the centre or pivot is the creator which guarantees the integrity/coherence of the system but also transcends it – in that it stands apart from the rules of the system.

Derrida points out that one bipolar term cannot exist without its pair – the meaning of one depends on the implicit presence of the other term. His method of 'deconstruction' is primarily an exposure of how these terms work in a discourse or philosophical system and how any emphasis on one side none the less implicates the other. The bipolar opposition in the co-presence of terms comprises a single structure, like the two wings of one bird perhaps. Through deconstruction, new relationships are seen to be inherent in what seemed a moral certainty and reconstruction with a differing emphasis is already foreshadowed in the very mode of structuring an argument.[21]

There can be no end to this process, which, depending on one's point of view can be read as destructive or constructive. Since meaning in any system, whether cultural or philosophical, depends on difference rather than reference, as Saussure had shown, there is an almost endless possibility of re-interpretation. Furthermore in conversation, or dispute, or philosophical argument, the fact of difference means that speakers have to negotiate to find a meaning that operates mutually to enabling communication to continue. It is thus necessarily so that in discourse the precise meaning of a word, sentence or attitude, is commonly deferred (put off) until such mutuality is achieved. Derrida calls this delaying procedure in creating meaningful discourse *differance*, a pun untranslatable in English, which reveals a further implication of difference. Derrida's work suggests that no ultimate meaning can be found because the possibilities of difference/differance (deferral) are unlimited and hence no final or absolutist ethical system can be found. To some this ultimate relativism destroys the possibility of establishing the good. To others however it suggests the unending fascination of exploratory discourse and continual experimentation in ways of being and doing.

If we take Derrida's philosophical viewpoint as the prime posture of contemporary thought, supported in many ways by Wittgenstein, then we find ourselves left in an ethical vacuum, one in which almost any moral position can be argued and lived but without any authentication from outside. All traditional religions become something like a matter of taste while New Age beliefs have the nature of fashions. Science can often account for a seeming causality within patterns of wholeness but the pivot for an ethical life remains a matter of choice – not unlike choosing a TV channel. This seems to be the contemporary form of nihilism and in the vastness of such a freedom many fear a void without meaning, fixate in unsupportable, defensive dogma or may run from it in despair.

EPILOGUE

After reading Jim's essay, the Buddha leaned back in his chair. He felt excited by what he had read and marvelled at what Richard Tarnas has called 'The Passion of the Western mind'. He felt the extraordinary pressure within Western philosophy to find a way through the problems provoked by 'nihilism', the logical death of the Christian 'God', and its overwhelming effects on European thought and culture. He realised that such worrying concern had simply not been present in the Indian and Chinese thought systems with which he had been familiar. Argument yes, deconstruction and reconstruction yes but no such culturally destructive nihilism as that leading to the great Cartesian split, the isolation of knowledge from value, the scientific materialism and utilitarianism of modern thought, the pragmatism of self-concerned greed in economics and the slow destruction of the natural planetary world. Yet, he also delighted in the extraordinary freedom into which Western philosophy had plunged. He saw here an opening through which remedies for the world crisis might be proposed.

He had begun to realise that his time on the Earth for this visit was now limited. Before departure, he wished to spend time in the far mountains and he had arranged to travel to remote monasteries in northern Bhutan where he felt he would meet old friends and encounter the ancient world of Buddhism as it survives today. Jim had agreed to put together their talks for public presentation and he felt that, at this time, there was not much more he could do. The world, like his original followers, would have to work out its own salvation with diligence.

One evening, strolling again along the embankment in the soft sunlight of an autumn evening witnessing the softly flowing river, the rotating London Eye, the excited tourists and the watchful police, Jim asked the Buddha, "So how, after all these studies and reflections, do you feel that Buddhist views relate to the modern world? What have they to offer?"

The Buddha took up the theme. "I am sure you are aware that the present crisis could be terminal. I mean in the sense that the current, consumer driven civilisation cannot last. We have already entered the end games of the present world. Fundamentally, the world view of this civilisation is profoundly faulted. All great civilisations have come to an end with the failure or emerging irrelevance of their founding ideas: Rome; the empire of the Incas; the Ottoman empire; the British empire and now the hegemony the U.S.A. Today the implications are far more serious because the fabric of the planet that has been the support of all these worlds is being destroyed. Your great grand children will open their eyes on a vastly poorer planet than the one we experience now. Much beauty will have disappeared."

"Do you see a fundamental cause for all this?" asked Jim.

"There are of course many causes in an interrelated mesh," replied the Buddha, "but the key to it all seems to lie in the profoundly schizoid division between Humanity and God, Nature and Culture, Science and Religion, which underpins so many quarrels and misunderstandings and which powers the failure to secure any kind of sustainability for life on the planet of the immediate future. This schism has a very ancient origin being anchored in the projection of the idea of God into a heaven distant from Man, which has led to the demanding of varying obediencies in differing cultures and conflicts between them. It began in the ancient split between the dualistic religions of Zoroaster, Yahweh, Christ and Mohammed and the holistic perspectives of the east in Hinduism, Taoism, Confucianism and Buddhism. In these latter, humanity and the universe were not split apart by a reification of self and deity as separate controllers of life: Universe and Humanity were co-determining. Western science indeed now reveals this Asian view to be an irrevocable conclusion to the debate but has thereby set up a deep quarrel between scientific understanding and the powerful Abrahamic religions of the Middle East and Europe-America. This split is being fought out between rational science and doctrinaire religiosity. It is far from clear whether the clarity of scientific understanding will prevail. The dogmatism of the capitalists, the Christian religious right and the fundamentalism of Islam could combine in mutual destruction to end our world in a whimper if not a self-created bang. An uncritically religious American president has preferred to ignore the rationality of science predicting catastrophe. We may simply allow our brilliantly civilised world to degenerate under the sheer weight of such ignorance. It all began a long time before Descartes!"

"How do these trends effect the individual?" asked Jim.

The Buddha paused before replying. "There is a profound relationship between these conflicts in thought and the suffering of individuals in our time," he said. "An extraordinary linkage connects the humanist belief in 'individualism', the cult of the self determining, wealth creating individual functioning within his own personal world of supposedly positive values, with the nihilism that comes from the questionable realisation that all values are relative, that there is no ultimate good and that everything depends on utilitarian choice. The freedom of the individual provokes a total uncertainty regarding personal values in a world of mere convention erroneously presented to us as nature. Here lies the ideological spin that sustains the illusion that the consumer society is the only one we can have. The painful psychology of alienation to which this freedom without value gives rise is becoming a marked feature of our civilisation, yet, driven by ego-satisfying bonuses and cunning incentives to work harder and harder, the talented employees of the transnational corporations strive blindly to keep the wheels of profit-making exploitation turning – even to the extent of not noticing the abundant corruption it so commonly supports.

"In emerging nations such as India, the rapid spread of these Western conventions may enrich the entrepreneurs who by luck or cunning have reached an adequate educational standard, but countless, poorly educated, young people remain jobless and disaffected, totally confused by the conflicts between the traditional, community values of their parents and the need for mobility, individual drive and forgetfulness of the past that allows social climbing within the new system transforming the countryside and uprooting traditional communal values. Pankar Mishra,[22] in his moving book, *The End of Suffering*, describes from personal experience the angry disillusion of those for whom inadequate education, social unrest and illusory ideals lead to a total disaffection from the surge of bourgeois wealth creation and an inclination towards incipient, hopeless revolution. Such people have no values from the past to sustain them and no hope for the future through which new values may be born. Nothing remains for them apart from a forlorn anger eager to latch on to any illusory project the demigods of violence may propose. Individualism, nihilism and the breakdown of communities are all ultimately the products of a capitalism in which the conflict between greed and value becomes ever more pronounced."

"Can Buddhist ideas help?" asked Jim.

"When I observe the suffering of the human race, the political discord and mismanagement, the selfishness of world economics, the thoughtlessness regarding the ecology of the planet and triviality of values I can see that what we call the Buddhist understanding of suffering is not only valid but that it is supported by much modern research and thought."

"How come?" asked Jim

" First of all, we can see that in the evolutionary story the biology of body and the emergence of mind relate closely to one another. Co-dependent evolution, one might call it. There is a holism increasingly in play that confirms a fundamental Buddhist orientation to the cosmos (Chapter 12). In the human case, we have seen that the self is created in conflict; the need to compromise is rooted in its essential nature and it has the innate mechanisms for repression. The construct we call 'self' has to protect itself in many ways if it is to grow to adulthood. Some children have a very bad time, others have it easy but the basic struggle is the same for all. Suffering, internalised in development, lies at the root of mental distress (Chapter 15, 16). It all circulates about the idea of me, myself. I want. I want. Such an egocentric focus may indeed have a biological underpinning within cognition. After all, dogs and cats, even without language, often show they have very clear 'ideas' of what they want or like. Among humans, the self begins as a representation of the needs of the body. We simply do not realise that each one of us is no more than an idea created by the cognitive functions of our own minds – there is nothing fixed or absolute. If we really want to, we can change. As the Buddha realised long ago, it is the reified idea of self that lies at the root of suffering. All the other manifestations of desire and the competitive violence arising from attachments depend on this. Here is the root ignorance."

"So you feel that the self concern of today is basically similar to the self concerns of 2500 years ago?" queried Jim.

"We can see that the desire to be permanently comfortable in ignorance of both the true nature of mind and the nature of time lies at the root of self concern. This appears to be the 'basic fault' in human life. Everything is actually impermanent and our personal disputes and even our wars count for little in the wide vista of the cosmos; our attachments to me and mine, our pride, our selfishness and sometimes our cruel rejection of others, remain rooted in buried resentments. The suffering all this causes is met today in the West by psychotherapy and social psychological processes of many kinds and the knowledge obtained in these ways is a tremendous asset to the Buddhist practitioner and teacher. Yet, in the main, these methods only attempt to adjust a person to his or her circumstances. They do not propose a radical insight into what it is that has these problems. For emancipation we need experiential knowledge of what we are, not only who we are."

Jim interrupted, " Do you really think that the yogic meditations of Buddhism can change the world. Only a few people can make really effective use of them?"

"You are right," the Buddha responded, "but the Dharma is not only understood through the advanced methods of which you speak. The root of Dharma practice is mindfulness, don't forget, not samadhi or brief moments of selfless bliss. One of the mistakes in modern Zen is that so many practitioners are galloping off towards a horizon beyond which they believe they can find some absolutely conclusive experience. Even a moment of enlightenment passes and leaves one, if not very careful indeed, wanting it again; the normal desire of course for something one has in retrospect enjoyed! Progress can come more in the awareness of self in walking, buying, selling, talking, and advising. Here we use our critical faculties as well as the presence of a calm mind to see what we can do. The practice of care-filled mindfulness is not difficult if you only pay proper attention to where you are and what you are doing in every moment. Here comes reflection – out goes reaction. It does need training of course."

'Yet,' interposed Jim, "if we look around we see people to be so conditioned in their social programmes, in their karma, so 'subjected' as Althuser would say, that it is difficult to believe many can set aside their preoccupations with themselves, their gains and losses, their beliefs in one or another God, the insults and mistreatments they have suffered. Instead of attempting to understand, they are happier in a casino, or on a beach, or in a cinema or prayer hall, or indeed in the creation of riots!"

"The power of what we have been calling ideological spin is indeed vicious," said the Buddha. "Only a few can perceive the functioning of power and the use of 'spin' in the persuasion of the gullible in politics and religion alike. This is especially so when everyone is looking outside themselves for salvation. Look at the media! Most of them fall for the conventional just as the French thinkers have argued. Fortunately, there are also the critics. We certainly need them. They expose the plots, excise the spin, publish the cartoons. They let people know how they are indeed subjected to the power of elites, the wealthy, the capitalist or religious institutions. Yet, if once someone looks within and sees her participatory continuity with the cosmos in heartfelt revelation, dualism is at once dead for her, there is a sudden freedom that transcends the options of politics. Without loosing our analytical capacities we need the old shamanic sense of how strangely wonderful the whole world is and how this illusory self is participant within it. No need for the external saviour once one can laugh at this primordial mistake.

"The European philosophers have been right to struggle with 'nihilism'. It has been so difficult because the necessity of 'God' had become so deeply entrenched. For a long time it seemed 'He' could only be replaced by an equally pivotal presence at the heart of a thought system, hence 'logocentrism'. The discovery of total relativity has been revolutionary but also deeply distressing for many. Within thought, there is no answer to this but once you discover the field of 'consciousness without an object' without fear you become aware of an expansiveness of mind previously locked up in words. This is an experiential revelation that makes it possible to conceive of life in a different way and in which merely idealised securities no longer have the pivotal place – for there is no pivotal place. Beyond locked doors lies freedom. Unfortunately, such revelation needs an awakening to the fact of locked doors and the quest for the keys to open them."

"It sounds as if you want to re-educate the world!"

"Precisely! How right you are. Yet truly it is only when the need for education strikes home that it can really produce some goods. And by goods, I mean values, sources for action that benefit all and preserve the world. Only the educated are capable of confronting the complexities of modern economics and the necessity of repairing the planet. The institutionalisation of greed is so engrained that only a revolution in social thought can tackle it. My fear is that the rot is going so fast that only a great catastrophe will generate sufficient motivation for serious change. May be it is through education that we have to proceed. Tinbergen was right to argue the case for a new type of citizen."

"Something a little beyond the three Rs, a touch of practical science, how to use a computer and behave politely, I presume!"

"Sure – it must begin and end in personal exploration – this fascinating world, these amazing inhabitants of our planet, our human treasures and cultural variety. Yet, the gaze must also be trained to look within, to subject all assumptions about oneself, all the self-supportive illusions of convention, to trained scrutiny, to probe the nature of personal and transpersonal consciousness.

"The fundamental problem of contemporary world education involves a quest for unifying values. Values originate in community and it is the breakdown of communities that has given rise to this increasingly worldwide alienation that can certainly destroy us. The problem is how to re-create a sense of belonging through which our forlorn loneliness may subside. Idealistic appeals along the lines of "Small is Beautiful", advocating the creation of small, interdependent communities, are insufficient. Schumacher made a good point but it is to the relationship

between small and big that we need to apply ourselves. Without an understanding of the functioning of a nation, the transactions of a village or
township will founder. In any case, small is often far from beautiful. Most
communes originate from idealistic groups within which the power of
individual idiosyncrasy and its potential for generating interpersonal discord is entirely forgotten – until strife breaks out in shrill recriminations.
In the present world, we have to focus on the global village. Unless we can
see that we are all truly in a great mess together, the potential for
negotiation within compassion is unlikely to develop. The goal of
education must be to find a way to generate an openess to one another
that can envelope the big as well as the small. The values one may hold
towards another need to be such that they can also embrace the all.

"All this needs practice on the ground at home and abroad. It needs
investigation – tsan tsan tsan – as the Chan masters say! But the main factor
in investigation has to be debate. We need great debaters who will
penetrate the ideological spin, the patterns of prejudice and how they
arise from fear; debaters who will turn the light around so that each student
sees her inner world, her motivation, and the manner in which she
values life. Action stems from this. Furthermore, it is only when one can
clear all this away to find oneself at ease that one can understand what
transcendental wisdom actually is. We no longer abide in caves. We have
to do it in the marketplace as well as in the hills - on the move as well as in
repose."

"So a debate about values is crucial?"

"Absolutely. Yet first it needs to be seen that values are not about what
I want or need so much as what may be the attitudes determining policies
that do good in the world. It is really only against such a background that
self-at-ease arises. The first debate must be about why it is not good to kill,
lie, steal, sexually damage someone or drug oneself silly. Modern illusions
have led our leaders into great mistakes in which at least the first three of
these vital precepts have been set aside in a cheap nonchalance based in
institutional gain. The Eightfold Path needs modern expression. We
need a profound moral reformation so that leaders do not only mouth
traditional values but also actually make use of them. This is the only way
the West as a whole or indeed a political party can regain its self-respect.

"Understanding this issue needs prior teaching in terms of history.
Our significant civilisations have been built around the way such precepts
have been applied, different though they may have been in contrasting
religions, eras and civilisations. Whether you call them the Ten
Commandments or the Five Precepts, they lie at the root of debates about
value. And this needs to be made personal. Abstract talk does nothing.

A vital requirement in developing a new worldview is the appreciation of the global shift in understanding culture that science has brought about. We have moved from Bakhtin's second phase of cultural history into the third (Chapters 10, 20, 24); meaning that all ideas about any ultimate understanding of existence have become relative. Science has revealed the vast omnipresence of mystery. No religion of any culture provides an unquestionable interpretation of why and how we are here. The dogmatisms of stage 2 religions are all unprovable. Neither Islam nor Christianity has a valid final claim on truth. This is why debate about how to run the world in the awareness of ultimate mystery becomes the pivot of modern education.

We need also to understand that people who have grown up witnessing terror based on religious dogma are very valuable. They need to share that terror with those who have led merely comfortable lives in front of television screens. Only through sharing, can love arise. Good hearted Islamists, Christians, post-Christians, agnostic scientists as well as Buddhists all need to meet one another in a debate aimed at world survival. We all have to wake up to become at long last responsible voters. Otherwise democracy will be a failure and all lost."

" So that's what it is all about – waking up!'

"It has only been when the people have been awake that the tyrants, the twisters, the demagogues, the priest-ridden hierarchies have been controlled. When we wake up, we start to think. Meditation and yoga are only the supports for thoughts that reach to heaven. Indeed, education, education, education – but how – and who will lead?"

End Notes

1. Toulmin, S. 1992. *Cosmopolis. The Hidden Agenda of Modernity*. University of Chicago Press. Chicago.
2. Wedgewood, C.V. 1999. (Original 1938). *The Thirty Years War*. Folio. London.
3. Scruton, R. 2001. *Kant: a very short introduction*. Oxford University Press. p. 14.
4. Scruton. *loc cit.*
5. Scruton: p. 76.
6. See discussion in Critchley, S. 2001. *Continental Philosophy: a very short Introduction*. Oxford. University Press: 26-27.
7. Tarnas, R. 1991. *The Passion of the Western Mind*. Ballantine. New York. p. 434.
8. See: Critchley, S. 2001. *Continental Philosophy: a very short Introduction*. Oxford University Press: 42-44.
9. Ott, H. 1993. *Martin Heidegger: a political life*. Harper Collins.London.
10. Batchelor, S. 1983. *Alone with Others: an existential approach to Buddhism*. Grove Press. New York.

11.   Morton, F. 2006. *A Nervous Splendour: Vienna 1888-1889.* Folio Society. London. (Originally 1979. Weidenfeld and Nicolson.)

12.   Grayling. A.C. 1996. *Wittgenstein: a very short introduction.* Oxford University Press.

13.   Wittgenstein, L.W. 1953. *Philosophical Investigations.* Blackwell. Oxford.

14.   "Upon that of which one cannot speak, thereof one must keep silent" The famous last line of the Tractatus.

15.   See: Kaufman, W. 1971. *The Portable Nietzsche.* Chatto and Windus. London. p. 106.

16.   For a good coverage see: Tanner M. 2000. *Nietzsche: a very short introduction.* Oxford

17.   For a lively introduction to the thought of Michel Foucault see 2003. *Society must be Defended: Lectures at the College de France.* 1975-1976. Penguin. London.

18.   Culler, J. 2002. *Barthes: a very short introduction.* Oxford University Press.

19.   Joseph, J.E. 2004. Root and branch: Pictet's roles in the crystallization of Sausaures's thought. *Times Literary Supplement.* January 9th. p.12-13.

20.   For a valuable discussion see: Doja, A. 2006. The predicament of heroic anthropology. *Anthropology Today.* 22.3:18-22.

21.   Belsey, C. 2002. *Poststructuralism: a very short introduction.* Oxford University Press.

22.   Mishra, P. 2004. *An End to Suffering: the Buddha in the World.* Picador. London.

PART IV

THE SEARCH FOR A FUTURE

If we look at humanity as a whole, we are social animals. Moreover, the structures of the modern economy, education and so on, illustrate that the world has become a smaller place and that we heavily depend on one another. Under such circumstances, I think the only option is to live and work together harmoniously and keep in our minds the interest of the whole of humanity. That is the only outlook and way we must adopt for our survival.

His Holiness the Fourteenth Dalai Lama. [1]

19

THE ORIGIN OF SUFFERING

INTRODUCTION

In placing Buddhist ideas in the forefront of modern thought we must challenge the manner in which they are most commonly described and by which they may be dismissed or subverted by the prevalence of a materialist world view. It seems essential to emphasize once again that the root ideas of Buddhism cannot be treated simply as just another 'religion'. Indeed, it would be more correct to argue that Buddhism belongs to Science, just as Science can inform Buddhism.

Buddhist ideas comprise a system of enquiry that has no end because it is bold enough to press beyond the confines of narrative into that mysterious silence that lies beyond thought. Although, as Kant rightly saw (Chapter 18), nothing can be said of such a realm, it can be experienced simply as the thought-less root of existential being known for example in yogic meditation training. Buddhist enquiry presses remorselessly into this realm because as identification with such spacious experience becomes unavoidable, so the relationship between narrative and the unknown becomes clarified in a unifying sense of belonging. Form is emptiness yet emptiness is expressed in form – as the Heart Sutra says. Here then is a view that has the potential to heal suffering arising from nihilism and alienation. Such enquiry is subjective empiricism with every much a right to be called science as does its objective corollary. Furthermore, since Science as mathematical narrative is dependent upon the characteristics of mind, it too is subject to buddhistic enquiry just as the mind/brain of subjectivity is open to objective research in narrative creation. Science and buddhistic enquiry thus form two poles of investigation by which we seek to see meaning in the mysterious universe of which we are both product and part. The current world crisis is fundamentally a crisis in the meanings that one-sided Western narratives have foisted on contemporary humanity. Unless we probe into the very roots of this malaise, we are unlikely to find any solution other than a patch-up that will soon be undone by planetary response.

In Part 1 of this book we outlined the severe problems that the contemporary Western world view has been unable to resolve. We suggested that in a globalised world we should at least pay greater attention to Eastern thought and in particular to the profound understanding of self and mind that originated with the Buddha. Can such inclusion help us to resolve some of the intractable issues that confront us? This book is an examination of this possibility. In Part 2 we presented an account of buddhist history and ideas and, in Part 3, a summary of key themes in the Western world view that relate to Buddhism, challenge it or are challenged by it. We imagined the Buddha revisiting the earth to find out how his ideas were received today. In this final part, we explore some of the implications that come from a joint consideration of buddhistic and scientific ideas. Can such an exploration begin to define a world view that can transcend the issues that bedevil us at the start of the current millennium?

In his first sermon to his five friends in the Deer Park at Sarnath, the Buddha had argued that life was suffering; not that life included suffering or gave rise to suffering but that it was suffering itself. The 'Noble Truths' argue that this is so because life consists of endless desire for security and meaning in a world that has no existence other than as an ever-changing flow of events in time. Human inability to accept this fact and to persist in an endless quest for a secure permanence for the self is what the Buddha called ignorance. Freedom from suffering could be found only when the attachments to illusory securities arising from this pivotal ignorance were laid aside. Unless attachments were abandoned in the walking of an enlightening path, suffering was endless, having no beginning and no ending.

We have been examining these ideas in the context of contemporary knowledge, in particular research into the origins of mental characteristics defining the self. Why did human ignorance evolve? Why does the self persist in its failure to understand its own nature in spite of its extraordinary capacity for the analysis of phenomena? Basic ignorance leads to suffering. How does this come about? Was the Buddha's insight fundamentally correct and does it hold today? Let us have a look at some of our conclusions.

BIOLOGICAL APPROACHES TO SUFFERING

In our review of evolutionary theory we have seen that once a feature of anatomy or social behaviour has become naturally selected it may subsequently play a role in determining the path of evolution that follows. These 'pre-adaptations' become elements in a series of linked changes like the successive steps of a staircase. A driven or 'autocatalytic' process is at work here whereby one step largely predetermines others that may follow within a frame provided by context. This is a developmental process likened to the movement of a ball down a slope – its direction depends on the tilt and shape of the incline down which it runs. In many respects, the Buddha's Law of Co-dependent Arising neatly encapsulates the principle here for logically it presupposes the possibility of natural selection.

In Chapters 15 and 16 we explored the fact that much human suffering is related to the dependency of the helpless child upon the mother and the behavioural constraints this imposes upon both parents and children. We can explain this today as a consequence of an autocatalytic sequence of changes set in motion very early in human history. Two key elements lie at the root of this sequence; bipedalism and social complexities in child development.

Some 5 million years ago when African forests retreated and savannah and desert land increased during an dry period, many species began to adapt to open country. Standing high on the back legs allowed early hominids to see across grasslands more easily and to develop a walking stride for travel and fast running. This freed the hands for holding, gripping and throwing and thus for tool making and the wielding of weapons. While the chimpanzees in forests remained essentially quadrapedal, sometimes walking on their knuckles and only standing high for observational or carrying purposes, the hominids gradually acquired bipedalism as their prime method of movement and this provided many advantages through the freeing of the hands for multiple uses.

Many animal species living in open country find that congregation in groups offers protection from predators and the sharing of information in the common search for food. Competition within such groups may lead to the formation of mutually supportive alliances commonly based on kinship. Social life becomes increasingly complex and 'Machiavellian' strategies enable individuals to manipulate others to their advantage. Clever animals engage in such activities with eventual reproductive success. Social intellegence increases, eventually leading to the capacity for realising that personal activity depends on mental agency – the prime ingredient of which is sensed as a relatively independent self. The self, as it were, is the cognitive representative of the body in a social world just as the body relates the mind to the physics of existence. Self-conception is a mental reification based on insightful awareness of the connections between many components of personal existence: sensation; perception; cognition and memory – as the Buddhists would say. Such cleverness depends on an evolutionary increase in the size of the computing brain.

The human brain is indeed notably larger in relation to body size than is the case in other primates. Furthermore, the rounded shape of the head, the tucking of the face under an expanded cranium and the pivoting of the skull on the spinal cord are consequences of the upright posture and the need for balance during bipedal movement, which has also necessitated changes in the shape and orientation of the pelvis producing problems for females at birth. While in quadrapedal baboons the baby passes through the birth canal in a movement directly front to back, in humans the brain and skull have begun enlargement in the mother's uterus and this necessitates a rotation through ninety degrees in passing the birth canal. Such a movement requires effort on the part of the mother and often assistance from a midwife.

In order to facilitate birth, the small human baby is born in an extremely undeveloped state. Indeed the child is completely dependent on maternal care for an extended period, the brain/skull continuing to grow for months after birth. The child gradually moves towards a degree of independence through infancy and childhood yet requires continuous education in social affairs and skills far into adulthood. Humans show a marked prolongation of life beyond the period of reproductive capability; an adaptation enabling accumulated wisdom to be passed from age to youth during the long period of maturation.

Human children, we have seen, are born into a situation of great social complexity and grow up within a network of competing adult interests that are highly variable according to circumstance. (Chapter 15) The dependency of child upon mother has affected the strategies whereby men and women attempt to maximise their reproductive fitness. Women are focussed on maximising the care given to their children while men, relatively free from such concerns, may or may not assist in rearing their children depending on circumstances and their opportunities for fathering children from additional women. We have seen how differing forms of marital relationship are linked to contrasting ecologies and livelihoods. The mother has skills whereby she endeavours to maintain the father's interest in her and in her children. Children likewise endeavour to increase their welfare through gaining support from parents and this may lead to conflict with mother and competition between siblings. Diversity of interests, skills and social orientations within a family tends to ensure that parents distribute their care in relation to the various assets children show, assets that may be related to their potential reproductive success. The initial, total dependence of children leaves them open to threats of rejection by mothers who, for whatever reason, may reduce or cease their involvement in a child's growth. In addition, father's demands on mother, his differential interest in his children and the risk of abandonment or even assault by him, increase the uncertainty with which a child's early relating is endowed. Children compete for their parents' care and cannot be certain that all will be well. A natural lack of ease is built into human procreation from the very start thereby producing diverse distortions in a child's sense of itself as an 'I' in the world. The Buddha's contention that life is suffering indeed has strong biological support.

Sigmund Freud's belief that the origin of human neurosis lies to a large extent within biology is generally supported by evidence gained in the study of human social evolution and, as we have seen (Chapter 15), John Bowlby's work has approached this theme directly. The whole process of human development is subject to threats to well-being, if not survival. The human self originates in a world beset with uncertainty. Human eyes open on a difficult scenario where nothing is certain. Although parents usually love their children, that love is always set within an atmosphere of perceivable ambivalence.

We have seen how the increased size of the human brain is essentially a response to the need for skill in managing social affairs through the intelligent appraisal of the utility and reliability of others. In a complex communal life, individuals need to be aware of their own personal existence as entities and agents in a world of competing others. The cognitive construction of the idea of a 'me' controlling and determining the actions of the body becomes the source of flexible strategies whereby innate tendencies of genetic origin find effective expression. The emergence of language facilitated the reification of self-knowledge through naming self versus others and mine versus yours, his or hers. The 'I' becomes an object, a John, a Betty or a Horatio; an agent in the world intent on its own fulfilment and ignorant of the complex processes that underlies its manifestation. 'I' appear to be one agent in a world of agents; entities quite solid and thing-like. The fact that 'I' am a reified cognitive construction is lost to view.

Social skills have required the evolution of enhanced brain capacity for handling information and providing an integrated continuity of experience in evaluating the passing scene. While the nature of consciousness as experience still evades us (Chapter 16), we can assume it has been a product of these evolutionary developments in social biology. Human minds are embodied cognitions through which we relate to the world and primarily to a social world.

This relatively recent bio-social perspective undermines the more traditional Cartesian dichotomy whereby the physical, biological or medical sciences are contrasted with humanistic or aesthetic interpretations of human life. We move here towards monist rather than dualist conceptions of the body-mind relationship. Contemporary evolutionary theory tends to bring about a convergence between the physiological and biological sciences on the one hand and psychological and historical studies on the other, even though much of the discourse in these fields of enquiry is still based in contrasting visions. Yet, we remain experientially in a dualistic world of observer and observed, thinker and thought. If we wish to establish truly consilient knowledge, such as E.O Wilson advocates, we need also to look within, to turn the gaze back, as it were, to observe the mind within the mirror. It is here that the phenomenological investigations of the Buddhist yogic approach can give us insights that go well beyond the discoveries of Husserl and the Western phenomenologists (Chapter 17). In particular, if we are to avoid the suffering that a collapse of civilisation would certainly entail, these insights cause us to reflect anew on the values we wish to establish as essential to our worldview of the future.

TRANSCENDING THE THING-SELF

The dependency of the young child has major effects on the developing mind. In the search for the origins of neurosis, psychoanalytical and psychotherapeutic schools have looked at the way in which the inevitable frustrations of wants and needs of baby lead eventually to repression and the development of a hidden, inner world of fear-filled resentments against the perpetrators of frustration. Suppressed anger is linked to deep needs for love, recognition and meaning for an emerging self with a name and an identity. The differing schools of thought all circle about these primal themes (Chapter 15). The repressed, inner conflicts of adults are rooted in our infancy and become the cause of subsequent failures in relating; failures themselves anchored in fantasies that may become almost explicit in dreams. In their studies of notable historical personalities, Alice Miller and others have demonstrated how the whole character and career of a human being is usually pivoted upon the social, especially the familial, circumstances of birth.

In an outstanding, concluding essay to her book *An Introduction to Object Relations*, Lavinia Gomez[2] points out that most Western, psychological thinkers are more concerned with the individual than with the vital importance of relationship in human development.[3] Their focus points primarily at personality examined separately from the community in which a person lives even though the subjective sense of self arises through the importation of social experience. The self as a cognitive construction is often viewed as a separate process from both its underlying biology and the community that surrounds it, although to do so is to perpetuate a dualism in which we 'have' a self rather than 'being' a self. The self is treated as a 'thing' separate from its context. Body and Mind thus remain distinct and their relationship unclear. Gomez writes: "*All these versions of duality are related to the physical and mental bases of our lives, without addressing this duality. Our physicality drives us towards food, shelter, sex; our subjectivity yearns for relationship, art, for meaning. While the western mind-body distinction forces us to differentiate between these aspects of ourselves, empirically they lie together in a single humanity. The subjective experience of our physicality renders it psychological; yet our split self concept stands in the way of unitary language.*"

She goes on to point out: "*Eastern thought has long been recognised as offering a different view of the self, less finite and less solid, and has been explored with devotion by westerners who feel boxed in by their social conditioning. Perhaps the self they hope to transcend is the thing-self, which we now conjecture as a defence against uncertainty which shields us from the fullness of experience.*"

Yet in modern French thought, particularly in Lacan and Sartre, we have come across a more unitary, less dualistic, version of the origins of suffering based in a developmental failure to recognise the basis upon which the construction of self rests (Chapter 18). As we have observed, Lacan sees the emergence of self as mistaking the social image-of-oneself-as-perceived-by-others as ones true being. It is as if one believes the face in the mirror is one's true face. The true basis of self, Lacan argues, is the lost unity of self and mother. Lacan speaks of a deep, unconscious sense of lack arising from the loss of maternal unity. Sartre saw consciousness as a vacuity, in which the objects of experience merely appear, and from the emptiness of which an individual flees in an endeavour to become something solid (Chapter 18). 'Bad faith' expressed in this flight can be cured only by a full encounter with vacuity itself. Of this however Sartre says nothing, remaining circling existentially around his founding ideas. For Sartre, a deep painful neediness in life arises from the lack of any rooted substantiality in experience.

Such notions of a profound sense of lack in human experience have also found expression in the work of pioneer psychoanalyst Alfred Adler (1870-1937) that has received a warm extension in the ideas of James Hillman. Adler based his psychology in the notion that physical inferiority, whether real or inferred, leads to feelings of negative self evaluation which demand compensation if the self is to feel at ease. Since any physical attribute can be judged inferior relative to the same feature in others, it follows that an inferiority complex must be a quite general problem for human beings. The defence of the ego requires the creation of guarding tendencies that protect the self against its own hidden fears.

One prime consequence in men is the 'masculine protest': a need to win or be perceived as 'one-up', having its origin in the development of a feeling in the necessarily small, dependent child that weakness is a sign of both inferiority and femininity. In a male dominated society, exaggerated heroism or bravado is thus a compensation for a lack of self-confidence in the face of unconsciously assumed inferiority. Such compensations may be socially effective depending on the manner by which the subject relates to the 'realities' of his social situation.

Adler was influenced by the philosophy of Hans Vaihinger, which argued for a fictional basis for subjectivity. The mind invents images and stories that come to act as healing fictions in compensation for the lack of self-confidence. These imaginary narratives play a major role in determining action in the world and contain configurations of the prime goals in a person's life. Mental disorder is thus constructed out of ineffective fictions that fail to compensate (or severely over-compensate) for the inner sense of inferiority. The therapeutic process consists in the reordering of such fictions to achieve a better balance in social relations.

In attempting to answer the question, "What does the soul want?" James Hillman argues that deep within mental development is a sense of inferiority that appears in deep psychic figures that seek to undermine the means by which compensation is being attempted. Such figures appear in dream, fantasy or in therapeutic interaction. In particular, they arise from real or imagined failures in erotic life wherein relative inferiority is especially easily stimulated. He argues that a need for compensation forms part of what he terms the soul and that a sense of loss is a permanent possibility. "*No psychological act can fully satisfy, no interpretation truly click like a key in a lock, no relationship of souls complete the lack and failure that reflects the essence of the psyche. Imperfection is in its essence, and we are complete only by being in want.*" He goes on: "*The whole therapeutic opus with its vision of perfection in the love of fellow-feeling can never leave the tiny beginning, the bit of gravel in the shoe that returns us to feelings of inferiority which are given with embodiment in our organic creatureliness.*" He concludes that the "*soul's eternal wanting is psychotherapy's eternal question.*" [4]

These views begin to approach the cardinal notion of Buddhism where, as David Loy, points out, the lack of insight into the 'emptiness', the non-substantiality of the impermanent self, is the prime cause of suffering – as the Buddha said. In Buddhism, the yogic enquiry into the nature of mind leads eventually to an uncovering of the absence of any substantial thing – like self. The whole basis of the cognised entity is questioned through the examination of its root in sensation prior to intentionality. In meditation, the narrative of self floats free in a space-like, open awareness wherein judgement or analysis no longer apply because these are both attributes solely of the narrative and not of its basis. Surprisingly, the prison of self-concern with its sense of inferiority, its prejudices and fixed views, is then found to have open doors and in such openness, a curious freedom is to be found. A positive, felt relationship with the bare suchness of existence is discovered precisely in this freedom. Training in the ability to sustain this insight leads to an equanimity in the face of life's perils that takes a practitioner far from the depressive states which Lacan and Sartre describe and which Hillman's grit in the shoe dramatises. A unifying, ultimately indescribable openness may replace the prisons of dualistic visioning which have become so marked a feature of the schizoid West stifled by the forms of its own narrative.

The simplicity whereby the Four Noble Truths are expressed should not lead us astray. It is indeed in the endless wanting for a condition that is not present, or not wanting that which is present, that lie the roots of suffering. Our modern knowledge of social psychological evolution and the dynamics of self are beginning to show us how this came to be. An understanding that goes to the very roots of our biological history may begin to point the way to plausible resolutions through filling out the buddhistic vision of self as desire.

End Notes

1. HH the Dalai Lama. 1999. *The Dalai Lama's Book of Wisdom*. Thorson. p.100. These are extracts from teachings given in London in May 1993.

2. Gomez, L. 1997. *An Introduction to Object Relations*. Free Association Books. London.

3. But see further: Hinde, R.A. 1979. *Towards understanding relationships*. Academic Press. London.

4. Hillman, J. 1983. *Healing fiction*. Station Hill Press. New York.

20

TINBERGEN'S DOUBT REVISITED

Tinbergen did not experience the severe dislocations that currently beset the world nor the optimistic hypocrisy by which the questionable values of consumer-dominated democracy are spun into seemingly inevitable and even desirable outcomes. Things have gotten worse since his time and it is increasingly apparent to any thinking person that they cannot go on as they are. It is not difficult to envisage a disastrous outcome to global 'development' should it remain uncorrected by new insights and alternative directions.

DOOMSDAY SCENARIOS

If limited global resources dwindle without adequate energy replacement or an acceptance of lowered and more equitably distributed standards of living, exploitation of the majority by a powerful minority may develop followed by an inevitable resistance taking an increasingly violent form driven by regression, bigotry and self-justification. Unless governments show an unhesitating wisdom, democracy itself may permit the election of salvationist tyrants whose policies quickly produce revolution. With modern weaponry and technology easily acquired, the result could be a collapse into a worldwide anarchy far more damaging than the Thirty Years War that devastated Europe during the demise of authoritarian Christianity. Any use of weapons of mass destruction would ensure not only the collapse of civilisation but also plausibly an extinction of the human species together with much of sentient life. The planet would be left for molluscs, flies and spiders to recreate.

Even without such a doomsday scenario, the likely solution would be the imposition of authoritarian regional or world governments devoted to the welfare only of their supporters and the suppression of all other cultural expressions. The freedoms we know today would disappear, self expression would be increasingly dangerous, cultures would become rigidified under self-righteous officialdoms, and underground resistance would express itself by continuous, unsuccessful terrorism without clearly formulated objectives. Such a situation could only hold the fort against planetary disaster for a limited period of time that might however last for centuries. To its inhabitants, the twentieth century would appear to have been paradise.

Unless humanity takes steps to alter its historical direction, something like the above scenario is an entirely plausible outcome. Tinbergen was therefore right in his anxieties about the future. The seductive benefits of technological science and its supporting world view are manifest in the high standards of living throughout parts of the developed world, the freedoms of expression under democratic Western governments and the exciting vistas of continuing research in all fields, yet the underlying anxieties cannot be resolved by existing philosophies of economics and society. The dangers to the desirable lifestyle of the wealthy are perhaps the most obvious threats: yet the contemporary obsession with both 'growth' and 'sustainable development' in a world of limiting resources is actually so contradictory that we can only hope that the roots of the obsession itself may be confronted.

There are indeed signs that this can be the case. The appallingly negative consequences of unrestrained corporate capitalism have not gone unnoticed. The destruction of local cultures, the pauperisation of those whose local industries have been destroyed, the problem of debt, the exploitation of small countries by the transnational corporations, the condition of Africa and the failures of the World Bank and the IMF in controlling financial collapses of formerly healthy economies, have lead to worldwide condemnation and the criticism of the global policies of institutions following a market philosophy. The over-exploitation and pollution of the planet primarily by the U.S.A. can only become enormously magnified as the full impact of the modernisation of China, India and South America is felt. Worldwide exploitation of planetary resources at the levels of U.S.A. is merely a pipe dream. New economic approaches are needed to repair the damage (Chapter 17) but the power of the 'religion of consumption' is such that any serious attempt to curtail the onward march of increasingly insupportable life styles will be dangerously resisted. The problem requires a vision of human fulfilment that can challenge the illusion that the human subject can ground him or her-self solely through material gain. Only the creation of such an alternative vision is likely to persuade humanity to adopt reasoned policies of self control that are the conditions for an 'enlightenment' of both an Eastern and a Western form.

The root of the matter is education. Those who confront the current evils of the world come from many origins and persuasions. There is little unifying understanding among them apart from a resistance to the manifest inadequacies of current global policies. There is no underlying philosophy of human nature from which world policies can be developed. This means that although what is wrong with global development is not so difficult to understand, a basis for its correction that can be universally accepted remains so far largely unconsidered. Piecemeal and fragmentary opposition does little to control the onward march of greedy development. The world seems to await a saviour but the days of saviours are over. We have to work this one out for ourselves.

Tinbergen wondered whether the psychology based in our biological origins on the African savannahs was adequate for the task, whether we were in fact sufficiently flexible to face up to the testing conditions of our own creation. He called for a "new type of citizen." (Chapter 1) This book, in common with the work of David Loy, has been arguing that Western philosophies alone seem unable to meet the challenge because at a fundamental level they have proved unable to tackle the fear of personal ungroundedness. Such fear underlies the quest for security that is the basis for our greed for illusory material solutions. The Western world has not recovered from the death of God and pursues policies with a potential for self-destruction.

THE PROBLEM OF RELIGIONS

Speaking of a 'vision of human fulfilment' suggests a religious argument. In the perspective of Western humanism, 'religions' are a disaster. Is the solution we are exploring therefore 'religious' or something else? Words are tricky and some clarification is again needed to avoid misunderstanding. The breaking of the domination of religion over creative thought in Europe has had immense consequences. The Western humanist tradition has been the source of extraordinary gains in understanding, in personal freedom, in scientific understanding. This is true in spite of its unfortunate closure around the rigidities of the Cartesian world view that has led to our alienation from nature and the crisis of unrestrained consumerism. Its values have included liberty, pursuit of knowledge for its own sake, cultivation of acceptable pleasure, free speech, tolerance of contrasting views, open friendship and a feeling of being a member of a human community oriented to general well being. These were the understood dimensions of the 'good' that sustained the humanist triumph until the mid twentieth century and to which philosopher Charles Taylor feels we need to find a way to return (Chapter 1). They are the very basis of our democratic values. The cost of their decay is not so much a loss of meaning and value in the post-modern world as a failure to address the fundamental post-Christian loss of a secure self. Underlying all the struggles to find an alternative to God is a confusion that all too easily accepts simplistic solutions and ends in merely self-serving interpretations of fulfilment that encourage dispute.

Humanist philosopher A.C. Grayling of Birkbeck College in the University of London argues that "*the real problem faced by the humanist project is the survival of religious beliefs and practices, and in particular their growth in parts of the world, especially Africa and Asia, where the fertile mixture of under-education, poverty, impotence and resentment makes the promises and quick psychological fixes of religion especially welcome.*"[1] He points particularly to fundamentalist forms of Christianity and Islam. "*All these forms of religious expression are essentially regressive, oppressive and at best medieval, and their dissonance with the modern world is a continual and too often terrible source of conflict.*" He argues that the toleration of such religions within a Western world of traditional liberal values favouring free speech and free worship is mistaken. The powerful and coercive 'religions of the book', Christianity, Islam and Judaism, all derived from a common Middle Eastern origin, have become mutually incompatible with one another and their bloody disagreements are allowed to thrive while generating endless confusion. He argues, "*All religions are such that, if they are pushed to their logical conclusion, or if their founding literatures and early traditions are taken literally, they will take the form of their respective fundamentalisms.*" In that each regards the others' teachings as falsely pernicious and that the only truth is their own way, the inevitable consequence is mutual crusade, jihad or fatwa. Even when suppressed by secular law, such antagonism and distrust leaves society in ferment. Such rampant stupidity is a major barrier to rational understanding of any kind.

Perhaps one of the most alarming aspects of the coercive aspects of fundamentalist Christianity is its penetration into the politics of the right in U.S.A. Naïve, born-again Christians include among their number a regenerated George. W. Bush whose crusading attitude towards sensitive world reform has sustained the Middle East in turmoil, created bloody chaos in Iraq and totally failed to understand that military might alone cannot possibly meet the challenge of fundamentalist Wahabism in Islam. Meanwhile, as his citizens become dubiously welcomed anywhere in the world, this foolish president campaigns politically through utilising the power of fear to suborn the intellegence of the citizens he appears to protect. Endlessly mouthing 'democracy' and 'freedom' he fails to understand the messages of Kofi Anand that the rule of law must begin at home. Cryptic totalitarian abuses in prisons are among other signs that the democratic conventions of the American past are weakening. The naïveté of evangelical Christianity in combination with the 'neo-conservative' political programme of economic imperialism suggests that the present culture of U.S.A. is a major contributor to world problems and very far from offering any solution. Yet, there is clearly hope as the mid-term elections 2006 and the control of Congress by the Democrats now indicates. US citizens have clearly rejected the nonsence inflicted upon them and are looking for a way out.

Religion, says Grayling, should be left to the personal sphere allowing public education to be entirely secular. The abandonment of support for faith schools and religious propaganda may allow dogmatic antagonisms to fade away and plausibly the French insistence on keeping religion out of school may be a wise policy. Uncritical, multicultural toleration may lead not to common understandings but to unending civil conflict and pernicious prejudice preventing necessary global reforms. Even so, Grayling's views need very cautious consideration because it is an inalienable right of democracy that individuals should have the openess of free speech and expression. Yet, when these rights are exploited for the expression of intolerance, authoritarianism and ideological control, freedom itself disappears. At present, the resentment of Islam at the West and the Western suspicion of Islam is polarising a dispute that needs sensitive understanding. It should be possible for moderate Islam, a religion of righteousness, to coexist reasonably both with a compassionate Christianity and scientific secularism but this can only come about through dialogue and respect on all sides. Interfaith dialogue requires a tolerance based in an underpinning that must be in itself philosophical.

It may well be that periodic upsurges of insight can only develop when defensive attachment to the forms of a religion is given up within a religious world view itself. The Desert Fathers knew this, apophatic and hesychast Christianity in the Greek and Russian churches understands it, Martin Buber in Judaism expresses it and so do the varying forms of Sufism, nominally part of Islam. The textual expressions of all these movements have many features in common. In reading them, one sees a common thread. Meister Eckhart, Martin Buber and the Sufi masters all transcend authoritarian discourse in ways that parallel the insights of the Buddha. Practitioners within these traditions of spiritual practice have a generosity based in their relative lack of attachment to ego concern that allows them to talk easily with one another. Aldous Huxley has called this a perennial philosophy that underpins religion.[2] There is hope in this view but its expression remains diverse and deeply contaminated by orthodox concerns with security through dogmatic belief.

We have noted that historical transitions between differing stages of religious development have been characterised by the Russian thinker

Michail Bakhtin as occurring in three phases of cultural change.[3] In the first phase, the 'ancient matrix', personal identity is relational, structured in terms of the immediate social world and environment of exploitation. The self is deeply participatory, involved within and pervaded by the unified life of the world system as perceived. Time is felt to be cyclic based on a harmony within nature, the human relationship with which is governed by detailed rules regulated by shamanic discourse including means for restoration when broken. The vehicle is mytho-poetic, 'shamanic' discourse, often revealed in trance states wherein representational fantasy reflects themes in both social and environmental relationships.

In the second phase, individualism is enhanced through an awareness of time in a personal becoming moving towards destinies distinct from the world matrix. This phase coincides with the appearance of class systems, state government and religions of personal salvation emphasising a separation between identity, the political world and the cosmos. The vehicle of thought is here anchored in reified usages of terms of self, identity, ethics and linear processes descriptive of commercial advance and personal salvation. The so-called 'great' world religions of today are mainly of this type.

The third phase develops through an emergent understanding of belief and world-view as contingent upon their context. A sense of the relativity of faith to the history of cultural change arises so that the monologic discourses of previous religions/philosophies are opened up through reflexive awareness. It is then realised that projections of reified abstract ideas upon a conceptual universe in no way necessarily relate to 'truth'. This last phase has it main contemporary expression in the humanism of the so-called post-modern period but it has a much earlier origin. An understanding of relativity allows older, even shamanic, discourses to be attributed new meanings within an ever moving discourse with 'reality' operating in many modes.

If we take a look at the major world religions, we can see that few of them have made this third transition. In particular the great monotheistic religions, Christianity (2.16 billion adherents worldwide), Islam (1.34 bn), Judaism (14 million) and the oldest, Zoroastrianism (2.6 million),[4] all reify the mystery of universal causation as a single eternal and omniscient 'God', an idea that provides the basis for moral judgement and acts as the core socio-ethical glue of the society of believers. The problem is that when such root ideas are threatened by critical analytical approaches and scientific studies of actual causation in the world, believers react with defensive aggression through excommunication, imprison-ment or even the slaughter of unbelievers. Such societies become highly conservative and unresponsive to social and economic changes to which in many cases they react by regression to fundamentalist simplicities oppressing a population with rigid rules lacking in humility, compassion or reason. Furthermore, since each faith holds its beliefs to be unchallengeably true, dialogue and negotiation between them becomes almost impossible and conflict inevitable.

It so happens that Asian religions, Hinduism (877126000 adherents), Buddhism (382155000) and Taoism, have retained a sense of human participation in the universal process that to a large extent avoids the conflicting dualisms of the monotheistic majority and, apart from local conflicts in the name of religion which have ethno-economic causes (*i.e.* Sri Lanka), are less likely to regress into widespread fundamentalism. These approaches have crossed the boundary between Bakhtin's second and third phases. In the case of Buddhism such transition is especially clear in a manner that allows Buddhism to claim a clear relationship with Western post-Christian humanism.[5]

Bearing these three orientations in mind, we can see that the objective study of 'faiths' must entail the relating of socio-economic study with the anthropology of custom and social structure. The world-view of a people needs detailed understanding through analysis of transcribed speech, ritual and trance utterance as well as of any textual material available. As a picture of the 'inner' world of the participants emerges we can see how meaning is attributed to self and social process in contrasting faiths and how ritual and other practices come to regulate communal life in relation to social tension and the supply and demand of commodities derived from the exploitation of nature. A worldwide education in the understanding of these processes is desperately needed to reduce the blind adherence to medieval moralities based in incompatible beliefs in arbitrary metaphysical entities. Such an education, plausibly, would bring about a lessening of tension without the need for laws favouring this or that solution.

HUMAN POTENTIAL

The key notions within Buddhism, the root ideas deriving from yogic investigation, express a transcendence of theistic duality peculiarly well. Of course, indigenous practices within Buddhism often take the form of dependent religiosity also – where the believer is dependent upon an attachment, worshiping the Buddha for example rather than following his example and his teaching. Yet, in the teachings of the masters, lamas and yogins, there is the clarity of a psychology anchored in a holistic perception of universe and self. This is a vision that, while solving nothing objectively, provides the subjective security of an open freedom. As Master Tung-shan said on attaining enlightenment through observing his reflection in a stream, "I am not it, yet it is all of me."[6] When the relationship of self and universe is seen in this light, the rigidifying attachments to protective concepts and dogmatic identifications melt away. If Western humanists came to see the universe in such a way, it would become possible to reformulate the materialism and ego-centred demands for the illusory 'goods' of today in new and curative ways. Could such a view become the basis for a new education system going beyond the utilitarian projects of the present time? Is a buddhistic version of humanism a way forward for our time?

While Tinbergen doubted whether the human capacity for adaptation was sufficient to cope with present demands, there are signs that human potential remains vast and, like an immense oilfield on the moon, untapped. Gloomy as so many predictions about the future may be, it is far from clear that human ingenuity is exhausted. The problem is how to activate this potential in a way that will correct the negativities of our time. To tap this field we will have to try out new approaches, in particular through working with new psychological dimensions that may open the way to potentialities currently viewed as impossible or suspect. The barriers to change inherent in the present system are enormous: not only is there a lack of vision in discontent but neither philosophers nor economists have yet seen a way to modify corporate capitalism in a way that could stop the spoliation of the planet before serious disasters begin to strike. Long-sight and timescales of several hundreds of years are needed. Yet, the modern world is an intellectual construct as much as it is a product of material history and the problem with the Western intellect is that it has been stuck for too long in the groove of the Cartesian vision. The mind is altogether bigger than this in its capacity for imagination, insight and subjective self-awareness. It is on these further reaches of the human mind that we will have to call.

End Notes

1. Grayling, A.C. 2003. *What is Good. The Search for the Best Way.* Phoenix. London. p. 233.
2. Huxley, A. 1954. *The Perennial Philosophy.* Chatto and Windus.London
3. Bakhtin, M. 1989. *The Dialogic Imagination.* University of Texas. Austin.
4. See: Faith: the facts. *The Independent.* London. April 14th 2006.
5. Crook, J.H. 2007. Shamans, Yogins and Indigenious Psychologies. In: Barrett, L. & R. Dunbar. *Handbook of Evolutionary Psychology.* Oxford.
6. Loori, J.D. 1999. *Teachings of the Insentient: Zen and the Environment.* Dharma Communication Press. Mt Tremper. NY. p. 47.

21

THE UNGROUNDED SELF
IN HISTORY

Much Buddhist discourse is concerned with the resolution of suffering in the minds of individuals yet the study of human history also implicates a grasping after an unobtainable security by humanity as a whole. Recently David Loy, an American philosopher for long resident in Japan and a Zen teacher, argues that much historical change has itself been driven by the search to resolve the hidden sense of lack that insecurity entails. This important thesis has the potential to revise our approach to the future radically.[1]

A QUESTION OF 'LACK'

David Loy begins by stressing that self-consciousness is not something that exists as an independent object with its own individual being. It is more like the surface of an ocean, he says, dependent upon its depth but unable to grasp that fact because it is itself the manifestation of that depth. When the self wishes to experience itself as an object in a world of determinable 'reality', it finds itself unable to do so with conviction. It is always shadowed by a sense of incompleteness or 'lack', which it tries to escape or avoid (Chapter 18). The conceptualised self, lacking groundedness, becomes subject to a nagging anxiety frequently repressed only to re-emerge as a compulsive search for something upon which to rely. Originating deep in the unconscious, imaginary solutions are projected on the world and for a time appear to fill the need. All such solutions are however, in the Buddhist view, failures to address the root problem – the actual emptiness of self. Once uncovered, this emptiness proves to be a surprising source of open creativity leading to an essentially spiritual realisation that 'I' am none other than such spacious freedom itself. Such a move is however frightening for those used to a more rigid conception of themselves; it will be avoided leading to further repression and escape into illusory security. When such illusory security becomes the root of a world view, anyone or any viewpoint that threatens it will become the enemy (Chapter 20). The trap snaps shut and the hunting dogs let loose.

Fear of the 'oceanic' leads humanity into a spiritual captivity that seems sacred only because it protects us from an apparently threatening nothingness. The truly spiritual quest is none other than the work needed to transform such captivity into freedom yet, sadly, such quests have often lead simply into yet another trap. Ever since the collapse of the ruling Christian myth began, we have witnessed powerful socio-political movements that have led to precisely this impasse. Loy explores these movements in considerable detail.

Medieval Christianity contained our lack of groundedness effectively through viewing it as sin. The world was still 'enchanted' by a world view ruled by God, rather as had the Roman Empire been ruled by a divine emperor. So long as one obeyed the rules the subject could experience unity within such a world. Any deviation, any doubt was sinful and led to holy retribution even excommunication. Yet Christ, by taking on the sins of humanity in personal sacrifice, had mercifully saved us from our sins. In worshipping him, believers expressed their thankfulness and their reunion with God. Christianity was thus able to channel the anxiety of believers into a spiritual realm where lack of groundedness as sin was forgiven and a sense of oneness with God's creation sustained.

The organic wholeness within medieval Christianity had been held together by a moral life that sustained a sense of groundedness within divine authority. As soon as early science broached such security by an intellectual undermining of Christian beliefs, a huge anxiety was released within the Western world. All cherished values were questioned and the philosophical struggle to come to terms with the fear of nihilism began in earnest. At less intellectually exalted levels, a dread of death emerged on centre stage necessitating the need for a strict morality that might ensure passage to a kingdom in heaven. As the Reformation challenged the spiritual authority of the ancient church and secular life began to develop in mercantile form, the traditional solutions fragmented. Since each fragment supposed itself to be a final solution inevitably wars began between them, not only verbal but horrifically actual. The Thirty Years War was a disaster with very long term consequences for Europe. A major emergence was Calvinism stressing the Lutheran emphasis on a personal relationship direct to God rather than through the corrupting mechanisms of the church. Yet, in this Calvinist view, original sin undermined humanity's freewill to do good, which meant that nothing could be done to ensure salvation. Only God's 'grace' could select the few divinely chosen for salvation. In such a world, where money making and economic success might indicate God's favour, the temptation to turn to secular expedients to resolve the anxieties of ungrounded-ness became attractive.

The humanity of the early Renaissance became distorted into mechanistic philosophising (Descartes, Hobbes) ending in utilitarianism and ultimately the ideals of socialism and communism. (Chapter 18). In that such movements temporarily resolved concerns with ungrounded-ness, they too were based in an ultimately spiritual quest. Loy argues that, on the way to these twentieth century outcomes, the divinity of kings, the nation state, numerous religious movements and idealisms emerged and passed away – all essentially compensations for the underlying lack of personal groundedness manifesting socially and politically.

After the Thirty Years War, reliance on the charisma of divinely appointed monarchs was replaced by the idea of the nation state. Yet, as the state become ever more complex and necessarily ruled by laws, so the communalism of earlier societies became replaced by a need to mesh local, factional, industrial, trading, and other competing loyalties under rules of law agreed between stake holding interests rooted essentially in individual property or capital. Trust became easily subverted by mutual suspicion. The focus on individual rights within a world of competitive relations yielded the extreme individualism ultimately characteristic of the West (Chapter 15). This however is a mode of being that can only find satisfaction in forms of achievement that few may actually attain. Ideas of nationality and citizenship provide some recompense for a loss of communality yet the continuing ungroundedness of the subject remains unaddressed. Its expression in unconscious fear continuously erupts in the comings and goings of fashion and escapist ideals: the ultimate holiday; varieties of Shangri-la; the perfect guru; bizarre communes; football fan clubs; alternative health; religion and anything you can think of, sexual identities; power dressing; choice; clubbism and drunkenness in the streets. All these fads and desires can be fed and maintained by their commodification leading to the subjection of the personal to the functioning of the consumer state – yet their result is continuing alienation.

The new forms of industrial collectivity were a social expression of agreements between gain-focussed individuals in their exploitation of resources. The first joint stock company was chartered in England in 1553. In a limited liability company the management is responsible to the stockholders who require a return on their investments. Today the transnational corporations have no other moral code and the stockholders usually have little interest in their effects on the world or control over the

ethics of management. Like nation states, the huge transnational
corporations have become self-justifying processes increasingly exploiting
world resources and devoted solely to their own interests. These financial
processes function within 'the economy' which, as Loy points out, is a
collective objectification of desire, not so much a desire to achieve ever
higher standards of living and ever widening choice but to find a solution
through money to our lack of groundedness. Preoccupation with
perpetual growth as an end in itself becomes socially dangerous in a
world that is actually limited in it's resources. Loy argues: "*The tomorrow
that-never-actually-comes gives us hope of resolving the lack that gnaws on us today;
the reality is however that our future orientation is a way of avoiding a present we are
unable to cope with.*"

If Loy is right and the economy is essentially an arena for illusory
solutions to ungroundedness then the whole of the consumerist world
view is anchored in a fundamental but unacknowledged anxiety.
Consumerism has a hidden spiritual objective, albeit an illusory one, in
the attempt to compensate for ungroundedness. It is our modern
'religion' and it has spread worldwide through a globalisation that has
proved irresistible. The notion of a 'secular' world is actually mistaken,
beneath the secular veneer spiritual needs actually dominate but in largely
unconscious ways. Loy suggests that 'God' has actually not disappeared
but rather re-appeared as the functioning of the nation state, the market
economy and our scientific projects as if they were a source for grounding
our activities in an objectified 'reality'. Yet, these societal functions are
inherently unstable, never profitable enough, and never empty the
world of problems. Like God, on examination, all are empty; victories of
means over ends, for the ends are not comprehended except as some
unformulated utopia of the imagination. The powers of nation states,
the market and technocracies are, in Loy's view, demonic in their
destructiveness because no limits are set on their use. They have become
political and economic compulsions: institutions that have taken on
lives of their own, subordinating individuals and indeed whole cultures
to their patterns while accepting no higher critique whatsoever. The
churches may sometimes groan but they too have been suborned. The
'deification' of the state, the market and scientific endeavour can in no
way settle our ungrounded anxieties. Meanwhile the twin terrorisms of
unbridled consumption of limited planetary resources and the mindless
resentment of the underclass continue unchecked.

So – what to do?

End Note

1.   Loy, D. 1999. Lack and transcendence: the problem of death and life in psychotherapy, existentialism and Buddhism. Humanity Books. New York.

Loy, D. 2002. A Buddhist History of the West. State University of New York Press. Albany.

Loy, D. 2003. The Great Awakening: a Buddhist Social Theory. Wisdom Publications. Somerville. MA.

22

HEART AND MIND:
THE BASIS FOR TRANSFORMATIVE
YOGA

GOOD SAMARITANS AND THE FEELING FOR THE WORLD

There are those who argue that the functioning of the market in the modern economy is a natural process. The market, consisting of limited liability companies and corporations all working hard to maintain their stockholders' investments, provides the funds whereby governments sustain their welfare plans by taxing profit. The system is unsurprisingly logical but these effects are no more than the inevitable consequences of a process that is far from being natural in any biological sense. It is a cultural creation and as such open to change through the adoption of different values. The so-called naturalness of the system is a result of its own closed logic.

We have been exploring what that logic is. As we have seen, the modern system originated in Great Britain following the land enclosures that dispossessed the agricultural peasant thereby generating a large, exploitable class of the poor for employment and exploitation in nascent factories. Capitalist ideas became dominant as huge fortunes began to be made and the suffering of the working class ignored or seen as an essential price to be paid for national progress. Protestant Calvinism thrived because hard won benefits of business were believed to indicate God's favour and hence the possibility of being among the elect destined for a heavenly kingdom. The gradual disappearance of God left the acquisition of money as the remaining 'good' that could ensure at least a comfortable life. Money thus became God and no limits were set on the competitive acquisition of the blessings of wealth. Indeed, much of the excitement of migrating to the United States lay in the idea that here was a land where anyone could become rich. Such a value system leads to highly addictive behaviour, which in a world lacking constraints has known no bounds. Yet, the early millionaires often used their money to create trusts for the general welfare. This seems rarely to be the case today when the culture of corporate capitalism usually lacks any serious ethical dimension. What appears 'natural' of course is that a wealthy man's inclusive fitness in terms of his genetic success is seemingly higher than that of the poor simply due to his more secure lifestyle, wider opportunities and acquired skills in competition. Wealth will not give up easily.

Biology is subtler than this. We have seen that under certain evolutionary conditions not only aggressive competition but also various types of altruism or mutualism appear (Chapter 14). In most human cultures a further extension of altruism has developed, the Good Samaritan principle, whereby even unrelated humans may aid each other when in distress. This extension of self-focussed altruism makes sense in terms of a widespread adoption of reciprocation that can in principle extend to the whole of humanity. We can envisage all humanity as kin. There is a balancing of opposites that allows general altruism to emerge within self-interest – depending however on circumstance. What appears to have happened, post Calvinism, is that the competitive element has gained almost complete ascendance over altruism leaving us with the illusion that the market economy is the only possible way of running the planet. Individual self-interest rules yet the underlying root, David Loy emphasises, is not actually economic desire but a repressed fear of ultimate meaninglessness for which wealth and its attendant delusions are compensation.

Feelings such as fear are often discounted or denied, a tendency related to the pronounced separation between mind and feeling within the Cartesian world view. Truth, it is erroneously assumed, can only be known by the mind; feeling is discounted. And yet, it is precisely a feeling that allows an individual to set himself aside and become a Good Samaritan. Think of those tireless young people working for Médecins sans Frontières in situations of extraordinary human tragedy and danger. Such help to others in distress is not calculated: many risk their lives. Ordinary folks may hire a lorry and at great expense and difficulty drive supplies to some disaster area. Why? There is a feeling here that a principle is at stake. The demands of such a 'hypergood', as Charles Taylor remarks, are not easily ignored.

This is not something so much thought about as driven by an inner demand, yet, in order to act in such a way, feeling may have to overrule accepted orthodoxies of reason. Many feel anguished by the faults of contemporary economic policies but, in the face of overwhelming reason, find it difficult to make an effective response. This heart-mind split is a curious effect of Cartesian world views. It has not been evident to a similar degree in any other culture.

In Chinese scriptures, for example, the word often translated into English as 'mind' actually has a much broader meaning that includes affect, feeling. The 'heart' is included in the term here. What is being talked about is a 'heart-mind' that contemporary Westerners have a problem both in translating and in experiencing. On a sunny summer evening, I may hear a Wood Pigeon cooing in counter song with a neighbour some way off. Being an ornithologist I know a good deal about bird calls and their function but, as I listen to the pigeon, that may not be the first thing that comes to mind. I find myself smiling at the seemingly self-contented cooing of this rather fat and comfortable bird. It seems like a well-off arboreal matron gently singing to herself and nattering to a neighbour. The smile arises from an imaginative projection and a sense of its absurdity—yet the quality of my awareness is at that moment determined by it. There is a touch of tenderness that in no way obscures any scientific analysis that remains available in my memory. I am simply present to a world perceived though my own heart's inclination.

If we examine our lives we will find that this sort of heart-mind evaluation is actually commonplace. Naturally, it is a seedbed of illusions that may need to be subjected to rational analysis, yet, much of the time, the enjoyment of life as well as its sadness and distress is determined by it. The heart-mind is actually fundamental. Descartes threw out a baby with the bathwater. Throughout much of recent history, the heart-mind has lost ground to the rational intellegence that often functions in abstracted isolation.

RELATING HEART AND MIND

As we have seen (Chapter 19), the Russian thinker Mikhail Bakhtin (1895-1975)[1] has suggested that three sociocultural periods are visible in human history and find expression in the literature and art of their periods as distinctive 'chronotopes'. In each period, time and space are experienced differently with related contrasts in human relationships. The earliest period was an essentially shamanic 'ancient matrix'. In the second phase, individuals, now participating in the birth of commerce, became aware of their personal development through time, a linear awareness in which becoming rather than being was pronounced. Mind and reason predominate. In the third phase, this marked individualism discovers its own relativity through reflexive insight into its origins and formation. In high culture, personal consciousness is then seen as a product of history and some of the older forms of thought and feeling may re-emerge or become open to new exploration. These forms of thought are however now understood as mind productions: subject and object are distinguished and the world as virtuality is more clearly understood.

In these three phases, heart and mind relate in contrasting ways. In the second, the constructed identity dominates feeling, while, in the third and emerging contemporary phase, self reflection opens again on heartfelt feeling, for example in the examination of Jungian archetypes and their role in emotion. In this third phase, multicultural influences interact to produce a complex pattern of ever varying interactions which do not permit easy formulation in closed systems of interpretation and in which heart returns in a complex relation to mind that has however lost none of its rationality. In such a world, the feeling for the pigeon has its place because such an affectionate regard may modify courses of action that might otherwise be purely determined by analytical logic. As this neglected aspect of human potential is once again explored there is a possibility for a re-enchantment of the world unimaginable in the black and white world of the tradition bound faiths of phase two.

If we are to create values that make a difference to the present course of history, it is precisely in this emerging relationship between heart and mind that we need to look. The demonstrations in Seattle and elsewhere come from the hearts of millions and such a collective manifestation of deep revulsion can empower people to insist on change whatever the logical arguments against them. For the heart has its logic too.

In asking what can replace the underlying nihilism and alienation of our times we have to seek for a mode of experiencing life that provides a felt sense of ultimate value or grounding, a 'hypergood' as Charles Taylor would say. It is here that Buddhism can help because the Buddhist approach points beyond mere intellectual analysis, opinion as belief and narratives of explanation, to the mysteriously silent root of the thinker's mind. The Western fear has been that such a root has no meaning. As we have seen, such fear arises from an unexamined experience suggesting that beyond thought is nothing but an uninterpretable void.

The Buddha and his successors realised that much of what appears to the mind is projection. We create virtual worlds and build our narratives of explanation upon an often-delusional basis arising from problems in childhood. Yet, in practising methods that quieten the agitation of the heart – mind, a relative peace can be found. The ancient Buddhists proceeded to examine this peace through a process of subtracting all mental engagements, attachments and explanations from it to see what remained when nothing at all was being thought, when nothing could be projected. Indeed, they found a void, an experience of 'nothingness' that can be scary. Yet they persisted, realising that what the mind had become empty of was merely thought. Experience remained – the experience of witnessing the very basis of the heart-mind free from the attachments of the judging, evaluating mind of discrimination. On returning to the world of thought, they could see that this emptiness, although free of thought, did have qualities. It was not the case that there was nothing-at-all there. There was a qualitative mode of being very difficult to describe simply because it was beyond all the categorisations of language. As we have seen, they used many terms and metaphors to describe this realm, the womb of experience, the unborn, no-mind, emptiness and so on. Such words were not actually predicates but descriptive terms for an essentially ineffable experience that none the less had undeniable existence.

It may at first seem strange that such an experience is commonly felt to be of inestimable value, often causing a shift in attitude and personal goals that are life changing. In part this is due to concomitant experiences of joy and bliss, freedom and silence, which appear as foundations both for being and becoming. One may suppose that when worrying identifications with thoughts are absent, the brain mechanisms of affect relax into a basic joyousness otherwise inhibited by the chemistry of anxiety. Similarly, we may suggest that aggressive and destructive behaviour may be a reflex response to competition or opposition rather than a root condition. When such stimulation is absent, there can be a return to a quieter frame of mind allowing insight and compassion to appear. Perhaps there is a homoeostatic system at work here with equilibrium around a condition of open tranquility. The realisation that such a mode of being, even when only occasionally known or rarely seen, is fundamental becomes pivotal. One begins to act from this point of reference. As Master Sheng-yen has put it – the ego gives way to wisdom. But could such an experience be no more than submergence in some illusory condition?

The fact is that such a state is not isolated from the world. In meditation, the senses are opened so that the world, as it were, comes into the vast clarity of the heart-mind and resides there without any form of prejudice. There are the woods and trees, there is the traffic and the sound of aircraft yet the experience has a 'silence' of its own. The cosmos simply turns as it must and the meditator experiences a feeling of fusion with it that has no horizons but rather endless depths. Logically, since the subject is an expression of the universe anyway, this need not be particularly surprising. Further-more, there is freedom because the universe lacks any form of intention. There is no strutting god here. The cosmos has no view, imposes nothing, like the great Mississippi river it just keeps rolling along: 'just this' – no imperatives.

Such experiences commonly labelled in the West as 'mystical' and beyond interpretation, occur potentially in any one. Often they arise in religious contexts where varying degrees of mental concentration have been attained. Usually they are then immediately interpreted within the closed system of ideas of a particular ideology and imprisoned in partial narratives. In Buddhism they are not captured by any metaphysical system for the Buddha did not seek to explain the world. Rather they are examined in the light of their further consequences and anchored in an open ended philosophy that lacks dogmatism, is focused on relief from suffering and related to a seemingly self-evident morality.

One of the key consequences of such experience is a caring awareness of other people and their unhappiness in attachments, prejudices and self-assertion. The heart-mind responds to such suffering with sorrow and a compassion that can inspire action. This action is not undertaken because of some ethical injunction but because feeling perhaps rooted in or derived from parental care demands it. No elaboration of metaphysics is called for here since action stems from the heart and is not dependent on an interpretation of the cosmos. Such a stance relates without opposition to the investigation of physical nature because objective science threatens no dogma here.

We can now see that the fear of a meaningless void is entirely misplaced. Beyond the constructions of religious belief and philosophy, a direct examination of the heart-mind through mental yoga reveals a positive spaciousness without easily definable characteristics but which finds expression in feelings of clarity, joy and bliss that easily turn to compassion towards others. In facing the vastness of the cosmos with a vastness of mind, there is no longer fear but awe and wonder. The river has discovered itself to be the ocean.

A heart-mind familiar with such a tradition of being is in contact with 'everything'. In contrast to the split condition of western awareness, a trained mind can now feel in touch with the world in such a way that it no longer wishes to destroy it. The whole capitalist denudation of the planet is seen irrefutably as a most terrible and inexcusable mistake. There is a feeling for the insentient, not only for the sentient. Rocks, stones, trees, waterfalls all have their messages and all are witnessed like the cooing pigeon high in the tree. Such feelings are not only to be found in meditation. John Daido Loori [2] points up their presence in Western poetry, in Wordsworth, in Whitman, in Snyder and now they appear in the fresh haibun poetry of Ken Jones and others. [3] Unfortunately, only a few young people know their way to it today. Their education is focussed on achievement not contemplation, on exams not viewing the sky, on exploitation and competition not on conservation and collaboration, on an uneasy equanimity in the destruction of their children's inheritance and not on the beauty of the heart-mind's potential. All too many seek refuge in the illusions of alcohol or cocaine. All this needs to be reversed if anything is to be saved.

End Notes

·1.   Bakhtin, M. 1981. *The Dialogic Imagination.* University of Texas Press. Austin.

2.   Loori, J.D. 1999. *Teachings of the insentient. Zen and the environment.* Dharma Communications Press. Mt. Tremper. New York: p. 31.

3.   Jones, K. 2003. *Stallion's Crag: haiku and haibun.* Iron Press. Cullercoats.

23

MEDITATION IN PRACTICE

Understanding such a way of being does not come easily. Beset with fears, anxieties, and fixed beliefs, the mind does not find it easy to let go into its own intrinsic peace. The practice of a method is usually required and this is especially so when the aim is to do something quite counter to the prevailing educational emphasis of our time. We need therefore a brief introduction to the nature and form of such practices. Nowadays they are collectively known as 'meditation', a word sometimes confused with 'contemplation'. Here I follow the Buddhist usage wherein meditation means a yogic practice or discipline while contemplation additionally involves reasoned reflection.

Currently there are many systems of meditation practice in use, some traditional and some containing mixtures of psychotherapy and eastern practice whether Indian, Chinese, Tibetan or Japanese. Such systems are not always based in the Buddhist view we have been describing but have sometimes fallen within closed systems of religious thought that capture meditation for their own purposes.

WESTERN CHAN PRACTICES

In this chapter, I will briefly describe the Chinese Zen system because not only is it traditional and fully anchored in the Buddhist view but also straight forward enough to be easily understood by Westerners. In the Western Chan Fellowship, my colleagues and I have created a system, which, while based in tradition, is also open to experimentation in a Western manner. [1] The charity functions by providing periodic retreats for around twenty people at a remote centre in rural Wales. Most participants also practice in small groups around the UK but there is no permanent residential centre. The fundamental teaching comes from the Linchi and Cao-dong traditions (Chapters 8 & 9.) as restored in China in the last century by the great Master Hsu-yun and represented today by Chan Master Sheng-yen of Dharma Drum Mountain, Taiwan. As well as providing entirely traditional retreats, we have constructed some new ones based in tradition but carefully suited to the condition of the Western mind. There are four types of retreats, the Western Zen Retreat, Silent Illumination, Koan and Mahamudra. Taken in series they introduce Mahayana practice and can become the basis for a life's fulfilment and a critique of contemporary life.

We like beginners to start with the Western Zen Retreat using the communication exercise (CE) of Charles Berner, an American who had created a Zen-based practice known as the 'Enlightenment Intensive'. The value of this practice is that it throws the participant immediately into self-confrontation through direct enquiry. More orthodox, Buddhist methods usually start with calming the mind and this may delay a very essential confrontation unnecessarily. The day is divided into periods of sitting meditation, watching the breath or simply being aware, periods of communication exercises (CE), walks, meals, exercise and rest. In the CE, two people work together on certain fundamental questions of which the first is "Who am I?" This is received from the partner as a request "Tell me who you are." One member of the pair asks the question and the other responds. They alternate in the roles of questioner and respondent every five minutes for either thirty or forty minutes. Each then takes a different partner but they continue with the same question. In a group of 15 say there are thus 14 -1 others to work with. There are strict rules because this is not a conversation. To allow the respondent complete freedom of expression, the questioner must not comment either verbally or non-verbally in any way on the respondent's offerings. The role reversal imposes a certain discipline. The respondent has to abandon self-concern every five minutes and give neutral but undivided attention to the other. In retreat, we persist with this practice for four or more days.

When a question has been "answered," the practitioner may take up a further question, often "What am I?" or "How is life fulfilled?" and experienced practitioners may move on to "What is love?" "What is another?" or to one of the Zen phrases from koan stories. The process of 'answering' is a demanding one for the repeated questioning is remorseless. In answering, "Who am I?" for example, people usually spend hours describing their roles: bank manager; electrician; secretary; lecturer; waiter; father; mother; carer; in quite an objective, explanatory mode, as one might indeed in any conversation. But soon one may be responding with – "Well, when I hear the news I often feel distressed." or – "When I remember my mother's death I feel like crying." or – "I laughed and laughed – never had I seen anything so funny." Feelings are being tentatively explored but soon, in the openness that the exercise permits, real feelings emerge or at least they become verbally explored. On day three a great deal of emotion usually rages around the room. The extraordinary fact is that, within the confines of the retreat, once an issue has been fully stated or shown to the other it does not return. The process of sharing becomes one in which one empties oneself of all concern progressively. Sharing is the essence of this process. Berner called it "emptying the barrel."

Gradually, as the exercise proceeds, there is less and less to talk about. The participant may become stuck knowing that an 'answer' has not appeared but finding nowhere to go, nothing to say. We call this 'crossing the desert'. Something remains that must be said and only when it has been said is there release. People come up against barriers of shame and guilt that are difficult to rehearse. Once someone does so, the partner is also released knowing that trust is possible because the partner has taken the risk. Truth in all its painful honesty is revealed and shared.

Finally, it is over. Often, quite suddenly, the practitioner sees that everything that has been said is nothing other than the expression of him or herself. In the acceptance of that, there is relief. "Hey – I am me and that's OK." may be one form of its expression. The feeling of release may be extreme, joy and laughter reign. For many, however, acceptance of one-self is not so easy as it means balancing the negative and the positive in a very honest manner. Guilt and shame are often deep barriers to be overcome only by courageous acceptance of what is true. Afterwards the individual feels free and open, often in a way never known before.

This acceptance of identity is only the first step in the process. Continuing to work with later questions may lead to a loss of one's egoic orientation in a feeling of oneness with the universe; the self as it were expands to include all things. This 'one mind' opens the heart-mind to awe and wonder. People often recognize this state as a fundamental root of their being, something many refer to as 'home'. When they return to our small retreat centre in the Welsh hills they often say they are 'coming home' and they mean to something in themselves not just to an ancient farmstead close to the wilderness. Yet, in the Zen perspective, this is not yet enlightenment.

In the Silent Illumination retreat, we practice the orthodox Chinese Zen methods of calming the mind together with insight into its nature. Hour after hour, in thirty-minute periods, intensive but alert sitting gradually quietens down the noise of the mind: the endless wandering of thought around differing aspects of one's personal narrative slows down.[2] As the hours pass, the practitioner begins to perceive patterns in his mind wandering. Perhaps he believed he was an unendingly interesting person only to discover that everything he thought about actually revolved around one, two or three issues merely elaborated upon in mental games.

One can collect ones thoughts, parcel them up according to theme and then discard the whole lot in one move. Slowly the mind becomes less obsessed with its own stories.

At intervals during the retreat, physical exercises promote a focus on the internal state of the body energy called 'chi'. Gradually one becomes aware of the totality of the body simply as sensation perched on a cushion. This sense of 'being – there' gradually cools into something approaching silence. When one then opens the ears or eyes to let in the world, everything meshes in one pervasive quietude. The feeling of oneness with everything comes over one in a great stillness that is not engaging with anything. 'Illumination' comes when, everything being dropped, this silence appears as a shining, characterless vastness in which, none the less, without any involvement with oneself, all things appear. Although this is a gradual process, it may resolve itself quite suddenly. Often a clear insight may occur outside the meditation hall, when driving home in traffic, or in the bath. This insight is simply a sudden, profound, awe filled and joyful immersion in detached equanimity. Any self-concern seems far away.

In the Koan retreat, we once again make use of verbal expressions as a focus for the meditative enquiry. These may be paradoxical stories of ancient master's lives or key phrases from such stories. In our version of this retreat, we take a stance that differs from current Chinese practice. Knowing that the Western mind is educated to seek out meanings and explanations, we allow this tendency to exhaust itself against the unsolvable problems of paradox. Practitioners are encouraged to find whatever meaning they can, to let them go and look again. Many interpretations may arise, especially if one happens to be a Jungian analyst, say! But the release from the Koan is not achieved in this way. The heart-mind gradually focuses with great attention on some word or phrase that comes to dominate one's awareness, forcing one into a 'great doubt' about its meaning. The mind is now highly one-pointed as in Silent Illumination. It is from such a state that insight may arise.

Our last form of retreat is classical Tibetan Mahamudra following a text given me by the Kargyudpa yogin, Khamtag Rimpoche, in the Himalayas.[3] This meditation practice is in fact very similar to Silent Illumination but presented in a highly detailed, step-by-step, fashion that maintains a close focus on what one is about throughout the practice. We present this method together with a simple introduction to tantric visualisation. These Tibetan visualisations open the heart to feelings of peace, clarity and compassion through evoking them as imagined icons with which the practitioner merges. In this retreat, therefore, the focus is more on feeling and its use in the transcendence of everyday thought. Tantra needs to be taught with great care and this retreat is open only to those who have practised in other retreats first.

This bare outline cannot give an inexperienced reader much of an insight into what happens on retreat. Fortunately, we have many reports that illustrate how practitioners actually feel during and after retreat. Excerpts from a few examples, each from a different practitioner, follow to give some impression of what the reader might experience should he or she attend such a retreat.

RETREAT EXPERIENCES

Silent illumination retreat, June 1994 [4]

" I always expect to find the first days of a retreat difficult but this time they were exceptionally so. Along with various physical symptoms, I experienced an overwhelming feeling of agitation and dread hard to describe and understand. Although weary, I was not at all ill. What was happening? I explored this with the teacher. I suspected that a deeply entrenched pattern, which had a strong connection with the powerful impressions of impermanence that I had had since childhood, had surfaced in me. The underlying anxiety was intense. In everyday life, I compensate for this very well, pointing to exterior circumstances as its cause. Here it was not due to anything exterior, it was created in my own mind,

The talk that evening made a profound impression on me. It addressed the reality of transience drawing on Dogen Zenji's 'Being time' sermon. I had a powerful insight into the identity of time and existence. Time does not happen to things – it is things. Time is the very fabric of the Universe. This was a gut-felt knowing no mere intellectual understanding. I also saw that the ego can only exist in a reference to the past and future but past and future play no part in being. For two days my practice sailed along.

But then, extraordinarily, on the final day of the retreat, the feeling of dread returned full force for no discernible reason. It was clear that Chan, far from allowing me to escape from my negativities, would confront me with them and force me to deal with them at the most fundamental level.

I had signed up for a mountain walk to follow the retreat. I wondered whether to go or not but fellow retreatants persuaded me that, if I was cracking up, I'd be better off hanging out with the Sangha in the wild mountains than back in the 'market place'. So I went.

During the three days we talked about the famous 'Mountains and Rivers Sutra' of Dogen. I cannot say I understand the sutra but, in some mysterious way, the words "green mountains walking" hit me like a thunderclap. For the rest of our time, the extraordinary natural world about me seemed alive in a shimmering, flowing way I had forgotten since childhood. Not just the skylarks and the heart rending beauty of the Red Kite that came to inspect us over the source of the Wye, but the very streams and mountains, even the sheep shit. The presence of my companions moved me too. We all seemed to be able to be what and who we were without fear of disapproval or criticism. We could discuss and disagree without a trace of rancour or point scoring. I think all of us were struck with how easily human beings could live together with the benefit of mindfulness and practice informing our lives."

Silent Illumination retreat, June 1994[5]

"I started off watching the breath. Things learnt on previous retreats proved helpful. I relaxed and gave my body to the cushion and my mind to the method. I watched the breath and watched thoughts coming and going. I found that I was able to let them through, let them be and let them go. I was not involved in great long trains of thought.

The middle day of the retreat was difficult. I wanted to find the serenity that I had experienced the previous day. I wanted to be in the space that I had been in before. I found I was fighting myself. I was tense and my legs were painful. I knew that I should drop wanting and drop resistance but couldn't. I began to wonder what on earth I was doing here. I thought about going home and abandoning Chan completely. Was I just conning myself? Wouldn't I be better off just getting on with life instead of trying to find all these spiritual experiences which none of my family understand anyway?

My job was dealing with the firewood. They were tough logs and I could not split them. The axe got stuck and I felt angry and helpless. After a while, Frank took over. I pottered about stacking logs. Then I was asked to split little logs into bundles of faggots using a little chopper. Making kindling requires mindfulness but little strength. The logs just split themselves. I was not splitting logs, it was 'logs splitting'.

Later, in the rest period, I noticed a quotation pinned to the wall of the bedroom. 'When we wish to teach and enlighten all things by ourselves we are deluded. When all things teach and enlighten us we are enlightened.' The logs taught me to tackle the things I can manage. To chip away at the edges. No heroics. I went back to watching the breath.

I find it difficult to write about how things continued. I was sitting in the Buddha room but I wasn't. Everything was just there in the sunlight. Quite OK; no worry; no hassle. The buttercups glowed in the grass. I noticed what it is like to be present with presence. Time sped by but what is time? There is no time. At one level I had an intuition about this. At another level reason took over – Of course there's time. Time, on the other hand, is just a fabrication of the human mind. It is impossible to reason about the intuition. It is so much at odds with the time we learn to live by. I can sit on the rocks by the sea at home. It is timeless – always changing but unchanged in a thousand years. I found 'freedom and ease of body and mind.' Indeed it had always been there."

The Maenllwyd. 2004. Solitary retreat

"I had come alone to the Maenllwyd for a few days partly to recalibrate after a hard period of work and partly to look over something I was writing. After a few sits the mind had calmed. There was a clarity about the air, the meditation hall, the autumnal woods – a clarity that had little to do with them. I should say my mind had become clear of the concerns I had come with. I was open to place and time.

For some weeks, I had been turning over one of Tai Hui's huatous. "It's not the Buddha, it's not the self, it's not the mind, it's not a thought – It's nothing at all. What is it?" I had gone to the library and was about to take a book from a shelf when, out of nowhere, the phrase repeated itself unobtrusively in my mind. Suddenly a laugh came up from nowhere – 'OH – of course, indeed its nothing at all! Absolutely. Gone altogether gone!' There really is no problem – not at all. Indescribable freedom. I was laughing and laughing and that is what I remember now as I write. I went into the Chan hall and prostrated three times to the Buddha chuckling all the time. Then I fell silent. There was unfathomable peace. I cannot find words and if I did, they would be misleading. Just no problem at all – and all this fuss!"

THE SIGNIFICANCE OF MEDITATION

We have been arguing that the deep malaise of the world dominated by Western thought and technology is rooted in the absence of grounding for the modern self. David Loy has referred to the doubts and insecurity that this entails as 'lack'. Can the practices we have been describing and others like them help to diminish or do away with such 'lack' to free us from the consequences of Western nihilism? If this were found to be the case we could argue that a new ontology for the Westernised mind was available that could underpin a new view of ethics in the conduct of world affairs.

Loy certainly believes this [6] *"Our hollowness is not so awful after all; it is not something that needs to be filled up. We cannot make ourselves real in the ways we have been trying... the bottomless pit swallows up all our efforts... but we can realise something about the nature of the hole that frees us from trying to fill it up... We do not need to make ourselves real, because we have always been real... I have always been grounded: not however as a separate, skin-encapsulated ego somewhere behind my eyes, for there has never been such a self. Rather, the bottomless, festering black hole can transform into a fountain ... gushing up at the core of my being. The bottomlessness of this spring means that I can never understand the source of this spring, for the simple reason that I am this spring. It is nothing other than my true nature...The point is to live that spring, to let my fountain gush forth. – The nothingness at my core turns out to be my freedom to ...do this, to do that."* He goes on to point out that this fountain is not separate from the world, the theme is not dualistic. Rather dualism disappears when I realise I do not have to grasp at anything out there in the world to ground myself. My nature is already the ground, its spontaneity is not so much mine as an expression of the universe of which I am a part and in which my formulation of me as a 'me', although not exactly an illusion, is itself delusory.

People may not be so easily persuaded. The theory looks good but the evidence being yogic is not so easily realised. The masters have told us that the depth of our personal realisations is inevitably linked to the extent of our delusion, that is to say the grip which cultural conditioning has upon us. Some, with seemingly flexible or loose minds, can experience these freedoms almost as soon as they have heard of them. Others need to work hard maybe for years. Yet again others may be so set in fixed forms of belief that their 'karma' prevents insight from arising–at least, as tradition puts it, in this life. For the majority of practitioners faith will be required and this can come only from the integrity of the teachers, lamas and masters who transmit this existential wisdom from generation to generation in ways that convince. Actual realisation is commonly partial but when this is combined with faith then wisdom can blossom forth. What then is the relation between wisdom and enlightenment?

Careful practice with a master can allow one to uncover the oneness of self and universe without too much difficulty and this is already a great gain. The separation of mind and life is already largely healed. Yet, these 'one mind' states are largely due to the expansion of the sense of self to cover all experience. Self-reference, although sometimes virtually invisible, none the less remains intact and quickly reappears yet, with good reason, the practitioner is pleased with his or her 'achievement'. This is however not yet a realisation that the ego itself is an imputation that may itself yield to a wider vision once it is set aside: for this is the realisation that finally confirms the total freedom from self conceptualisation lying at the root of experience.

Master Sheng-yen has pointed out that this can only arise when all attachment to self as concept and world as thing disappears. It is not thought that is the problem: attachments are the glue. Here is the great paradox, because if one wishes to find such a state it will be precluded by the very fact of desire. Desire implicates an ego and so long as desire continues, the ego cannot disappear. When this does happen, it is never by will or wanting. The one-pointed mind is more or less accidentally tripped over by some brief but startling stimulus, either external or internal, and falls suddenly out of all self-referencing. The experience is a shock for something has gone absent. The mind appears vacant, its occupier has left, yet the world in its oneness shines, the breeze blows, the trains rumble, experience goes on. The hallmark of this moment is an awareness of absence, which itself becomes a sense of loss as the self-concerned mentality begins to return. Classical cases of this 'enlightenment experience', this glimpse of no-self, this 'seeing the nature', all seem to have these characteristics yet there are many experiences that are not so clear and even a fine master may have difficulty in confirming them. Master Sheng-yen is much more cautious than most before doing so. We need one or two examples to bring out these features.

'SEEING THE NATURE'

Nowhere perhaps is the clarity of the relationship between science and Buddhism better exemplified than in James Austin's mammoth enquiry into 'Zen and the Brain'. [7] An accomplished professor of neurology, Austin has published extensively in the fields of neurochemistry, neuropharmacology and clinical neurology. His book concerns the plausible brain mechanisms that underlie Zen practice and experience. It is a detailed text, by no means an easy read for anyone not acquainted with the complex architecture and processes of the brain but outstandingly original in that Austin knows personally, through direct experience, what he is talking about. This blend of subjective and objective points to the direction this field must take increasingly.

One day on the way to a short Zen Retreat in London led by Irmgard Schloegl (The Venerable Nun Myoko-ni), an Austrian woman who had trained extensively in Rinzai Zen in Japan, Austin experienced 'seeing the nature', the goal of Zen. He had been travelling by train to the retreat on a balmy Sunday morning but, being somewhat absent minded, found himself at the wrong station. It was an ordinary dingy station, rather grimy buildings, nothing special. He stood on the empty platform as the rattle of the train faded into the distance. Waiting for another train, Austin turned and gazed down the tracks in the general direction of the Thames. Then - it happened. The entire view shifted into what he later described as 'absolute reality, intrinsic rightness, ultimate perfection'. Here was a condition of clarity that felt totally and revealingly real without any contamination, completely appropriate and beautiful.

"The new scene is set gently, not fixed on hold. It conveys a slightly enhanced sense of immediacy. Despite the other qualities infusing it, the purely optical aspects of the scene are in no way different from the way they were a split second before. The pale-grey sky, no bluer, the light, no brighter, the detail no finer grained... It is being viewed directly with all the cool, clinical detachment of a mirror as it witnesses a landscape bathed in moonlight... But there is no viewer. The scene is utterly empty, stripped of every last extension of an I-me-mine. Vanished in one split second is the familiar sense that this person is viewing an ordinary city scene. The new viewing proceeds impersonally, not pausing to register the further paradox that no human subject is doing it. Its vision of profound, implicit, perfect reality, continues for a few seconds...."

The experience then reveals a series of insights. This is an eternal insight. Everything has always been just this way, remains so even when lost, continues indefinitely. Furthermore, this is it – there is nothing more to do. Everything is complete and valid in itself. No further intervention by whoever-might-be-inferred-to-be-there is required. Austin felt totally released mentally, he felt especially good inside and deeply grateful. He called the experience 'objective vision' in that no subject was apparent within it. He felt awed, deepened and calm with a profound sense of intellectual illumination as he began his retreat.

When Irmgard heard his account she leant back, smiled and said kindly "I'm very happy for you!" She warned him to move on and not get attached to the memory.

In another account, a participant from a recent retreat is driving his car not far from New York.[8] He is listening to a tape of a talk given during the retreat. The talk was discussing the question "Who am I?" and the speaker had just asked, "Are you that question?"

"The question triggered something that caused me to exclaim, "That's it!" My mind's vision of what I am shifted to the entity asking the question. It was like a merging of the conventional I with an indefinable *** asking the question. I cannot come up with any words to describe the ***. 'Nothing' comes to mind but not quite. For some time there was only the *** doing the driving and it was the only thing in my consciousness. Simultaneously my body seemed to be merged with the *** which proceeded to play with gestures, vocalisations and gleeful observation of the surrounding countryside as *** was driving along. Distances appeared flattened as if on a movie screen. The experience filled me with joy, a feeling of freedom and release from all anxiety. This lasted all afternoon and evening."

This experience was confirmed subsequently by Master Sheng yen.

Another account comes from an expedition in the Himalayas. *"With three companions I had spent three days in July 1977 crossing the immense ice field of the 18000 foot Umasi-la pass into the Zanskar Valley of Ladakh. We had arrived at the first inhabited outpost, the little monastery of Dzongkhul Gompa. As we were*

being given tea in the upper hall of the gompa I had glanced out of the window. The
mountain-side opposite was falling away as ice-laden water rushed down in a massive
waterfall from the glacier above. Again emptiness of self came over me and the great
space of the mountain seemed to fill me with itself. I wandered alone for half an hour
up and down the flat monastery roof until I felt myself gradually returning as thought
once more created self-concern." (Confirmed by Master Sheng yen)[9]

Lastly, here is an account of a brief glimpse that none the less shows the same experiential characteristics of ego disappearance. A solitary retreatant at Gaia House in Devon was sitting as part of a routine practice when suddenly she felt a qualitative shift in her experience. There was no longer a self that was meditating. She got up and looked in a mirror. There was a reflection but no one was looking at it. The experience passed in a few minutes as a sense of me and mine returned. The practitioner said afterwards that this experience clarified all the puzzles of the Dharma she had worried about previously during a long period of practice. [10]

These accounts all show characteristics that appear to be diagnostic of 'seeing the nature'. First and foremost, there is an experience of absence and what is absent is realised as being the 'I', the normal subject of awareness. Instead, there is simply a bare awareness that is deeply clarifying, felt to be in some sense timeless, beautiful and confirming. Often there is some trigger that in taking the mind by surprise seems to bring about the shift. The experience often foreshadows considerable changes in life style and orientation. When such features are absent, it may be doubted whether an experience can be considered to be '*kensho*'. Events of this kind are relatively rare.

WISDOM AND THE HEALING OF THE WORLD

Such 'enlightenment experiences' are however followed by the return of self-concern. The self is not gone; indeed, if it were gone there would be only madness, a disconnection from the world. There must therefore be a form of 'post-satori practice' [11] to be followed after the event. There are problems here. Instead of a desire to reach a future but unknown state, the practitioner may now have a desire to return to what she has found. Of course, this does not work and deep confusion may arise unless good teaching is at hand. Alternatively, the returning ego may be so enhanced by false beliefs enshrining oneself as a Buddha that arrogant, far from enlightening, self advertisement may begin to the delusion of all, especially oneself.

Whether the practitioner has had an enlightenment experience or not, the need is the same, the cultivation of wisdom. Wisdom arises in the mindful awareness of the relation between practice and the everyday world. Gradually one perceives the relations that obtain between one's practice and the manner in which one lives one's life. The obstinacy of stupidities, prejudices and anxieties are examined in the context of a meditative peace and insight of whatever depth that has been arising. It becomes important to understand one's karmic conditioning, to accept it as such and then to work with it in many overlapping ways. It is important to be extremely realistic about one's inadequacies and to accept them not in forms of acquiescence but as the basis upon which one has to work. Envy of those with deeper experiences is seen as especially delusional and non-productive. Humility in relation to the teachings brings greater ease of mind. As one sits on the cushion there is a need to ask, "What am I on about now?" consulting the heart-mind, allowing unconscious themes to arise into thought, reflecting on what to do or how to set them aside. With a clear perception of motive one can then let it be such as it is, and enter the yogic practice.

There are important guidelines in the teachings. The cultivation of the 'perfections' is one of them. The endeavour is to generate the four 'sublime states' of Loving Kindness, Compassion, Altruistic Joy and Equanimity which are the result of ten qualities leading to Buddhahood: giving; moral behaviour; renunciation of luxury and mere 'wants'; insight into one's own behaviour and nature; energy in living; patience with oneself and others; truthfulness in all things; resolution to succeed; loving kindness to all sentient beings and equanimity. [12] Each can be the basis for meditation and reflection. These are basically practical matters: some will-power is needed but reflection can usually begin a process of correction, returning from a deviation to the main path. The taking of the Precepts can be helpful together with contemplation of their wider meanings. No killing, stealing, lying, no harmful sex, alcoholic or drug addiction – all these have wider metaphorical meanings that become koans for examination. Has one killed another's joy or stolen someone's hope? Has one misled another in justifying some action? Sex can be self indulgent rather than a joyous relating with another. The unwise glass of beer may lead to an exchange of insults. One can ponder these precepts in relation to politics, social life, and education as well as in applications to one's own conduct. The outcome is the growth of self-understanding and a capacity to choose where previously there had only been thoughtless impulsion. Reflection begins to replace habitual reaction.

Such reflection is the basis for a wisdom that becomes increasingly informed both by the discoveries on the cushion and by the consequences that meditation begins to have in one's life. Contemplative wisdom and an understanding of the meanings of 'enlightenment' go together to yield a freedom that is both engaged and detached at once. In detachment, in silent observation, the motives and sorrows of others are clearly seen and more often correctly interpreted. One begins to see possible ways others might follow as well as those that apply to oneself. A wish to help others reduce their anxious suffering increases but a concomitant understanding of the need for tact cautions one against interference. The quest for enlightenment is married to the cautious wish to 'save' others from their delusions. In the language of Buddhism one begins to walk the path of a Bodhisattva cultivating the mind of insight (*bodhicitta*) for the release and benefit of others. Wisdom yields the flower of ethical living.

Even a limited understanding of the path can lead to the wisdom of following the Bodhisattva's path. It is not dependent on 'achieving' special states or insights. These provide depth and certainty but the 'good' one seeks is not dependent upon them. For those who are beginners in the way faith is an essential: faith in the logic of the teaching; in the experience of the teacher; and most of all, faith in the potential of oneself and of all human beings. Faith and wisdom show enlightenment to be a never-ending path.

End Notes

1. See: www.Westernchanfellowship.org. Also the journal New Chan Forum available from this web site.

2. One of the best introductions to the methodology of sitting meditation is to be found in Katsuki Sekeda's *Zen training: methods and philosophy*. Shambala 2005 originally published in 1985. The introduction by biologist A.V. Grimstone is especially helpful. Also see Crook, J.H. (Eds.). 2002. Illuminating Silence. Watkins. London.

3. Crook, J.H. and J. Low. 1997. *The Yogins of Ladakh*. Motilal Banarsidass. Delhi. Chapter 17. See further: Chang, G.C.C. 1963. *Six Yogas of Naropa and teachings on Mahamudra*. Snow Lion. New York.

4. See *New Chan Forum*, 11, p.23. www.westernchanfellowship.org

5. See *New Chan Forum*, 11, p.30. www.westernchanfellowship.org

6. Loy, D. 2003. *The Great Awakening: a Buddhist Social Theory*. Wisdom. Boston. p. 30

7. Austin, J.H. 1999. *Zen and the Brain*. MIT Press. Cambridge, Mass.

8. Personal communication.

9. See: Crook, J.H. and J. Low. 1997. *The Yogins of Ladakh*. Motilal Banarsidass. Delhi.
    Also Li, R. (Ed.). 2002. Chan comes West. Dharma Drum Publications New York. p. 36

10. Personal communication.

11. Waddell, N. 1999. *Wild Ivy: the spiritual autobiography of Zen master Hakuin*. Shambala Boston and London. p.48.

12. Nyanatiloka. 1972. *Buddhist Dictionary*. Frewin. Colombo. p.125.

24

TRANSFORMATIVE EDUCATION

ATTITUDES AND DENSITY DEPENDENCE

An education capable of counteracting the beguiling attractions of worldwide consumerism will have to be fundamental providing not only a fresh world view of global application but also including practices in economics and psychology that fulfil not only human needs but also meet human aspirations for a fulfilling life.[1] A viable world view has to provide alternatives to the rampant ecological spoliation of the planet, the failure of local cultures to maintain themselves in the face of the global market and the poor development of conservation in energy use. In seeking to replace the present form of market capitalism, it will also have to provide a sense of self that is no longer closely defined by money, status or celebrity to be won through competitive greed. It must produce a personal fulfilment countering the deep alienation of the young and offer means of negotiation with deeply rooted, superstitious faiths. Nothing less will make much difference: the effect needs to be manifest at personal, social, cultural and economic levels of human activity. If Tinbergen's doubt is to be resolved, only a change of this order will do it. Such a turn around will be difficult to achieve because addiction to a seeming self-fulfilment through the acquisition of ego enhancing commodities or to security through superstition has become so deeply rooted.

Formerly, in many traditional communities, persons defined themselves in terms of mutual assistance, participation and sharing, rather than in terms of competition and one-upmanship.[2]. Of course, once immediate needs have been met, money obtained through the competitive sale of products or services is undeniably useful. So much can be done with money that is valuable: clinics; schools; hospitals; and the chance to travel, to be informed as a world citizen. Profit can fund the research and development that drives our unending quest for more of whatever supplies increasing opportunities for gain. Yet the cost of all this lies today in the isolation of individuals within a loosely defined world of casual acquaintanceship, personhood defined by job, life sequences defined by money, the loss of a strong sense of community and the absence of moral purpose other than the instrumentality of perpetual gain. There is also the growing and guilty grief at the poverty of Africa, the chaos in the Middle East, the disappearance of even common species of birds and plants, the awareness of the diminishing rain forests and melting ice sheets. Both a growing alienation from politics and the current global trend lead to profound inner dissatisfaction, depression and a loss of confidence that allows resentment to breed. Oddly, life in the developed world often no longer feels as 'good' as it used to be however much money is in the bank.

Hope for change lies precisely in many fragmentary movements that increasingly recognise that new values are needed. Once a numerical threshold is surpassed, people-power is very effective as the fall of the Berlin Wall, the demonstrations against IMF and World Bank policies, shareholder resistance to fat-cat payouts in unsuccessful companies and the elections in India are showing. Confused people looking for clarity are however also understandably wary of loosing the gains that the Western humanist enlightenment has supplied and such fear can produce stagnation.

The awareness of the need for change needs some clarifying contextualisation. Why is it that so many people feel this way? There is something in the air deeper than the arguments of politicians, the self-righteous claims for an elusive democracy or even the fact of a globalising Islamic terrorism. The genocides in Rwanda, Kosovo and the Sudan point to something more fundamental. An ecological viewpoint helps us here.

We have already mentioned how animal populations are controlled by factors that may be related to their density (Chapter 1) As the population increases, reproduction slows due to increasing constraint while, when population falls, resources may be freed that allow it to increase again. Competition tends to increase when there are high numbers in a restricted habitat. The successful strategy then is for individuals to put more energy into careful maintenance, optimisation rather than maximisation, and the production of offspring with a competitive edge.

We know that humanity has largely filled our usable planetary habitat. After centuries of expansion resources are now limiting. Our huge population is restricting our opportunities and there is a pressure to develop planet wide controls in the regulation of populations. Yet, the legacy of Western expansionism continues to be an economic theory and a psychology appropriate to conditions when resources were seen as unlimited and the frontier far away. The emerging ecological facts and our inadequate response to them are a measure of our failure to foresee them and to adapt to them.

EDUCABILITY

If our social and psychological maladaptation continues, Tinbergen's worst fears are likely to be realised (Chapter 1). Do we have the potential to develop strategic means of sustaining our populations and our welfare on an overcrowded planet? Global industrialisation and the emergence of exploitation by corporate capitalism has developed so fast that humanist theorising has largely failed to respond, only just becoming urgently aware of the need to do so. There are of course two plausible routes to the controls needed: forced and arbitrary implementation by the authoritarian rule of a dominant class, clique or faction (*i.e.* contemporary China) or, alternatively, communally, internationally and democratically agreed rules based on social and personal wisdom respecting individual rights (*i.e* the Western enlightenment ideal). Here we have the context of our contemporary cultural malaise and a definition of the task a new educational system must face.

Education necessarily relates to the educability of a population and there are reasons to suppose that this may vary. The presentation of an educational programme may be more effective in one culture than in another. The corrosive effects of consumerism have perhaps damaged quite seriously the educability of the young in some modern cultures and the take-up of a new world view may therefore be more easily accomplished in those cultures least affected but for whom the need is correspondingly less obvious. Susan Greenfield's fear that electronic lifestyles of the future may so dumb-down initiative and creativity as to yield fundamentally inadaptable cultures is not implausible (Chapter 1). She appears to have been influenced by the fate of humanity in H.G. Wells story of *The Time Machine*. There are already some signs that the contemporary erosion of creativity among the educated youth in Britain tends in this direction. Academic life has changed its tone within the lifetime of professors retiring today. University courses are now more commonly filled with those only interested in gaining wealth-creating jobs than with students fascinated to learn about and contribute to their subjects. Nowhere is this perhaps so strongly the case as in the competitive society of Japan, in some senses our most modern nation. The implication is that Government policy will need to back educational changes and that state schooling should be a prime target. There are big issues here.

The ethics of communities with developed economics (Europe, U.S.A.) have been based in the values of the humanist enlightenment. Such values include respect for the individual, freedom of opinion and self expression, rights to life and the qualities of life, freedom from oppression and exploitations of many kinds, democratic governance, evaluations by reason and consensus and the protection of rights and values by law when necessary. Free thinking reason outside the prejudice of state, church or sect, has played the major role in producing the founding documents that enshrine these values, such as the American Constitution or the Charter of the United Nations. These values remain of the greatest importance to humanity providing they can be related to the self-control that will be needed under increasing population density in an ecological crisis.

A major point in all this is that humanist values have been based in a moral ontology; that is in a sense of moral being in the experience of having a standpoint in a personal life. Indeed to discuss the self outside this consideration is to undervalue an essential element in what it means to be human. The decreasing significance of an agreed moral ontology in personal life is a major ingredient in the contemporary pudding of discontent and it is precisely here that the debate needs first to focus.

MORALITY AS WILL

In his wise and scholarly study of the *Sources of the Self,* Charles Taylor set himself the gargantuan task of tracing out the roots of the forces moulding modern ,essentially Western, identities.[3] His conclusions merit serious attention because he shows that the turbulence of our lives is linked as much to our confused and unreflective morality as it does to seemingly external pressures from the environment, population or economy. It seems reasonable to suggest that the anguish reflected in Peter Reason's student's essay with which we began this discussion (Chapter 1) lies in the absence of a moral viewpoint or, rather, the sense that without one that can make a difference life is not worth having. Yet, where does a moral ontology, the sense of being good or participating in the 'good', originate?

We have seen that an evolutionary scenario traces the origin of ethics to universals such as the forms of altruism operating in the maintenance of an individual's inclusive fitness (Chapters 14, 17). Such psycho-biological research provides valuable insight but tends to lead to programmatic, instrumentalist understandings of ethics that merely exist to maintain the public good through individual advantage – as in utilitarianism for example. The moral sensibility that underlies much of human action is rooted, Taylor argues, in a deeper intuition of the 'good' than this alone.

Western humanist values focus on respect for others whoever they may be, freedom from oppression and suffering in general and an affirmation of the importance of the ordinary life of family, business, work and play. Our ethics are programmes for the maintenance of these 'freedoms'. Such an orientation is very different from one that roots personal being in a relationship to some transcending power, god or whatever with a morality based in keeping his rules, his rituals or whatever is needed for placation or salvation. In assuming responsibility for personal actions within a socially contractual understanding, we have cut ourselves off from the illusions, inhibitions and graces such earlier beliefs in deity allowed. The world of course is lonelier and the question of what our morality is *based in* becomes critical by the very fact of its avoidance or denial. As we have been arguing, it is of course the Cartesian understanding of knowledge and the sheer brilliance of material science that projects us into this instrumentality, this controlling of the inward through its denial. The fear here is of a meaninglessness implying that the everyday adds up to no practical point.

Taylor points out that within our frameworks of morality some distinctions, qualitative rather than quantitative in nature, are felt to be incomparably more vital than others. These are intuitions that some modes of life or feeling are higher and of an over-riding significance. At one time, the 'honour' of warriors was experienced in this way – something deeply obligatory to fail in which meant shame and disgrace. In later times, the notion of the 'English gentleman' carried similar obligations that were often felt rather than articulated. Another such value enshrines the notion of self-mastery, the capacity to disengage from social, political or other pressures to affirm a distinctive distance and self-possession based in an objectification of emotions and inclinations. Such self-mastery was a key theme in stoicism and reappears in the 'authenticity' of many humanists today. Christian ideals of altruism also command deep respect and are similarly rooted. Here we are not speaking of the calculating altruisms of sociobiology whereby an animal aids another only in relation to a return or a reproductive gain but rather of a disinterested altruism that includes all people, maybe even all-sentient beings as in the Buddhist case, effectively treating all beings as kin. Although such altruism can be given an extended sociobiological interpretation, it is not such explanation that accounts for the charisma that a total altruist, Mother Teresa for example, may inspire. Putting another's case or needs before one's own is seen as a 'hypergood' in Taylor's terminology as it can exist only as a transformation of the will, a move from a lower to an higher condition of personal being, the adoption of a transformed stance in life. In such cases, and others like them, morality involves 'higher' goals or states seen as 'incomparably good'. To fail in such respects would entail deep shame rather than guilt or regret.

In such examples, the attitudes and behaviours expressing a stance in life become the root of traditions. Furthermore, because they express the possibility of an humanity with a potential to surpass its normal limitations, they may sometimes be considered sacred. Values such as these have evolved during the maturation of cultural trends over many centuries and they remain with us as sources of personal power. Taylor sees contemporary moral consciousness to lie in a conflict between instrumental applications, good things to do in the conventional operations of everyday life, and the call of such 'higher' transformations. Values that may be crucial for some are totally denied or even scorned by others and the tension leads to an ambivalence in which the simplistic operations of a contemporary utilitarianism subservient to the market provide too easy a way out.

The utilitarian mindset is born from a philosophy that separates mind and matter and then interprets mind as if it were matter. It operates only with what can be seen to be advantageous in the everyday. This does not lack significance. We need to slow down at traffic lights and to ensure they keep working. As a root for all values, however, it fathers the morality, if one can call it that, of consumer capitalism, which unlike communism ensures the uneven distribution of poverty.[4] Taylor comments, "*a utilitarian outlook – entrenched in the institutions of a commercial, capitalist and finally a bureaucratic mode of existence, tends to empty life of its richness, depth or meaning. The experiential charge takes various forms: that there is no more room for heroism, or aristocratic virtues, or high purposes in life, or things worth dying for nothing is left that can give life a deep and powerful sense of purpose, there is a loss of passion ... The instrumental society may bring this about through the images of life it offers and celebrates, just by occluding deeper meanings and making them hard to discern.*"[5]

EDUCATION TO MAKE A DIFFERENCE

Does present day, Westernised humanity have the capacity to surpass its limitations, to create indeed a "new type of citizen"? It seems clear that any education to make a difference must focus on the development of the will to change and to act so as to correct the severe imbalances that currently afflict the world. A transformative education will have to take on all this and the resistance will be considerable. Yet if appropriate action in the material world demands constraint, a lowered standard of living for the rich in the developed world, a more even distribution world wide of goods and resources, then it demands actions based in a morality that accepts forms of apparent personal disadvantage. Education of the will involves rather more than the mere imparting of information or techniques. Only a transforming ethic can tackle the engrained selfishness that is one major part of our inheritance. Transformation is an act of will that can only happen if the basis for such action is not only clear but also "incomparably good". It needs to be based not only in accurate information and critical opinion but in a heart felt sense of necessity.

A sense of history becomes significant here. The great shifts in ethical thought known as 'axial ages' [6] have occurred during period of economic and cultural transition when old ways of economic exploitation, wealth creation and modes of cultural life have broken down producing conflict and social disruption coupled with a profound questioning of values and ethics. Into such a situation, new thinking emerges suggesting an insightful solution that is rapidly adopted, becoming the common standard of thought and opinion. We can see such principles operating in various ways during the emergence of Buddhism, Christianity, the Italian renaissance and the 'age of enlightenment' in Europe following the Thirty Years War. The conditions of breakdown and conflict are certainly present today and there is no lack of questioning. We may surmise that the time is ripe for a new world view based in reinterpretations of the old.

A helpful perspective on the roles of heart and mind in these dilemmas comes again from the vision of Michail Bakhtin[7], the Russian philosopher whom we encountered earlier (Chapter 20). He argued, we may recall, that the meaning and evaluation of a culture is not contained within social groups, persons or language in isolation but rather co-emerges between them. In his view, the history of cultural evolution can be seen as falling into three phases. The earliest was the 'ancient matrix' in which the self is deeply participatory, involved within and pervaded by the unified life of the world system as perceived; time is felt as cyclic based on a harmony within nature, the relationship with which is governed by detailed rules regulated by shamanic discourse including means for restoration when broken. The social vision is contained within a mytho-poetic discourse, often revealed in trance states wherein fantasy reflects themes in both social and environmental relationships. Heart predominates over mind. The second phase coincides with the appearance of states with more developed agricultural economies, class systems and religions of personal salvation that emphasise a separation between person and cosmos. Individualism is enhanced through an awareness of time as a personal becoming moving towards destinies distinct from the world matrix. Thought becomes anchored in reified usages of terms expressing divinity, self, identity, ethics and the linear process descriptive of commercial advance and personal salvation. Mind predominates over heart. The third phase is one in which there is an emerging and

sophisticated awareness that personal beliefs and world views are
contingent upon their context rather than as being in some sense
'absolute'. Such a 'situationist' awareness is necessarily associated with a
sense of the relativity of faith and opinion in which the monologic
discourses of previous religions/philosophies are opened up to
questioning through reflexive awareness. Earlier ideas are now seen more
as metaphors for life or mind rather than objective existants. Critical
humanist debate diminishes beliefs in an absolute deity, unchallengeable
saints or popes with infallibly true insights, thereby enabling an open
investigation of the very foundations of thought, self-identity and
consciousness that escapes the control of authoritarian dogma. Heart and
mind function together in such reflection. Clearly, this third phase
characterises the emerging present but, deep in history, such themes
have been previously debated during the contacts between Indian, Greek
and Persian thought leading to the philosophical insights of the yogic
traditions within Buddhism.[8]

Within the European thought of the last several centuries the problems
for phase two thinkers (Christian apologists) faced with the emergence
of phase three thought (in science and humanism) have found expression
in the agonised debates around 'nihilism' as the imagined opponent of
Christianity. As we have discussed (Chapter 18), such issues, not being
resolved within European thought, have lead to the present philosophical
crisis. It is here that the significance of buddhistic thought becomes
apparent in that it supplies a deep insight into the 'suchness' of universal
mystery without requiring the posing of a reified, even personalised, entity
or divinity as the cause. The dualism that lies deep in the schizoid
mentality of the West is thereby overcome. The result is a holistic vision
that promotes a spiritual practice as the basis for personal values while
avoiding the conflict between religion and science, which, especially in
U.S.A., remains otherwise so destructive.

A world view capable of underpinning new world citizenship would
seem therefore to require a clarity engaging the trends apparent in
Bakhtin's third phase of cultural history. Such fulfilment does not
necessarily demand that individuals abandon beliefs in whatever divinity
they may propose as an ultimate universal cause nor the abandonment of
personal ethics based in prophetic visions; it does however require an
understanding that such beliefs are relative to the personal, cultural or
ethnic contexts which birth provides as a life situation. Personal belief is
then no longer claimed as absolute; a tolerant understanding of alternative
visions becomes possible and conflict based in the intolerance of difference
can cease. For those whose 'nihilism' seemingly fails to provide a basis for

value, there is here none the less the possibility of spiritual practice based in an openess to universal mystery unavoidably already present through holistic participation in life itself.[9]

Any such pervasive toleration through agreements to differ in personal belief could provide a basis for the intensive negotiation that will be required to restore a balance between human life and the planetary environment. Without such underlying tolerance and willingness to negotiate in support of the common good, there will be a continual struggle within social environments of threat, intimidation, exploitation and coercion. We simply do not have time to waste on such issues when the planet is burning, the seas rising, huge storms brewing and the welfare of future generations deeply at stake. To reverse such trends is the greatest educational challenge possible, one to which educationists must respond or prove themselves useless in the course of time. Let us now consider some issues, many of them difficult and non-consensual, which educationists need consider in order to create some appropriate response.

TEACHING REALITY

Rarely are children and young people taught in school the broad 'realities' of the world that the consistent findings of modern thought have uncovered for us and which we have briefly reviewed in Part 3 of this book. They are thereby denied the opportunity for debate based in current ideas and the possibility of forming their own opinions. Tinbergen himself pointed out the failure of many schools to invest adequately in the creativity of children as opposed to their capacity merely to pass exams. So much education is directed merely at university entry requirements and the production of persons suited to the needs of the 'economy', often generating square pegs to fit round holes. The requirement is not only for the provision of an adequate education in science but also for the teaching of science within the context of the evolution and needs of the human mind and the ecological limits of the planet. In this perspective, 'faith schools' can be expected to transmit little more than the prejudices of superstition as a sad basis for ethics that may differ in application between 'us' and 'them'. Children in faith schools, rather than debating ethics that may match the planetary crisis, commonly receive only the simplistic propaganda of pre-modern religions. In state schools, they may get no more than an optimistically bland survey of world cultures that provides little guidance for forming an opinion or creating understanding.

Teaching 'realities' is not the same process as teaching a science or explaining someone's philosophy. It is a matter of looking directly into the reasonableness of points of view, the evidence for credibility, and the presence of uncertainty. It is a matter of teaching children how to debate. Such teaching would allow young people to be open to the diversity of viewpoints on offer with a capacity to evaluate them and thus to participate actively in modern life. Such an education is needed if young people are to create futures they will inherit rather than risk alienation from them. It can become the basis for leadership.

Many schools still offer classes in RE, so called 'Religious Education'. Teachers often express frustration at not knowing what to stress in such classes especially in a multicultural and largely post-Christian society such as exists now in Great Britain. The result is often a poorly taught comparative survey of religion heavily biased in favour of the teacher's own belief or that of most of the parents. A great opportunity is being wasted here. The vigour of the modern debate concerning the meaning of human life is entirely passed by. We need to replace these vaguely oriented classes by an honest, teacher-led discussion of modern thought in all its ambiguity and complexity. Young people would then be in a much better position to participate truly in the ongoing debates that will define their futures. In the process, they will encounter much that will be extremely critical of the assumptions current in the everyday world that surrounds them. Their response may make uncomfortable viewing for those who seek to create new generations of consumers blindly led into cultural subjection by the guile of advertising agencies and political spin doctors One may even expect a political resistance to implementation because such education could lead to a changed perspective threatening the prevailing social subjection to the market. It may indeed produce a critical mass of people that could alter the course of history. What then might be taught in such a desirable syllabus?

Children are plausibly better equipped than adults at accepting life as an open field of adventure. There is nothing more involving for young people than true exploration, especially when based in careful preparation. Exploration implies unknowing. The adventure of knowledge is an adventure into a mysterious cosmos, which in spite of all our intellectual achievement we still by no means understand. The vastness, the mysterious emptiness of space, the circling planets, the narrative of the big bang and the futures of galaxies and big holes are matters that can open a sense of wonder and mystery in a child and create an exploratory mind very different from one conditioned by the dogmas of some convention. Having a view on the heavens can create an open security within a wondering exploration of knowledge rather than a repeated falling back into opinion always threatened by doubt. Doubt indeed may be built positively into a confidence that examines the world.

An education in self-exploration is particularly essential to provide the realisation that inner work is needed to create a meaningful self. Such teaching needs to include much that is experiential rather than merely didactic. Exploring contrasting ways of being in the world, the waxing and waning of feelings, the way to deal with uncertainty, the discovery of inner peace, all need to be investigated through the forms of subjective empiricism with which much of this book has been concerned. Buddhistic themes are strikingly relevant. Ways of teaching these outside the formal constraints of the past need study; such education needs to be tested and effects measured. In limited experiments so far, children take easily to well-presented meditation. Here they can find a security in a not-knowing that is a route to unbiased discoveries of what can be known: an acceptance of uncertainty that can be voiced rather than feared and which can be seen as a truth within understanding. The unusual silence and peace of the meditation room can become the home base for life's expeditions, a tool to use in balancing emotional intellegence.

The world needs to be explored anew, literally. A great expansion of educational travel under supervision is essential even though reducing the carbon emissions of air travel would not be helped by it and special allowances need to be made. Ladakhi women who had developed an excessive admiration for the ways of the West were taken abroad and shown both the wealth and the poverty of western cities. They have been enabled to appreciate their own rural existence from a clearer, personal experience. Teenagers need exposure to reality in the same way. Bernie Glassman's Zen retreats in which participants join the down-and-outs of American cities sleeping rough in the streets without money, adequate food or shelter for a period of several days is perhaps too much for children – but the idea is exemplary. School trips abroad need to be prepared thematically. There is more to Granada, Moscow, Beijing or Paris than the tourist sights. Trekking in the Himalayas requires sojourns in remote villages, eating indigenous foods, enduring primitive hygiene, and catching a flea or a bedbug or two. Carefully guided visits to Auschwitz provide important cautionary tales. Without such understanding, the children of the well-off have problems in understanding the condition of the world's poor and are denied the possibility of discovering that happiness can be found even under conditions of little comfort. Teamwork and mutual sharing during hard and tiring treks has the additional merit of inculcating a capacity for empathy with others in a manner rather different from the shared machismo of a rugby team – fine though that too can sometimes be.

Apart from the experiencing of new habitats and ways of life, expeditions can include valuable 'inner journeys'. A visit to the Sahara should include a day or two walking alone in the silence of the great dunes. A visit to British national parks should include periods of silent appreciation, maybe 'landscape meditation' where the views are good. As Ken Jones has found, people respond well to his teaching of the great Japanese monk Dogen's 'Mountains and Rivers Sutra' through inviting them to spend a day alone in a restricted area of a Welsh mountain - whatever the weather.[10] Amerindian vision quests and similar forms of training in the natural environment are excellent in this respect, testing a person's courage in the face of solitude, adverse weather, limited resources and a need for creative resourcefulness. National Parks need to provide facilities for such forms of training as well as those for more muscular sports, climbing, mountain biking, and riding. Remote and solitary huts for such use need to be established and made available to those who are practising self-discovery in this way. Athonite monks or Tibetan yogins need not be the only ones to discover the value of solitude but the teaching to back it up will need to be carefully prepared.

There will be risks in such expeditions. Instead of the current tendency to litigation every time a teacher slips up in pupil protection, there needs to be a more rational acceptance of the fact that no adventure is possible without risk, no such learning possible without hardship. The recent closures of riding schools for fear of litigation are lamentably to the point. Riding horses is not without risk and total safety is unreasonable in many such learning situations. New principles need to be established here to provide security around the forms of responsibility demanded in parent -teacher relationships. A nanny state produces merely molly-coddled citizens jumpy at every unusual sound.

Adventures in the field need also to be related to courses in 'ecoliteracy' focussing academically and practically on all aspects of natural ecology, the analysis of systems, the current environmental problems and the causes of change both in the countryside and in urban contexts. The Centre for Ecoliteracy in California advised by Fritjof Capra is producing exemplary programmes that need to be linked with education in self-knowledge and social democracy. These are absolutely essential paths to the recovery of sustainability.[11] A number of institutions in Brazil and India are following this excellent example. Stephen Harding's visionary exercises in approaching the problems of the planetary crisis are usefully provocative as are the courses provided by him and others at the Schumacher College at Dartington, UK.[12]

The schoolroom classes formerly entitled Religious Education need then to be replaced by courses that might be called simply 'Humanity' or 'Science and Ethics' and perhaps subtitled 'World Renewal' or some similar expression. The inner and outer adventures we have been advocating can open the minds of teenagers to the extraordinary diversity of human life, the gradations in wealth and welfare and the fact that happiness is to a significant degree independent of money so long a certain subsistence requirements for life and procreation are met. As children become teenagers, their education needs to emphasise their own responsibility for the future. Their wider understanding of human diversity can encourage a heart-feeling that all of us are in the broadest sense kin and that through kinship we are all responsible for one another. This can be the beginning of the critique of modern individualism with all its concomitant ailments, alienation and thoughtlessness. A real sense of the 'global village' can become the basis for a revived sense of community that takes into its embrace the whole of humanity. Once caring for the world community becomes a clear necessity, a realisation of the inadequacy of the contemporary economic philosophy of globalised capitalism can come into play through an acceptance that we cannot sustain the current levels of planetary exploitation without severe risk to all of us. Such a realisation may force the restructuring of capitalism so that it may at last seek to conserve our resources, limit our competitive destructiveness, allow concern for all to replace the concern for me and mine and create an economic perspective that matches the needs of humanity to a sustainable environment. Without acknowledging the total necessity of such a change, any education for the future will fail. Needless to say however, any promotion of education along such lines will require considerable financial investment, currently only likely to arise through private means. The importance of education as a critical contribution to world improvement merits extensive state support and political demands for this will have to be made.

A major barrier to such teaching will be the engrained conservatism of the orthodox Abrahamic religions; a barrier made insurmountable by the inherent quarrelling and mutual destructiveness between them. The deconstructive approach we have offered here, whereby the idea of a reified 'god' is perceived to be a human projection, will alarm those of more fundamentalist inclinations. There is however in each system a minority tendency to see divinity as essentially the same as self, as in neo-Dionysian Christianity, Sufism and in Jewish mysticism. Here there is sufficient common ground with Buddhism to allow friendly discourse. In any global, educational programme, it will be essential that the ideas we have been examining be presented with a tolerance allowing for a wide range of metaphysical interpretations that form bases for personal faith. Believers in metaphysical positions need to feel welcomed and not excluded from such debates and discussions.

The key principles and orientations to be considered in such a course might be as follows:

(1) *Historical context.* The predominant cultural context of our time is the philosophy of science that has shifted our understanding of ultimate reality from the dogmas of religions, particularly the Abrahamic religions, to the openess of universal mystery that is the present day subject of both objective and subjective empiricism. The basis for a global education needs to be an openess to creative thought that the freedom of such mystery allows.

(2) *Our home in the Universe.* The limitations of knowledge. Space and time. Big bang. Galaxies and Black Holes. The ultimate unknown. These topics can be taught as general ideas rather than in the context of the actual teaching of Physics.

(3) *How do we know?* The methods of objective conjecture. What is evidence? What is science? What is philosophy? The self as the subject of objective exploration. Phenomena as a creation of the mind. What is the self? Self as narrative and exploration. The unending enquiry. There is no need here to trudge through a list of relevant philosophers. The ideas themselves need to be faced, eyeball-to-eyeball.

(4) *The evolution and history of humanity.* The nature of evolution. The life of Charles Darwin. The origins of human peculiarities. Why "intellegent design" is no explanation. Cultural differences and adaptations to ecology.

(5) *The nature of morality, its origins.* Ethics. Distinctions between wants and needs. The idea of the 'good'. Comparative belief. Religion as a path of transformation. Self transformation in the achievement of the good. Will, idea and directed change in a world using up its resources.

(6) *Life and Suffering.* The development of personal practices of reflection through meditation and direct experience. How does suffering arise? The Four Noble Truths of the Buddha. Witnessing the obsessions of the ego. Calming the mind and apprehending the real. Practice of compassion and sharing. Encounter and sensitivity groups for examining mental and personal conflict. Relating to other people's points of view. Theoretical and practical classes in conflict resolution. Finding a basis for interfaith discussion.

(7) *The Global Crisis.* Disputes concerning economics. Market capitalism versus Keynesian perspectives. Ethics in economics. Justice and sustainability. The contemporary debate in the search for alternatives. The planetary, ecological crisis. Possibilities for cooperation.[13]

(8) *Moral choice.* Precepts, vows, practice. Social criticism. Addictive sex. Sexual restraint. Vulgarity of voice. The use of wealth. Social futures.

The uneven distribution of poverty and the problem of sustainability. The risks of human futures. Alternative paths. Participation and the fulfilling life versus alienation. The requirement for honesty and preceptually based action by politicians. The critique of spin. The search for a future.

(9) *Fieldwork.* Visits to other countries, experience of differing economic conditions, working through difficult experiences in such situations, retreats and solitary sojourns in the wilderness. Bird and mammal watching. Practical and theoretical ecoliteracy. Pass-crossing and climbing mountains. Interchange between groups of differing culture and race.

The essential feature of such a course would be open exploration at all levels without dogmatism. While the teacher must be a source of information, he/she should also be a leader of carefully directed, open discussion. The outcome needs to be class rather than teacher based. The presentation of ideas needs to enable pupils/students to debate and work out their own positions in a way that rejects prejudice, is governed by evidence, respects reason and discusses what is 'reasonable'. Practice in the use of such principles will be important. A careful balance between reason based in objectivity and reason based in feeling should be maintained especially in discussing cultural issues. What is found to be common between cultures, especially in multicultural settings? Can there be a universal humanistic approach to global problems? What should it be? What is the role of yogic meditation in the discernment of the real? How should inter-faith discussion be managed? Several levels of the course need to be constructed for presentation to different age groups and experiential exploration encouraged as a basis for discussion.

Such a course would enable a trained teacher to integrate objective and subjective approaches to knowledge and understanding so that a holistic post-Cartesian perspective can arise giving an appropriately broad picture of the human dilemma. Methods that are experiential will be as important as talk teaching. Beginners' classes in meditation, visits to the wilderness practicing mindfulness are all significant. In doing this the key ideas of the Buddha, will necessarily play a major role in opening up the study of the self, selflessness, the cause of suffering, the motivation for altruism and the anchoring of the mind in equanimity through yogic means. These essential roots of human being can then be matched to Western notions in the philosophy of mind and in psychotherapeutic approaches to personal distress. A genuinely buddhistic humanism can be a sure basis for the study of justice with sustainability but this does not imply indoctrination in Buddhism as a system in itself. Statues of Sakyamuni and Socrates as representative of the deep traditions of East and West may perhaps stand alert in such classrooms and their lives well studied. How about acting out debates between these two?

Where should such a course be taught? The answer must be worldwide in order to respect the globalisation of culture under the prevailing influence of Western economic practice and the need for its criticism. From Scotland to Malaysia from New York to Nairobi, from San Francisco to Mumbai, there are already common methods of teaching many subjects, especially the sciences. Such a course in what might be truly called 'moral science' would allow students worldwide to explore what they have in common, to explore the acceptable universals of humanity, to understand the origins of prejudice. Courses, furthermore, can be self-generating-that is to say, the focus can vary from place to place so that the students in relation to gifted teaching can themselves construct syllabuses creatively and continuously. And there's the rub, teachers of an adequate quality will need training and the whole structure of teacher training for a less consuming and less addictive world examined. Where will these leaders be found? How can governments and educational institutions come to adopt such suggestions for the welfare of the world? Perhaps a start may be made through comprehensive conferences on the essential need for an education for change as their main focus. Who then will start the process?

End Notes

1. Perhaps a beginning can be seen in Jon Kabat-Zinn's endeavours to 'mainstream' the meditation techniques of Buddhism within American hospitals, prisons and welfare schemes Undoubtedly this 'mainstreaming' is beneficial and may lead some to investigate the buddhist ideas upon which meditation is based. Yet, as Ken Jones indicates (in 'The New Social Face of Buddhism') in the relative absence of a founding ontology and ethical teaching, the fact of its benefits may turn it too easily into a commodity and open it to market manipulation so that it is simply absorbed back into the prevailing consumer ideology – much as yoga in beauty parlours has lost its spiritual base. Something more fundamental is required that shifts both attitudes and economic practice at familial, national and cultural levels. Only an alternative worldview can do this.

2. Norberg-Hodge. H. 1991 *Ancient Futures: learning from Ladakh.* Rider. London

3. Taylor, C. 1989. *Sources of the Self. The Making of Modern Identity.* Cambridge University Press. Cambridge.

4. A Brahmin friend once described communism to me as "the even distribution of poverty."

5. Taylor. ibid. *Sources of the Self.* p.500.

6. Lipson, L. 1993. *The Ethical Crises of Civilization: Moral Meltdown or Advance.* Sage. London.

7. Bakhtin M. 1981. *The Dialogic Imagination.* University of Texas. Austin.

8. McEvilley, T. 2002. *The Shape of Ancient Thought.* Allworth. New York. Crook J.H. 2007 in press. Shamans, yogins and indigenous psychologies. In: Dunbar, R. and L. Barrett (Eds.). *The Oxford Handbook of Evolutionary Psychology.*

9. Harding, S. 2006. *Animate Earth: Science, Intuition and Gaia.* Green Books. Totnes.

10. Jones, K. 2002. Green mountains walking. A training in landscape intimacy: the evaluation. of an experimental retreat. *New Chan Forum* 27:27-32. See: www.westernchanfellowship.org

11. See: Ecoliteracy: dancing earth. Several authors in *Resurgence,* 226. October 2004. Also www.ecoliteracy.org

12. Harding, S. 2006. loc cit above.

13. See: Hinde, R.A. and J. Groebel. 1991. *Cooperation and prosocial behaviour.* Cambridge University Press.

25

HOPES FOR WORLD RENEWAL

Tinbergen's doubt pivoted on the thought that the human capacity for adaptation was perhaps insufficient to cope with the increasing viability gap "between what our new habitat requires us to do and what we are actually doing." He went on to argue – "*The scientist will have to point out that the prevention of a breakdown, and the building of a new society is a matter of enlightened self-interest, of ensuring survival, health and happiness of the children and grandchildren of all of us... of people we know and love.*" (Chapter 1) It has perhaps become clear that by 'enlightened self-interest' Tinbergen could only have meant the development of a capacity for restraint so that the unbridled selfishness of wealth creation based in unsustainable planetary exploitation coupled with ever increasing differentials between rich and poor is brought to an end. He rightly supposed that this would require a "new type of citizen."

This book has proposed that a serious consideration of Buddhist thought can contribute much to the failing humanist vision by providing a holistic perspective on human destiny that does not depend on the projection of a metaphysical being, a god or gods, as a universal cause. The viewpoint entails an acceptance of endless change as the source of universal causation wherein all changes mutually interact with one another within a single, seamless cosmos. A sense of participation in the universal process, honed through yogic meditation, becomes the basis for an acceptance of the wonder and suchness of things reaching well beyond the divisive dualisms of Abrahamic religious world views. A spiritual understanding of this kind rooted in meditational participation encourages empathy for all beings, indeed all things, as belonging to a world that also defines one's own existence. The schizoid mentality of the West, its extreme ethical relativity, and its illusory 'nihilism' attributed to science, can be replaced by a unifying viewpoint in which ethics evolve naturally from a reasoned understanding of personal existence within the participatory universe itself. In such a Buddhistic view, the scattered concerns of those actively resisting the genuine nihilism of our destructive consumer culture can plausibly find a profound and common root.

Our survey of contemporary Western values suggests that there are
three principle barriers to any practical development of any such Buddhist
humanism. The first and most embracing one is that in a democracy few
will vote for any suggestion that limits their financial capacity as property
owners. Furthermore, in the undeveloped world few will accept the view
that they need to curb their development before it can approach the
standards of living in the richest parts of the developed world, U.S.A.,
Europe and Japan. The economic impetus for the maximization of wealth
will continue so long as citizens of the world do not effectively oppose it.
It is exactly this unrestrained capitalism that must surely bring disaster.

The second barrier lies in the widespread belief that ever increasing
wealth can bring happiness and a sense of personal meaning. So long as
this illusory ideology is sustained, any capacity for a more enlightened self-
interest will be precluded. Economic sufficiency is of course a necessity if
higher aims are to be realised, yet working with questions concerning the
nature and possibility of restraint on global exploitation is now more than
urgent. Can capitalism transform itself? What is 'sustainable' development'?

The third barrier consists in the increasing influence of religious
fundamentalism that persists in attempting to establish bigoted and
prejudiced world and life interpretations with potentially damaging global
significance. The first of these is operative primarily among the deprived
of the Middle East, the second, mainly in the heart of wealthy America.
While capable of using modern technology for their purposes, persons of
such attitudes are intellectually incapable of relating to the scientific and
philosophical insights available in humanist democracy and may indeed
deny some of their most important findings. The combined approach of
neo-conservatism in the current US administration with the illusory moral
certainties of evangelical Christianity US style might indeed lead to strife
between religions driven by ideologues incapable of mutual
understanding. A Christian dialogue with moderate Islam is an essential
start to easing tensions. The relationship between these faiths within the
educational perspective proposed here may take a long time to determine.
There are a great many vested interests at stake.

Underlying these three barriers is the overriding presence of the
personal, institutional, national or religious 'self' and the assumption
that the satisfaction of its wants is essential for meaning. The challenge of
the Buddha has been to point out that no versions of self exist as the kinds
of entity they are assumed to be. This challenge is reinforced by the
direction taken by Western philosophy and psychology in seeking to
understand the alienation and stress of our times. Yet, there is hope.
Mankind may be foolish a lot of the time but insights have a way of recurring.

Duped for so long by capitalist advertising, the consumer, hungry for self-enhancing commodities, remains largely the 'subject' of the few multi-million pound executives who run the worldwide industrial-military complex. Yet, such dominance is being challenged. Education, vigorous and critical news reporting in investigative journalism, the spread of information on the web, together with the rise of heart-felt resentment, is generating a mass movement soon perhaps to become as significant as Solidarity in Poland, Glasnost in the Soviet Union or the popular surge that destroyed the Berlin wall. Already investors are resisting the fat-cat bonuses given to executives of huge corporations who have not only failed to sustain the viability of their concerns but who have employed secretive and corrupt methods in the attempt to do so. Corruption in the U.S.A. involves such vast sums of money that small states could survive for a year or more upon them. The embezzlement of funds intended for the reconstruction of Iraq seems to know no end.[1] Such persistent corruption in high places, the awareness of the inherent evils in the market, failure to relieve the debt of the third world, the continuing loss of rain forests and biodiversity, and the visible alterations in climate are stimulating more than unease. The urge for change is beginning to set the agenda.

Some certainly see that the only move that can seriously shift self-focused economics would be a view of being in the world that was not so dependent upon money, on maximization linked to the careless disregard of the ills that assail us. The advantages of the buddhistic view that we have been exploring is that it supplies just such a perspective and can be perceived as being a companion to objective science in providing a basis for meaning. A buddhistic humanism becomes a genuine possibility as the subjective and objective poles of human enquiry begin to meet. The beauty of such a view is that the cosmos is no longer interpreted through reifying projection. The universe lacks any intentionality. It functions as it must, creates its own laws and we are one of the products of this process. The extraordinary fact is that the Universe becomes in a sense aware of itself through sentient life. Maybe this happens elsewhere in the cosmos but for the present, we seem to be alone. Meaning resides therefore in making a go of it, finding a way beyond the destructiveness of ignorance. The cosmos remains an awesome mystery but we are not apart from it, we participate in it. "I am not it but it is all of me." When the heart-mind grasps this intuition, many insights follow. Human history does show ways whereby a different kind of citizenry could come to be. Increasingly we must examine them.

To begin with, we have seen that the biological basis of human nature is markedly bipolar. In common with other animals, human individuals are genetically primed to behave in ways that tend to maximize their survival and their reproductive success. This inevitably involves competition, aggressiveness, assertion, cheating and the Machiavellian manipulation of others. Yet, in addition, altruistic behaviour towards kin and reciprocation with helpers is often found, yielding a softer, familial way of life. These twin tendencies are found throughout humanity. Communal wisdom arises when ways of balancing them are created that operate for the general benefit as well as (or even contrary to) benefits to self-alone. Sometimes a personal loss can be a general gain in which one participates. The enhancement of practices that lead in this direction is commonly called spiritual. A general acceptance of the restraint essential to heal the world would indeed comprise the 'self-enlightened behaviour' Tinbergen calls for. The Buddhist system of values focuses exactly on this. Wisdom is not one-sided nor is it particularly idealistic. It seeks a balance between the forces it witnesses as being there, to create a position that can be the basis for a way forward. After all, it is the 'Middle Way'.

The practices of altruism, perceived biologically as selected strategies of sharing with relatives, may be extended through culture so as to cover sharing throughout humanity. In effect, this means identifying all fellow human beings as kin: a profoundly meaningful move if ethics other than those of self-interest are to prevail. Indeed a move in this direction is shown by the deliberate use of kin terms in Christian monasticism where senior monks and nuns are 'fathers' or 'mothers' and junior monks and nuns are ' brothers' or 'sisters'; terms clearly indicating a deliberate reference to family unity and the idea of sharing. Brotherhood is also a vital aspect of Islamic integrity. The brotherhood of mankind was a founding idea in various socialist movements and this aspect of nineteenth century idealism remains valid long after the politics of communist state control have passed away.

These ideas are in any case not new. Ever since the time of Emperor Asoka, attempts have been made to create a Buddhist statehood in which the principles of the Buddha were enshrined in law and public conduct. Mostly these ventures have occurred in S.E. Asia with varying success. Indeed, in these countries, a suspicion of the selfishness and social evils of capitalism remain part of public consciousness and warmly debated by inspired reformers such as Buddhadasa Bhikkhu and Sulak Sivaraksa.[2] The most developed social movement has undoubtedly been the Sarvodaya Sramadana movement in Sri Lanka led by A.T. Ariyaratne. It is a comprehensive effort to improve village life through the adoption of Buddhist principles in emphasising basic needs for welfare and personal fulfilment in a grass roots endeavour aiming at an economics of self sufficiency highly critical of both communism and capitalism and influenced by the example of Mahatma Gandhi in India, who indeed may be considered the father of many such trends. In contemporary Japan with its strong communal traditions, various companies have made efforts in their management philosophies to incorporate principles of benefit to employees and society alike quite apart from those accruing to shareholders. These ventures had their successes prior to the severe downturn in the economies of Japan and SE Asia generally and prior to the upsurge in globalisation led by the transnational commercial giants. The Wall Street Journal of 1997 saw the Asian collapse as a total vindication of the short termism of American capitalism versus the 'communitarian' economics of Asia.[3] The current, emerging problems in world economics suggest however that the last word has by no means been said.

In his 2006 Reith lectures, Daniel Barenboim, the celebrated pianist and conductor, drawing on both the rich humanist tradition of Europe and on the Jewish thinkers Spinoza and Martin Buber, reflected on the parallels between music and life. Music comes out of silence and returns to silence. So does life. Music is ephemeral; it quickly passes and is gone. So does life. In a rich musical work, opposed themes appear antagonistic yet they resolve into a surpassing unity. So can life. Yet, such resolution depends on the players in the orchestra. They need to listen to one another. One theme may be poorly expressed without insight, becoming unrelated to the work as a whole; one instrument may produce too much power and overwhelm others. True musical strength lies in the mutual interplay of the many parts in a drive towards resolution in unity. The players must know the last note when they play the first. If a civilisation is to endure, if a life of quality is to be maintained, similar insight needs to be followed. Barenboim gave his last two lectures in Remallah and Jerusalem respectively, applying his theme to the Arab-Israeli conflict that remains pivotal in the argument between Islam and the West, yet it applies equally to our world situation as a whole.

Do current circumstances offer a millennial opportunity? Could it be that the present social, economic and political pressures might give rise to a new 'axial age' in which major changes in our understanding of the way we have to live on the planet may come about? No doubt, great changes are needed and these must all be linked to the way in which we understand ourselves as economic beings. The schizoid, Western split between, on the one hand, an anachronistic religious base and, on the other, a humanist, science-based culture created by inventive genius but lacking ethics apart from personal gain, has proven disastrous. The puerility of so much political expression demonstrates how bankrupt our society has become.

Such bankruptcy feeds mindless prejudice and an inability to face the daunting challenges of overpopulation, planetary pollution and world governance.

Where might such a change in understanding begin to manifest? Sadly, one can discount those regions of the world sunk in a religious conservatism not unlike that of ancient Egypt. Perhaps a newly enlightened U.S.A. may emerge as a true world leader rather than the main cause of the present crisis. Indeed the bleak rule of neoconservatism is already dying as the mid tem elections of November 2006 have shown. With the democrats again exercising real power, the opportunities for serious change have appeared at last.

Indeed, we should not be pessimistic. The democratic liberalism within the US population has a potential for initiating insightful change The magnificently endowed educational institutions of the USA employ some of the most brilliant of living scholars and by far the majority support social, democratic politics. They have the power and the influence to shift the debate and the whole world is waiting for them to do so. America's friends have not forgotten the passion and creativity of the sixties and seventies when American teachers and group leaders fanned out over Europe with their exciting ideas wonderfully confronting old conservatisms. The U.S.A. may well re assert its ethical leadership in ways now most severely needed.

India, the homeland of so much spiritual insight, is currently split between rapid modern industrialisation and it's backdrop of an immensely poor and backward population. Without a solution to the population problem, India will have little strength to take a global lead yet its economic development means it is becoming a major world power of the future. A lively democracy rules and deep spirituality remains. India has the capacity to provide an intellectual lead linking the prime ideas of both East and West.

China is clearly a possibility. Within a century, China may challenge America as the planet's No 1 power and plausibly may exercise its strength with discretion. Chinese thought has always emphasized two main themes, the family and Confucian ethics and has also been deeply influenced by Buddhist self-reflection. The cautious growth of democracy will continue and China never moves fast. There is a chance that China's increasingly pervasive influence may encourage a peaceful containment of violence throughout the world, perhaps, however, with an authoritarian tendency that may limit its creativity. The Confucian democracy of Singapore is perhaps an example of the way it may go: yet such an optimistic view may become illusory if the Chinese leaders seek the false fruits of global power in an effort towards global dominance. Unfortunately the record of

Chinese governance in Central Asia, particularly Tibet, has been cruel and exploitative in the extreme.[4] We should be warned and take precautions.

What of Europe? The cradle of most of our difficulties is currently undergoing a remarkable transformation from a collection of brilliantly creative but quarrelling states to a unified socio-political and economic region.. In the last half century, some of the most creative social democratic thinking has emerged within Europe. This historic turn is generating vigorous debate within and between the various components; a debate in which Great Britain should participate far more energetically, setting aside her retrograde memories of empire and rethinking the currently dubious 'special relationship' with the States. The post-Marxist, mostly German, thinkers of the Frankfurt School have critically re-evaluated social theory with acumen and depth.. [5] In Britain, the reflective influence of Wittgenstein remains strong philosophically and the efforts of New Labour to bring socialism and Thatcherism into some sort of relationship should not be dismissed. The Stern report and new initiatives suggest a fresh political awakening.Yet, it is in France that perhaps the most dynamic thinking of the last century has taken place, albeit against a background of uninspiring politics. The great masters, Sartre, Lacan, Foucault have been followed by other towering intellectual contributions from thinkers such as Aron, Ladurie, Derrida and Bourdieu. Much of this thinking has remained rather inwardly focussed as France regrets the passing of past glories but the principles involved are capable of much wider application. The capacity of French thinkers to engage directly with social movements is especially noticeable, Bourdieu, for example, being very involved in the lively resistance to IMF and World bank policies and the support of a vigorous journal debating these issues. The passion and attack of French thought remains as vivid as ever and it seems likely that both creative and controversial ideas for the future will continue to emerge from France. Yet, here again, conservatism has generated social divisions with the needs of a large immigrant population left unmet. The government is surprisingly clumsy and unrelated to the intellectual genius of so many savants.

As Leslie Lipson has argued,[6] European thought has once before emerged with a vigour that changed the world but only after stimulation from the tragedy of the Thirty Years War. He supposes that such a shift may occur again in a third great 'axial' change. Yet, what can shake the political world out of its inability to respond to the resistance to change inherent in the three barriers we have discussed? The answer is perhaps only another great tragedy, a catastrophe sufficient to collapse the old order and bring on the new – a unified planet running on hydrogen, eco-

literate and attempting to restore the terrible damage of the last
two centuries, democratically structured around an United Nations
government and with effective forums for resolving conflict, a self-aware
world of which we at this time can only dream. We have examined the role
Buddhist humanism might play in this great task. Western humanism
with an Eastern spiritual base not at all at odds with science may heal the
split mind into which Western hegemonies have led us. The way can only
be along a path of disciplined renunciation that none the less takes
compassionate care of the world.

At the end of Jean Giraudoux' play, Electra,[7] three characters are
gathered together on what one may well suppose to be a terrace. A series
of great tragedies have just come to an end. Electra, her old nurse and a
beggar representing the infirm, the blind and the lame have witnessed
terrible times. The nurse says, "Tell me. Explain. I can never grasp things
quickly. I can see that something is happening but I'm not sure I
understand. What do you call it when the day is breaking, like today, and
everything is spoiled, everything is ruined, and yet you can still breathe
the air, and everything has been lost, the city is burning, the innocents are
slaughtering each other and the guilty are dying in the early morning
light?"

Electra tells her, "Ask the beggar, he knows."

The beggar replies, "All that has a very beautiful name. It's called the
Dawn."

End Notes

1. Harriman, E. 2006. Cronyism and kickbacks: on the economics of reconstruction
   in Iraq. *London Review of Books* 28.2:14-16. – Referring to US General Accountability
   Office and other documents. See:www.gao.gov/www.sigir.mil/www.iamb.info.

2. Swearer, D.K. 1995. *The Buddhist World of Southeast Asia.* State University of New
   York Press. New York.
   Sivaraksa, S. 1992. *Seeds of Peace: A Buddhist Vision for Renewing Society.* Parralax.
   Berkeley

3. Harvey, P. 2000. *An Introduction to Buddhist Ethics.* Cambridge University Press.
   Cambridge. Chapter 5.

4. The Environment and Development Desk. 2000. *Tibet 2000 Environment and
   development issues.* CTA. Dharamsala.

5. Held, D. 1980. *Introduction to Critical Theory: Horkheimer to Habermas.* Hutchinson.
   London.

6. Lipson, L. 1993. *The Ethical crises of Civilization. Moral meltdown or advance.* Sage.
   London.

7. Giraudoux, J. 1959. *Theatre.* Grasset. Paris. p.112.

POSTSCRIPT

Times change and we with the times – so runs an ancient saying. Nothing could be more true of the present period. This book was written during the key years of the Bush administration in the USA and reflects the alarm and despondency many felt then. Today, the citizens of America in an outstanding demonstration of the value of democracy have elected Barack Obama as their new president. This heralds a total change in US policies following a campaign marked by optimism, good will and a major reversal of racist prejudice by a vast electoral majority leading to a 'black' family in the White House. This 'Mandela' moment alone points to an era of new opportunities for diplomacy, action in the Middle East and policies ensuring environmental preservation.

Even so, this wonderful election comes at a time of developing world recession on a grand scale, an economic catastrophe indeed. All the questions raised in this book remain unanswered, the injustices unresolved, the religious conflicts unequalled, Africa in chaos, women's rights limited in many parts of the world and a lack of democratic institutions based in public education in several powerful nations. A new worldview and a new basis for world thinking, especially with respect to global economics in relation to climate change, is never more important.

The greatest shift may well be a renewed respect for the United States and a resumption of diplomatic leadership by the U.S.A. The plausible sources for global change discussed in Chapter 25 may well become centered on the White House, with Britain and Europe in strong support. The core values of the European 'enlightenment' may at last begin to encounter the enlightened vision of Asia to produce global change. This at least must be our hope and it remains our challenge. Could this be the Dawn the beggar foresaw? Together we can do it.

Nov 5th 2008. US Election day.

INDEX